An Atlas of the
Birds
of the Western Palaearctic

An Atlas of the
Birds
of the Western Palaearctic

Colin Harrison

Design and Cartography by Crispin Fisher

Collins

St James's Place, London

William Collins Sons & Co Ltd
London · Glasgow · Sydney · Auckland
Toronto · Johannesburg

To KAREL VOOUS, whose work on his
Atlas of European Birds, and on various
individual species, was both a
help and an inspiration.

First published 1982

© Colin Harrison 1982

ISBN 0 00 219729 4

Filmset by Jolly & Barber Ltd, Rugby

Made and printed in Great Britain by
William Collins Sons & Co Ltd, Glasgow

Contents

The Drawings

A book consisting mainly of a series of maps showing the distribution of a large number of different species presents a special difficulty. Few people can carry a mental picture in their minds of all the species involved, and most will sooner or later find themselves confronted by a map, with very little idea of the appearance of the creature whose geographical distribution is shown. In order to link the maps to the living birds, this book carries a small monochrome sketch of each of the species mapped: 810 birds in all. It is not intended that this should be a kind of substitute field guide, but rather that the sketch should remind the reader of the appearance of the bird. Where a number of related species are shown, the illustrations may also help to indicate the degree of similarity or difference within the group.

The black-and-white illustrations of the bird species were drawn by the following artists:

Norman Arlott   warblers, goldcrests, flycatchers, babblers

Leslie Baker   divers, grebes, swallows and martins, tits

Dr C.J.F. Coombs   crows

Rob Hume   herons to flamingos, raptors, gulls and terns, buntings to snowfinches

Mick Loates   gamebirds

David Thelwell   cormorants to pelicans, cuckoos, kingfishers to woodpeckers, waxwings to dunnocks, thrushes, nuthatches to sunbirds, orioles and starlings

Laurel Tucker   tropicbirds, waterfowl, cranes to bustards, auks, parrots

Ray Turley   sandgrouse, pigeons, owls to swifts

Ian Wallace   petrels and shearwaters, waders, skuas, larks, pipits and wagtails

Introduction

This book is intended to be a companion work to *The Birds of Britain and Europe* by H. Heinzel, R. Fitter and J. Parslow. I have therefore followed, for the most part, the sequence of species used in that book. The sequence used by those authors was to some extent dictated by the grouping of species on the colour plates. In similar fashion, because I wished to group certain maps together so that they could be available for comparison as a group, I have made a few minor rearrangements of my own, but in general the two sequences are similar.

A book like this must inevitably reflect some slight bias of interest on the part of the author. When it was first suggested to me that I should prepare an atlas of European birds it seemed to me that there was relatively little that I could add to what had already been done in the past, but on further consideration there appeared to be two needs that might be satisfied. First, since birds are creatures capable of moving rapidly, for long distances, and of reacting promptly to changing conditions, there was a need to update the existing information. These attributes of birds do, of course, make them difficult to map satisfactorily, and also indicate that further changes may occur in the near future, perhaps even between the time that I finish this work and the actual point of publication (the manuscript was mainly completed by mid-1978).

The other, and perhaps the more interesting aspect of this work, as far as I am concerned, had been in my mind for a long time. Studying other collections of maps of European bird distribution I had been intrigued by the way in which the ranges of some species were confined to Europe while in other cases a species showed a small range just entering the boundary of the region mapped. In the first instance I found it difficult to believe that the species with the finite range did not have a counterpart or replacement species in similar habitats elsewhere, and in the second I wanted to know whether the limited borderline range represented almost the complete limits of the species, or whether it was just the tip of an extensive but extralimital range. Some of the last information is given in the excellent earlier *Atlas of*

European Birds by Professor K. Voous, but this work gives only the breeding ranges, on a world basis, of a more narrowly defined list of European species. I wanted to try a broader and slightly different approach.

Our problem is that for birds Europe is not a zoogeographical unit. What we are examining is the western end of a large Eurasian landmass which zoogeographically is known as the Palaearctic. It is the latter that represents the regional entity within which most distributions are contained, while in exceptional instances the range of a species may continue through North America, the Nearctic region. These two northern regions together are known as the Holarctic. If there is any real boundary to the western region of the Palaearctic it has become apparent from these maps that for birds it would lie somewhere to the east of the centre, through the region of the Altai or Lake Baikal. Sinkiang and the central Himalayas.

In this book, by using the whole Eurasian region where it seemed appropriate, I have tried to show the distribution of European birds in a broader setting and, where possible, to relate their distribution to that of the species group of which they are a part. Where this is not shown on maps I have indicated such apparent relationships in the text summary of each group of species.

What started out as an atlas of European birds has now become an atlas of Western Palaearctic birds with information on some aspects of the Palaearctic as a whole. I hope that in addition to updating our knowledge of bird distribution in Europe this book will also help people to see these birds in their wider setting, and to view them as part of a continuous pattern of distribution and replacement which utilises virtually the whole of the climatically tolerable parts of the earth's surface.

Because I have used this wider field, the number of species is larger than the title of the book might suggest: 639 species are covered in both maps and individual text; another 167 extralimital species are also shown in full or in part on maps, but only referred to, more briefly, in the introductory texts for species

groups. Various other species apparently forming part of the replacement patterns in other
regions, including the North American counterparts of the main species within our present
region, are briefly referred to in the group
texts and have been included in the index.

In compiling the information I have given
here, I have used the most recent authoritative
sources available to me, and a selective list of
references is given. I am very grateful to those
people who have generously helped me with
information on apparent changes in the distribution of various species. In particular I should
like to acknowledge my considerable debt to
Frances Warr, who has not only helped considerably through her knowledge of birds of
the Middle East, and by her contact with

people studying birds in that region, but whose
assistance during the initial period with the
drafting of maps and assembling of data provided much of the original impetus for this
book.

I am also deeply indebted to Crispin Fisher
who has organised the illustrations and the
layout and made the maps acceptable to the
printers; creating a better book than was
originally envisaged.

In the introductory section which follows I
have given information on how to use the
maps and accompanying text, and then the
information which will aid an interpretation
of the picture which the maps provide, together with a few comments on its limitations.

Using the Text

The maps do not, in themselves, give sufficient information on distribution other than in a most generalised form, and without further comment they may sometimes be misleading. They are therefore accompanied by short pieces of text.

The sequence of species is broken down into the separate families, as scientifically classified (see Contents list), and since in most instances these are large units they have been subdivided into smaller and more easily identified groups of species. For each group there is an introductory text which gives an indication of the type of birds involved, and which comments on the general pattern of distribution and replacement, and may give information on distributions extending outside the limits of the maps. These introductory sections are the only place in the text where the extralimital species which may appear on some of the maps are dealt with, the species text being confined to the Western Palaearctic species. Where similar species or apparent ecological counterparts occur in North America any reference to them will be in this section.

To some extent the occurrence of birds within the range indicated on the map is determined by their need for a particular type of nest site, and the nest site is either mentioned in this introductory section if it is common to the whole group, or may be referred to in the text for the species where it is more specialised.

There are other factors which may limit and control the occurrence of birds within their general range as shown on the maps, and these are dealt with in the text on individual species. The status – resident, migrant, nomadic, etc. – is given, and the broad climatic zone of the general ranges for breeding and wintering are indicated. The final clue to locating a bird is the habitat, which includes the site, vegetation and altitude required for existence in any particular area. Without such information the maps are of limited use, and this therefore forms the major part of the text. There is a limitation on the latter in that within the short space available for comment, generalisations about habitat are inevitable, and it may be found that within a particular area a species may be more conservative in its habitat tolerance than the text suggests.

One example of the need for text with the maps may be cited. To make the range of a bird reasonably visible on the map it may be necessary to exaggerate the distribution slightly in places. On a small map the narrowest line of colour may be several miles wide, and where a bird is confined to coastlines this can only be indicated on the map in a way that is immediately obvious to all eyes by using a broader line of colour which might seem to suggest that in such a species the birds also occur further inland. It is in such instances that the text helps to correct the picture given by the map.

Interpreting the Maps: Problems and Possibilities

Most people will turn to this book in the first instance for information on two or three things. It may be to find out where a particular species might be found, to discover if a bird should occur in a particular place, or to check on what birds would normally make up the avifauna of a particular area. By producing this series of maps we appear to give a general 'yes' or 'no' answer to such questions, but although the information seems simple and straightforward there are many hidden problems in presenting information by means of maps. In the following section I shall comment on the problem posed by the mobility of birds, the difficulty of showing their distribution on maps, and the factors which may influence such distribution; and also on the inferences that we can draw from recurring distribution patterns.

To draw a line round the geographical range of a bird species is like trying to define the edge of a wave, or like mapping a puddle that tomorrow might be bigger, or smaller, have changed its shape, or disappeared altogether. The important respect in which birds differ from most of the other living organisms which we try to map is that they are highly mobile and if necessary may travel a long distance in a short time. Most birds would only need two or three days, perhaps less in some cases, to traverse the entire European area that we are considering in this book. In such circumstances the surprising fact is not that birds can move for long distances, but that they remain for periods of time in areas sufficiently circumscribed to be represented on a map with any consistent degree of accuracy. Arising from this inherent unpredictability of birds are two aspects of the failure to conform to boundaries which merit special mention: one is the problem of strays, the other the occurrence of irruptions.

STRAYS

One result of the extreme mobility of birds is the tendency for individuals, or in some instances small flocks, to occur for brief periods in areas far outside their normal range; in places where they should not, in theory, be found. Once birds start to fly determinedly, or drift on wind currents, they can travel for considerable distances. A tendency to wander is present in many immature birds which sometimes results in a random occurrence in unlikely places. Such movements may be linked in part with the accidental results of wind and weather, and it is certainly true that these factors affect the more extreme strays.

A long-distance flier may be driven far off course by storms and strong winds. Persistent strong westerly winds may bring stray seabirds far inland, and in autumn may transport North American migrants, including small songbirds, to the western seaboard of Europe. It is alleged that some of these are helped a little by eastbound ships. Easterly winds may bring Siberian strays across, often unnoticed until they reach their land limit on the small islands of the west coast. Some eastern Eurasian species occur with some regularity, during migratory and non-breeding periods, in European localities far removed from their normal breeding and wintering ranges. The majority of these breed in northern Siberia and winter further south and might suffer from wind drift, but this does not seem to be the complete explanation.

Major movements of night migrants may be drifted off course when the wind changes after they have begun their flight, and by morning they may appear where they are not normally seen. An exceptionally warm and sunny spell of weather in spring, when migrants are moving north, may cause some to travel further than they normally do, and a few may nest outside the usual range. In addition to these there are some individuals in which the sense of direction appears to break down, and which may continue to move further from their usual area of occurrence.

Some of these stray occurrences may be the earliest indications of long-term changes in distribution taking place in response to gradual changes in weather or modification of the required habitat; but they say that it takes more than one swallow to make a summer, and it takes more than one stray bird to make a change in distribution. It is only when the rare visits change to a regular habit that they become important in this respect. In the type of map used here such strays cannot usefully be included. To extend the range to encompass them would be erroneous, and to indicate each recorded occurrence would merely produce a spatter of spots around each mapped range which would probably only indicate the extent to which birdwatching occurred in these areas. In this book I have limited myself to the usual and typical geographical range of each species; and readers must accept that straying individuals can, and will, occur far from the areas in which they would normally be expected. This unpredictable possibility is, after all, one of the pleasures of birdwatching.

IRRUPTIONS

An irruption is the name given to a type of intermittent movement by a large number of individuals of a particular species, resulting in their exceptional and unexpected appearance outside their home range. The movement is often on a large scale and may resemble more typical migratory movements, but is of a dispersive type and occurs only at unpredictable and often infrequent intervals.

It is typical of species which exist in large numbers in extensive and relatively uniform habitats, and in most instances appears to be linked with a temporary failure of a basic source of food. The movement takes the form of a spread into regions not normally inhabited, and sometimes at periods when normal migration would not occur. The birds may gradually return to their usual range, but in some instances a number may remain and breed for a season or more before returning.

In the tundra and Subarctic zones the numbers of small rodents increase rapidly over a period of several years and then decline drastically for a year or two. While the numbers rise, raptors such as the Snowy Owl (map 325) and Rough-legged Buzzard (120) also increase in number, but with the advent of a sudden food shortage they disperse southwards. In the northern forest zone a large proportion of the more resident species are likely to irrupt to varying degrees, but the more regular, if sporadic, occurrences involve birds feeding mainly on seed or berry crops. Typical species involved in irruptive behaviour are the Waxwing (428), Common Crossbill (625) and slender-billed form of the Nutcracker (658). The Common Crossbill has colonised the conifer plantations of southern England during such irruptions, and in recent years the Waxwing has occurred so frequently in the west that the pattern is beginning to resemble a migration.

Another region producing irruptive species is the steppes of southern Russia, Kazakhstan and Turkestan. Here again several species, such as Pallas's Sandgrouse (308) and the Rosy Starling (656), have been notorious as irruptive species; but other birds from this region also show a greater tendency to spread temporarily westwards than do those of other regions.

MAP PROBLEMS

1. Projections

It is impossible to represent accurately a large portion of the curved surface of the earth on flat paper. This is a fundamental problem of all maps. Where a map covers only a small area this does not matter greatly, but where a large sector of the world is shown this becomes a major problem. The most accurate way would be to split the surface into a series of long, elliptical shapes, like the external view of segments of an orange, and to leave them joined along the Equator. However, it is difficult to connect mentally the scattered pieces of information which such a plan would show, and these pieces are therefore joined in a variety of ways, or more usually stretched at their narrower ends to join up with each other and form a continuous picture. These map projec-

 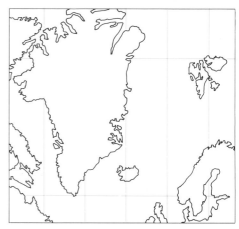

Map A. Greenland and Scandinavia shown (with Britain on the same scale in each) in two projections: one (left) based on the Pole, the other a Mercator projection based on the equator.

tions are selected for presenting the particular information required as accurately as possible.

Probably the best-known projection for world maps is Mercator's, and the present map is a modification of this. Its advantage is that it shows northern and southern, or eastern and western, points on the map in their correct relationship to each other, and gives correct lateral and longitudinal aspects of distribution. Its disadvantage is that while it is reasonably correct around the Equator, and the relative size and shapes of landmasses in the Mediterranean and southern European areas are fairly accurate, the relative east/west widths of areas become greatly exaggerated as one approaches the North Pole, and to prevent them becoming completely unrecognisable the north-to-south length of them is also exaggerated. An example of what happens is shown in Map A. This distortion will not affect the overall pattern of distribution of any particular species, but in studying such maps one must be aware that the apparent size of the northerly part of any extensive range is exaggerated, particularly along the lateral axis, in comparison with the southern end. As a result the species of Boreal, Subarctic and Arctic zones appear to occur over far greater areas than species in more temperate zones, even when the measured area of distribution is approximately the same.

This has some relevance to the earlier comments on strays. On the maps a species breeding in north-eastern Eurasia will appear to have traversed a very great distance to occur as a stray in western Europe, whereas from a global viewpoint the actual distance travelled is nothing like as far. On our map the distance from the Faeroes to Kamchatka in the north appears a little further than that from eastern Morocco to Japan in the south, but in measured units it is only about half the distance.

A variety of map projections is used in various publications, and in comparing one map with another it must be remembered that similar areas of distribution may show differences due to the use of different projections and the distortions involved.

2. Scale

Most bird species have requirements for feeding, shelter and nesting which do not obtain everywhere within their area of occurrence, and within the distribution ranges shown the actual presence of the birds may be sporadic. The information available is not sufficiently detailed for us to differentiate between areas where birds are numerous and those where they are present but scarce. In addition to variations in species density the special requirements of each species limit its occurrence, so that a large-scale map of its range would probably show a broken, highly discontinuous pattern, or perhaps just a few patches indicating the birds' presence. For the Common Sandpiper or Common Kingfisher the large-scale pattern of distribution would be a map of the streams, rivers and open waters.

By such standards the present maps are small-scale ones. The further you move away from any group of objects, the more difficult it becomes to see the smaller details and to separate one object from another. Just as the stripes on a zebra merge at a distance into a general greyish blur, so the spots and lines of a large-scale distribution map coalesce and lose their identity to produce larger patches of uniform colour. To help overcome this problem I have provided in the short text for each species information on the habitats within the species range where it may be found.

3. Regional variation in information

Through Europe, and over Eurasia as a whole, information on bird distribution varies in quantity and detail from one region to another. In general the situation is that detailed information on bird distribution is available for north-western Europe, and tends to become less detailed and more generalised as one proceeds eastwards or southwards. Admittedly, the work needed to provide a detailed survey is considerable. The mapping of the breeding birds of Britain by the British Trust for Ornithology involved some 8,000 ornithologists, most of them amateurs, over a five-year period. Most north-western countries have

now produced similar surveys, but in the Mediterranean region only Italy has done so. More generalised but new studies of bird distribution in Iran have also helped to clarify the pattern in that region. However, there are still extensive areas of the east and south where information is poor. From what we now know it is likely that in most instances new information from such areas will indicate that the ranges are smaller than was originally thought. In the absence of better information it is always easier to link some scattered records by filling in a whole area than to try and guess a pattern. Limitation within the range of the habitat required, and increased activity by man, are both likely to make birds scarcer than was thought; and to my regret most of the revision of maps is done with an eraser.

When looking at a map there is a tendency to assume unconsciously that the coverage of information is uniform, and that any differences apparent between one area and another are equally valid and accurate. Unfortunately this is not so, and one must take account of the comments made here in trying to assess the validity of the map.

ECOLOGICAL COUNTERPARTS AND REPLACEMENT SPECIES

In mapping the distribution of any European bird I have also looked for the presence of similar species outside its range. In any area a particular major habitat – forest, grassland or marsh, for instance – may provide a variety of smaller ecological niches which can be utilised by birds, often with a different species in each. If similar niches occur in two different areas, and if the species I am studying occurs in only one of these, then I would hope to find another similar species occupying the niche in the second area. In fact two such species may have evolved slight differences in habitat preference during isolation and may overlap to some degree in their ranges. The more exceptional instances in which no counterpart occurs I would suspect to be either the result of some past occurrence, such as a climate change, which has wiped out an earlier form which has not yet been replaced; or an indication of an impoverishment of the environment as a result of which a species, in order to survive, may occupy a series of niches which

elsewhere might accommodate several different forms.

Where I think that I have identified a counterpart of the species I am mapping I have referred to it in the text, and in a number of instances included it on the map. In some cases more than two species are involved. The species apparently acting as a replacement in a similar habitat I have usually referred to as an **ecological counterpart**. The two or more species will not necessarily be members of the same genus, or even of the same family, although they usually are; but they will replace each other in apparently similar ecological niches.

There is a different type of species replacement shown on some of the maps. In this a closely related group of species have become adapted to different types of habitats, and as a result replace each other where the habitats change. In this way they may effectively utilise most of the area available. Species involved in patterns of this type, and those which occur outside the Eurasian limits in areas where eco-

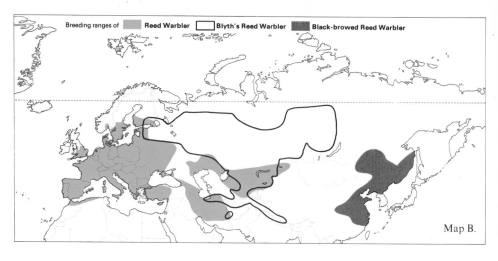

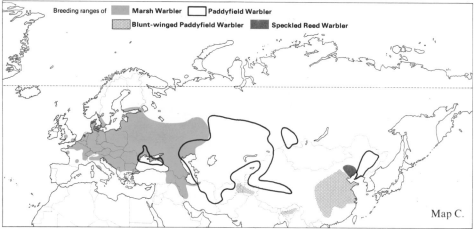

logical comparisons are uncertain, I have referred to simply as **replacement species**.

For the non-passerine species, where species groups are small, it has usually been possible to show either kind of distribution where it occurred and to comment in the text on the interpretation where necessary. However, in some passerine groups, where large numbers of similar species occur, one can find both types of distribution within one group. For mapping these a choice must be made. In these instances the maps which show the neatest pattern of replacement of one species by another are the second kind: those in which the boundaries of the distribution mark a well-defined change in habitat. In preference to such patterns I have chosen to show those in which species with similar habitat requirements are grouped together.

An example can be seen in the maps of the plain-backed *Acrocephalus* warblers. Of the four western species there are two pairs, one in more wooded habitats, the other in more marshy areas. The two maps (B and C) shown here divide the pairs and regroup them so that the species replace each other more neatly along well-defined boundaries of overall change in habitat. In the main sequence of maps (450 and 453) the same species are shown paired by habitat preference, with a more extensive overlap of range where they meet which probably indicates small differences in habitat utilisation that allow some degree of co-existence.

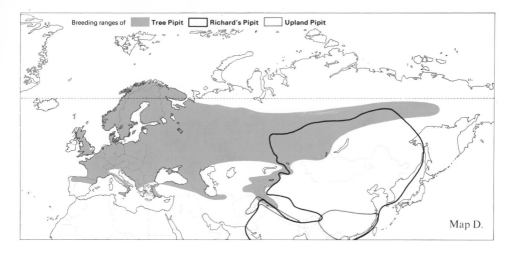

Map D.

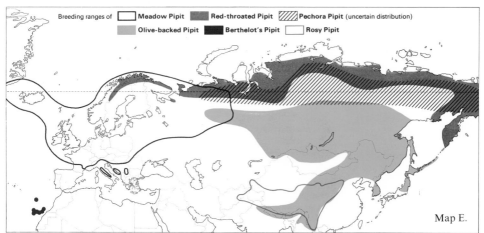

Map E.

A similar but slightly different problem arose with the pipits where the choice lay between grouping large and small species (D and E) or those of grassland and partly wooded habitats (413 and 421).

CLIMATE

Climate appears to be a primary factor governing the distribution of birds. There are two different factors involved which usually interact – variation in temperature and variation in wetness, including both the presence of surface water in streams, rivers, ponds and lakes, and in moist and marshy soils.

Temperature is the more obvious of the two, but while we know that it often controls the distribution of a species to some degree,

this is difficult to demonstrate. The prevailing temperature or changes of temperature produce secondary effects in a region, such as changes in the type or growth of vegetation, and the availability of seeds or insects, or open water for feeding. It is hard to separate the effects of these secondary conditions from the direct effect of temperature variation. We can only be sure about this in cases where we can see that in areas of relatively uniform habitat

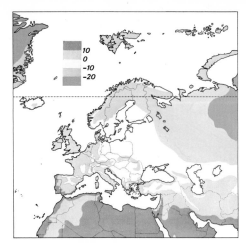
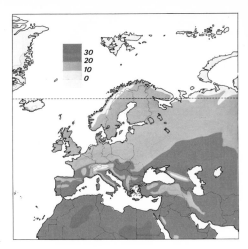

Temperature. Map F (*left*) January, and Map G (*right*) July: isotherms in degrees Centigrade.

extending to north or to south the distribution of a bird species fluctuates around some invisible line across this zone.

A more obvious aspect of response to temperature, in which the reaction of birds can more easily be studied, is that involving seasonal change. Winter cold renders many northern regions temporarily unsuitable for most birds, and the majority of species which inhabit them must leave them. For many Arctic, Boreal and Temperate breeding species annual migration to warmer winter quarters is a part of the typical distribution pattern. Some may leave our area completely, and most of these move south into Africa. Others, but much fewer, go south-east to India or

South-East Asia, and for those species with a wide breeding range the wintering area may help to indicate the general direction from which the original extension in range occurred.

In addition, a number of species may leave the northerly parts of their total range while others of the same species in less inhospitable areas remain present the whole year round. The migrants may either join the latter populations or bypass them on their way to winter quarters further south. It is not only a north-to-south movement that is involved, for, particularly with these partial migrants, there are also westerly and south-westerly movements to areas of milder winter climate.

Just as there are problems in judging cli-

Rainfall. Map H (*left*) November to April, and Map I (*right*) May to October: isohyets in centimetres.

matic effects, so there are problems in judging moistness as a quality of a region. It is easy enough to separate habitats with and without open water. It is much more difficult to judge relative wetness, and one suspects that secondary factors such as the type of vegetation and its growth, and the type of food present, may be more critical in determining the presence or absence of certain birds.

1. Climatic zones (see also section on Vegetation)

In order to use these climatic variations I have referred to a series of broad climatic zones, occurring in a series from north to south, which are determined by a temperature gradient, but more often recognised in practice by the landscape produced by its secondary effects. Although the terms listed below are widely used, the definitions are hazy and sometimes vary; and they are in any case theoretical divisions which in practice merge into each other along ill-defined lines. They should be regarded as generalised divisions intended to help clarify the overall picture of distribution, rather than hard and fast definitions. The temperatures referred to in places are mean temperatures, and the extremes may vary considerably on either side of these.

ARCTIC ZONE. Winter temperatures well below freezing, summer mean below 15°C. Ground frozen with permafrost, thawing at the surface in summer. Where not permanent snow or rock, usually tundra; moss or lichen tundra grading into shrub tundra.

ALPINE ZONE. This often has tundra-like vegetation on cold, high mountain areas, and may attract similar bird species. It appears to be an altitudinal equivalent of the Arctic zone and the two are often linked as the Arctic/Alpine zone; but the Alpine zone has a climate modified to some extent by that of the lower altitude areas around it.

SUBARCTIC ZONE. A slightly milder zone, usually with low birch and willow shrub tundra grading into birch scrub and forest tundra on the borders of the Boreal zone.

BOREAL ZONE. Winter mean −3°C, summer mean above 15°C. A zone with cold winters and cool summers with more rain in summer. Recognisable as the broad northern zone of conifer forest.

TEMPERATE ZONE. Winter mean above −3°C, summer mean below 21°C. In western Europe less than six months with a mean

temperature below 6°C, but with longer, colder winters further east. Rainfall more evenly spread in the west, mainly in summer in the east. A zone of generally milder winters and warmer summers, characterised over most of Europe by broadleaf forest.

WARM TEMPERATE ZONE. Winter mean above 4°C, summer mean 21–27°C. A zone of mild wet winters and dry hot summers. Evergreen broadleaf forest is typical of some of the zone, which may otherwise be characterised by dry areas with sparse vegetation.

SUBTROPICAL ZONE. Winter mean above 10°C, summer mean above 27°C. Within our range this is mainly an arid zone of high temperatures and little rainfall.

TROPICAL ZONE. Winter and summer means above 21°C. A zone of consistently high temperature and high rainfall. Characterised by tropical forest.

These zones are helpful when discussing the general distribution of birds, but it will be apparent from both text and maps that the distribution does not fall neatly into these divisions; although there is some evidence of latitudinal replacement which might be linked with temperature in the grebes (map 8), Whooper and Bewick's Swans (58, 59), grey geese (61), *Aythya* ducks (84–8), sea eagles (104), buzzards (118), larger falcons (144), ringed plovers (193), small owls (334), skylarks (387), pipits (421) and ravens (664–5). There have been past attempts to define bird distribution in terms of temperature by using summer and winter isotherms (lines connecting points with the same mean temperature) as range boundaries. However, the actual limits of species distributions depart from these lines so frequently that I believe other factors such as vegetation and land surface features to be more important in determining them.

2. West to east variation; the ocean influence

An idealised pattern of bird distribution controlled by temperature would be a series of regular transverse zones extending from the Pole to the Equator, as indicated by the divisions listed above, but other factors also play a part. One is the oceanic effect. The oceans, with their circulating currents, tend to have a modifying effect on the areas of land bordering them, cooling it a little in summer, and warming it a little in winter. Add to this the mainly westerly movement of air currents over oceans in the northern hemisphere, bringing not only milder but moister oceanic air over the western sides of continents; and such regions have both a milder and wetter climate. Europe is the western extremity of a continental landmass, and the presence of the Atlantic Ocean on its western side creates moister and milder conditions in the west, while drier and more extreme climatic conditions – hotter summers and colder winters – characterise the eastern parts. As with other aspects of bird distribution in Europe a response to such conditions is modified by other factors but some east/west division of this type is apparent.

Secondary factors are again possible determinants of distribution, and one must make allowance for the likelihood that south-western and Iberian isolates may reflect distributional history rather than present climatic influences, and for some groups, such as birds of prey, absence in the west may have been brought about by man. In instances which might be related to climate (see also western and eastern faunal groups p. 36) and which do not appear to be due to a belated spread, or to pressure of a competing species, we may list for the eastern species the Red-necked Grebe (7), Red-footed Falcon (155), Little Crake (187), European Roller (360), Lesser Grey Shrike (435), River Warbler (447), Barred Warbler (471), Red-breasted Flycatcher (507) and Penduline Tit (560). Purely western species, allowing for the alternative factors suggested above, are very few, perhaps only the Dartford Warbler (487) and possibly the Firecrest (502).

The eastern birds are mainly migrants which take advantage of a hot summer and avoid the cold winter. Few birds appear closely linked with the mild western region for breeding only, but the amelioration of winter weather by the oceanic influence, enhanced still further by the effect of the warm North Atlantic Drift current, is much more significant. The most obvious evidence of this climatic modification can be seen in the position of the 0°C isotherm, indicating roughly the division between frozen and ice-free water, and frozen and unfrozen ground. The line can be seen on the winter temperature map (Map F, p. 18) to cross southern Europe in the east, but swing north in central Europe, indicating warmer conditions to the west of it. This allows western populations of more widespread species to remain resident, and eastern populations may move westwards to join them. Evidence of this can

be seen in the position of the line dividing summer and resident distributions on fifty-two of the maps; and the present distribution of some species such as the Fan-tailed Warbler (459), Cetti's Warbler (461) and Cirl Bunting (594) appear to be determined partly by this.

3. North Atlantic Drift current (Map J)

The main Atlantic currents circulate clockwise around the ocean. Part of the north-east flowing Gulf Stream occurring off eastern North America continues north-east where it divides at the Azores. It brings warmer water to the west coast of Europe and extends between Britain and Greenland to the south-western edge of Spitzbergen and the sea north of Scandinavia. Its immediate effect is to produce an ice-free coast with warmer waters than would be anticipated for those latitudes, and allows coastal feeding and breeding species, and seabirds, to occur much further north in these parts than elsewhere. This can be seen for the Storm Petrel (18), Great Cormorant (23), Shag (26, 27), Grey Heron (35), Common Shelduck (73) and Redshank (226). In some instances the breeding range is encompassed by the area directly within the zone of the current, as in the Great Northern Diver (1), Fulmar (12), Manx Shearwater (14), Leach's Petrel (19), and Gannet (31).

Along its northern edge the current meets a cold current flowing from the Arctic along the east coast of Greenland. Some Arctic species such as the Glaucous Gull (271), Ivory Gull (280), Brünnich's Guillemot (298) and Little Auk (301) tend to migrate mainly westwards

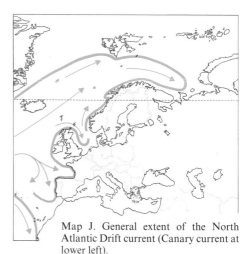

Map J. General extent of the North Atlantic Drift current (Canary current at lower left).

along this current and only to a limited extent southwards into the warmer water. This is linked with the fact that along the edges of this warm current the waters mix with cooler waters to produce conditions that nourish a rich concentration of plankton and fish. This source of food has as important an effect on the distribution and populations of the seabird species as does the climate amelioration.

There is a distributional phenomenon which occurs in this area and might be linked with these special conditions, although it cannot be proven. There are several coastal species which throughout the Holarctic region are limited to the Arctic zone, but in this region extend southwards from their otherwise circumscribed range. These are the Common Eider (89), Ringed Plover (194), Kittiwake (279) and Arctic Tern (286). One cannot argue that they need warmer waters but a rich food supply might be a significant factor.

4. Altitude (Map K)

One important cause of the irregular patterns of distribution shown by birds is the variation in the height of land, and the occurrence of hills and mountain ranges. The latter may affect the flow of air over the land and the pattern of rainfall, producing a wetter zone on their western slopes and a more arid area to the east of them. In addition they provide, in miniature, the type of gradation of temperature zones apparent in different latitudes. At greater altitudes the temperature is lower, and the rainfall sometimes greater; and although the higher land is influenced by the same general weather conditions as the lower areas surrounding it, it may also create conditions of its own and produce a series of cooler zones within a warm one. In ascending high mountains in the Warm Temperate zone one may pass through a broadleaf forest zone of a temperate type, conifer forest of a boreal type, higher subalpine scrub and meadows, and possibly tundra-like conditions on the mountain top.

These altitudinal zones may enable birds to extend their range into areas which might otherwise be unsuitable, and will also create conditions where the more typical species of the region around are absent. The link between altitudinal and latitudinal zones can be seen in those species which occur in colder zones at low altitudes in the north and recur in similar habitats on mountains further south. Examples are the Ptarmigan (158), Shorelark (402), and Ring Ouzel (552). The Dotterel (204) should belong here, but has eccentrically nested on one recent occasion on the Netherland polders. The Rock/Water Pipit has evolved two distinct subspecies in isolation. The Rock Pipit (418) occurs on rocky coasts in the north, while the Water Pipit (419) occupies an ecological equivalent in rocky alpine meadows in the south.

An altitude distribution pattern can be seen in the extension of some otherwise arctic species along the southward-extending mountain ridge of Scandinavia. This can be seen in the Scaup (85), Common Scoter (94), Long-tailed Skua (261), Snowy Owl (325) and Snow and Lapland Buntings (585 and 586). In some

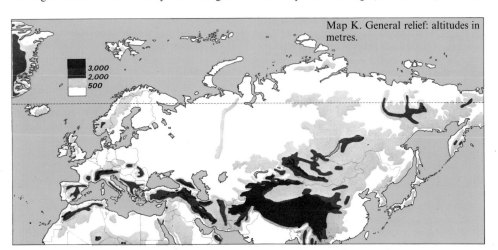

Map K. General relief: altitudes in metres.

3,000
2,000
500

of these there is a further extension to the Scottish highlands. The occurrence of conifer forest enables some species to extend further south in Europe in mountain areas, for example the Capercaillie (160), Hazelhen (163), Pygmy Owl (334), Three-toed Woodpecker (366) and Nutcracker (658).

In Europe, and in Eurasia generally, the higher mountain ranges mostly occur along the southern part of these regions. These enable some birds, in particular birds of temperate broadleaf and mixed forests, to extend their range southwards over a greater area than might be expected. In many species the range begins in lowlands in the north and terminates in mountain areas in the south. In addition some species are totally limited to mountain areas. These mostly occur in higher rocky areas, and although they would have had a more continuous distribution in a cooler past their present discontinuous range is determined by the occurrence of the higher mountain ranges. Examples are the snowcocks (164–5), Alpine Dunnock (443), Wallcreeper (577), Snowfinch (651) and Alpine Chough (673).

VEGETATION

The most important factor which helps to determine the birds present in any area is the dominant type of vegetation there. A few species of birds appear to be wholly linked with a particular plant species, as in the case of the Bearded Reedling (map 554) and reedbeds (*Phragmites*). However, care is needed in proposing such correlations. In Europe the range of the Eurasian Jay (659) has been shown to be closely coincident with that of the oaks (*Quercus* spp.) which provide its typical winter food, but in Siberia it is associated with conifer forest; while the Middle Spotted Woodpecker (369), which is also closely associated with oak forest, has a northern European range which follows very closely that of the Hornbeam (*Carpinus betulus*).

For the majority, however, the link between birds and certain plants is less apparent, or absent. For most birds the choice of a habitat seems to depend more on the general structure of the vegetation; for example in the size and spacing of shrubs or trees, the thickness and type of foliage, and distribution and height of herbage. A particular species of bird may occur in several habitats where the general appearance of the vegetation is similar but where the plant species involved are quite different.

For some species distribution has been aided by man. One effect of human modification of vegetation is to create a large number of small and varied units mixed together; and these may give some birds a wider but more discontinuous distribution. There is another factor which complicates efforts to link birds with a particular vegetational zone. Where a uniform plant habitat such as conifer forest or grassland occurs, it is found that the places preferred by the species which occupy it are those along the border of the zone rather than sites well within it. In this way the birds benefit from the variety and interaction of the two types of vegetation instead of only one. This is sometimes referred to as the "edge effect" and is well known to those who study bird territories. As a result species are more likely to occur along the borders of major zones or in areas of mixed and broken vegetation types. This again makes it difficult to correlate directly birds and major vegetation zones.

The zones themselves are rather artificial divisions. One type of vegetation tends to graduate into another, and the questions of where the line is drawn between two zones, and how many subdivisions are recognised, are highly subjective decisions. The list of vegetation types that follows is a convenient series of the more obvious divisions in the very complex and man-modified vegetation of Europe. In this list, and in the text of the book, I have tried to avoid introducing too many specialised or local terms in describing vegetation and habitats.

Since the majority of birds inhabit more than one zone, and since their distribution is further complicated by the "edge effect", it does not seem useful to include in the following list the names of those species with a more circumscribed range which are endemic to a particular zone.

TUNDRA. This is essentially an area where plant growth is inhibited by low temperatures, a short growing season and a frozen subsoil.

The main virtue of the region is that it offers a rich insect fauna in summer for breeding species.

MOSS TUNDRA. This is usually swampy and low-lying, with many pools, and has a vegetation mainly of sphagnum mosses, but mixed with grasses and other herbage.

LICHEN AND ROCK TUNDRA. This occurs on rocky and more well-drained areas such as ridges. It tends to be poor in vegetation and food.

SHRUB TUNDRA. This occurs in slightly warmer areas and consists mainly of dwarfed willow (*Salix*) and birch (*Betula*). Shrubby growth may also occur along waterways through open tundra.

FOREST TUNDRA. This is found along the northern edge of the conifer forest zone, and consists of scattered trees and groups of trees (conifers and birches) in areas of otherwise open tundra.

BIRCH SCRUB. This is an intermediate area between shrub tundra and forest, usually better drained than the former and ranging from open shrubby growth to more continuous low forest.

HIGH MOORLAND. This is on montane areas where climate and/or constant grazing have prevented tree and shrub growth. It produces cold open areas with ground vegetation dominated by Ling (*Calluna*) or grasses.

CONIFER FOREST. A zone of cone-bearing and mainly evergreen trees. In the extreme west pine (*Pinus*) predominates, with spruce (*Picea*) soon appearing a little further east, and other genera such as larches (*Larix*) and firs (*Abies*) becoming more important in the east. This type of forest is frequently thick, with little undergrowth, but in places, particularly by water, it may be mixed with broadleaf trees. Much of the region in which it occurs was modified by Pleistocene glaciation and numerous lakes and swamps are characteristic of some areas. It has been cleared for cultivation and pasture in many areas, but less extensively than the broadleaf forests.

BROADLEAF FOREST. This was the typical vegetation covering most of temperate Europe in the past. It is often a mixture of species, but may vary from oak (*Quercus*) forest with a rich growth of shrubs and herbage, to stands of pure beech (*Fagus*) or hornbeam (*Carpinus*) which permit little growth beneath them. It is rich in tree and shrub species. It has been more extensively cleared for cultivation and pastures than most other vegetative zones, and in many parts of Europe it is limited to shelterbelts, or small areas retained for timber, and is referred to in places in the text as "woodland". Scattered trees occur more frequently in cleared areas. The effect of this clearing and modification of the landscape by man has resulted in the artificial production of types of vegetation which may occur more naturally elsewhere.

PARKLAND. This usually involves broadleaf trees and consists of widely-spaced, well-grown trees with open and usually grassy space between them. Shrubby growth may be absent or only present in very limited areas.

SCRUB. This is a very variable type of vegetation. It usually consists of a thick growth of shrubs and trees, often low-growing. It occurs naturally where soil or climate does not permit full forest growth, and also as a temporary stage in areas where forest is regenerating after clearance, or is continually prevented from achieving a more climax stage.

HEATHLAND. This is a temperate equivalent of high moorland. It is mainly open grassland, heathers (*Erica* spp.) or mixed herbage with some low shrubs and sometimes scattered trees. It often occurs on stony or sandy areas with poor soil but may also be maintained at this stage in more fertile areas by grazing.

ARTIFICIAL FOREST. Under this heading I would include plantations, which are stands of usually single species, close-growing, uniform in height and not allowed to decay or achieve maturity; and orchards, which are patches of an open and low forest, again usually of controlled growth.

EVERGREEN FOREST. This is the natural forest of warm temperate regions; usually occurring in the lowlands, and extensively reduced by cultivation and continual grazing. In the Mediterranean it consists mainly of evergreen oaks, sometimes mixed with heat-tolerant conifers. In this zone orchards tend to be replaced by citrus fruit groves, and in many areas olive groves provide open stands of trees which are allowed to mature and often contain many cavities.

MAQUIS. The name is used here for the mainly Mediterranean, warm temperate equivalent of the more northerly heathland. It may occur on dry or rocky areas of poor soils or as a result of constant grazing, replacing evergreen forest.

It consists of low shrubs, often prickly and drought-resistant, and varies from a tall, thick and continuous cover to lower and more open growth, often with herbaceous plants. It grades into a low, sparse and scattered growth with bare open ground between, known in this region as garigue.

SEMI-DESERT. This occurs in regions where the rainfall is extremely low and erratic. It is characterised by extensive areas of bare, dry ground, and vegetation may only cover about half the ground area. It tends to consist of well-spaced drought-resistant shrubs, or (rarely) trees, and scattered clumps of herbage.

DESERT. This is a further stage than the last, where the extremely small amount of rainfall cannot sustain a vegetative cover. Much of the ground is bare, and vegetation may consist of scattered shrubs or herbage tufts, often confined to slightly better sites such as ravines and wadis.

DISTRIBUTION AND THE EFFECTS OF TIME

In these introductory pages I have emphasised the facts that birds are mobile and to some extent unpredictable and difficult to map. I have pointed out that they respond to changing conditions and that their distribution is controlled to some degree by climate, altitude and more particularly by the vegetation present. We know that at present we experience small changes in climate over a period of years, that greater changes have occurred within recorded history, and that in the prehistoric glacial (Pleistocene) period considerable fluctuations took place both in European climate and in the distribution of vegetation associated with it. We can be reasonably certain that birds responded to such changes, and that these variations in climate helped to produce the present patterns of distribution.

1. Fossil evidence

We can deduce some of the distributional changes that have occurred in the past from the bones found in deposits of the Pleistocene and post-Pleistocene periods. Z. Bochenski has produced maps of some of these and the three illustrated show the present distribution (orange) and the past records (red spots) of a southern species, the Black Vulture, which occurred further north; a northern species, the Willow Grouse, which extended south; and in the third species, the Ptarmigan, how the present isolated populations may have been joined in the past.

The last map shows how a cold-tolerant species occurred in the past further south and at lower altitudes. As the European climate became warmer it would be forced to shift further north or into the higher, colder zones of mountains. For these species shown here we

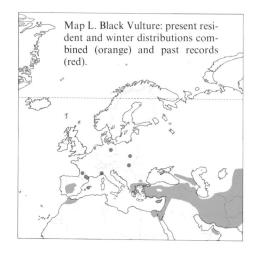

Map L. Black Vulture: present resident and winter distributions combined (orange) and past records (red).

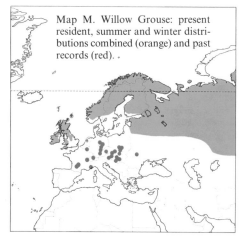

Map M. Willow Grouse: present resident, summer and winter distributions combined (orange) and past records (red).

Map N. Ptarmigan: present resident distribution (orange) and past records (red).

can see how the changes of climate in the past have helped to produce the present distribution, and if it has affected these species then all species are likely to have been influenced in some ways.

2. Glaciation: refuges and re-invasion

From a study of other living things, both plants and animals, we already have a reasonable, but by no means wholly finalised, picture of the climate of Eurasia in the recent past. For a period of nearly two million years there has been a succession of fluctuating cold and warm periods. The problem is that a massive advance of glacial ice and tundra conditions over more southerly areas can eliminate much of the evidence of what has gone before. The maximum advance of ice occurred in what is generally referred to as the next-to-last glaciation (the Riss, Saalian, or Wolstonian Glaciation) which covered much of northern Eurasia (Map O) and extended tundra-type conditions well to the south. This was followed by a warmer interglacial period (the Riss/Wurm, Eemian or Ipswichian Interglacial) when conditions improved and forest was found much further north (Map P), while tundra and ice were much reduced; but from recent information it would appear that even during this period there were at least three short but very cold phases. There was then another glacial period (Wurm, Weichselian or Devensian Glaciation) in which the ice did not advance so far south (Map Q) that it erased the evidence of the earlier glaciation. This period ended *c.* 10,000 years ago and is usually known as the last glaciation; but there is some doubt as to whether these alternating cold and warmer periods have ceased, or whether we now live in another interglacial period. The last suggestion is not as odd as it might seem.

Map O. Vegetation zones at coldest period of next-to-last ('Riss') glaciation.

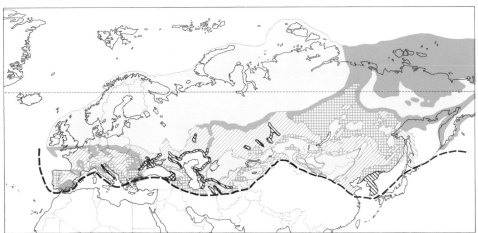

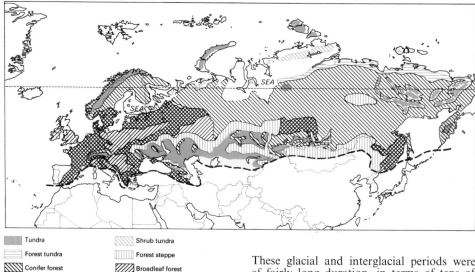

Tundra		Shrub tundra	
Forest tundra		Forest steppe	
Conifer forest		Broadleaf forest	
Steppe		Desert	

Map P (*above*). Vegetation during warmer periods of last interglacial.

Map Q (*below*). Vegetation zones at coldest periods of last glaciation.

Ice	Tundra/cold steppe
Shrub tundra/steppe	Shrub/forest tundra
Forest tundra/forest steppe	
Cold loess steppe with birch scrub	
Cold steppe with riverine or conifer forest	
Conifer forest	Mixed forest
Steppe	Desert

These glacial and interglacial periods were of fairly long duration, in terms of tens of thousands of years, and certainly longer than the time that has elapsed since; but, whatever the future, we have evidence of a series of very cold periods in the past, alternating with periods as warm as, or warmer than, those which we now enjoy.

In a long-term view the distribution of plants and animals through the Eurasian region in the Pleistocene can be seen as a dynamic pattern of ceaseless ebb and flow, although in human terms the process is so slow that even over a period of several successive generations of men little change might be apparent. Plants cannot move as do animals, but there is a constant and gradual shift of boundaries as

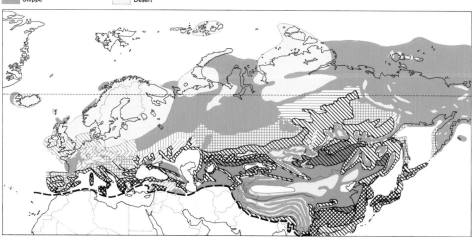

one species colonises an area at the expense of another. With large-scale temperature and climate changes these could occur on a larger scale. In considerably less than 3,000 years, conifer trees, with their wind-blown seeds, could have shifted their distribution north from the borders of the Mediterranean to the extreme north of Scandinavia, merely by establishing new seedlings annually a kilometre further than in the previous year. The time is a short one within the very long period under consideration, but long enough in human terms for the change to go unrecorded. When the boundaries of plant distribution change, the distribution of birds also changes, and for birds whose limits are defined directly by climate the move can take place before the plants have responded.

If we compare the map of present-day plant distribution in Europe (Map R), with that of a glacial period, it is apparent that during colder times a vegetation type such as forest, for example, could no longer survive in northern areas and occurred only in more southerly regions bordering the Mediterranean, while forest birds would have made a corresponding southward shift. The geography of the southern region is such that it does not allow a broad and unbroken zone of forest. It is interrupted by seas and mountain ranges, and the forest becomes broken into a series of separate areas, isolated from the others to varying degrees. It is when populations of birds become isolated in refuges such as these that the evolution of new species and subspecies can occur.

A small population of birds, with an inheritance of genes more limited than that which occurred in the original widespread population, may be isolated in such circumstances for thousands of years and for as many bird generations. The population may develop differences in colour and perhaps in size and shape, compared with other related but isolated populations. When conditions finally change and the forest can spread again, these populations may spread back with it and meet each other.

If the changes within the population have been slight (and they tend to increase with the length of time that the group was isolated) then birds of a single species may interbreed and merge together again in a single range. Where this has occurred it will be difficult to find evidence of it now. If within a species with a wide continuous range there are small con-

Map R. Simplified map of modern vegetation zones (ignoring effects of agriculture).

Ice	
Tundra	Shrub tundra
Forest tundra	Conifer forest
Mixed forest	Forest steppe
Grass steppe	M Mountain steppe
G Swamp grassland	High altitude grass and steppe
Semi-desert, desert, salt and shrub steppes	
Mediterranean scrub, maquis	Mediterranean evergreen forest
Jungle scrub and open tropical scrub	
Tropical rain forest	

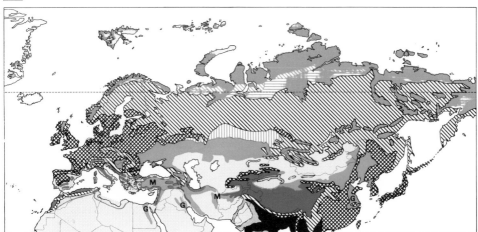

sistent and local variations, one cannot distinguish differences arising from possible early isolation from those which may have evolved since the present range was occupied.

When an isolated population has evolved more distinct differences these will be retained in the regions into which the birds subsequently spread. The birds will interbreed with other subspecific populations of the same species when they meet; but in some instances the areas of distribution are distinct and the zone of interbreeding very narrow. This might indicate that the different forms had only recently re-encountered each other, or alternatively suggests that they may have also evolved some small preferences for habitat or temperature which control their spread to some degree.

Some of these subspecies are so distinctive in appearance that in the past they have been regarded at times as separate species. They often help to show patterns of replacement which may give an indication of their probable areas of evolution. Such patterns may be seen here in maps of the Black Kite (107), Pied (422) and Yellow Wagtails (424), Red-backed Shrike (431), Stonechat (513), Black Redstart (538), Bluethroat (541), Great Tit (571), Common Nuthatch (574), Reed Bunting (591), Goldfinch (617), Nutcracker (658), Eurasian Jay (659) and Crow (668).

The patterns of isolation and subsequent re-encounter are similar for the populations which have become separate species, but here patterns may be confused by the possibility of overlap in distribution, and perhaps a greater passage of time necessary for this degree of divergence. However, in some groups it is possible to see replacement patterns similar to those of the distinctive subspecies; as in the cormorants (26), sea eagles (104), pied woodpeckers (367), tree pipits (421), bulbuls (430) and starlings (654).

These changing patterns of climate and vegetation have been mentioned only with reference to forests, but this subdivision, isolation, spread and reunion occurred at intervals, during the Pleistocene and after, in virtually all the different types of bird habitats. In some respects the interglacial periods show converse patterns, with the colder tundra and steppe habitats which in the glacial periods had dominated Eurasia reduced to smaller scattered northern areas.

From what I have said it follows that a knowledge of the changes of habitat distribution during the Pleistocene period may help us to understand the evolution and present distribution of species and subspecies. There is, however, one major problem. We may be able to infer what must have happened in the past, and perhaps guess at the existence of several successive stages, but what we now see is the aftermath of only the last of a repeated sequence of great climatic events, and we have no way of gauging how much of the present pattern is the result of the immediate past, and how much is the relic of a succession of earlier events. It is known that at least six major glaciations and their intervening interglacials have occurred in the Pleistocene period, and from new information that is becoming available it would seem that the period contained many more alternating periods of extremes of climate. Any one such period might bring about the kind of events I have discussed here, and the only effects we can assess with any certainty are those for the last glaciation and the subsequent period of time.

Apparent evidence of a secondary pattern of subspeciation superimposed on an earlier one producing several species can be seen on the maps of the kites (107) and pied wagtails (422).

3. Distribution patterns

In the past history of climate change in Europe there have been long periods when the habitats required by many bird species were reduced to small and sometimes isolated areas. We know that fragmentation and isolation of this kind in bird populations has produced new and separate species or subspecies. By comparing the distribution of different species in various groups, certain recurring distribution patterns can be seen. The occurrence of such patterns, in unrelated groups, may indicate the sites of past refuge areas and the probable path of subsequent spread from them. Using these patterns we may be able to construct at least a part of the recent history of speciation and distribution in this region. In the section which follows I have tried to select the more obvious patterns and to use them for this purpose.

Pair patterns. The simplest and commonest pattern is that in which the single division from north to south produces separate eastern and western populations which may be species or subspecies. Usually the whole broad stretch of Eurasia is involved. In addition to the presence of mainly uninhabited northern regions during glacial periods, similar areas of cold and ice occurred in higher mountain areas. Many of these were isolated icecaps, but in central Eurasia the high areas of Altai, Pamirs, Himalayas and Tibetan plateau formed a wedge of inhospitable country that divided the main region into two.

This pattern can be seen in a wide range of species. East and west pairs of species occur in the sparrowhawks, spotted eagles (129–30), Montagu's and Pied Harriers, capercaillies (160), corncrakes, Caspian and Oriental Plovers (197), golden plovers, curlews (234), Snipe and Pin-tailed Snipe (244), rock doves (309), turtle doves (316), European and Jungle Nightjars (343), green woodpeckers (376), tree pipits (421), red-backed shrikes (431), dunnocks (439), *Locustella* warblers (444–7), *Cettia* warblers (460–1), pied flycatchers (504–6), spotted flycatchers (508–9), redstarts (535), Redwing and Naumann's Thrush (548), Blue and Azure Tits (562–3), dippers (581), reed buntings (591), Yellowhammer and Pine Bunting (592), Chaffinch and Brambling (608), and jackdaws (671).

There are other species in which a similar divide in distribution is apparent but involves two subspecies. These are the White Stork, Harlequin (93), Velvet and Common Scoters, Marsh Harrier, Red-footed Falcon, Common Pheasant (172), Pied Wagtail (422), Red-breasted Flycatcher (507), Stonechat (514), Blue Rock Thrush (520), Black Redstart (538), Bluethroat (541), Black-throated/Red-throated Thrush (550), Rock Bunting (604), Azure-winged Magpie (662) and Rook. A division into eastern and western populations, which is possibly recent since it has produced no apparent differences between the two, occurs in the Lesser Kestrel, Whimbrel (234), Marsh Sandpiper, Marsh Tit (568) and Siskin (611).

In some instances the pairs of forms remain separated (fig. 1A), the Azure-winged Magpie or perhaps the Harlequin being the most extreme examples of this. In many cases, however, they have spread back and meet again or overlap in range. Subspecies, if they meet again, may form an apparently continuous range (fig. 1B) with the past separation indicated by such characters as plumage variation and possible differences in migration routes and winter quarters. Species, however, may evolve small differences in their ecological requirements which allow them to overlap extensively in range when they meet again (fig. 1C).

For many pairs of forms the mountains of central Eurasia are the line along which they meet, and may continue to create a distribution gap between the two. However, in a number of instances the division between such a pair of species may occur not in Eurasia but far to the east or west, suggesting that at times other factors may affect this distribution pattern,

A number of species with a broad Eurasian distribution have a closely related second

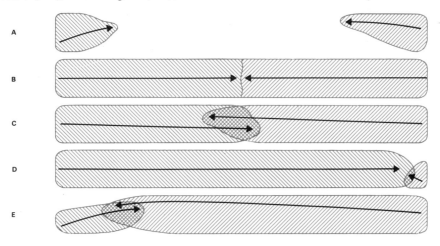

Fig. 1. Pair patterns

species occurring only on the extreme edge of the range in the east (fig. 1D). These are usually in eastern China, south-east Siberia or Japan; and sometimes with a very restricted range. Examples can be found in Great and Temminck's Cormorants (23, 26), little egrets, spoonbills, shelducks, Ferruginous Duck and Bauer's Pochard (86), mergansers, sea eagles (104), pheasants (172), little gulls, Common and Black-tailed Gulls, crested and Chinese Crested Terns, Ringed and Long-billed Ringed Plovers (193), Lapwing and Grey-headed Plover (205, 208), lesser spotted woodpeckers (fig. 3), pygmy woodpeckers (fig. 3), and waxwings. Some of the more typical species pairs discussed earlier have an additional eastern species with restricted range; as in the green woodpeckers (376), shrikes (431), dunnocks (439), grasshopper warblers (445), reed warblers (450), *Cettia* warblers (460), pied flycatchers (504), spotted flycatchers (509), robins (539), reed buntings (591), and crows (668).

The converse situation, in which species occur with a long range from eastern Eurasia through to Europe where they meet and usually overlap with a second species with a more restricted south-western range (fig. 1E), can be seen in the Spotted and Lesser Spotted Eagles (129–30), kites (107), European and Red-necked Nightjars (343–4), Great Spotted, Middle Spotted and Syrian Woodpeckers (367), Grey-headed and Green Woodpeckers (376), Eurasian and Short-toed Treecreepers (578), Cirl Bunting and Yellowhammer (592), and Common and Spotless Starlings (653–5).

Similar patterns occur in the subspecies of some forest birds such as Common Nuthatch (574), Nutcracker (658) and Eurasian Jay (659). This pattern of a long westward extension, even where the European western counterpart does not occur, is seen in a number of northern forest species including Hazelhen (163), Pygmy Owl (334), White-backed and Lesser Spotted Woodpeckers, Red-flanked Bluetail (544) and some buntings (587–9).

Several alternative explanations can be suggested for these uneven distributions. It might simply be a matter of the distribution of the required habitat. This might be a reasonable argument in the case of forest birds of the second type of distribution, since western forms are more often linked to broadleaf habitats and eastern forms to conifer forest; but this does not seem convincing for some of the

water birds of the first group, nor for the subspecies of widespread species which show the second pattern. Alternatively it can be suggested that while in scattered refuge areas birds may become adapted to the general temperature of the refuge. If one refuge was cooler than another, then the birds from the cooler refuge might be able to react more quickly as the regions warm up after a glaciation and to colonise an area before the birds in warmer refuges had responded to the climatic change. This explanation might fit a number of instances but would not explain them all.

The third possibility concerns the size of the original refuge. The argument here is that if two forms originate from a large and a small refuge respectively, the large refuge will produce a more rapid increase and surplus in numbers, and so enable that population to spread much more rapidly than the other in the small refuge. Having done so, it may inhibit the subsequent spread of the latter. This again would be more clearly applicable in the case of the forest species, since the maps show a large forest refuge in eastern Eurasia during the glaciations, while in Europe only very small areas persisted, mostly around the Mediterranean region. Water birds from the west might also fit this hypothesis to some extent, since during the glaciations the Caspian, Aral and Black Seas covered a much greater area and may have carried larger populations.

Trio patterns. Another type of pattern, which often has the appearance of a species pair pattern with a southern addition, is the trio pattern (fig. 2A). The typical one would show a pair of species occupying much of the Eurasian range and usually originating from opposite ends as in the previous pattern. In addition, when the two populations had been divided in east and west, a third population was sometimes pushed southwards into the Indian region. When the various forms spread back again in warmer periods the Indian birds appear to have been prevented from spreading north by the Himalayas and the Tibetan plateau. They either ended their range at the mountain slopes or spread to a lesser extent along the coastal regions towards the Persian Gulf or into northern Indonesia and/or southern China. Examples occur in the pond herons (42), small sparrowhawks (114), quails (166), partridges (167), rock doves (309), cuckoos

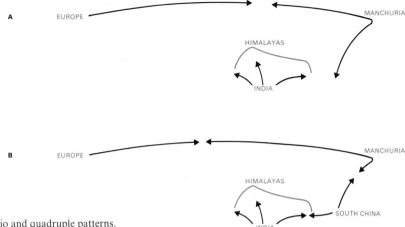

Fig. 2. Trio and quadruple patterns.

(320–1), great reed warblers (449), treecreepers (578), greenfinches (618) and orioles (652).

It is a pattern which may also occur in subspecies, as shown by the Black Kite (107) and the Great Tit (571). In the latter the three major populations interbreed in the areas where they meet, and form intermediate populations. Trios consisting of two species, one of which has a pair of well-marked subspecies, occur in varying patterns in the honey buzzards (123) with two eastern subspecies, the red-backed shrikes (431) with two western subspecies, and the red-breasted flycatchers (507) with two northern subspecies. The existence of these mixed patterns indicates that these must be at least second stages in repeated patterns of isolation and spread

Other species groups which exhibit trio patterns that do not fit so neatly into the basic distribution pattern described above are the griffon vultures (137), pratincoles (252), tree pipits (421), pied wagtails (422), redstarts (535), robins and rubythroats (539), nightingales (543), black-headed and red-headed buntings (603), rock buntings (604) and crows (668).

In several instances there is a slightly different pattern, with the third species in southern China or Indochina, as in the francolins (169) and whinchats (512), which may relate to the next pattern group.

Quadruple pattern. This pattern (fig. 2B), involving eastern species, is similar to the last but differs because in an earlier period eastern

China appears to have had two refuges, the northern Manchuria and south-east Siberian refuge, and another in the south-east. This pattern, with the extra south-eastern species, can be seen in the little bitterns (47), shrikes (431), rock thrushes (519), starlings (654), and also the crows (668) if the Indian species is added. Subspecific patterns of this kind occur in the Common Nuthatch (574), Nutcracker (658) and Eurasian Jay (659).

South-eastern edge, and Himalayas. The south-eastern edge of the region covered in this book when Eurasia is discussed, borders on a southern region of usually warm and moist climate, rich forest vegetation and a complex of northern mountain ranges. The area is one with a high potential for producing and maintaining a very large number and variety of species. On a number of the maps where several species of a group occur in southern Eurasia, a line enclosing a relatively small region of the Himalayas and Indochina encloses the total range of not just one, but a number of species in that group. The situation is often too complicated to map adequately on a small scale.

The potential of the northern part of this region for a forest group such as the woodpeckers is shown in fig. 3 and involves only those species associated with temperate forest habitats, and omits the endemic ones. Four European species appear to originate after the last glaciation from eastern Eurasia; and the figure shows the species groups for each in the south-east part of the range. All four species

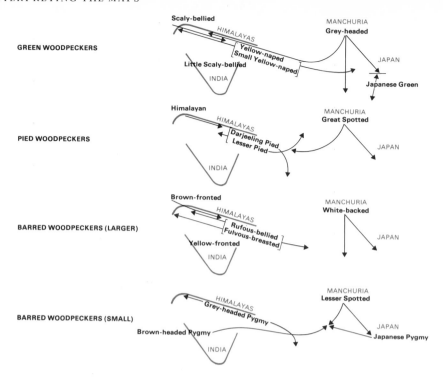

Fig. 3. Recurring distribution patterns in eastern woodpeckers.

also spread southwards into China and Japan, where two encounter related Japanese species. One reaches the Himalayas and another extends through the range. Of the four groups, three have a representative species in lowland India, three have a western Himalayan species, and these three also have two other species extending through much of the Himalayas from the east.

There is an underlying pattern here which reveals the presence of a more complex pattern of refuge areas than within the main area under discussion, and is possibly associated with the upper parts of river basins. Mercifully it lies mainly outside our area. There are some other indications of parts of this pattern elsewhere in our maps. It can be seen in the bullfinches; and the presence of a western Himalayan species also occurs in the red-breasted flycatchers (507), coal tits (565), and jays (659), while similar subspecific patterns are apparent in the Common Nuthatch (574) and Nutcracker (658).

Southern glacial refuges (Map S). The patterns discussed above reveal the presence of a chain of potential refuges along the southerly borders of Eurasia, in Japan, northern China, southern China, India and southern Europe. These appear to be the lowland refuges to which birds retreated during glaciations. If we now examine some groups of species which occur through these more southern parts, and which are non-migratory and with small ranges, we see that they produce a large number of forms suggesting the existence of a chain of such refuges. The combination of distributions in fig. 4 shows the pattern involved. It is probably a little crude and inaccurate since it is not always clear from which refuges a population is derived; and since different birds have different needs, the area which constitutes a refuge must inevitably vary to some extent.

The extreme instance of the last comment is that shown by the parrotbills (554) where, in species requiring large reedbeds, relatively

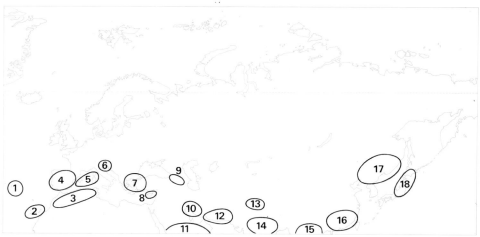

Map S. Potential southern edge refuge areas (probably incomplete or oversimplified for 14–18, south-eastern Eurasia). 1 Azores. 2 Canary Islands. 3 North-west Africa. 4 Iberian Peninsula. 5 Western Mediterranean Islands. 6 Adriatic. 7 Aegean. 8 Cyprus. 9 Southern Caucasus. 10 Persian Gulf. 11 Arabia. 12 Southern Iran/Pakistan borders. 13 Western Himalayas. 14 India. 15 Indochina. 16 Southern China. 17 Northern China. Manchuria, south-east Siberia. 18 Japan.

Species groups or species	1. NORTH AFRICA	2. IBERIA and S.W. EUROPE	3. ADRIATIC and CENTRAL EUROPE	4. AEGEAN and EASTERN EUROPE	5. MIDDLE EAST	6. ARABIA	7. IRAN/AFGHANISTAN/PAKISTAN BORDERS	8. WESTERN HIMALAYAS	9. INDIA	10. NORTHERN INDOCHINA	11. SOUTHERN CHINA	12. NORTHERN CHINA	13. JAPAN
SHAGS	—	*	—	—	—	—	*	—	*	—	—	*	*
RED-LEGGED PARTRIDGES	*	*	—	*	—	*	—	*	—	—	—	—	—
NIGHTJARS	*	*	*	—	—	*	*	—	*	—	—	—	—
PIED WOODPECKERS	O	—	*	—	*	*	*	*	—	*	—	*	—
GREEN WOODPECKERS	*	*	—	—	—	—	—	*	*	—	—	*	*
BULBULS	*	—	—	—	—	*	*	*	*	*	—	—	—
HIPPOLAIS WARBLER	*	*	—	*	*	—	*	—	—	—	—	—	—
PIED FLYCATCHERS	*	O	—	—	O	—	—	—	—	—	*	*	*
BABBLERS	*	—	—	—	*	*	*	*	*	—	—	—	—
THIN-BILLED NUTHATCHES	*	*	—	—	*	—	—	*	—	—	*	—	*
ORTOLAN BUNTING GROUP	—	*	—	*	*	—	*	—	—	—	—	—	—
Eurasian Jay	O	O	—	—	O	—	—	*	—	O	O	O	O

Fig 4. Southern refuge areas and some species groups. An asterisk represents the presence of a species in the area. Where the same species is present in more than one area, the asterisks are linked by a line. Well-defined subspecies are represented by circles.

limited sectors of Chinese river valleys appear to have provided the isolation necessary for speciation.

Even allowing for these problems, we can see from figure 4 that within widespread groups of sedentary species there is evidence of isolation and the development of new subspecies or species in a large number of refuge areas. Thirteen are identifiable from the table. An examination of other species patterns provides additional evidence for these, and in the European region indicates several others. The potential European refuge areas along the southern edge of the region, likely to have been important at the height of glaciations, can be identified by endemic species or subspecies of limited distribution. There appear to be twelve within the broader European, or Western Palaearctic region. With the indicator forms listed these are:

AZORES. One well-defined subspecies of Bullfinch (610).

CANARY ISLANDS. Long-toed Pigeon (312), Laurel Pigeon (313), Plain Swift (350), Berthelot's Pipit (413), Canary Islands Chat (515), Blue Chaffinch (608), Canary (613). Distinct subspecies of Firecrest (502).

NORTH-WEST AFRICA. Barbary Partridge (168), Levaillant's Woodpecker (379), Tristram's Warbler (489), Moussier's Redstart (537), Kabylie Nuthatch (573). Subspecies of Eurasian Jay (659).

NORTH-WEST AFRICA AND SOUTHERN IBERIAN PENINSULA. Crested Coot (180), Red-necked Nightjar (344), Dupont's Lark (399), Spotless Starling (655). Subspecies of Purple Gallinule (181), Thekla Lark (391) and Azure-winged Magpie (662).

WESTERN MEDITERRANEAN ISLANDS. Marmora's Warbler (488), Corsican Nuthatch (573).

ADRIATIC. Rock Partridge (168), ?Middle Spotted Woodpecker (369), Italian Sparrow (644). Subspecies of Yellow Wagtail (424).

AEGEAN. Olive-tree Warbler (466), Rüppell's Warbler (478), Cretzschmar's Bunting (599).

CYPRUS. Cyprus Warbler (476).

SOUTHERN CAUCASUS. Caucasian Black Grouse (162), Caucasian Snowcock (164), Green Warbler (496), ?Sombre Tit (566), Krüper's Nuthatch (573). Subspecies of Chiffchaff (493) and Bluethroat (541).

PERSIAN GULF. Black-shafted Tern (291), Grey Hypocolius (429), White-eared Bulbul (430), Iraq Babbler (557).

ARABIA. (The list is limited to the species occurring within our area.) ?Socotra Cormorant (28), Arabian Partridge (168), Philby's Partridge (168), Sand Partridge (173), ?Sooty Gull (263), Arabian Woodpecker (367), Arabian Babbler (556). Subspecies of the Common Bulbul (430).

SOUTHERN IRAN/PAKISTAN BORDERS. See-see Partridge (173), Sykes's Nightjar (346), Hume's Lesser Whitethroat (486), Plain Willow Warbler (497), Hume's Wheatear (533), Eastern Pied Wheatear (534), Eastern Rock Nuthatch (576), Sind Jungle Sparrow (647), Pleske's Ground Chough (663).

Northern glacial refuges (Map T). Although the birds that are adapted to exploit the tundra and other cold regions must have had very restricted opportunities during the warmer interglacial periods in Europe, they show little evidence of refuge patterns compared with the southern species. This might be linked with the fact that they are mostly migratory and usually cover long distances. Most of them have extensive distributions with little variation in populations, and a high proportion have a circumpolar range.

The frozen winter sea, now and in the past, has resulted in the separation of some species in the two oceans. It has produced a series of birds with Atlantic and Pacific forms, reinvading Eurasia to varying degrees during the summer. This situation occurs in the Brent Goose (67), Harlequin (93), Barrow's Goldeneye, Common and Velvet Scoters, and Guillemot and Brünnich's Guillemot. In other instances pairs of closely related species occur with a counterpart in each ocean, as in the Great Black-backed and Slaty-backed Gulls, Black and Pigeon Guillemots, and Puffin and Horned Puffin.

There is only one area of this northern region which appears to produce a refuge distribution pattern comparable with those found in the south. This is in the centre of the tundra zone and encompasses the estuarine areas of the Ob and Yenesei Rivers and the Taymyr Peninsula. This area had offshore tundra islands during the last interglacial and during the last glaciation the rivers retained a persistent tundra area between two great icecaps.

The Red-breasted Goose (66) has a breeding distribution confined to this area. It is a

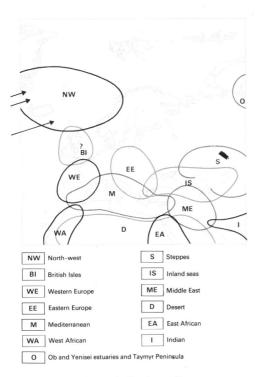

NW	North-west
BI	British Isles
WE	Western Europe
EE	Eastern Europe
M	Mediterranean
WA	West African
O	Ob and Yenisei estuaries and Taymyr Peninsula

S	Steppes
IS	Inland seas
ME	Middle East
D	Desert
EA	East African
I	Indian

Map T. Faunal areas indicating earlier refuge or invasion patterns.

north of the British Isles. Within this region are found the Pink-footed Goose (63), Barnacle Goose (69), Lesser Black-backed Gull (275) and possibly some other species (see p. 36). These three all have related species occurring in the northern European region and some isolating factor must have been present in the past to allow speciation to occur.

Larger faunal areas (Map T). In addition to the small refuge areas which can be identified from the species distributions, there are larger and less clearly defined areas with endemic faunas which suggest a past separation and which probably contain within their limits the more circumscribed areas which were the keys to survival in these regions. Some of these larger areas towards the margins of the European region may contain species which have invaded from outside the limits, rather than having evolved within the area. It is not possible to do more here than to identify such areas and to list the species which appear peculiar to them. In doing this I have not attempted to categorise those species with wide ranges which do not immediately fit into the pattern of distribution discussed here.

MEDITERRANEAN. The Mediterranean sea and its borders is an obvious area providing suitable habitat conditions for some birds with special requirements. Typical species not already mentioned in the list of refuges are Eleonora's Falcon (151), Mediterranean Gull (268), Audouin's Gull (276), Pallid Swift (349), Subalpine Warbler (481), Spectacled Warbler (482), Bonelli's Warbler (490), Black-eared Wheatear (524), Black Wheatear (531), intermediate-billed Reed Bunting (591), Syrian Serin (611), large-billed Crossbill (625).

CASPIAN AND MEDITERRANEAN. During colder periods the Caspian, and at times the other inland seas, were considerably larger than they are now (Maps O–Q). They appear to have persisted as potential refuge areas through these periods of change and a number of species have a distribution which wholly or partly embraces both the Mediterranean and the Caspian regions. These are the Pygmy Cormorant (29), White Pelican (33), Squacco Heron (42), Marbled Teal (82), Red-crested Pochard (83), White-headed Duck (101), Collared Pratincole (252), Slender-billed Gull (277), Calandra Lark (382), Moustached Warbler (457), Olivaceous Warbler (469) and·

bird of more inland wooded tundra, but has failed to spread to east or west. The Lesser White-fronted Goose (64) has similar habitat requirements and may also have evolved or survived in this area but now occurs from northern Scandinavia to the Bering Straits. The Curlew Sandpiper (218) has a limited breeding distribution in this refuge area, in contrast to the similar but more widespread Dunlin (218). The Little Stint (219) has a limited coastal range, although it extends west of this area, but it is still confined in contrast to that of Temminck's Stint (219).

The only other obvious northern refuge is around a sea area, involving the south-east Greenland coast, Iceland and the Scandinavian coasts. It is not certain what areas might have been available for survival here during the glacial periods, although in the last glaciation there appears to have been some coastal land along the Scandinavian coast north of the ice, and possibly around islands off the

Spanish Sparrow (645).

STEPPES. To the north and east of the Caspian are the steppe zones. These are areas of short grass, sparse shrubby growth or semi-desert, and as steppes they have persisted through the more recent glacial periods and occur within this general area (Maps O–Q). They appear to have offered a persistent refuge to some species. Three – the White-tailed Plover (209), Eastern Stock Dove (310), and Pander's Ground Chough (663) – occur in the semi-desert steppes, although the first will certainly select moister sites within it. The remainder are on grass steppes or occur more widely through the region. They are the Pallid Harrier (142), Caspian Plover (197), Sociable Plover (208), Slender-billed Curlew (234), Black-winged Pratincole (252), Great Black-headed Gull (262), Black-bellied Sandgrouse (307), Pallas's Sandgrouse (308), Black Lark (382), White-winged Lark (382), yellow-headed form of Yellow Wagtail (424), thick-billed form of Reed Bunting (591), Red-headed Bunting (603), Rosy Starling (656).

MIDDLE EAST. This is another complex region. It is obvious that it was the speciation centre for some birds, but difficult to know what aspects it presented in the past. As a general refuge area it may well have been centred around the Tigris and Euphrates valleys and the Persian Gulf, but the eastern Mediterranean side must also have offered favourable conditions. With the increasing aridity of the area species will have moved out from it and I have listed a number of forms from the dry upland, steppe-type areas south of the Caucasus and Caspian which I suspect from their present distribution may have had their origin in a more southerly and central area. The species listed for this region are the Levant Sparrowhawk (115), Hume's Tawny Owl (339), Syrian Woodpecker (370), black-headed form of the Yellow Wagtail (424), Masked Shrike (433), Radde's Dunnock (442), Upcher's Warbler (468), Ménétries's Warbler (479), Hooded Wheatear (522), Finsch's Wheatear (527), White-throated Robin (545), Rock Nuthatch (575), Orange-tufted Sunbird (584), Cinereous Bunting (601), Scrub Sparrow (647), Pale Rock Sparrow (649), dark-crowned form of Eurasian Jay (659).

WESTERN EUROPE. In addition to the birds which must have moved northwards in the Middle East there are also those which moved northwards in Europe without a wider lateral dispersal. I have already commented, when discussing climate, on the very small number of western European endemics. The following are in this category – Red-legged Partridge (168), Melodious Warbler (465), Dartford Warbler (487), Cirl Bunting (594), black form of Crow (668).

EASTERN EUROPE. Eastern Europe, also commented on earlier, boasts a longer list, with Lesser Spotted Eagle (130), Aquatic Warbler (458), subspecies of Collared Flycatcher (506), subspecies of Red-breasted Flycatcher (507), Black-headed Bunting (602), subspecies of Nutcracker (658), and possibly the grey-bodied form of the Crow (668).

MID-TUNDRA. This area of the lower Ob and Yenesei Rivers and Taymyr Peninsula is possibly better categorised as a small refuge containing Lesser White-fronted Goose (64), Red-breasted Goose (68), Curlew Sandpiper (218), Little Stint (219). The first and last have wider ranges but I suspect they are linked with this area; and all migrate from it in the winter.

NORTH-WESTERN AREA. This borders on Greenland, Iceland and Europe and appears to have constituted a cool refuge for Pink-footed Goose (63), Barnacle Goose (69), subspecies of Brent Goose (67), Golden Plover (202), Lesser Black-backed Gull (275), ?Razorbill (296), ?Little Auk (301).

NORTH AMERICAN INVADERS. The favourable conditions of the North Atlantic Drift area appear to have produced an incursion from North America of a number of northern species. These are Great Northern Diver (1), Leach's Petrel (19), Harlequin (93), Barrow's Goldeneye (97), Iceland Gull (273).

BRITISH ISLES. As an isolated area the British Isles has four distinct endemic forms. It is possible the Red Grouse (159) and Scottish Crossbill (626) evolved their distinctive characters after the sea cut off the islands from the continental mainland. The subspecies of the Pied (422) and Yellow Wagtails (424) may be of earlier origin but it is difficult to determine where they would have maintained their separate identities from their conspecifics during the last glaciation.

DESERT. The southern desert region might be regarded as a relatively stable area, but it would have had a cooler and moister climate in the cold Pleistocene periods, and in the historic past has become increasingly arid, with a spread of true desert conditions. The presence of pairs of species with similar distributions and only slightly different ecological requirements suggests that at least two refuge areas existed. The pairs are Spotted and Crowned Sandgrouse (302–3), Pin-tailed and Black-bellied Sandgrouse (305, 307), Desert and Bar-tailed Desert Larks (397–8), and Short-toed and Lesser Short-toed Larks (395–6).

Apart from these, the general distribution of species through the North African and Arabian deserts appears to fall into three zones. There are the species of the main true desert region, probably with sporadic distribution within this area but poorly documented. These are the Cream-coloured Courser (255), Spotted Sandgrouse (302), Crowned Sandgrouse (303), Egyptian Nightjar (345), Desert Lark (397), Bar-tailed Desert Lark (398), Hoopoe Lark (401), Pale Crag Martin (406), Desert Warbler (480), Red-rumped Wheatear (529), White-crowned Black Wheatear (532), Fulvous Babbler (555), House Bunting (604), Trumpeter Finch (631), Desert Sparrow (647), Brown-necked Raven (665).

On the northern edge of this region is another narrow zone of desert to semi-desert, which for some species extends southwards in the region of the Red Sea. The typical species are Barbary Falcon (149), Sooty Falcon (150), Houbara Bustard (191), Pin-tailed Sandgrouse (305), Black-bellied Sandgrouse (307). Little Swift (353), Thick-billed Lark (381), Short-toed Lark (395), Lesser Short-toed Lark (396), Temminck's Horned Lark (403), Striated Scrub Warbler (463), Desert Wheatear (525), Mourning Wheatear (528).

The third zone is along the southern side of the deserts and only partly extends into the area of these maps. Species within our limits are Lichtenstein's Sandgrouse (304), Chestnut-bellied Sandgrouse (306), Black-crowned Finch Lark (392), Dunn's Lark (400), African Silverbill (640), Yellow-throated Sparrow (650).

AFROTROPICAL (PREVIOUSLY ETHIOPIAN) FAUNA. Species from the bird fauna of Africa occur on either side of the arid Saharan zone, extending towards the Mediterranean. A few species such as the Dark Chanting Goshawk (117), Lappet-faced Vulture (134), African Collared Dove (315), Namaqua Dove (318) and Common Bulbul (430) occur on both sides; but in general the western species are part of the western fauna that in the past

extended right up the west coast to Morocco but has been cut off by the westward spread of desert and now leaves isolated populations of species that mainly occur further south. Examples of this are the Tufted Guineafowl (174), Common Buttonquail (175), Crested Coot (180), Arabian Bustard (190), African Marsh Owl (330), White-rumped Swift (351), and Black-headed Bush Shrike (437).

The eastern species that occur along the Nile valley and Red Sea region and may invade Arabia to some extent have a more continuous connection with their southern populations. They include the Sacred Ibis (51), Egyptian Goose (71), Verreaux's Eagle (128), Rüppell's Griffon (139), Kittlitz Sandplover (198), Senegal Thick-knee (251), Egyptian Plover (257), Nubian Nightjar (347), Rosy-patched Shrike (438), Black Bushchat (517), Shining Sunbird (583), Pygmy Sunbird (584), Fan-tailed Raven (666).

In addition, a larger range of African species which extend into south-western Arabia is now known to extend further north in the mountain regions bordering the Red Sea. Recent information from M. Jennings suggests that a number occur just north of the 20° line that forms the base of the maps. These include Pink-backed Pelican *Pelecanus rufescens*, Hammerkop *Scopus umbretta*, Bruce's Green Pigeon *Treron waalia*, Senegal Scops Owl *Otus senegalensis*, Grey-headed Kingfisher *Halcyon leucocephala*, Grey Hornbill *Tockus narsutus*, Red-capped Lark *Calandrella cinerea*, Red-breasted Wheatear *Oenanthe bottae*, Gamboge Dusky Flycatcher *Muscicapa gambogae*, White-breasted White-eye *Zosterops abyssinica*, Rüppell's Weaver *Ploceus galbula*, Arabian Golden Sparrow *Passer euchloris*, Amythyst Starling *Cinnyricinclus leucogaster*, Yemen Linnet *Carduelis yemenensis*, Olive-rumped Serin *Serinus rothschildi* and Cinnamon-breasted Bunting *Emberiza tahapisi*.

ORIENTAL FAUNA. The Indian region has a large and complex avifauna but only a small number of species, usually adapted to drier conditions, have extended eastwards into the Iranian region. They include Indian Shag (26), Darter (30), Shikra (116), Indian White-backed Vulture (136), Red-headed Merlin (153), grey-headed subspecies of the Purple Gallinule (181), Red-wattled Lapwing (207), Great Stone Curlew (250), Ring-necked Parakeet (323), Brown Fish Owl (326), Spotted Little

Owl (335), Smyrna Kingfisher (355), Indian Roller (362), Indian Sand Lark (394), Bay-backed Shrike (434), Common Babbler (558), Purple Sunbird (584), Indian Silverbill (641), Common Mynah (657).

MOUNTAINS (Map K). The effect of mountains on bird distribution has been discussed earlier from a climatic point of view. In the Pleistocene, mountain ranges produced cold and ice-capped barriers that obstructed movement of species; but they also provided at other times refuges for cold-tolerant species during the interglacial and post-glacial warming of climate. Populations of some species which retreated northwards were left in such refuges as evidence of earlier southern distributions. Some examples are the Gyrfalcon (145), Ptarmigan (158), Lesser Sandplover (200), Dotterel (204), Ural Owl (341), Three-toed Woodpecker (366), Rock/Water Pipit (418–9), Siberian Rubythroat (540), Ring Ouzel (552), White's Thrush (553).

Within the south of the Eurasian region the main mountain ranges tend to run from east to west and thus reduce the frequency with which local isolate forms might be produced. A number of species extend with little change across most of the region, including Lammergeier (133), Griffon Vulture (137), Dotterel (204), Alpine Swift (352), Rock Thrush (518–9), Wallcreeper (577), Common Dipper (581), Rock Bunting (605), Crimson-winged Finch (630), Snowfinch (651), Red-billed Chough (672), Alpine Chough (673).

For the evolution of a species adapted to cool high altitudes in a species group where others prefer warmer lowland conditions, it must presumably be trapped in a refuge area where it cannot move south to warmer regions but must remain and adapt to lower temperatures. Such a refuge would presumably be on the northerly side of a large mountain area, but not subject to the worst extremes of climate.

In the Tibetan region such a process appears to have produced a wide range of cold-adapted species which have subsequently colonised the Tibetan plateau. These include the Bar-headed Goose, Pallas's Sea Eagle (104), Upland Buzzard (118), Tibetan Partridge (167), Wood Snipe (244), Brown-headed Gull (263), Snow Pigeon (309), Tibetan Sandgrouse (308), Long-billed Calandra Lark (382), Rosy Pipit (413), Brown Dunnock (439),

Himalayan Rubythroat (539), Black Crested Tit (565) and Tibetan Serin (611).

In Europe we appear to have only one species, the Citril Finch (614), an offshoot of the serin group (611) occurring on the western side of the Alps. The Bald Ibis (50) requires mountains for nesting and has relict populations in north-west Africa and Turkey. It would appear to be another Western Palaearctic relic.

Further east, in the highlands extending from eastern Turkey and the Caucasus across northern Iran to Afghanistan and the Pamirs, there is a more extensive list of species: the snowcocks (164–5), Bimaculated Lark (382), Red-tailed Wheatear (530), Güldenstädt's Redstart (537), Grey-necked Bunting (597), Red-fronted Serin (616), Sinai Rosefinch (633), Great Rosefinch (633). The snowcocks are interesting since they have produced a chain of high-altitude species – in the northern Altai, Tibet, Himalayas, Turkish/Iranian mountains and Caucasus – but never appear to have invaded Europe. The distribution of the two rosefinches may be significant. It is possible that the southwestern relict populations indicate the early separate speciation areas from which the two have spread to overlap extensively in general range in the Mongolian and Tibetan regions (633).

Further east still, the high central Eurasian ranges of the Altai and Pamirs are inhabited not only by the wide-ranging species listed above, but also by those of the Turkish-Iranian highlands. In addition there are other endemic forms such as the Black-throated Dunnock (439), Olivaceous Willow Warbler (500), Blue-headed Redstart (537), White-winged Grosbeak (638) and Biddulph's Ground Chough (663). The more forested western slopes of these mountains also influence the ranges of a large number of other species, particularly passerines, as can be seen from the maps.

4. Results of glaciation

From deduction and actual evidence we can assert that the previous two million years, the Ice Age or Pleistocene, was one in which bird populations became repeatedly fragmented, in which subspecies and species evolved in isolated areas, and what was probably at an earlier period a continuous distribution of a single species could become a complex pattern of different bird forms. We can also see that since the last glaciation many of these forms have spread back for only a limited distance, allowing us to reconstruct a picture of what probably occurred in the past.

Where a species is now widespread we can only speculate on its past history. We might also speculate on the reasons why that particular species was so successful. Why, of all the wheatear species, was it only the Eurasian Wheatear which moved north to occupy Europe and colonise a broad range from Greenland to Alaska? Why only one starling?

The post-glacial spread has been influenced in some species by the presence of closely related species spreading from elsewhere. In other cases it has been limited by the availability of suitable habitat. From the evidence of the past we must suspect that the distribution of birds which we now see is only part of a still changing overall pattern. We know that as we move towards the polar region we find that the bird fauna becomes increasingly one in which there are larger populations of fewer but more widespread species. Even so, when we compare different parts of the world we may reasonably suspect that our temperate and boreal bird faunas are still impoverished in variety of species as a result of the glaciations. It has been suggested that some changes, such as the apparently persistent but slow westerly extension of range of some boreal species, may be evidence of a post-glacial reassembly of a bird fauna that is still in process and will not be complete for a long while yet.

RECENT CHANGES

As I have suggested in the last section, changes in bird distribution are still occurring and will continue to occur. Admittedly those that we see are smaller and less dramatic than those of the Pleistocene, but then so is the present degree of variation in climate and vegetation. The ebb and flow of smaller cycles of change still continues, and we can identify two main factors. One is climatically controlled change, the other is the result of man's interference with his surroundings.

1. Recent climatic change

Any study of recent climatic changes is limited by the amount of past information, and while the history of man in western Europe, however inadequate, extends back for over a thousand years, the history of bird distribution only extends for about a century, and good climatic information for not much longer. In general we know that for most of northern Europe the period from the fourteenth century to the present day was colder and wetter than it had been previously. We have little information on the changes in wildlife that this brought about, but we should remember, when we study the lists of bird remains from archaeological sites that existed prior to this period, that the conditions may have been more favourable for many species then than was the case for some hundreds of years afterwards.

During the first half of the twentieth century Europe experienced a slow warming-up of the general climate. A gradual response to this by birds became apparent, and was most obvious in the latter part of this period in the 1940s when the spread of more southerly species was most evident at their northern limits in countries such as Iceland and Scandinavia. This period of climatic improvement is indicated by the scattered comments on extension of range in the text on various species; and in the early 1950s James Fisher was able to list forty-two species that were spreading in Scandinavia from the south or east.

Since the 1950s a colder cycle of years has occurred. A visible result of this has been a southward shift at the northern end of Europe. Shifts of this kind are difficult to study because the nature of bird-watching is such that absences are never as well documented as new occurrences. However, the rarer breeding birds now in northern Scotland are in a large number of instances those which, twenty years ago, it would have been necessary to travel at least to central Scandinavia to find. By an odd chance western Europe has also enjoyed a series of mild winters, and the overall picture is confused by the fact that relatively cold-sensitive species such as the Fan-tailed Warbler, Cetti's Warbler, Penduline Tit and Serin continue to spread in the north-west. However, one really cold winter could change all this.

Some of the recent climatic changes outside

or marginal to our area have affected our bird populations. The droughts on the southern side of the Sahara have affected the survival of wintering populations of migrant species such as Whitethroat and Sand Martin. When a bird population is reduced it is birds in marginal areas or barely suitable breeding sites that tend to move out. A similar effect has been noticed where the recent cold cycle has affected the northern limits of the range of some species. Birds tend to remain in scattered localities which for some reason are more favourable for them long after they have deserted the less satisfactory areas. A restriction in range is therefore more likely to be apparent as an increasingly sparse and scattered distribution rather than a steadily retreating boundary, and extensions of range may show the same pattern.

2. The effects of human activity

From a bird's point of view man's activities in Europe over the last few thousand years have been apparent largely as a major alteration of the vegetation. Probably the most significant change he brought about was the steady reduction of forest and the cultivation of land. Within previously forested areas this must have enormously benefited such groups of birds as finches, buntings and larks, which could utilise the weed seeds and exposed insects, and increasingly restricted the species that could not live outside a forest environment.

To some extent man's buildings offered new nest sites to replace tree cavities for Jackdaw, Barn Owl and Common Starling, and alternatives to rock crevices for Swift and Black Redstart. In addition species of forest or forest edge, such as Robin, Dunnock, Blackbird and tits, adapted to the new environment.

The constant draining of marshes has restricted and reduced the habitat of waterbirds right up to the present day, and it has only partly been ameliorated by the greater provision of artificial lakes and reservoirs, and the coastal reclamation which provides moist meadows and drainage ditches. The increase in grazing animals has also had considerable impact in reducing forest and maintaining areas of open grassland and heathland.

Theoretically the effect of all this activity on birds should have been merely to modify the fauna by altering the availability of habitat.

Unfortunately the general attitude to wild creatures until well into the present century has been that these should be destroyed as actual or potential competitors, or exploited for food or amusement. We can see one unfortunate result of this in the otherwise inexplicable absence of so many of the larger birds of prey from the populated areas of north-western Europe. This tendency to slaughter the more conspicuous or rarer birds as soon as they appeared makes it more difficult to evaluate some recent distributional changes in north-western Europe. The apparent spread in breeding range of some species may be an aspect of a new human tolerance or protection rather than an indication of ecological factors governing the distribution of the birds concerned.

A probable example of this is the spread of the Kittiwake and some other northern seabirds during the present century which has been attributed, in part at least, to a cessation of persecution at the breeding colonies.

Some of the more startling extensions of range by birds in recent years have been attributed to the indirect effects of man's activities. The Collared Dove occurred naturally in the last century no further west than Turkey, but may have been introduced by the Turks into the Balkan Peninsula. Within the present century it spread with increasing speed until by the middle of the century its range extended north-westwards across the whole of Europe. It tends to occur, and to thrive best, where food such as grain is put out for farm animals, and its successful colonisation is closely associated with human settlement. The spread of the Fulmar in much the same period has been linked with changes in fishing methods and an increased availability of waste food from these sources.

Although these species are exceptional in the extent of their spread and the size of population increases, their movements coincided with those of other species. The Collared Dove spread at about the same period as the northward spread of the Serin in Europe, from the Mediterranean to the English Channel; and the Syrian Woodpecker spread into and through most of south-eastern Europe. The spread of the Fulmar occurred with that of the Kittiwake and Gannet. Man's part in all this may have been merely to provide more favourable conditions and an extra impetus for species already involved in extensions of range.

The future activities of man seem likely to involve the increasing urbanisation of large areas, greater uniformity in the arrangement and landscaping of farmland, forest, and water storage; and the continuing and increasing use of chemicals to eliminate unwanted insects and plants. The overall effect is likely to be a drastic reduction in the extent and the variety of cover, food and nest-sites for birds as well as most other living creatures. The first pre- requisite for preserving our bird life is a greater tolerance of birds around us, and a determination not to harm or interfere unless it is really necessary; but in addition, in order to retain some remnants of what we now possess, some positive action is necessary deliberately to preserve, create and maintain as large a variety as possible of the habitats that occur naturally; so that although we may suffer some reduction in the richness of the wild life around us we may not lose some species altogether.

Using the Maps

There are basically two types of map in this book. One type gives information on a single species. The other shows a group of species together, indicating how they relate to each other in distribution. Usually the latter type only shows the breeding distribution since this appears to be the key to the general pattern, but if only two or occasionally three species are involved it has sometimes been possible to give the more complete information on distribution as used for single species.

COLOURS. On the first type of map **where only a single species** is involved the code of colours is simple. Areas where a species occurs only in summer are **orange**; areas where it is likely to occur all year are **brown**; and areas where it normally occurs only in winter are **blue**. Where a bird may occur on passage between summer and winter areas the intervening area is **hatched blue**. If the species shows periodic invasions or fairly regular irruptions into surrounding areas which are not permanently colonised, this is shown by the use of **coloured arrows**. **Single black arrows** may be used to indicate the direction of normal migration where this is helpful.

Where **several species occur on one map** I have used mainly **red** and **black**. These colours have been chosen to avoid confusion with the orange/brown/blue system used to show the complete annual information for a single species. This distinction is the more necessary because on some maps (e.g. map 166) the main species' orange/brown/blue information is supported by and contrasted with red and/ or black information about ranges of other species.

Birds: A Systematic Text to Amplify the Maps

DIVERS *Gaviidae*

Breed in Tundra to Boreal zones, winter on sea coasts, usually further south. There are four species; two large, two smaller, apparently overlapping considerably in distribution but separated by size and depth of waters used. The larger two are more tolerant of cold and form a species pair, with the White-billed on large waters in the tundra and the great Northern Diver on large waters of tundra and the more open forest lakes (Map 1). The latter probably evolved in North America in the Pleistocene, in the region south of the glaciated zone. The former may have evolved as a separate species in another refuge north of the ice sheet in the Bering Strait area where a cold-tolerant form could survive and, with amelioration of climate, spread east and west along the tundra. Red-throated Diver breeds on small to very small lakes and pools, mainly on tundra, but also on moors and open forest areas, feeding on larger stretches of water nearby. Black-throated Diver breeds on smaller forest waters with vegetated edges. The nest is a bare site or vegetated mound at the water's edge.

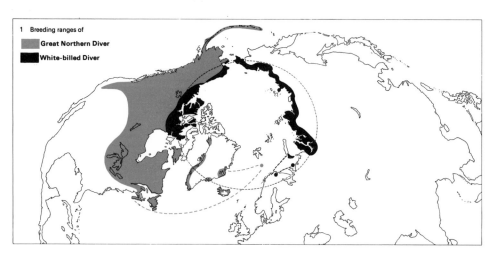

1 Breeding ranges of

Great Northern Diver

White-billed Diver

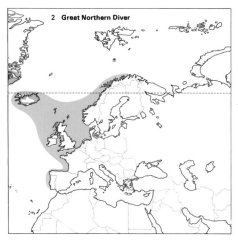

2 Great Northern Diver

Great Northern Diver *Gavia immer*
(Maps 1, 2)
Migrant; breeding in both Tundra and Boreal forest zones in North America, but within our present limits in Iceland and Greenland occupies only the former. The typical breeding habitat is on the larger deep lakes with still or running water, in open tundra or conifer forest, usually lacking tall shore vegetation. Birds dive usually 7–20 m. It winters at sea, in waters of the continental shelf, often near shore, occasionally occurring on large lakes, reservoirs and rivers. Non-breeding birds may summer on coastal waters. In the present area nesting is between limits of 3–10°C July isotherms, but in North America occurs south to 24°C July isotherm.

Great Northern Diver

White-billed Diver

White-billed Diver *Gavia adamsii* (Maps 1, 3)
Migrant; breeding on tundra on larger lakes,
river estuaries and deltas, and on coasts. It
nests in between limits of 0–10°C July isotherms. It does not move far in winter and
usually remains in coastal Arctic waters, only
stray individuals occurring further south.

3 White-billed Diver

Black-throated Diver *Gavia arctica* (Map 4)
A migrant, breeding in Tundra zone and conifer and birch regions of Boreal zone, throughout Holarctic. It is smaller than the previous
two species and the North American race is
smaller than the Eurasian bird. General distribution overlaps that of other species, but ecological preferences differ. It breeds on deep
lakes and fresh waters, large but usually smaller in extent than those of the previous two
species, and will tolerate lakes with overgrown
shores. Less frequent in bare tundra regions.
Birds dive usually to *c.* 7 m. Nesting is between limits of 4–24°C July isotherms. It winters at sea, more frequently on inshore waters,
or on enclosed seas, and occurs on rivers and
lakes during passage.

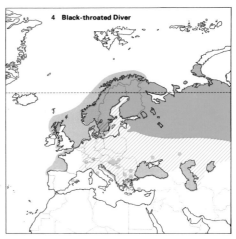

4 Black-throated Diver

Red-throated Diver *Gavia stellata* (Map 5)
Migrant; in breeding typically a tundra moorland species with a range extending into the
open forest of the Boreal zone. It nests on
shallow lakes and pools with open, bare aspect,
on open or shrub tundra, bare rocky places or
moorland. It will use very small areas of water
for nesting, flying to larger areas such as estuaries, large lakes or sea coasts to feed. Birds
dive to *c.* 10 m. Breeding is between limits of
0–18°C July isotherms. It winters at sea near
coasts, and on large areas of inland water.

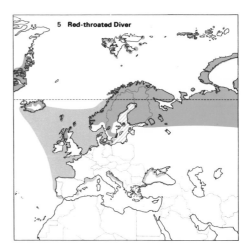

5 Red-throated Diver

Black-throated Diver

Red-throated Diver

GREBES *Podicipedidae*

Waterbirds, with a floating nest in herbage growing in water. There are five species, two large, two medium and one small; through most zones other than tundra. The Red-necked Grebe is the only one of the larger two that occurs in North America (possibly originating there?) and has a discontinuous east and west distribution in Eurasia. The two larger species overlap but with some ecological separation, the Great Crested Grebe requiring a larger area of open water, the Red-necked Grebe using smaller and more overgrown waters and, particularly in eastern Asia, with a more northerly distribution like that of the Slavonian Grebe. The two medium-sized species use smaller, shallower and partly over-grown waters, replacing each other geographically with the Slavonian further north than the Black-necked Grebe (map 8). The Dabchick uses smaller open waters with tall vegetation near the shore. In winter species migrate to the south of 0°C frost-line isotherm.

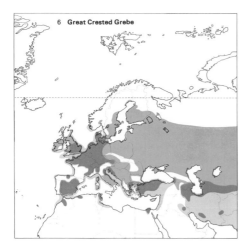

6 Great Crested Grebe

Great Crested Grebe *Podiceps cristatus* (Map 6)

Partly migratory; in Boreal to Warm Temperate zones, where suitable waters are present. Usually occurs on large stretches of fairly deep open water. It breeds on still fresh water, rarely on slow-moving rivers or estuaries; but in Asia may occur on brackish or salt water. Water chosen usually has a border or area of reeds or similar plants growing in water and the nest is typically a floating structure within these. Occurrence may also relate to the availability of fish of a suitable size. General breeding distribution is between July isotherms of *c*. 15° and *c*. 27° C. Migrants may appear in winter on both fresh and salt waters, without bordering vegetation, on coastal lagoons, or on the sea coast close inshore.

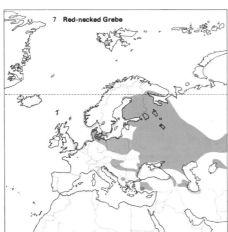

7 Red-necked Grebe

Red-necked Grebe *Podiceps grisegena* (Map 7)

Mainly migratory. Distribution irregular, in places extending further north than the Great Crested Grebe to *c*. 10°C July isotherm and south to the southern edge of the Temperate zone; absent from most of western Europe and mid-Siberia, producing two discrete populations. It will tolerate smaller areas of water with thicker vegetation on its borders than does the Great Crested Grebe, preferring still, fresh waters with rich submerged vegetation on the bottom, including pools north to shrub tundra. More migratory than former species, moving westwards as well as southwards. It winters at sea in coastal waters more frequently than the Great Crested Grebe.

Great Crested Grebe

Red-necked Grebe

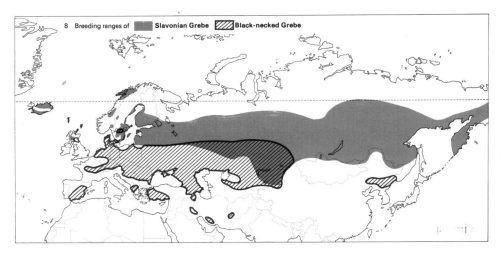

8 Breeding ranges of Slavonian Grebe Black-necked Grebe

Slavonian Grebe   *Podiceps auritus*
(Maps 8, 9)

Migrant; breeding distribution through the Boreal zone, between July isotherms 10°C and 21°C. It breeds on isolated and often small pools of fresh water, preferably shallow, with a luxuriant submerged growth, which may be overgrown with taller vegetation such as reeds, in which the nest is placed. In winter it disperses west and south to estuaries and in-shore coastal waters; it is more tolerant of colder waters than the Black-necked Grebe.

9 Slavonian Grebe

Black-necked Grebe   *Podiceps nigricollis*
(Maps 8, 10)

Partly migrant; in Warm Temperate and Temperate zones and southern edge of Boreal zone. North to July isotherm of *c*. 16°C. Also present in South and East Africa and might be regarded as a species with a greater range fragmented by the spread of desert and arid habitats. More specialised breeding habitat requirements may also produce the rather discontinuous range. There was some north-westerly range expansion into Scandinavia and the British Isles at the beginning of the century. It breeds, often colonially, in shallow freshwater marshes and brackish lagoons where there is a luxuriant growth of submerged plants providing insect food, tall herbage growing in water and small patches of open water. In winter it tends to move to similar waters further south and west.

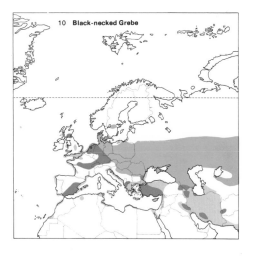

10 Black-necked Grebe

Slavonian Grebe

Black-necked Grebe

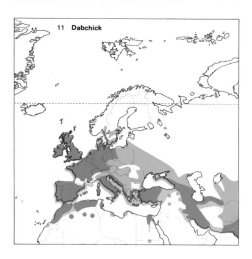

11 Dabchick

Dabchick *Tachybaptus ruficollis* (Map 11)
Partly migrant; distributed through Temperate, Warm Temperate, Subtropical and Tropical zones; through Europe, southern Asia, Africa south of the Sahara and most of Indonesia to Australasia; but in most of Australasia replaced by a very similar counterpart, the Australian Dabchick *T. novaehollandiae*. Northern limit at *c*. 15°C July isotherm. It breeds usually on small to very small waters, sometimes on the edges of larger waters. It occurs in shallower water with a luxuriant growth of submerged plants, and tall plants growing in water. It can co-exist with larger grebe species. In winter it may disperse onto fresh and brackish waters of all kinds, but rarely on the sea.

PETRELS AND SHEARWATERS
Procellariidae

A family of marine seabirds, only coming to land at coastal nest-sites; and at other times at sea, often far out in the oceans, some species making extensive circumoceanic journeys outside the breeding season. In terms of breeding sites, there is one larger Arctic/Boreal species, extending now into Temperate zones, a medium-sized Boreal to Warm Temperate species, a larger Warm Temperate to Tropical species, and three, one medium-sized and two small, centred on the Canaries and Madeira and mainly Tropical. As with other seabirds, however, the sea temperatures of the nesting

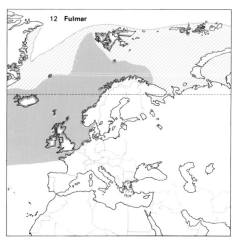

12 Fulmar

areas are modified by the warm North Atlantic Drift current. The Fulmar nests on open ledges, the other species in holes or cavities, natural or excavated. Breeding distribution is sometimes uncertain because of the secretive and nocturnal behaviour of some species. Food is taken under water or on the surface. In addition to the North Atlantic form of the Fulmar another subspecies occurs in the North Pacific. An ecological counterpart, the Antarctic Fulmar *F. glacialoides*, occurs in Antarctic waters. Cory's Shearwater is also an Atlantic bird. The Great Shearwater *P. gravis*, nesting at 36° south latitude on Tristan da Cunha, appears to be a South Atlantic replacement species, with the Sooty Shearwater *P. griseus* in similar southern Pacific latitudes. Outside their breeding seasons all three large shearwaters may occur inshore in the North Atlantic.

Fulmar *Fulmarus glacialis* (Map 12)
An Arctic/Boreal species which has extended into temperate regions in recent times. A century ago its southern limit was St. Kilda Island, but it now occurs south to Brittany. The spread is attributed to food availability, suggesting that temperature is not a limiting factor with this species. It nests in scattered groups of pairs, usually on cliff ledges, more rarely on level coastal sites or rock ledges a few miles inland. When not nesting it wanders at sea, usually from north of 50° latitude up to the Arctic ice.

Dabchick

Fulmar

Cory's Shearwater   *Calonectris diomedea*
(Map 13)
A Warm Temperate to Tropical species, nesting in colonies on cliffs and rocky islands in
the Canaries, Madeira and Azores (also south
to the Cape Verde Islands) and through the
Mediterranean. Mediterranean birds are smaller and with a less heavy bill than Atlantic
island birds. Outside the breeding season birds
may wander north and around the British
Isles, usually occupying temperate to tropical
waters with a 15–26°C surface temperature in
August. The breeding range is 35°–45° north
latitudes.

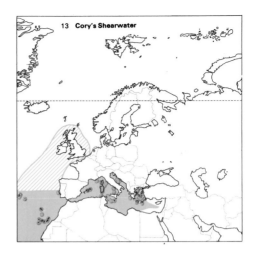

Manx Shearwater   *Puffinus puffinus* (Map 14)
A medium-sized species breeding in Boreal to
Warm Temperate zones. It nests on rocky or
hilly islands, usually in large colonies. It is
nocturnal in coming to land. It ranges from
Madeira, the Desertas and Azores, into the
Mediterranean, and north to Iceland. Birds
from North Atlantic breeding sites have a
post-breeding transequatorial passage to a
main wintering area off the eastern coast of
southern South America. Birds breeding in
the Mediterranean are recognised as two races
based on colour, and many winter in that sea.
Outside the area it has nested on the western
side of the Atlantic in Bermuda, and more
recently there has been a single record from an
island off north-eastern U.S.A. Populations
from Baja California, Hawaii, and New Zealand, otherwise treated as separate species, are
regarded by some authorities as races of this
species.

Little Shearwater   *Puffinus assimilis* (Map 15)
A small species of Warm Temperate waters.
It breeds on rocky island shores on Grand
Canary, Tenerife, Graciosa and Montana
Clara in the Canaries, the Salvages, Madeira,
the Desertas and Azores. Outside our area it
is present in the Cape Verde Islands, in the
South Atlantic on Gough Island and Tristan
da Cunha, and in the South Pacific around
Australasia. In post-breeding dispersal it is a

Cory's Shearwater

Manx Shearwater   Little Shearwater

16 Soft-plumaged Petrel

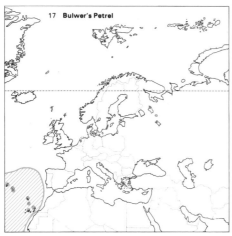

17 Bulwer's Petrel

cooler water form, replaced in warm tropical waters by the similar Audubon's Shearwater *P. lherminieri*. In the North Atlantic a small number stray north to inshore waters as far as southern Britain and Denmark.

Soft-plumaged Petrel *Pterodroma mollis* (Map 16)
A medium-sized species of mainly Warm Temperate to Tropical zones. It breeds on Madeira and the Desertas. Two populations appear to be involved. A smaller, Warm Temperate race, nesting in summer on high ground above the forest inland in Madeira, and a larger, Subtropical race nesting in winter on ledges and in crevices on rocky islands in the Desertas and further south in the Cape Verde Islands. Outside the area it also breeds on Gough Island and Tristan da Cunha in similar latitudes of the South Atlantic, and on Marion Island in the southern Indian Ocean.

Bulwer's Petrel *Bulweria bulwerii* (Map 17)
A small petrel of Warm Temperate to Tropical zones; breeding on Madeira, the Desertas, Salvages, Canaries and Azores. Outside the area it occurs on the Cape Verde Islands, and there are other populations on islands in the Pacific; while in the northern Indian Ocean it is replaced by the similar but larger *B. fallax*. The nests are in cavities or burrows, on rocky or sandy coasts. Outside the breeding season it occurs mostly well out at sea, rarely inshore.

STORM PETRELS *Hydrobatidae*

Like the previous family these are marine seabirds, only coming to land at coastal nest-sites; at other times at sea, often far out in the oceans, but in periods of strong westerly gales birds may be driven inland in western Europe. All are small. In terms of breeding areas there is a widespread Boreal to Warm Temperate species, a Boreal species, and two Warm Temperate to Tropical species. Within these zones, however, the sea temperatures are modified by the warm North Atlantic Drift. They nest in holes and cavities, natural or excavated, and are nocturnal in their visits to land, making information on precise distribution difficult to obtain. They feed by picking food from the surface of the water.

Soft-plumaged Petrel

Bulwer's Petrel

Storm Petrel *Hydrobates pelagicus* (Map 18)
This is the most widespread storm petrel in the area, in Boreal to Warm Temperate zones; present only on the western side of the Atlantic. It nests on rocky islands and small coastal islets; from Iceland and the Lofotens, around western Britain, Brittany and Biscay, through most of the western Mediterranean and in the eastern Canaries. In winter it occurs in the Mediterranean, moving into the eastern parts and occasionally into the Black Sea. More northern birds migrate south along the West African coast to South Africa and often around the Cape and up the eastern coast to the Zambezi.

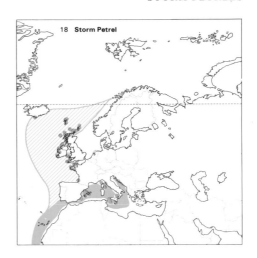

Leach's Petrel *Oceanodroma leucorhoa*
(Map 19)
Breeding is in the North Atlantic Drift waters of the Boreal zone. It occurs mainly in the North Pacific and in the western North Atlantic where the major concentration is from southern Labrador to Massachusetts; and it may be a more recent coloniser of the eastern North Atlantic in the regions of the North Atlantic Drift current. In this area it is present from Iceland and the Lofotens to islands off north-western Scotland, and may nest off western Ireland. Nests are on rocky and wooded islands and on rocky shores. After breeding it disperses widely, mainly moving in a southerly direction into subtropical waters, sometimes as far as South Africa. It is present in northern waters late enough in the year to suffer if the weather is bad.

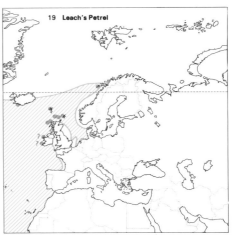

Madeiran Petrel *Oceanodroma castro*
(Map 20)
Breeding in Warm Temperate to Tropical zones; it occurs on the Azores, Madeira and Salvages. Also further south in the Atlantic on the Cape Verde Islands, St. Helena, Ascension and possibly West African islands; and in the Pacific on the Galapagos, Hawaiian Islands and islands off Japan. It breeds on rocky or grassy islands. After breeding there is no evidence of wide dispersal or migration but it may occasionally stray for long distances.

Frigate Petrel *Pelagodroma marina*
(Map 21)
Breeding is in the Warm Temperate zone, on the Salvage Islands. Elsewhere it occurs in the Atlantic on the Cape Verde Islands and

Storm Petrel   Leach's Petrel   Madeiran Petrel   Frigate Petrel

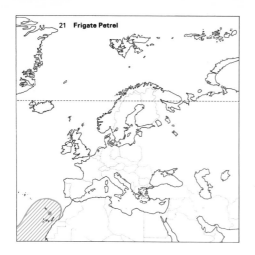

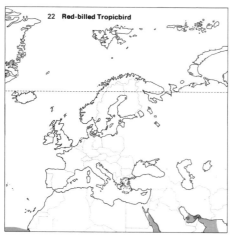

Tristan da Cunha; also on islands around Australasia and in the past in the southern Indian Ocean. It nests on small rocky islands and in breeding may compete for holes with the Madeiran Petrel. After breeding it disperses through warmer seas.

TROPICBIRDS   *Phaethontidae*

The family comprises three fairly similar species with one occurring marginally in the Palaearctic. The Red-tailed Tropicbird *Phaethon rubricauda* occurs in the southern tropical Indian Ocean and tropical Pacific, while the smaller White-tailed Tropicbird *P. lepturus* occurs in the south-west Pacific, Indian, and Atlantic Oceans and the Caribbean, overlapping in range with the Red-billed Tropicbird.

Red-billed Tropicbird   *Phaethon aethereus* (Map 22)

Resident and dispersive; in Subtropical and Tropical zones in ocean areas between 25° latitudes, from mid Indian Ocean westwards to western American seaboard. It feeds at sea by plunge-diving for prey. Breeding is in scattered pairs in rock crevices on shores or inland crags of islands. Except when nesting the birds are usually well out at sea. Birds occurring within Palaearctic waters also breed in the southern Red Sea and on the Cape Verde Islands.

CORMORANTS   *Phalacrocoracidae*

Six species are present. The typical regional pattern is of three overlapping forms; a large form of inland and shallow coastal waters, a medium-sized form of deeper marine waters and a small form of inland waters. The large Great or Common Cormorant (map 23) extends across the whole region as a shallow-water species, but in eastern Asia the closely related and large Temminck's Cormorant *P. capillatus* (map 26) occurs as a coastal deep-water species. In North America the Great Cormorant has colonised the coasts of the north-east, but the Double-crested Cormorant *P. auritus* takes its place over most of inland North America. The Pygmy Cormor-

ant (map 29) of south-eastern Europe to Uzbekistan is replaced in Africa south of the Sahara by the Long-tailed Cormorant, and in the Indian region and south-eastwards by the Little Cormorant, the three sometimes grouped in a separate genus *Halietor*. The medium-sized marine species (map 26) are represented by the common Shag in Europe and the Socotra Cormorant in the Persian Gulf and around eastern Arabia. The larger Temminck's Cormorant mentioned above appears to fill this niche around Japan and Korea, and further east the Pelagic Cormorant *P. pelagicus* extends around the northern Pacific from Japan to California. In the intervening Asian region there is no species occupying this marine niche, the medium-sized

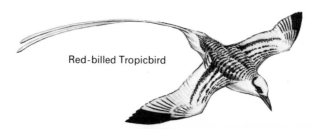

Red-billed Tropicbird

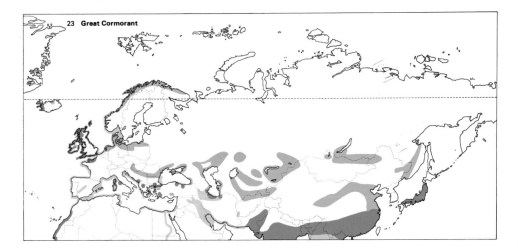

23 Great Cormorant

Indian Shag *P. fuscicollis* occurring in this region as a bird of inland waters which it shares with the larger and smaller species. All species are aquatic birds feeding on fish caught under water, but require perching places above water level when resting.

Great Cormorant   *Phalacrocorax carbo*
(Map 23)
Resident and migrant; with broad sporadic distribution through much of the Old World in Temperate to Tropical zones, between 50° latitudes; but the marine population in the Atlantic extends north to *c.* 70° latitude, especially in the region of the North Atlantic Drift. Inland distribution is fragmented by the absence of suitable waters. It is a bird of shal-

lower waters. It occurs on fresh, brackish and salt waters; on coasts and all kinds of large inland waters including rivers, and swamps with open water. When coastal it prefers shallow waters, fishing near or on the sea bottom, and avoiding deep water. It nests, usually sociably, on cliff ledges, rocky islands, trees and occasionally ground areas of swamps. It migrates from the northern part of the range in winter, with increasing numbers on coasts, and disperses in the resident parts of the range after breeding. It avoids long sea crossings, but will follow watercourses far inland.

Long-tailed Cormorant
Phalacrocorax africanus (Map 24)
Resident, but dispersive within range; in

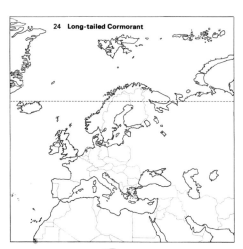

24 Long-tailed Cormorant

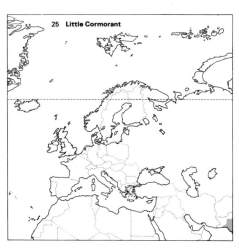

25 Little Cormorant

Great Cormorant

Long-tailed Cormorant

Little Cormorant

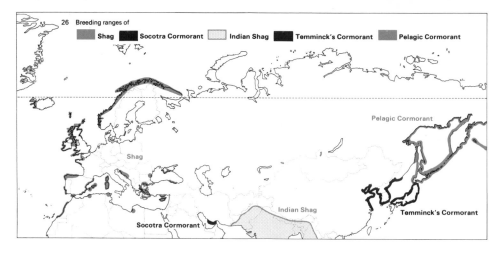

26 Breeding ranges of

Shag   Socotra Cormorant   Indian Shag   Temminck's Cormorant   Pelagic Cormorant

27 Shag

Tropical to Warm Temperate zones through Africa south of the Sahara. It occupies similar habitats to the Pygmy Cormorant but also occurs in estuaries and creeks and on sea coasts and offshore islands, in brackish and salt waters. It is sociable, breeding and roosting colonially in trees and reedbeds and occasionally on rocky ledges, often roosting with other waterbirds. At present it only occurs in the Palaearctic region in Mauritania, but in the last century it was also found in Egypt up to the Delta. The Little Cormorant *P. niger* (map 25) replaces the other small species from northern India through Indochina, Malaysia and Indonesia. It has similar behaviour and occupies similar habitats, including saline tidal estuaries, but not coasts.

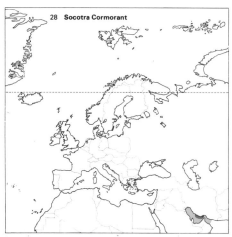

28 Socotra Cormorant

Shag *Phalacrocorax aristotelis*
(Maps 26, 27)
Resident and dispersive; in Subarctic to Subtropical zones. Confined to Europe but part of a series of medium-sized marine forms (map 26). It is a coastal species fishing in deeper waters than the Great Cormorant, but usually within reach of a coast or island, in waters with a summer surface temperature of 4–26°C. It nests sociably, but more scattered, often in sheltered rocky crevices, on coasts and islands. It leaves extreme northerly nesting range in winter but otherwise tends to disperse along coasts around nesting sites, young birds moving further than adults. There are accidental occurrences in various parts of Europe and the eastern Mediterranean.

Shag

Socotra Cormorant

Indian Shag

Temminck's Cormorant

Socotra Cormorant
Phalacrocorax nigrogularis (Maps 26, 28)
Resident and dispersive; in the Subtropical zone. It is a marine species, the counterpart of the Shag in this area. It breeds on islands in the Persian Gulf and possibly on others off eastern Arabia. Very sociable, nesting in large colonies on the ground among boulders.

Pygmy Cormorant   *Phalacrocorax pygmaeus* (Map 29)
Resident and migrant; in Warm Temperate to dry Subtropical zones; north to 48° latitude with July isotherm of 23–24°C. It occurs in fresh water of low-lying areas, usually in larger shallow waters, still or slow-moving, of larger rivers, lakes, swamps, flooded areas and ricefields. It prefers well-vegetated regions, roosting and breeding in large colonies in trees and reedbeds, often with other waterbirds. It migrates from some northern parts of range in winter. The general range is decreasing gradually through drainage. Previously it bred in Hungary and Algeria, and occurs accidentally further north and west.

DARTERS   *Anhingidae*

There are only two species, the New World Anhinga *A. anhinga* and the Old World Darter, very similar but showing some plumage and osteological differences. The Old World bird has been regarded as three species at times, the African, Asiatic and Australian forms being separated.

Darter   *Anhinga melanogaster* (Map 30)
Resident in Subtropical to Tropical zones, between the 37° latitudes. It occurs on slow-moving or still fresh waters of all kinds, including swamps with open waters, and more infrequently on brackish waters or sheltered saltwater creeks. It is found usually on shallow, tree-fringed waters, catching fish underwater but resting on higher perches. It roosts and nests sociably in trees, more rarely in reeds, often with other waterbirds. In Eurasia west of India it is now present only in the Iraq marshes, but until recent times it bred in southeast Turkey at Amik Gölü, where most birds moved south to Israel in winter. The latter colony was destroyed by drainage.

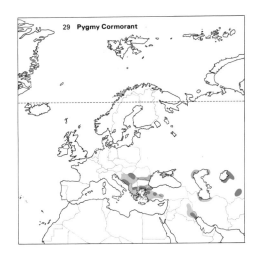

29   Pygmy Cormorant

30   Darter

GANNETS AND BOOBIES
Sulidae

Two genera of larger seabirds. There are three gannets, *Morus* species, so similar that they have been regarded as conspecific, differing only in small features such as the extent of black on the plumage and assumption of adult plumage by the young. The Northern Gannet *M. bassanus* occurs in the North Atlantic, the Cape Gannet *M. capensis* around South Africa and the Australian Gannet *M. serrator* around Australia and New Zealand. The three occur between the 30° and 50° latitudes except in the Palaearctic where the presence of the warm North Atlantic Drift current appears to enable the northern bird to extend further

Pygmy Cormorant

Pelagic Cormorant

Darter

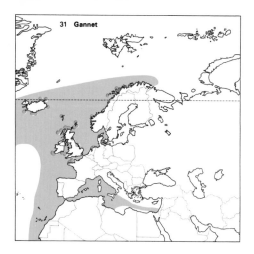

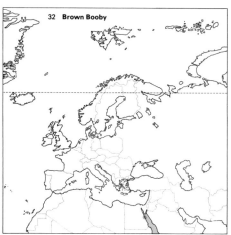

north. The six slightly smaller boobies, *Sula* species, are brown or black and white in colour with brightly coloured skin on face and feet. They occur in Subtropical and Tropical zones and overlap in distribution. All feed by plunge-diving for fish.

Gannet   *Morus bassanus* (Map 31)
Resident and dispersive; breeding in Temperate waters but extending into Boreal and Subarctic zones in the regions of the North Atlantic Drift. It nests on islands, rock stacks and cliffs, in colonies on level raised areas or broad ledges. It has increased in the twentieth century, extending to the Channel Islands, France and Norway since 1939. Except when breeding it is mainly a marine bird, but usually within the limits of the continental shelf, rarely close inshore or far out at sea. It is dispersive in winter, extending down the west coast of Africa to about Senegal.

Brown Booby   *Sula leucogaster* (Map 32)
Resident and dispersive; in Subtropical to Tropical zones, between 25° latitudes. Widely distributed in all three oceans. It bred on small islands in the northern Red Sea (but no recent confirmation), and also on the Cape Verde Islands. More coastal in occurrence than other *Sula* species, it will feed in both deep waters and shallow inshore waters, including coastal surf. It can perch on branches and will roost in trees. It nests colonially or in scattered pairs, on islands, on the ground or on rock ledges or niches.

PELICANS   *Pelecanidae*

Very large waterbirds. There are two similar large species present, occupying the same range over most of Eurasia. They are vulnerable to hunting and intolerant of disturbance when nesting, which, as much as drainage, probably caused a reduction in range. The loss of range by the Dalmatian Pelican in historic times probably disguises the difference between this, a more northerly species with greater habitat tolerance, and the White Pelican with a more southerly distribution and limited lowland range. South of the range of the former, in Africa south of the Sahara, the smaller Pink-backed Pelican *P. rufescens* overlaps in distribution with the White Pelican. Another smaller species, the Spot-billed Pelican *P. philippensis* of South-east Asia, is related to the Dalmatian Pelican and sometimes regarded as conspecific. The American White Pelican *P. erythrorhynchus* is a replacement for the White Pelican in inland North America, where the smaller Brown Pelican *P. occidentalis* occurs in coastal habitats. Both Eurasian species breed colonially on level sites, usually in thick vegetation in marshy sites or on islands.

White Pelican   *Pelecanus onocrotalus* (Map 33)
Mainly migrant in the Palaearctic, but further south resident and dispersive; in Warm Temperate to Tropical zones. In the Palaearctic it

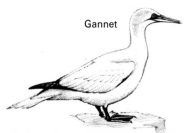

Gannet

Brown Booby

breeds on larger, low-lying shallow waters in a restricted zone between Greece and the western end of Mongolia. Through most of this range it migrates south to winter in Africa, the Middle East and Northern India. In the last century it bred west to Hungary and Yugoslavia, and also in Iraq and Kuwait. It also breeds at present through Africa south of the Sahara. It requires large areas of shallow warm waters, preferably fresh, but it can tolerate brackish or saline conditions. It is usually restricted to large marshes with open water, deltas, shores of inland seas and lakes, large estuaries and coastal lagoons.

Dalmatian Pelican *Pelecanus crispus*
(Map 34)

Migrant, or resident and partly dispersive in south-west of range; in Warm Temperate to Subtropical zones. The present range is more restricted than in the past. It was present in southern England in the Iron Age, in Germany and the Netherlands in Roman times, and still present in Hungary in the last century. Its original range may therefore have been from the Temperate zone southwards. The Spot-billed Pelican *P. philippensis*, occurring from India south to the Philippines and east to south-east China, has been regarded by some as conspecific with the present species. The Dalmatian Pelican occurs with the White Pelican in similar scattered sites but extends further east to western China. It has similar habitat requirements, but is more tolerant of smaller waters at higher altitudes and in more hilly country, and will breed as smaller units. It may also occur in flooded areas and on sheltered coasts. It is mainly migratory, the eastern populations migrating to northern India and southern China.

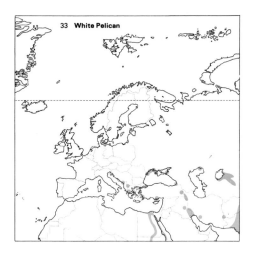

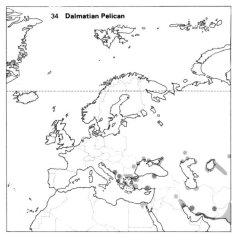

HERONS, EGRETS AND BITTERNS *Ardeidae*

There are twelve species in the region, occurring from Temperate to Tropical zones, associated with open waters or swamps. A widespread family, all are long-legged wading birds feeding mainly on fish or amphibians and similar prey. There is considerable size variation from about one to five feet (30–150 cm). Typical herons, *Ardea* species, have a form near most waters in the warmer Boreal to Tropical zones, one on waters with taller vegetation cover in Temperate to Tropical zones, and one on large waters in Subtropical to Tropical zones. A group of mainly white egrets, *Egretta* species, has two forms of open shallow waters in Warm Temperate to Tropical zones; and a form in coastal waters of Subtropical to Tropical zones. The Cattle Egret occurs on wet grasslands of Warm Temperate to Tropical zones.

The similar Squacco Heron is one of a series of pond-herons, *Ardeola* species, in Warm Temperate to Tropical zones on mainly still waters with thick surrounding vegetation. The Little Green Heron, of Subtropical to Tropical zones, has similar habitat preferences but usually by flowing water, and also occurs on the

White Pelican

Dalmatian Pelican

coast; while the Black-crowned Night Heron usually occurs on flowing water with nearby vegetation in Warm Temperate to Tropical zones. The Eurasian Bittern occurs in warmer Boreal to Warm Temperate zones in swampy areas with thick vegetation, and the Little Bittern occurs in similar habitats but extends into the Tropical zone and is part of a series of species through Eurasia.

TYPICAL HERONS *Ardea* species
Three larger, long-legged species. The Grey Heron has the widest range, and feeding varies from dry land to belly-deep water. All three species utilise long legs for deep wading and in the other two species this may help determine habitat. The Grey Heron is replaced through

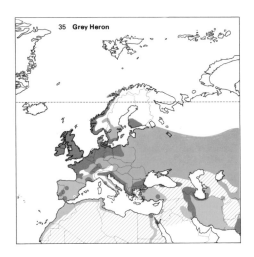

35　Grey Heron

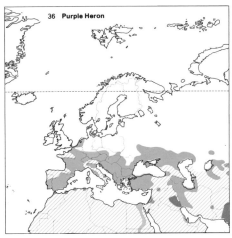

36　Purple Heron

North America by the similar Great Blue Heron *A. herodius*. In Africa south of the Sahara the Grey Heron overlaps in distribution with the Black-headed Heron *A. melanocephala*, but the latter is adapted to drier habitats and feeds more away from water. This may provide an adequate ecological separation of the two species. The slightly smaller Purple Heron is more adapted to life in and around reedbeds and also limited to warmer conditions. The very large Goliath Heron is confined to the Ethiopian region and Iraq. Another very large Heron, the Great White-bellied Heron *A. insignis*, occurs in north-eastern India and in Burma.

Grey Heron　*Ardea cinerea* (Map 35)
Dispersive, partly migratory and migratory; in Warm Boreal to Tropical zones with northward extension on the warmer western fringe. It occurs on the edges of all types of shallow waters, preferably fresh, but brackish and salt waters are also used. It avoids very abruptly steep or heavily overgrown margins, but otherwise it is found on all types from ditches to rivers, pools to lakes, from small wet patches to swamps, on coasts and estuaries, and at varying altitudes. Normally it prefers more open waters with nearby trees for roosting and nesting sites, but will nest on the ground or on rocks by water. It breeds colonially or in scattered pairs. Northern breeding limit is close to the 15°C July isotherm. The young disperse after fledging. North of *c.* 40° latitude it is migratory except in western Europe where with the likely availability of ice-free water for most of the winter it becomes locally dispersive in many areas. Some European birds are trans-Saharan migrants. It has expanded north-west in Scandinavia in recent times and has bred sporadically in areas of north-west Africa.

Purple Heron　*Ardea purpurea* (Map 36)
Dispersive and migratory; from warmer parts of Temperate zone to Tropical zone. It occurs where tall vegetation such as reeds and thick scrub or forest border freshwater marshes or slow-moving rivers, preferring to feed near, and breed in, such cover. It will utilise more open places in winter. Distribution is to some extent limited by the need for extensive areas of such habitats, and it is intolerant of human disturbance and drainage. It breeds in small colonies or scattered pairs in trees or on the

Purple Heron

Grey Heron

ground in cover. The young disperse after fledging. Apart from the Netherlands population, it normally occurs south of 51° latitude. It is resident through South-east Asia, Indonesia and parts of Africa, but the Palaearctic population is migratory, wintering on the southern side of the Sahara.

Goliath Heron   *Ardea goliath* (Map 37)
Resident, and possibly dispersive; in Subtropical to Tropical zones of Ethiopian region between *c.* 33° latitudes. It occurs on fresh, brackish or salt water, usually on the edges of large rivers and lakes, and in open coastal sites. Also to be found in the edges of tall stands of vegetation or mangroves. Usually nests in ground vegetation, sometimes in trees.

37   Goliath Heron

WHITE EGRETS *Egretta* and *Bubulcus* species
Four large to medium-sized species. Slender, long-legged wading birds, feeding actively in open sites, mainly in shallow water. Mostly with extensive, near-cosmopolitan, distribution. The Great White Egret is the large form with a world-wide distribution between 50° latitudes, mainly resident in the Southern Hemisphere, partly migratory in the north. The slightly smaller Plumed or Intermediate Egret *E. intermedia* is also present in similar habitats from India to Japan and south to Australia, and in Africa south of the Sahara. The Little Egret is smaller again and a bird of similar habitats with a range between 48° latitudes but in the Old World only, being replaced in the Americas by the extremely similar Snowy Egret *E. thula*. At the extreme east of its range the Little Egret overlaps in distribution with the Chinese Egret *E. eulophotes*, an apparently closely related species differing in slightly larger size and yellow bill. The latter has a very restricted range, mostly near the coast in extreme south-east China and at times north to Korea. It is probably an evolved isolate of that region with the Little Egret a later invader.

The Western Reef Heron is a purely coastal species, feeding along the shore from West Africa to Ceylon and the southern tip of India but absent from Somalia. When breeding it has a crest of two elongated feathers. The Eastern Reef Heron *E. sacra*, with a bushy crest, is an otherwise similar species occurring from the east coast of the Bay of Bengal east to Japan and south from the Philippines to New

Zealand. Of possible New World equivalents, the similar-sized Louisiana Heron *Hydranassa tricolor* and more restricted Reddish Egret *Dicromanassa rufescens*, the latter with a white-plumaged phase, are both sea-coast species.

The Cattle Egret is a stouter species with similar active feeding habits to the others, but is adapted to feeding in grassland mainly away from water. It has undergone a considerable extension of range in which respect it now resembles the first two egrets, but may have been much more restricted in the past.

Great White Egret   *Egretta alba* (Map 38)
Migrant and dispersive; in Warm Temperate to Tropical zones. It occurs in large areas of

38   Great White Egret

Goliath Heron

Great White Egret

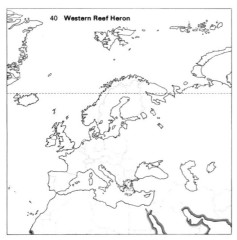

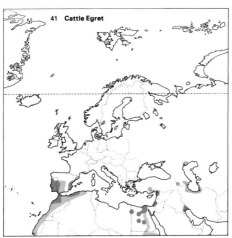

usually lowland waters; in marshes, and on the edges of all kinds and sizes of fresh waters, but also on estuaries and coastal salt waters in winter. It feeds in open areas but breeds colonially in tall dense growth of vegetation, reeds or shrubs, usually on the ground. European birds probably migrate only to the circum-Mediterranean wintering area. It has decreased in range through persecution and drainage, and the range in Europe may have been much more extensive in the past.

Little Egret   *Egretta garzetta* (Map 39)
Migrant and dispersive; in Warm Temperate to Tropical zones. Occurs by shallow lowland water, fresh, brackish or saline, still or slow-moving, including saltpans, ricefields and flood waters. Roosts and nests in trees or low vegetation, rarely on rock ledges. The young disperse after fledging. Mainly migrant in Europe and trans-Saharan migration occurs. It has increased after an earlier ranged decrease.

Western Reef Heron   *Egretta gularis* (Map 40)
Resident and dispersive; in Subtropical to Tropical zones, between West Africa and Ceylon, except on the Somalia coast, and between the latitudes of 4°–31° north. It occurs on reefs, and rocky and sandy coasts; less frequently on coastal lagoons, or muddy coasts of estuaries, saltmarshes, mudflats and creeks. It feeds in shallow surf or rockpools. It nests colonially in trees such as mangroves, and in low vegetation, often on islands.

Cattle Egret   *Bubulcus ibis* (Map 41)
Migrant, partial migrant and dispersive; in Warm Temperate to Tropical zones. It occurs in a variety of habitats, from the edges of shallow fresh waters to grassland, wet and dry, pastures and arable fields, and open groves. Associated with grazing animals, feeding on disturbed insects. The egrets roost and breed in trees and thickets. There is wide dispersal of young, but also erratic expansive colonisation. In the present century it has spread through the Americas, and into Australia and New Zealand, possibly aided by large-scale grazing agriculture. In Europe there has been a slight spread. Israel was colonised in 1950, but there has been some decrease in Algeria and Tunisia.

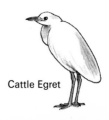

Little Egret   Western Reef Heron   Cattle Egret

SKULKING HERONS *Ardeola,*
Butorides and *Nycticorax* species

These are medium to small herons which prefer waters by or in thick vegetation and tend to be secretive and skulking. They are usually solitary in feeding. More typical of warm climates, occurring in Europe as summer visitors. The Squacco Heron is a small species preferring still water with thick surrounding vegetation. It is a European/Western Palaearctic and African species, replaced in the Indian region by the Indian Pond Heron *Ardeola grayii* and in China by the Chinese Pond Heron *A. bacchus* (map 42). The Javan Pond Heron *A. speciosa* occurs from Indochina to Java, and the Madagascan Squacco Heron *A. idae* on Madagascar. The species vary in the colours of mantle and breast and in the head plumes. The Yellow-crowned Night Heron *Nycticorax violacea* might be an American equivalent. The Little Green Heron is a small skulking form of fresh and salt, flowing and coastal waters, resident in Tropical and Subtropical regions around much of the world, with a summer population in eastern China and Japan. It is absent from most of the Western Palaearctic; and from North America where the possibly conspecific Green Heron *Butorides virescens* is present. The larger Black-crowned Night Heron is almost cosmopolitan in range, but is replaced in Australasia by the Nankeen Night Heron *N. caledonicus* which has a brown and buff body colour.

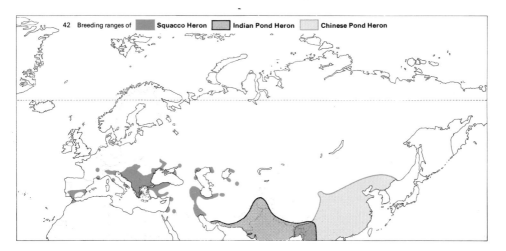

42 Breeding ranges of ▨ Squacco Heron ▨ Indian Pond Heron ▨ Chinese Pond Heron

Squacco Heron   *Ardeola ralloides*
(Maps 42, 43)

Migrant and dispersive; in Warm Temperate to Tropical zones. It occurs mostly by still fresh waters, ponds and ditches, bordered by thick vegetation usually including shrubs and trees, and feeds in and by such cover. It will also occur in more open sites on floodwater and ricefields, and also in marshland and on estuaries, shallow coasts and inshore islands. It is skulking in habit and more active at dusk. Breeding is sociably in colonies with other small herons or other waterbirds, in trees, shrubs or occasionally reedbeds. The young disperse early, before main migration. It decreased considerably in the last century and early twentieth century through persecution,

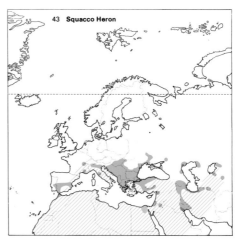

43 Squacco Heron

Squacco Heron

Indian Pond Heron

Chinese Pond Heron

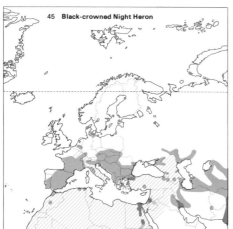

but has increased again in the last forty years. In the past it has bred more extensively in North Africa.

Little Green Heron   *Butorides striatus*
(Map 44)
Only just into the southern limits of the Palaearctic region, where it is resident, in Subtropical to Tropical zones. It occurs in mainly moving fresh, brackish and salt waters of streams, rivers, swamps, creeks, estuaries, lagoons and reefs. It is found more in the open than the Little Bittern but less so than other herons; usually near thick and tangled cover in which it can skulk and hide when disturbed. It nests in low bushes, usually over water and in mangroves, in scattered pairs or sometimes sociably.

Black-crowned Night Heron   *Nycticorax nycticorax* (Map 45)
Migrant and dispersive; in warmer Temperate to Tropical zones. It occurs by still and slow-moving fresh waters of all kinds and in swamps, occasionally on floodwaters and ricefields, or in grasslands. It roosts and nests in trees, usually but not always near water; occasionally in reedbeds or similar vegetation. Nests colonially, often with other waterbirds. The young disperse widely before autumn migration. Breeding distribution may vary irregularly from one area to another, with temporary extensions and contractions.

BITTERNS *Botaurus* and *Ixobrychus* species
The bitterns are skulking species of reedbeds and marsh vegetation, and are mainly crepuscular. The smaller species have a greater range of habitats and are more arboreal. A large and a small species normally occur in any one area, except in South-east Asia. The large bitterns form a group of four similar species, replacing each other geographically. The Eurasian Bittern occurs across Eurasia, with a population in southern Africa, the Australian Bittern *Botaurus poiciloptilus* replacing it in Australia, the American Bittern *B. lentiginosus* in North America and the Pinnated Bittern *B. pinnatus* in South America. The little bitterns show a more complex pattern

(map 47). The Little Bittern occurs in the Western Palaearctic, northern India, Africa and Australia. Schrenck's Bittern *Ixobrychus eurythmus* occurs from south-eastern Siberia through China and northern Japan. The Chestnut Bittern *I. cinnamomeus* and Yellow Bittern *I. sinensis* show a common range through India, Burma and southern China, both overlapping the range of the Little Bittern in northern India at lower altitudes and in China that of Schrenck's Bittern. Of the two the Yellow Bittern extends further north in China and also through Japan. Hence in parts of eastern Asia there are three similar small bitterns with no obvious differences in habitat and ecology. The Least Bittern *I. exilis* is a North American replacement species similar

Little Green Heron

Black-crowned Night Heron

Eurasian Bittern

to the Little Bittern, and the Stripe-backed
Bittern *I. involucris* is a South American
counterpart.

Eurasian Bittern *Botaurus stellaris*
(Map 46)
Resident, partial migrant or dispersive; in
warmer Boreal to Warm Temperate zones. It
occurs in swamps and large wetland areas
where large stands of tall vegetation such as
reedbeds create thick cover by sheltered pools
and ditches. It emerges to feed in open water
but otherwise remains within the vegetation,
rarely in sparser growth and on brackish or
saltwater areas. It is polygamous, breeding in
spaced territories, with nests on the ground in
thick vegetation. The northern breeding limit

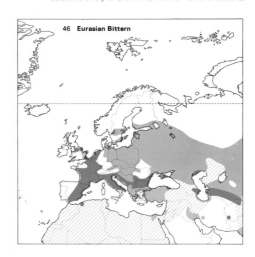

46 Eurasian Bittern

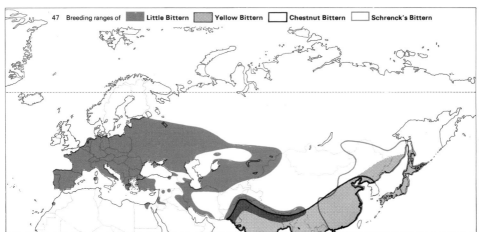

47 Breeding ranges of ▓ Little Bittern ▨ Yellow Bittern ☐ Chestnut Bittern ☐ Schrenck's Bittern

is close to the 16°C July isotherm. In south and
west Europe a resident on usually ice-free
waters, but through much of the range a migrant, or possibly more accurately a cold
weather disperser, to unfrozen waters. The
range was reduced in the last century through
damage and persecution. In Britain the species
was re-established in 1911 after a half-century.
More recently it has spread, or spread back,
into Scandinavia, but disappeared as a breeder
on the southern edge of the range in Greece,
Sicily and Portugal.

Little Bittern *Ixobrychus minutus*
(Maps 47, 48)
Migrant and dispersive; in Temperate to
Tropical zones. It occurs where thick but not

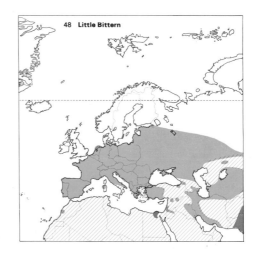

48 Little Bittern

Little Bittern

Yellow Bittern

Chestnut Bittern

Schrenck's Bittern

necessarily extensive stands of vegetation such as reeds, or shrubs and trees, occur in freshwater swamps or bordering and overhanging pools, lakes, rivers and streams. It nests in scattered pairs in shrubs, trees or tall vegetation either growing in or overhanging water. The young disperse after fledging and before the main trans-Saharan migration. It has bred in the past in northern Algeria and Tunisia and in Sicily and is suspected of breeding in south-east England.

IBISES AND SPOONBILLS
Threskiornithidae

Large to medium-sized wading birds with specialised bills, the ibises being smaller species with curved bills, taking a range of small creatures in wet and dry habitats, the spoonbills with a long, broad-tipped bill for filter-feeding, limited to large shallow waters.

The Glossy Ibis which occurs on the larger lakes and wetlands has a very sporadic and discontinuous distribution through the Old World and also occurs in the Caribbean and eastern North America. In south-western North America and South America it is replaced by the White-faced Ibis *Plegadis chihi*, differing only in a narrow white line round the eye, with a dark-faced isolate *P. ridgewayi* in the Andes. The Sacred Ibis of marshy areas is an Ethiopian species, once present in Egypt, with an isolated population in Iraq. There are several similar Old World replacement species, the Black-headed Ibis *Threskiornis melanocephala* (map 52) from India to Japan and south to Indochina, the White Ibis *T. molucca* from Indonesia to Australia, and the more distinct Straw-necked Ibis *T. spinicollis* in Australia. The Bald or Hermit Ibis is a relict species adapted for drier and rocky habitats and once present in Europe. A very closely related species also called the Bald Ibis, *Geronticus calvus*, is present in a few similar areas of southern Africa. There are five species of Spoonbill, mostly replacing each other, with the Old World species differing mainly in the colour and extent of bare facial skin and bill. The Eurasian Spoonbill occurs across Eurasia and in India and Somalia. The Black-faced Spoonbill *Platelea minor* with black face and grey bill replaces it in China and the Philippines, the African Spoonbill *P. alba* with red face and greyish-red bill in Africa, the Royal Spoonbill *P. regia* with black face and bill from Indonesia to Australia, and the Yellow-billed Spoonbill *P. flavipes* with a blue face in Australia. The Americas have the Roseate Spoonbill *Ajaia ajaja*, with bald head and pink plumage.

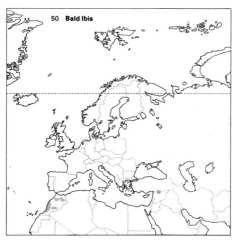

Glossy Ibis   *Plegadis falcinellus* (Map 49)
Migrant and dispersive; in Warm Temperate to Tropical zones. It occurs mainly on fresh, occasionally brackish or salt, waters of lowland lakes, lagoons, slow-moving rivers and estuaries, floodlands, ricefields and irrigated

Glossy Ibis

Bald Ibis

Sacred Ibis

areas. More rarely it is found on shallow coasts. It breeds colonially and with other waterbirds in tall vegetation and low trees, in large swampy wetlands. There is considerable dispersal and nomadism after breeding, with a wide range of accidental occurrences. The western range has contracted, probably through drainage and disturbance. It once bred in Spain, France, Austria, Czechoslovakia and Hungary, and in Morocco and Algeria.

Bald Ibis   *Geronticus eremita* (Map 50)
Migrant and dispersive; in dry Warm Temperate to Subtropical zones. It occurs in rugged, rocky habitats, usually dry, but also on high meadows and near water in mountains. It nests colonially on rock ledges. Movements and wintering areas are very imperfectly known. Until the seventeenth century it bred in southern Germany, Switzerland and Austria. It ceased breeding in Syria recently, and has bred in northern Algeria. Now reduced to a dangerously low world population.

Sacred Ibis   *Threskiornis aethiopicus*
(Map 51)
Resident and dispersive; in Subtropical to Tropical zones. It occurs in a large range of habitats near water, from lakes to estuaries and tidal pools, and on cultivated areas. It nests colonially, sites varying from trees to bare islands. Bred in Egypt until the 1850s.

Black-headed Ibis   *Threskiornis melanocephala* (Map 52)
Resident and dispersive; in Subtropical to Tropical zones. Like the Sacred Ibis it occurs on lowland plains and upland plateaus in a large range of habitats near water, from marshes, lakes and rivers to coastal lagoons and mudflats; and on wet cultivated areas. It nests colonially in trees or bushes, at times in colonies of other waterbirds.

Eurasian Spoonbill   *Platelea leucorodia*
(Map 53)
Migrant and dispersive; in Temperate to Subtropical zones. Distribution is limited by special feeding needs. It occurs on lowland waters and coasts, exceptionally at a higher altitude in south, requiring extensive slow-moving or disturbed shallow water. Water may be fresh or salt, but fast-moving or stagnant water unsuitable. It breeds colonially by

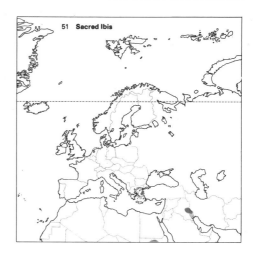

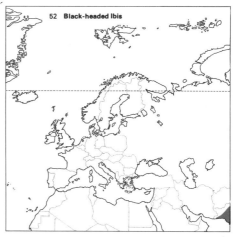

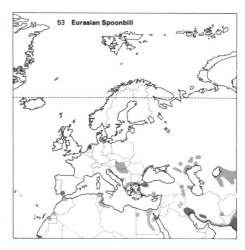

Black-headed Ibis

Eurasian Spoonbill

water in dense stands of vegetation mixed with shrub and trees. It is sensitive to disturbance when breeding. Some dispersal of young occurs after fledging. The range has been reduced in the west and north-west. Up to *c*. seventeenth century it bred in Britain, France, Italy and Portugal. In the present century it has attempted to breed, with varying success, in Denmark, West Germany, Czechoslovakia, Portugal and Israel.

STORKS *Ciconiidae*

Large, long-legged and long-billed birds, feeding on amphibians, fish and other small creatures in shallow water or swampy areas. The two species, White Stork and Black Stork, occur in summer through similar zones between latitudes 30°–60° but are separated by different ecological preferences, one in open areas, the other by waters and swampy areas in forest. The availability of these habitats may affect the overall distribution, although the differentiation of the Chinese population of the White Stork into a black-billed form which has been regarded by some as a separate species *C. boyciana* may indicate differences of distributional history in the Late Pleistocene period. Both species migrate to China, India and Africa south of the Sahara. Small breeding populations of both in southern Africa are said to be of migrant origin.

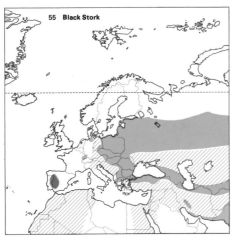

54 White Stork

White Stork   *Ciconia ciconia* (Map 54)
Migrant; in warmer Boreal to Warm Temperate zones. It occurs in more open wetlands, preferably where pools, slow streams or lagoons are present, in grasslands, steppe, tree savannah, ricefield and cultivation. Mostly in lowlands, occasionally at higher altitudes in the south of the range. The overall distribution is highly discontinuous, the southern U.S.S.R. population partly shown on the map ending south of Lake Balkhash, with another population isolated in eastern China (see comment above). It breeds in pairs or small groups on trees, buildings, rocks or similar raised sites; and migrates in flocks, avoiding large areas of open water and therefore concentrating at points such as the Bosphorus and either end of the Mediterranean. It has decreased in north and west, last bred in Britain in the fifteenth century, in Belgium in the nineteenth century, in Switzerland in the 1940's and in Sweden in the 1950's. It has bred occasionally in recent times in Italy and Israel.

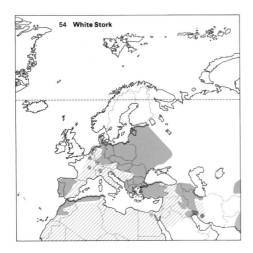

55 Black Stork

Black Stork   *Ciconia nigra* (Map 55)
Migrant and dispersive; in warmer Boreal to Warm Temperate zones. It occurs in older undisturbed forest by open waters, streams, pools or banks of rivers or lakes; or else in small swampy areas or damp meadows in clearings. It extends through the forest zone across most of Siberia to Sakhalin and into northern China. It prefers cover and freedom from human disturbance. It nests in large trees, but will use rock outcrops or caves in mountains,

White Stork

Black Stork

usually in scattered pairs. The young disperse after fledging and before the autumn migration, which is less concentrated in a few routes than that of the White Stork. It has decreased in the west, disappearing from Belgium and south-west Germany in the last century and Denmark and Sweden in the early 1950's.

FLAMINGOS   *Phoenicopteridae*

Large, long-legged birds with bills adapted for filter-feeding on fine organisms in salt or alkaline waters. Distribution is very limited by the scanty availability of suitable large waters, and leads to long distance movements. The Greater Flamingo is the most generalised and widespread form, occurring in the Western Palaearctic and Africa, with another race in the Caribbean and Galapagos Islands. The Smaller Chilean Flamingo *Phoenicopterus chilensis* of South America is sometimes regarded as conspecific. The more specialised algae feeders are more restricted, the Lesser Flamingo overlapping in range with the Greater in Africa and India, and the two *Phoenicoparrus* species with the Chilean Flamingo in South America.

Greater Flamingo   *Phoenicopterus ruber*
(Map 56)
Resident, migrant, partial migrant and dispersive; in drier Warm Temperate to Tropical zones, not occurring in Eurasia east of the areas shown on the map. It occurs where there are extensive areas of saline or alkaline waters on inland lakes, large lagoons, deltas, and more rarely on shallow tidal flats. This limits the distribution and even where conditions are apparently suitable and birds usually present, long flights may be made between localities, depending on conditions of salinity and water level. Breeding is highly colonial, on mud nests by or in very shallow water, but birds are highly sensitive to disturbance and weather and may desert. Breeding is erratic and sporadic and it is possible that the birds may use several localities according to prevailing conditions.

56   Greater Flamingo

SWANS, GEESE AND DUCKS
Anatidae

Large to small swimming waterbirds, usually short-legged with longish necks and broad bills primarily adapted for filter-feeding but in some species secondarily modified for grazing and fish-eating. The large swans feed mainly on submerged weeds. The *Anser* geese are grazers of open grassland areas, while *Branta* species occur on shore, steppes and in forest. The shelducks are gooselike forms. The medium-to-small ducks occupy a variety of niches as surface-dabblers, divers in fresh and sea waters and fish-eaters.

SWANS *Cygnus* species
Three species of large, long-necked birds in this region, feeding mainly on submerged vegetation, but also grazing. They nest on the ground at the water's edge. The three mainly replace each other. Bewick's Swan *Cygnus columbianus bewickii* together with the North American Whistling Swan *C. c. columbianus* (the two sometimes regarded as separate species) have a circumpolar distribution on arctic tundra. The distribution pattern suggests a possible speciation in a Pleistocene Bering Straits refuge north of the American glaciation. The Whooper Swan and its slightly larger, black-billed North American counterpart, the Trumpeter Swan *C. buccinator*, occupy Subarctic to Boreal zones when nesting,

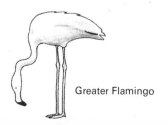

Greater Flamingo

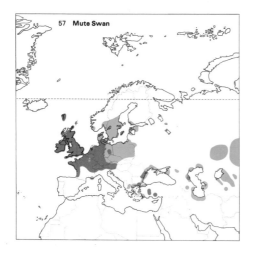

57 Mute Swan

58 Bewick's Swan

59 Whooper Swan

with a broader distribution in Siberia than in Europe which may reflect human interference. The Mute Swan occurs in warmer Boreal to Temperate zones with a discontinuous distribution that frequently overlaps the southern edge of the range of the former species.

Mute Swan *Cygnus olor* (Map 57)
Resident, partly migrant and migrant, in the Temperate zone, extending into the warmer Boreal in northern Europe. It occurs on fresh to salt waters of large shallow lakes, slow-flowing rivers, estuaries, lagoons and creeks, deltas, sheltered coasts and floodwaters. It has become domesticated and adapted to all types of small waters where aquatic plants occur. Usually in scattered pairs but non-breeders may be sociable. It is migratory in the east and elsewhere may be forced to make short movements if water freezes. Deliberate introduction and encouragement has influenced distribution, but there has been a general increase and spread in Europe in the present century, particularly in the last two decades.

Bewick's Swan *Cygnus columbianus* (Map 58)
Migrant; breeding in the Arctic, and wintering in Boreal to Temperate zones. It breeds on arctic tundra in swampy areas with pools and lakes, less frequently on slow-flowing rivers, estuaries or sea coasts. It breeds in scattered pairs but is sociable in winter, and winters on quieter lowland waters, lakes, reservoirs, pools, floodland and rivers with grassland grazing nearby. It may occur on coasts on migration. European wintering birds represent the population west of the Taymyr Peninsula; more easterly populations wintering in China and Japan. There has been some shift of wintering grounds from southern U.S.S.R. and Germany in the present century; and in Britain a shift from Scotland to England.

Whooper Swan *Cygnus cygnus* (Map 59)
Migrant, but partly resident in Iceland; breeding in Subarctic to Boreal zones, and wintering mostly in Temperate zone. It occurs when breeding on undisturbed shallow lakes, ponds and small pools in swamps, reedbeds, grassland, heath and forest, usually in lowlands, occasionally at higher altitudes; sometimes on lagoons, estuaries or inlets. It nests in scattered pairs, but is sociable in winter. In winter

Mute Swan

Bewick's Swan

it occurs on a wide range of waters, and will also use sea inlets and inland seas. Non-breeders sometimes remain for the summer in Britain and the Baltic. Lost in past centuries from Faeroes and Britain and reduced in range in Scandinavia through human persecution, it has spread again recently in the last region.

GREY GEESE *Anser* species

Five medium-sized grazing species of open grassland and marshes. Populations tend to have distinct breeding and wintering areas which tend to maintain separate types. They are sociable in winter, with family groups maintained within flocks. The Greylag Goose occurs in warmer Boreal to Temperate zones, extending further north on the coasts of northern Europe. The Bean Goose replaces it as a breeding species in the Arctic and colder Boreal zones (map 61). Two forms of it are recognisable, a more heavily built, stouter tundra form and a more slender-billed forest form. The Pink-footed Goose is a very closely related isolate at the western end of the range of the Bean Goose and is sometimes regarded as conspecific. These geese do not occur in North America and Voous has suggested that the Blue/Snow Goose complex replaces the tundra form of the Bean Goose, and the Canada Goose replaces the forest form. The White-fronted Goose is a circumpolar low-land tundra species, while the Lesser White-fronted Goose is confined to Eurasia in a narrow zone on the edge of the tundra, in wooded tundra and montane habitats.

Greylag Goose   *Anser anser* (Maps 60, 61)
Resident and migrant; breeding in warmer Boreal to Temperate zones, wintering in Temperate to Warm Temperate zones. It usually occurs where open fresh waters are bordered by grassland, cultivation or swamp, but within these limits it occupies a large range of habitats from near-tundra and heathland to steppe and swamp, with a wide range of altitudes. The nest is usually on the ground in a sheltered site, rarely on ledges or tree sites; and it nests in small groups of pairs. In winter it uses larger waters with nearby grazing, including brackish and salt waters. Iceland birds migrate to Britain, and Scandinavian birds to south-west Europe. Range much reduced by human activity. Extensively reintroduced in England.

60 Greylag Goose

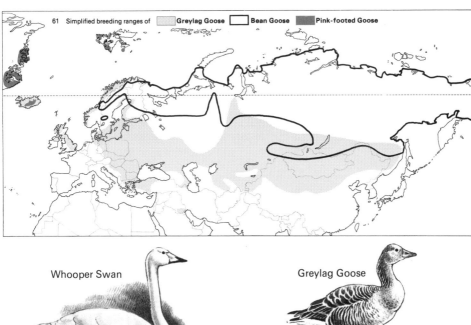

61 Simplified breeding ranges of ▨ Greylag Goose ☐ Bean Goose ▩ Pink-footed Goose

Whooper Swan

Greylag Goose

Bean Goose   *Anser fabalis* (Maps 61, 62)
Migrant; breeding in Arctic to colder Boreal zones and wintering in Temperate zone. The tundra form breeds on lowland tundra and offshore arctic islands, but the forest form may breed in thick birch or conifer forest, or on higher rocky ground with sparser trees, usually near water of some kind. It nests usually in scattered pairs on the ground. It is sociable in winter, occurring on grassland, steppes, cultivation and the edges of larger waters, both fresh and salt. The range has contracted in Norway and Sweden in recent times.

Pink-footed Goose   *Anser brachyrhynchus* (Maps 61, 63)
Migrant; breeding in the Arctic and wintering in the Temperate zone. It breeds on higher ground in tundra regions, on low mounds, and on ledges and tops of rock outcrops, rocky gorges, and low cliffs. It breeds colonially or in scattered pairs. It winters on estuaries, sea coasts, lakes, or rarely on inland moors; feeding in cultivated areas on stubble, potatoes and grassland. Iceland breeders winter in Britain, being more concentrated in Scotland in recent years, and those from Spitzbergen mostly in the Netherlands.

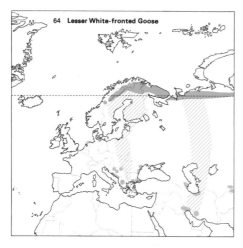

Lesser White-fronted Goose
Anser erythropus (Map 64)
Migrant; breeding in a narrow Arctic zone, and wintering in the Warm Temperate zone. It breeds on the shrub and forest edge of tundra, and on rocky slopes of hills and along streams; and shifts to larger open waters to moult. In winter it occurs on grasslands, from pastures to semi-arid steppes, and on cultivation, roosting in nearby swamps with reedy growth or open waters, lakes and rivers. It tends to use drier and more inland habitats than other geese. The main migration routes are south-easterly but stray birds move westwards with other species.

Bean Goose

Pink-footed Goose

White-fronted Goose *Anser albifrons*
(Map 65)

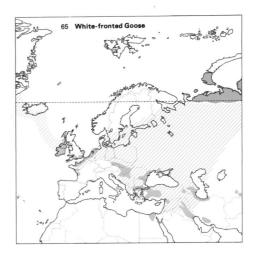

65 White-fronted Goose

Migrant; breeding in the Arctic zone, wintering in Temperate to Warm Temperate zones. It breeds on low, shrubby tundra near water, preferably fresh water; also on offshore islands. The Greenland race occurs on higher ground, on bogs or heathland by lakes. In winter the White-fronted Goose uses a wide range of grasslands, from bogs to arid steppes, and cultivated land with cereals and clover. The dark-plumaged, orange-billed west Greenland race winters mainly in Ireland and Scotland. The paler, pink-billed typical form in Europe occurs as a series of separate wintering populations, some of uncertain breeding origin, but those from around the southern North Sea originate mostly between Arkhangel and Novaya Zemlya.

BLACK AND WHITE GEESE *Branta* species

Four species occur, three of them smallish, arctic-breeding birds, and the fourth a large introduced species, the Canada Goose, which occupies a presumably underexploited inland wooded niche. Of the others, the Brent Goose is a bird of arctic tundra wintering on Temperate coastal mudflats. The species has a circumpolar distribution, subdivided into populations with separate breeding and wintering grounds (maps 66, 67), with the Red-breasted Goose occupying a more inland breeding habitat where the two Eurasian populations separate at the Taymyr Peninsula. The habitat specialisation of the Red-breasted Goose, with the more restricted distribution, is somewhat comparable to that of the Lesser White-fronted Goose. The Barnacle Goose has a restricted Greenland to Franz-Josef Land distribution, resembling the Pink-footed Goose in both the limited western distribution and the use of steep, rocky breeding sites.

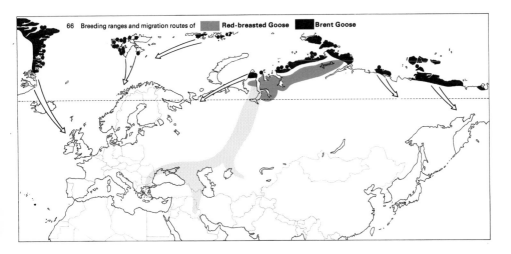

66 Breeding ranges and migration routes of ▨ Red-breasted Goose ■ Brent Goose

Lesser White-fronted Goose   White-fronted Goose

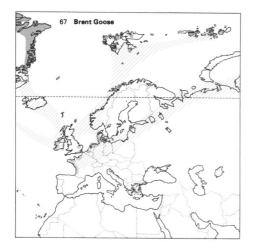

Brent Goose   *Branta bernicla* (Maps 66, 67)
Migrant; breeding in the Arctic zone, wintering in the Temperate zone. It breeds on low grassy tundra with freshwater pools, near rivers and the coast. The pale-breasted form also uses large and small offshore islands. In winter it feeds on coastal mudflats. Three distinct forms occur in Eurasia, a pale-breasted bird from Greenland to Franz-Josef Land, wintering in Britain and Denmark; a dark-breasted bird from the Yamaul to Taymyr Peninsulas of Siberia, wintering from the Netherlands to France, and a very dark bird of Siberia east of the Taymyr Peninsula, wintering around the north Pacific.

Red-breasted Goose   *Branta ruficollis*
(Maps 66, 68)
Migrant; breeding in the Arctic zone, and wintering in the Temperate zone. It breeds on steep slopes and rocky outcrops of tundra edge or wooded tundra, or occasionally on small islets; usually close to water and grazing. It winters on salt and semi-arid steppes as well as drier pastures, usually but not invariably near large shallow waters. It is suspected to be a relict species with a wider distribution at an earlier period. There is a marked decrease in the population due to destruction of birds and habitat.

Barnacle Goose   *Branta leucopsis* (Map 69)
Migrant; breeding in the Arctic zone, wintering in the Temperate zone. It breeds on steep cliffs and outcrops near water, or on small rocky islands; feeding on grass and herbage by water. In winter it feeds on grassland and stubbles. The Greenland birds winter in Ireland and north-west Scotland; Spitzbergen birds on the Solway in Scotland; and Novaya Zemlya birds in the Netherlands.

Brent Goose

Red-breasted Goose

Barnacle Goose

Canada Goose *Branta canadensis* (Map 70)
Introduced resident and migrant; breeding and wintering in the colder Temperate to Boreal zones. It occurs on various small and ornamental waters, usually among trees but not overgrown and with grazing nearby, and exceptionally at more open sites. It feeds on grassland and crops near water. Movements are mostly short but moult migration to Scotland appears to be evolving in British birds, while Swedish birds move south in winter.

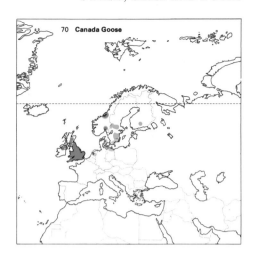

SHELDGEESE AND SHELDUCKS
Alopochen and *Tadorna* species
Longer-legged and more terrestrial waterfowl, feeding largely on land. The nest is in a hole, burrow or cavity of some kind, often some distance from water. The Egyptian Goose is an Ethiopian species, introduced and established in Britain. The two shelducks occupy widely overlapping ranges, with the Ruddy Shelduck better adapted to drier and warmer habitats and the Common Shelduck to more saline conditions which enable it to exploit the sea coasts and the lakes of semi-arid regions. Both species extend across Eurasia but have ranges terminating in western China. The Crested Shelduck *Tadorna cristata* appears to have had a very limited range on the eastern seaboard. It is known only from Korea and the coastal region north to Vladivostok, but may have had a wider range in the past and is now believed extinct. It may have been a replacement species; probably of the Ruddy Shelduck in this region.

Egyptian Goose *Alopochen aegyptiacus* (Map 71)
Resident; in Subtropical to Tropical zones in Africa south of the Sahara, introduced into the Temperate zone in eastern England. It occurs in Africa by inland waters at various altitudes into mountain regions, often on rugged and partly wooded areas. In England it occurs on mixed pastures, parkland and woodland by fresh water, and grazes on grassland and crops. It will perch in, and fly among, trees. Nest sites also include thick ground cover, old tree nests and rock ledges.

Canada Goose

Egyptian Goose

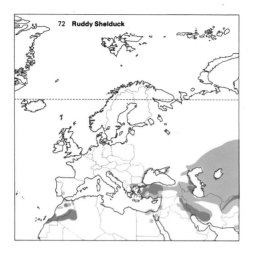

Map 72 Ruddy Shelduck

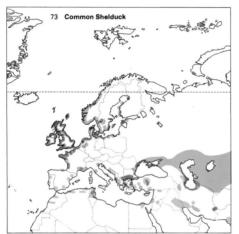

Map 73 Common Shelduck

Map 74 Mandarin Duck

Ruddy Shelduck   *Tadorna ferruginea*
(Map 72)
Resident, dispersive and migrant; in drier Warm Temperate to Subtropical zones in the west, extending into the Temperate zone in summer in Asia. It occurs by all types of fresh and saline inland waters at a wide range of altitudes, up to 5,000 m in Asia, extending into drier steppe and semi-desert. It prefers waters with sparsely vegetated surroundings, feeding and grazing on land in open areas, sometimes where very little water is present. The range has shrunk in the west.

Common Shelduck   *Tadorna tadorna*
(Map 73)
Resident, dispersive, partial migrant and migrant; in Temperate to Warm Temperate zones, extending into the Boreal zone in coastal regions of the warm North Atlantic Drift. In the west it is mainly a coastal bird of muddy and sandy tidal flats of shores and estuaries, where it feeds. Further east it occurs in drier areas on inland saline or brackish waters or marshes; exceptionally on fresh water. It feeds mainly on mud or in shallow water, rarely on dry land. In western Europe most of the otherwise resident birds make a late summer moult migration to the Waddensee of the German North Sea coast, and a few to the Severn estuary in south-west England. It bred in the past in north-west Africa and Italy, and has recently re-colonised Finland.

WOOD DUCKS *Aix* species

Mandarin   *Aix galericulata* (Map 74)
Introduced into Britain where resident, native to extreme eastern Asia where it is migrant or dispersive; in the Temperate zone. It occurs on still or slow-moving fresh waters bordered by overhanging vegetation, in broadleaf forest; and perches in trees. It feeds mainly along overgrown edges of waters or on forest streams. It nests usually in a raised tree hole.

Ruddy Shelduck   Common Shelduck

DABBLING DUCKS *Anas* and *Marmaronetta* species

Eight species, feeding mostly on fresh water, at or just below the surface, and in the latter case usually up-ending. The Wigeon also commonly grazes. Nest usually on the ground in vegetation near water, the birds breeding in scattered pairs but sociable in winter. Five are medium-sized and three small, these being the Teal, Garganey and Marbled Teal. Generally all except the last have a broad distribution, continuous across Eurasia, and mainly share a Boreal to Temperate distribution. Separation is maintained by small differences in feeding habits. In breeding distribution the Wigeon, Teal and Pintail are more northerly, with Mallard, Garganey and Shoveler a little more southerly, and Gadwall more southerly still. The Marbled Teal has a very limited Warm Temperate to Subtropical distribution. The Garganey is more migratory than the others. In the south-east the Mallard is partly replaced by the Spot-billed Duck *Anas poecilorhyncha*. The latter's breeding range from India to China, Japan and a corner of Siberia overlaps with the extreme south-eastern part of the Mallard's, and both share much of their wintering area in the east. The Teal has a broad range across to the Bering Sea. At the eastern end two related but slightly larger species share the range; the Baikal Teal *A. formosa* breeding in the north-east, south to Lake Baikal, while the Falcated Teal *A. falcata* occurs to the south of this but overlaps a little with the previous species, and both overlap with the Teal. Mallard, Gadwall, Teal, Pintail and Shoveler all occur also in North America. The Wigeon has a counterpart in North America in the very similar American Wigeon *A. americana*; and the Garganey is replaced by the Blue-winged Teal *A. discors*.

Mallard   *Anas platyrhynchos* (Map 75)

Resident and migrant; in Subarctic to Warm Temperate zones. It prefers still, shallow fresh water, but will occur on the edge of fresh, brackish or salt waters, from small pools and ditches to large lakes and rivers; and swampy and overgrown areas are also used. It has adapted well to man-made habitats, and will use raised and artificial nest sites, sometimes at a little distance from water. It has spread northwards in Norway since the last century, and has bred in Cyprus.

Gadwall   *Anas strepera* (Map 76)

Resident and migrant; mainly in Temperate to Warm Temperate zones. It prefers open, inland fresh waters, still or slow-moving, with emergent vegetation for cover, and dry banks or islands. It will feed on pastures and cultivation, sometimes well away from water, and nests in similar sites. It winters mainly in shallow, sheltered areas of larger lakes, lagoons, estuaries or similar wetlands. Icelandic birds winter in Britain, and northern European populations around the North Sea. It has spread westwards, colonising Britain, France and West Germany in the present century; and has occasionally bred in countries further north and south of the range.

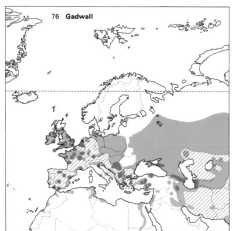

Mandarin   Mallard   Gadwall

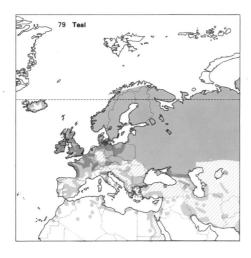

Wigeon *Anas penelope* (Map 77)
Mainly migrant, resident in parts of Britain; breeding mainly in Subarctic to Boreal zones, but extending into the Temperate in places. For breeding it prefers shallow, open fresh waters with submerged and floating vegetation, but will use saline or alkaline waters, usually in lowland sites bordered with open woodland or heathland. It moves to large open waters to moult, and winters mainly on shallow sea coasts, feeding on mudflats and saltmarshes, but also uses lagoons and floodland. Most Iceland birds winter in Britain, northern birds east to the Yenesei winter in west to south-west Europe, and mid-Siberian birds in the eastern Mediterranean, Caspian and Gulf areas.

Garganey *Anas querquedula* (Map 78)
Migrant; breeding in Boreal to Temperate zones, wintering in Subtropical zone. It is scarce in persistently wet or cold western areas, in upland regions or thick forest. For breeding it prefers shallow, still fresh waters of irregular shape, sometimes small, having abundant emergent and floating vegetation not too dense for easy passage, merging into grassland, floodland or marshy vegetation. It uses similar habitats in winter but also occurs on more open, sparsely vegetated ponds, ditches and small waters. It utilises open waters of steppes and semi-desert. Most Western Palaearctic birds winter in Africa on the southern side of the Sahara.

Teal *Anas crecca* (Map 79)
Resident and migrant; breeding in Subarctic to Temperate zones, wintering in Warm Temperate to Subtropical zones, into the edges of the Boreal zone in western Europe. It occurs on small fresh waters, shallow, and still or slow-moving; often isolated but sometimes part of a larger wetland system. Thick vegetation around the water's edge and emergent plants in the water are preferred. The nest may be in ground cover well away from water. On passage and in winter it frequently uses more open sites such as marshes, fresh and salt, lagoons, estuaries and shallow sea coasts. Iceland birds winter in Britain and Ireland, but otherwise the autumn migrations are mainly south-westerly, with additional movements in hard weather.

Wigeon   Garganey   Teal

Pintail *Anas acuta* (Map 80)
Mainly migrant, resident in a few north-westerly sites; breeding in Subarctic to cooler Temperate zones, wintering in Temperate to Subtropical zones. It prefers breeding at large, open shallow waters in lowland grasslands and pastures. It will use similar but smaller areas of suitable habitat in more varied areas. The nest is in ground cover in an open site near water. In late summer moult may occur on estuaries, lakes, deltas and saltmarshes, and in winter on estuaries, floodlands and open waters by shallow sea coasts. It will feed on cultivation and stubbles. Iceland birds migrate to Britain and Ireland, others move mainly south-west; but large numbers occur in West Africa. Considerable random movements and local fluctuations occur. Sporadic nesting occurs round the west and south of the main range, into most of the countries of southern Europe.

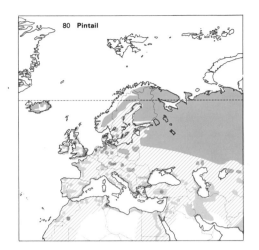

Shoveler *Anas clypeata* (Map 81)
Resident in the south-west, otherwise migrant; breeding in Boreal to Temperate zones, wintering in Warm Temperate to Subtropical zones. It occurs on mainly fresh, sometimes brackish or saline waters, but not normally on the sea; in lowland grasslands and reedy areas, also extending into open forest and into drier steppeland. It also occurs on shallow waters such as ricefields and sewage farms where feeding conditions are right. It uses similar waters on passage and in winter. The main migration movement is south-westerly, with some trans-Saharan migration.

Marbled Teal *Marmaronetta angustirostris* (Map 82)
Dispersive around breeding sites, and migrant; in drier Warm Temperate zone. It occurs mainly on small to medium-sized freshwater pools, sometimes with floating vegetation and typically bordered with dense emergent vegetation. Where suitable cover is present it may also occur on slow-moving rivers and oxbows, reservoirs and ditches, floodlands, and shallow brackish, saline or alkaline waters such as lagoons. Dispersal may occur as shallow sites dry out in summer; and limitation of suitable areas produces the sporadic range.

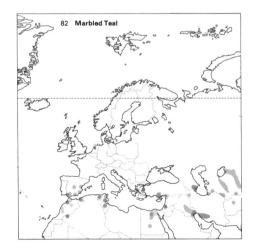

Pintail

Shoveler

Marbled Teal

TYPICAL DIVING DUCKS *Netta* and *Aythya* species

A group of diving ducks of mainly still fresh waters of 1–15 m depth, feeding on vegetable and animal food usually taken from the bottom. The Scaup is exceptional in having a mainly marine winter habitat. They breed in waterside vegetation. There are five species. Distributionally the Scaup, Pochard and Red-crested Pochard replace each other in breeding range from north to south, while the Tufted Duck has a range encompassing that of most of the first two and the Ferruginous Duck occurs to the south of it. The latter extends across into western China with an apparent replacement species, Bauer's Pochard *Aythya baueri*, with green-glossed head, occurring in north-eastern China (map 86). In North America the Tufted Duck is replaced by the Ring-necked Duck *A. collaris*, a similar species without the tuft; and Ferruginous Duck and Red-crested Pochard are absent but scaup and pochard are represented by pairs of species. The mainly coastal Scaup is present together with a smaller species, the Lesser Scaup *A. affinis*, on inland waters; and the Pochard is replaced by the very similar Redhead *A. americana* and a larger form, the Canvasback *A. valisneria*.

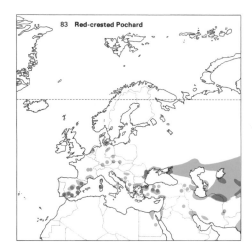

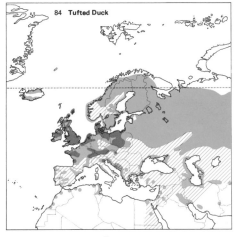

Red-crested Pochard *Netta rufina* (Map 83)

Migrant and partial migrant; in the Warm Temperate zone, also breeding sparsely in western parts of the Temperate zone. It occurs in the east on larger open waters, fairly deep and rich in submerged vegetation and bordered with reeds. In Europe it may use much smaller pools, otherwise similar but with more emergent vegetation and bordering trees. It dives to 2–4 m to feed, but also feeds by up-ending at the surface. It may occur on inland seas and sea coasts in winter. Most of the occupation of western Europe has occurred in the present century. Escaped birds occasionally occur and breed elsewhere.

Tufted Duck *Aythya fuligula* (Map 84)

Mainly migrant, but resident in much of Europe; breeding in cool Boreal to cool Temperate zones, wintering in Temperate to Warm Temperate zones. It occurs on lowland open waters, usually fresh, sometimes saline, often with little bordering vegetation, feeding at depths of 3–14 m. It uses deeper ponds, gravel pits, reservoirs, quiet rivers and sheltered coastal waters. It usually breeds on shallower fresh waters of 3–5 m. It winters on lakes, reservoirs, estuaries and calmer coastal waters. Most of the spread into western Europe has occurred since the late nineteenth century.

Scaup *Aythya marila* (Map 85)

Migrant; breeding in Arctic to Subarctic zones, wintering in Boreal to Temperate zones. It occurs when breeding on open fresh waters with some bordering cover, small to large, and

Red-crested Pochard

Tufted Duck

Scaup

on slow rivers; in tundra and forest tundra and into Boreal forest edges and in Scandinavia in montane birch forest. It feeds in up to 3 m depth, rarely up to 7 m. In winter it flocks on mainly shallow sea coasts and inland seas, occasionally occurring on brackish or fresh waters.

Ferruginous Duck   *Aythya nyroca*
(Maps 86, 87)
Mainly migrant, resident in a few south-eastern areas; breeding in drier Temperate to Warm Temperate zones, wintering in Warm Temperate to Subtropical zones. It prefers steppe-type habitats with still, shallow fresh-waters containing submerged and floating vegetation and a thick bordering growth of

85 Scaup

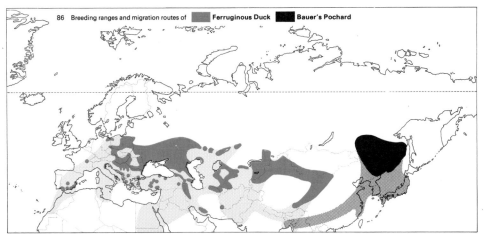

86 Breeding ranges and migration routes of ▨ Ferruginous Duck ■ Bauer's Pochard

emergent vegetation, often with shrubs. It may occur on very small waters of this type and can use saline or alkaline waters. It nests on float-ing vegetation or at the water's edge. It may occur on lagoons, coasts or inland seas on passage or in winter. It increased in the last century, but has subsequently decreased in the west and south-west of its range. Over the range as a whole it is frequently affected by varying water levels.

Pochard   *Aythya ferina* (Map 88)
Resident, partial migrant and migrant; breed-ing in Warm Boreal to Temperate zones, wintering in Temperate to Subtropical zones, the latter distribution in the west correlated with mainly ice-free waters. It occurs on

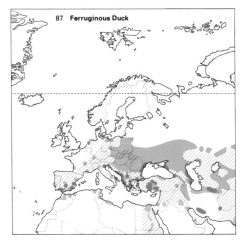

87 Ferruginous Duck

Ferruginous Duck   Bauer's Pochard   Pochard

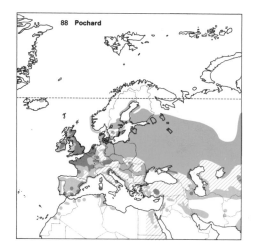

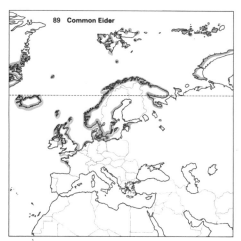

medium-sized open waters without floating vegetation, but in the breeding season requires a thick marginal growth of emergent and waterside vegetation, and preferably overgrown islands. It will use small waters where it is numerous, and in the south of its range occurs at times at higher altitudes. It feeds in depths of 1–2.5 m and prefers fresh waters but can utilise saline or alkaline water. It will sometimes use slow-moving rivers and estuaries, and rarely sheltered coastal sites. It winters on more open waters, lakes, reservoirs, and sometimes estuaries. It has spread west and north, since the mid-nineteenth century, into Scandinavia, Iceland, Ireland, Netherlands, Belgium, France, Switzerland, Austria and southern Bavaria.

EIDERS *Somateria* and *Polysticta* species
These are three heavily built diving ducks of shallow, northern and mainly Arctic coastal waters, feeding on molluscs and crustacea. They are ground nesters, often on open sites, and in the Common Eider often colonial nesters. They are mainly Arctic in distribution, only the Common Eider extending into the Boreal zone. The Common Eider is present in eastern Siberia and in North America, and the King Eider is circumpolar. Both the Spectacled Eider *Somateria fischeri*, which only accidentally occurs in the Palaearctic, and Steller's Eider are centred on the Bering Sea, occurring in extreme north-west North America and in eastern Siberia. Steller's Eider is a much smaller species than the others. Where the similar-sized Common and King Eiders overlap in range the latter breeds further inland and feeds further out at sea.

Common Eider *Somateria mollissima* (Map 89)
Resident, dispersive and partial migrant; in Arctic to Boreal zones. It occurs on sea coasts, preferably with some shelter from islands or rock skerries, and these may be used for nesting. It feeds in partly sheltered sea water at depths of 0–3 m. In winter it mainly disperses around the vicinity of breeding sites, with some coastal movement south-westwards in western Europe.

King Eider *Somateria spectabilis* (Map 90)
Migrant; breeding in the Arctic zone and wintering in Arctic seas on ice-free coasts. It

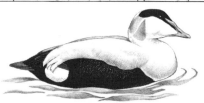

Common Eider

King Eider

breeds on tundra, further inland than the Common Eider, on freshwater pools, lagoons and sometimes rivers, or on muddy estuaries and bays. In winter it usually feeds in deeper water on sea coasts than the Common Eider. It occurs right up to the edge of the sea ice. Occasionally birds may summer further south, and have hybridised with the Common Eider.

Steller's Eider *Polysticta stelleri* (Map 91)
Migrant; breeding in the Arctic zone and wintering in Arctic seas on ice-free coasts. It breeds on tundra, nesting inland on swampy tundra with freshwater pools. In winter feeds in clear waters off rocky shores, and where fresh water enters the sea. It also occurs around sea ice. The apparent decrease of wintering birds since the last century might be due to warmer conditions.

COASTAL DIVING DUCKS *Clangula, Histrionicus, Melanitta* and *Bucephala* species
A group of six medium-sized to small ducks of northern latitudes, with the common characters of diving for food, nesting inland and wintering on sea coasts. The Long-tailed Duck is a circumpolar tundra nester. The Harlequin summers on fast-flowing fresh waters, and has a large population on either side of the north Pacific and a smaller Atlantic population in north-east Canada, Greenland and Iceland. The goldeneyes are boreal region birds, nesting in cavities. The common Goldeneye is Holarctic, occurring through North America; while Barrow's Goldeneye can utilise the colder, treeless zones and has a similar distribution to the Harlequin, the two goldeneyes overlapping in part of western North America. A third species, the smaller Bufflehead *B. albeola*, co-exists with the Goldeneye in North America. The two scoters overlap extensively, with the Common Scoter a breeder of more open tundra and salt waters, and the Velvet Scoter in more wooded freshwater zones, the two having slightly different coastal preferences in winter. In both species the Eurasian populations split into two in mid-Siberia. There are differences of bill-structure and pattern and in each the eastern Asiatic population resembles that of western North America, producing a pattern of double populations centred on the North Atlantic and North Pacific and regarded by some as separate species. The general distribution pattern

91 Steller's Eider

has a resemblance to that of Harlequin and Barrow's Goldeneye.

Long-tailed Duck *Clangula hyemalis* (Map 92)
Migrant; breeding in Arctic to Subarctic zones and wintering in Warmer Arctic to Boreal zones. It occurs when breeding on offshore islands, promontories and coastal tundra, and where fresh water is present on drier tundra; and in Scandinavia in the Arctic/Alpine zone of montane shrub tundra. In winter it usually occurs on sea coasts, also in fjords and occasionally on fresh water. In Europe it winters mainly in the southern Baltic. It usually feeds at depths of 3–10 m but has been caught up in nets at much greater depths.

92 Long-tailed Duck

Steller's Eider

Long-tailed Duck

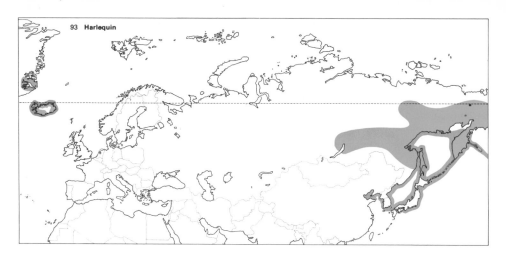

Harlequin   *Histrionicus histrionicus*
(Map 93)
Migrant, and partial migrant, for short distances; in Subarctic to Boreal zones. Distribution is limited by the need when breeding for cold, turbulent fast-flowing rivers, with nest-site at the water's edge. Migration follows the course of rivers and may be only to the nearest coast. It winters in rough waters on sea coasts, resting on rocky shores. It usually feeds at depths of 1–4 m.

Common Scoter   *Melanitta nigra* (Map 94)
Migrant; sometimes barely more than dispersive; breeding in Arctic to Boreal zones and wintering in coastal Boreal to Subtropical zones. It breeds on islets and promontories in coastal tundra and on slow-moving rivers, and further inland on freshwater lakes and pools in tundra and heathland, and at times in uplands and mountains on more open Arctic/ Alpine areas. Nests may be well away from water. It feeds at a depth of 0–4 m. In winter it occurs at sea on open stretches of more shallow inshore waters up to 2 km from shore, in depths of 10–20 m, but appears to travel further out to deeper waters for a late summer moult. The western form, east to about the River Lena, migrates west along the Arctic coast, the eastern form with a large area of yellow on the bill migrates east to the Pacific. Since the mid-nineteenth century the species has spread to Britain and Ireland, and bred occasionally in Spitzbergen and Faeroes, but has decreased in Scandinavia.

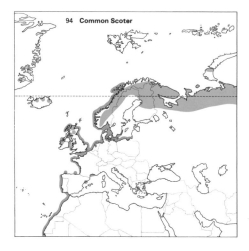

Harlequin

Common Scoter

Velvet Scoter *Melanitta fusca* (Map 95)
Migrant; breeding in Arctic to Boreal zones
and wintering in the coastal Boreal zone.
When breeding, it occurs on inland fresh
waters, lakes, pools and rivers; in more forested
habitat than the Common Scoter, rarely extending to more open tundra. In the Baltic it
occurs on islands and forested shores. It more
frequently occurs on fresh or brackish waters
as a breeder or passage migrant than the previous species. It feeds at depths of *c.* 5 m or
more. Like the Common Scoter it winters at
sea offshore, but occurs more often in the less
open waters among rocks and islands, and
nearer the coast. There are two Eurasian
populations. The western form east to the Ob
River basin migrates westwards; the eastern
form, with its stouter, reddish-patched bill,
migrates to the Pacific.

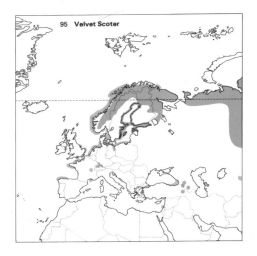

Goldeneye *Bucephala clangula* (Map 96)
Migrant and dispersive; breeding in the Boreal
to cool Temperate zones, wintering in Boreal
to Warm Temperate zones. It occurs in places
where forest with tree holes for nesting occurs
near fresh water, pools, lakes or rivers with
little aquatic vegetation; mainly in Boreal
forest extending into wooded steppe and tundra, and Arctic/Alpine uplands. On passage it
occurs on all types of waters, and winters
mainly on estuaries, sheltered bays and sea
coasts, but will also use suitable open fresh
waters. It feeds at depths of 0–4 m.

Barrow's Goldeneye *Bucephala islandica*
(Map 97)
Resident in the Palaearctic; breeding in the
Arctic zone. It breeds on cold inland fresh
waters, pools or lakes of moderate depth. Also
on fast-flowing rivers, but it is less limited to
fast-moving water than the Harlequin. It nests
in a variety of cavities and sites. It migrates
only as far as ice-free water, still or flowing
fresh water, and sheltered parts of coasts.

Velvet Scoter

Goldeneye

Barrow's Goldeneye

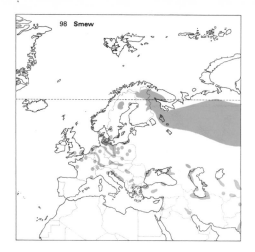

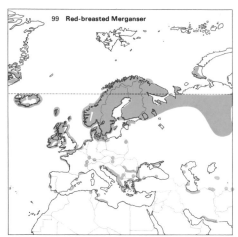

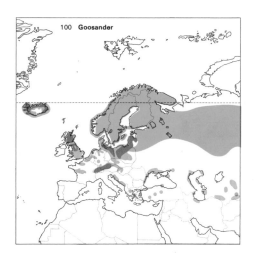

SAWBILL DUCKS *Mergus* species

Three species present. These are slender-billed, fish-eating birds of northern latitudes, catching their prey under water, usually in depths of less than 4 m. They nest in holes, cavities or under thick cover. They overlap extensively in range. The larger Goosander and medium-sized Red-breasted Merganser have a Holarctic distribution. In eastern China the latter overlaps with the similar-sized Chinese Merganser *Mergus squamatus*, a rare species with a limited distribution. The smaller Smew occurs across Eurasia but is absent from North America where the small but longer-billed Hooded Merganser *M. cucullatus* is a replacement species on mainly small inland waters.

Smew *Mergus albellus* (Map 98)
Migrant; breeding in the Boreal zone and wintering in Temperate to Warm Temperate zones. It breeds in forest areas with well-grown trees with holes, near cool fresh waters, and uses small to moderate pools and flooded woodland or oxbows, and slow-moving rivers. It feeds in water up to 4–6 m deep. On migration it occurs on many small fresh waters. It winters mainly on freshwater lakes, reservoirs and similar deep still waters, occasionally feeding on estuaries, sea inlets or sheltered coasts.

Red-breasted Merganser *Mergus serrator* (Map 99)
Migrant, and partial migrant to coastal waters; breeding in Arctic to Boreal zones, wintering in Temperate to Warm Temperate zones, and in ice-free Boreal to Subarctic coastal waters. It breeds in sea inlets and sheltered bays, or on small islands, in saline estuaries and on fresh or brackish rivers. It prefers clear water, and wooded or shrubby cover for nesting. It winters mostly on sea coasts in bays and sheltered waters and in estuaries. It appears to be increasing in numbers with some slight spread.

Goosander *Mergus merganser* (Map 100)
Resident, partial migrant and migrant; in Subarctic to Temperate zones, extending to the Warm Temperate zone in winter. It breeds on fresh waters of larger pools and lakes of montane and forest regions, inland seas, and the upper reaches of larger rivers, and prefers clear, colder waters. It nests in tree, rock and

Smew   Red-breasted Merganser   Goosander

ground cavities. In winter it occurs on deeper open fresh waters, lakes, reservoirs and more exceptionally on sea inlets. It has spread into England and Ireland in recent times.

––––––––––––––––––––––––––

STIFFTAIL DUCKS *Oxyura* species
Small, squat, large-headed diving ducks of mainly fresh water. They are mostly species of warmer regions. The White-headed Duck occurs through the warmer parts of western Eurasia in the steppe zone, with a discontinuous distribution. Another species, The Maccoa Duck *O. maccoa*, occurs just south of the Palaearctic in Africa south of the Sahara. The Ruddy Duck is widespread through the Americas and the white-cheeked North American form has been introduced and has established itself in south-western Britain.

White-headed Duck   *Oxyura leucocephala*
(Map 101)
Resident, partial migrant and migrant; in the Warm Temperate zone. It breeds on large fresh to brackish lakes and lagoons with extensive shallow water bordered by thick emergent vegetation and with waterplants. It will use small pools in such places. It will feed in water less than 1 m deep. It winters on similar waters and also sometimes uses sheltered bays of sea coasts. It normally avoids swift-flowing water but may use rivers on passage. Its range has contracted and it has disappeared from most of south-eastern Europe and some areas of the western Mediterranean since the last century.

Ruddy Duck   *Oxyura jamaicensis* (Map 102)
Resident or dispersive; introduced into the Temperate zone in Britain. It occurs mainly on still, shallow fresh waters bordered with thick emergent vegetation such as reeds, and with floating and submerged plants; typically on pools, lakes and gravel pits, but in North America occurs at times in slow-moving saline estuaries and on sheltered sea coasts. In Britain it now moves to larger fresh waters in winter. It has bred recently in Ireland.

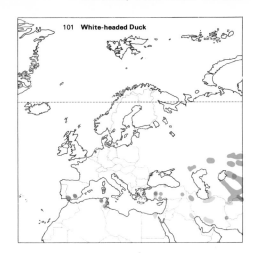

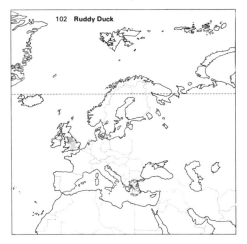

White-headed Duck   Ruddy Duck

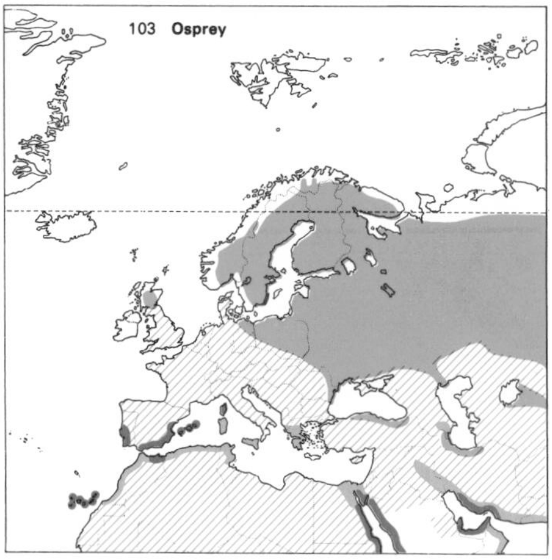

OSPREY *Pandionidae*

Osprey *Pandion haliaetus* (Map 103)
Mainly migrant, breeding in Boreal to Subtropical zones. A specialist feeder on fish caught by plunge-diving. It occurs around lakes and larger rivers and along sea coasts, usually in widely scattered pairs, in tropical regions in small rocky sea islets, coastal rocks or mangroves. Outside the region it may nest on estuaries more colonially. It occurs on all types of waters on passage, and may winter on coasts and large lakes. Absence from most of Europe is probably due to extermination by man. The distribution extends right across Eurasia, and into the Philippines and Australasia, in North America and sporadically in Africa.

HAWKS, EAGLES AND VULTURES *Accipitridae*

Large to medium birds, occupying a variety of habitats and in all temperature zones. They mostly take live prey of various kinds, but some are partial scavengers and others, such as vultures, completely so. Nests, usually large twig cups, are on trees or shrubs, rock ledges, or on the ground. Some species-groups have patterns of ecological separation and replacement, but often less obvious than in other families, the species often broadly overlapping in distribution, with minor habitat preferences and separated by differences in the principal prey selected. Vultures show a size-hierarchy resulting in dominance at carcases.

SEA AND FISH EAGLES *Haliaeetus* species

A group of mainly large eagles (map 104), feeding principally on fish, but also taking other prey and scavenging. The White-tailed Sea Eagle is a Subarctic to Temperate zone species right across Eurasia. The slightly smaller Pallas's Sea Eagle appears to be a more southerly Temperate to Tropical zone representative in eastern Asia. The larger Steller's

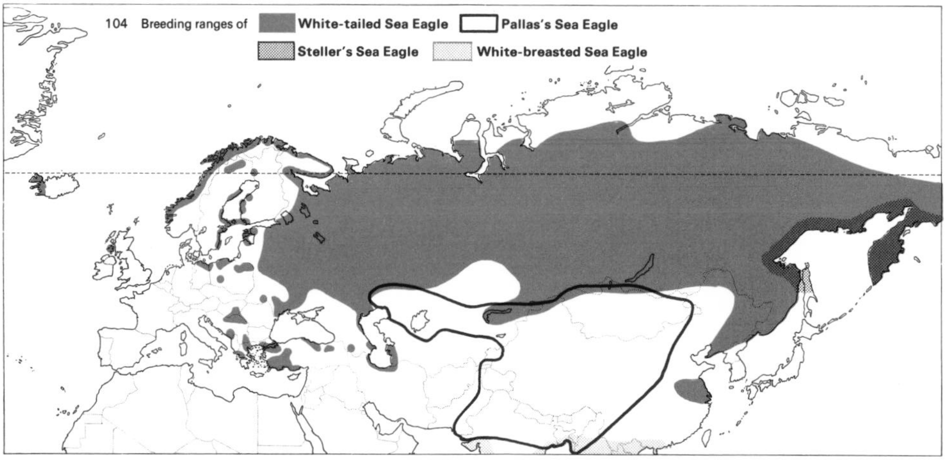

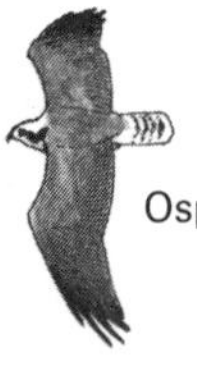
Osprey

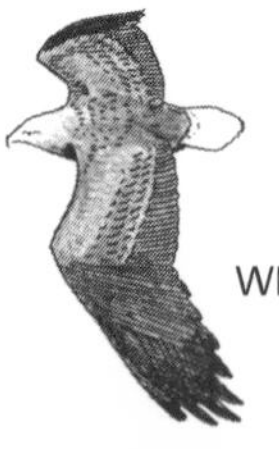
White-tailed Sea Eagle

Sea Eagle *H. pelagicus* overlaps in range with the White-tailed Sea Eagle in the extreme east of the latter's range round the Sea of Okhotsk. The White-breasted Sea Eagle *H. leucogaster* is a replacement species on the coast and the open larger rivers of India and Burma, and through Indochina and Malaysia to Australasia. On the forested rivers and lakes inland in the Indian region the Sea Eagles are replaced by the two fish eagles of the genus *Ichthyophaga*.

White-tailed Sea Eagle   *Haliaeetus albicilla* (Maps 104, 105)

Mainly resident in Subarctic to Temperate or possibly Warm Temperate zones. It occurs on sea coasts, and larger rivers and lakes, and may occur in suitable habitats up to 2,000 m in mountains. It is a vagrant rather than migrant and young birds may temporarily disperse beyond the usual limits. It probably occurred over most of Europe in earlier times and was exterminated by man. It last bred in Britain in 1908, but attempts are being made to reintroduce it.

Pallas's Sea Eagle   *Haliaeetus leucoryphus* (Maps 104, 106)

Part resident, part migrant, in Southern Temperate to Tropical zones. It occurs on inland rivers, lakes, marsh pools, coastal creeks and estuaries. In the present area it occurs mainly on steppe rivers and lakes in Temperate to Warm Temperate zones, but in the Indian region extends into Tropical zones and up to altitudes of 4,650–5,000 m in the Tibetan region. Interaction with other species in areas of overlap does not appear to have been studied, but it is suggested that slight differences in habitat preference may keep them apart.

TYPICAL KITES   *Milvus* species

Medium-sized, mainly scavenging birds. Two species probably evolving during an earlier division and isolation of a population, possibly in an early glaciation (map 107). From present distribution the Red Kite probably evolved in the west while the Black Kite appears to have had an eastern origin. In a secondary isolation with the Red Kite as a single unit, perhaps in the Iberian region, the

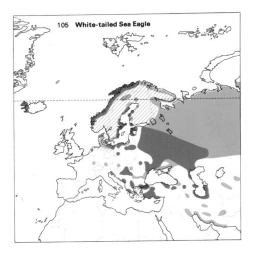

105   White-tailed Sea Eagle

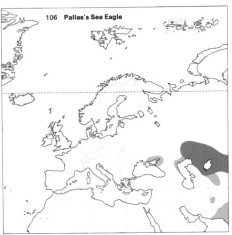

106   Pallas's Sea Eagle

Black Kite has undergone wider separation and isolation, producing distinct forms with small differences of plumage and bill colour, now regarded as subspecies. These show a distribution pattern resembling that shown by groups of species in some other genera, with eastern and western Eurasian forms, an Indian form and another in north-east Africa and southern Arabia.

Red Kite   *Milvus milvus* (Maps 107, 108)

Part resident, part migrant, in southern Boreal to Warm Temperate zones; migrating from most of the range outside the Warm Temperate. It occurs mostly in partly forested country

Pallas's Sea Eagle

Steller's Sea Eagle

White-breasted Sea Eagle

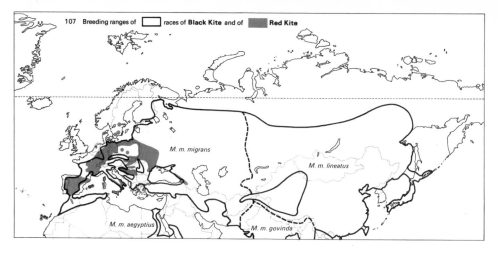

107   Breeding ranges of □ races of **Black Kite** and of ▨ **Red Kite**

M. m. migrans

M. m. lineatus

M. m. aegyptius

M. m. govinda

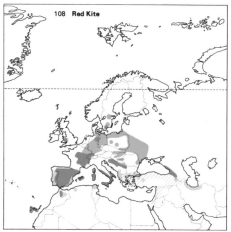

108   **Red Kite**

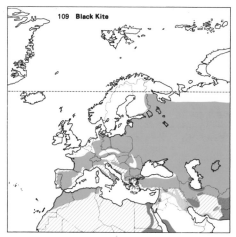

109   **Black Kite**

or parkland, preferring valleys with wooded slopes. It is associated with broadleaf forest, more frequently occurring in hilly country and less often near water than the Black Kite. Young birds of resident populations tend to be vagrant for a time. It can be a predator of young poultry and has been exterminated in parts of northern and western Europe, disappearing from most of Britain, Denmark and southern Scandinavia in the last century.

Black Kite   *Milvus migrans* (Maps 107, 109)
Mainly migrant, partly resident, in Boreal to Tropical zones. It occurs in a wide variety of habitats, often in association with man, but most frequently in the vicinity of water and differing in this respect from the previous species. In recent times it has shown a slight north-westerly extension of range. It is often gregarious in feeding and breeding.

Black-winged Kite   *Elanus caeruleus*
(Map 110)
Resident. This is a small bird of Subtropical to Tropical zones, with an Old World distribution between the 90° latitudes. It occurs throughout Africa apart from the Sahara, and from India through Malaysia and Indonesia; replaced in Australasia by the very similar Black-shouldered Kite *E. notatus* and in parts of the Americas by the equally similar White-tailed Kite *E. leucurus*. The Black-winged Kite is typically a bird of savannah with scattered trees or shrubs, but also occurs in other similar habitats from open forest to semi-desert.

Red Kite

Black Kite

Black-winged Kite

Short-toed Eagle   *Circaetus gallicus*
(Map 111)
Migrant. A largish bird of Temperate to Subtropical zones, Tropical in India. Its distribution extends eastwards to mid-Siberia
(Novosibirsk) and the Indian region. It migrates to the savannah zone bordering the
southern Sahara and to Indonesia. It feeds
especially on snakes, which to some extent
governs its distribution and the need to migrate. It occurs in open country with scattered
trees, in broken forest or forest edge, and into
steppes and mountain foothills. The reason
for its absence from north-western Europe is
unknown unless, as with other species, man
has been responsible for exterminating it.

––––––––––––––––––––––––––––––––

SPARROWHAWKS *Accipiter* species
Small to medium-sized birds of forest and
scrub, taking small prey, especially birds, by
surprising them in rapid flight. Males are distinctly smaller than females, thus reducing
direct food competition by utilising a different
size of prey. The largest species, the Goshawk,
occurs from Subarctic to Temperate or occasionally Warm Temperate zones throughout Eurasia, and also in the Boreal zone of
North America. In the east it has an isolate
population to the south-western side of the
Tibetan massif. The Crested Goshawk *A. tri-
virgatus* occurs through India, Burma and
Indochina south of this range and appears to
be a replacement species, although not closely
related. The Sparrowhawk is a smaller and
more active species with a similar distribution
range to the Goshawk, but extending into
eastern and southern Africa, and replaced in
the Americas by the Sharp-shinned Hawk
A. striatus. It too has an isolate population,
along the eastern side of the Tibetan massif in
the Himalayas. The Besra Sparrowhawk *A.
virgatus* appears to be a replacement species
in milder climates. It is very similar to the
Sparrowhawk. The northern limit of its range
extends westwards from northern China and
extreme south-east Siberia to the upper
Yenesei and northern Mongolia; and the
southern limit through northern Burma and
along the Himalayas. Where the two species
overlap in Siberia the Sparrowhawk occurs
in spruce forest and the Besra Sparrowhawk
in broadleaf forest. Where the two have a
narrow distribution through the Himalayas

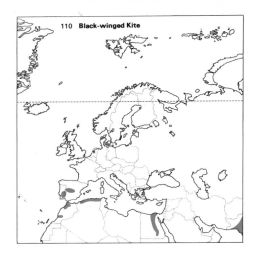

110 Black-winged Kite

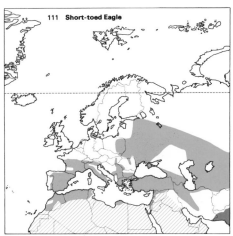

111 Short-toed Eagle

the Sparrowhawk occurs at higher altitudes.
   A group of three small species are related
birds occupying warmer, drier and more open
country than the previous species (map 114).
The Levant Sparrowhawk occurs around the
northern Aegean and in Iran south of the
Caucasus. A related species, the Grey Frog
Hawk *A. soloensis*, breeds from Korea through
eastern China. Between the two the Shikra
occurs in the Indian region and through
Burma and Indochina. It extends north-east
to the Aral Sea and Lake Baikal, and westwards through northern Iran to overlap in
distribution with the Levant Sparrowhawk at
the southern end of the Caspian Sea. It is not
known to what extent the two species interact
at at this point. The Shikra also occurs through

Short-toed Eagle

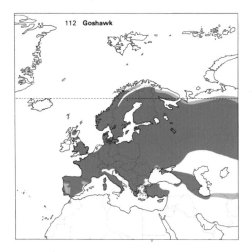

112 Goshawk

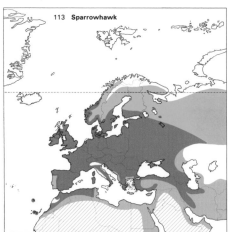

113 Sparrowhawk

most of Africa south of the Sahara and the two populations have probably been separated by increasing aridity in Arabia during post-glacial times.

Goshawk   *Accipiter gentilis* (Map 112)
Resident and partly migrant, in Subarctic to Warm Temperate zones. It occurs in wooded country, mainly coniferous forest; in open forest, and discontinuous forest and plantations; preferring more mature tree growth. It extends into more open country in the extreme north of its range where taller trees are absent, and may occur elsewhere in similar country or in scrub in winter. It is an agile hunter taking larger birds or mammals, usually from a perch or on the ground. It usually keeps within woodland but may soar and fly high on migration.

Sparrowhawk   *Accipiter nisus* (Map 113)
Resident and partly migrant; in Subarctic to Warm Temperate zones, migrating from more northerly parts of range and occurring in Warm Temperate to Subtropical zones in winter. It occurs in forest where some open space or clearings are present, or in discontinuous woodland or plantations, or small scattered groups of trees, preferably dense and not too widely spaced. It prefers younger tree growth than the previous species. The need for open space is linked with hunting methods, the principal food being small birds observed from a distance, surprised and seized, often in the air. Like the Goshawk it tends to stay low but often soars high on migration.

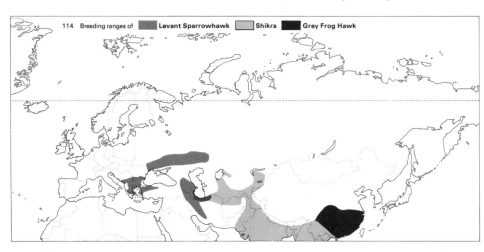

114 Breeding ranges of   Levant Sparrowhawk   Shikra   Grey Frog Hawk

Goshawk

Sparrowhawk

Levant Sparrowhawk

Levant Sparrowhawk *Accipiter brevipes* (Maps 114, 115)

Migrant; breeding in Warm Temperate zone and migrating to Subtropical zones. It breeds through grassland, steppe and mountain regions, occurring in broadleaf open forest, stands of taller trees in lower growth, orchards and olive groves, scattered trees in cultivated areas and trees or scrub on hilly slopes or in open places. It hunts less vigorously than Sparrowhawk, taking a larger range of prey including lizards and insects.

Shikra *Accipiter badius* (Maps 114, 116)

Resident and partly migrant; in Warm Temperate to Subtropical zones, from steppe to tropical broadleaf forest. It occurs in similar habitats to previous species – open forest, forest edge, parkland, orchards and scattered trees in cultivated areas. In the steppes it is usually in woodland, plantations or scrub by water. It ranges from sea level to 1,500 m in the Himalayas. It hunts more like Sparrowhawk than the previous species, but takes a similar large range of prey.

———————————————————

CHANTING GOSHAWKS *Melierax* species

Dark Chanting Goshawk *Melierax metabates* (Map 117)

Resident; in dry Subtropical to Tropical zones. It occurs in dry savannah and in thorn scrub, where a few tall trees are present for perches, but telegraph poles may suffice. The principal range is through Africa south of the Sahara where the dry habitat is present. The small Moroccan population is a relict of a western Saharan edge population. In the east it extends to Upper Egypt and the adjacent part of Arabia. It hunts in sparrowhawk fashion and nests in trees or shrubs.

———————————————————

BUZZARDS *Buteo* species (Map 118)

There are three west Eurasian species, overlapping marginally in range when breeding but mainly replacing each other latitudinally. Climate may help to determine the difference between species with feathered legs (cold), bare legs (temperate), long bare legs (terrestrial in warmer steppes) and long partly-feathered legs (terrestrial in colder steppes). The Rough-legged Buzzard is a mainly tundra species with cold adaptation and has a con-

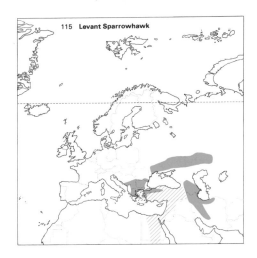

115 Levant Sparrowhawk

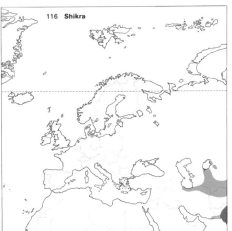

116 Shikra

117 Dark Chanting Goshawk

Shikra

Grey Frog Hawk

Dark Chanting Goshawk

tinuous Holarctic distribution which suggests a possible origin in a Bering Strait glacial refuge with later dispersal in both directions. The Common Buzzard is a forest species with a Boreal to Temperate distribution. An isolate population on the south side of the Tibetan massif suggests a wider range at an earlier period. The Long-legged Buzzard is a bird of open steppe and savannah from Temperate to Subtropical zones. In the east of its range in Tibet, on upland steppe and in more mountainous regions, it is replaced by a similar but cold-adapted form with partly feathered long legs, the Upland Buzzard *Buteo hemilasius*. Theoretically these last two replace each other altitudinally, but in some areas the situation is more complex. In North America the Rough-

legged Buzzard is present, and the Common Buzzard replaced in part by the similar but larger Red-tailed Hawk *B. jamaicensis*; but in eastern U.S.A. two smaller forest species are also present, the Red-shouldered Hawk *B. lineatus* in open mixed and broadleaf forest, and the still smaller Broad-winged Hawk *B. platypterus* in thick stands of forest. The Ferruginous Hawk *B. regalis* of the dry open western region may correspond ecologically to the Long-legged Buzzard in Eurasia.

Common Buzzard　*Buteo buteo*
(Maps 118, 119)
Resident and migrant; breeding in Boreal to Temperate zones and wintering in western Temperate to Warm Temperate zones. It is a

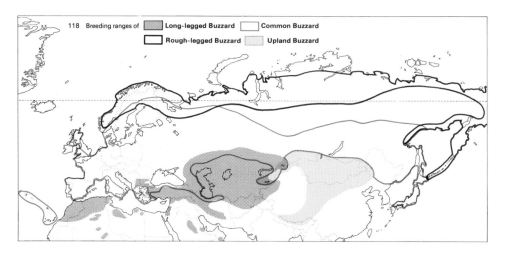

118　Breeding ranges of　███ Long-legged Buzzard　□ Common Buzzard
　　□ Rough-legged Buzzard　▒ Upland Buzzard

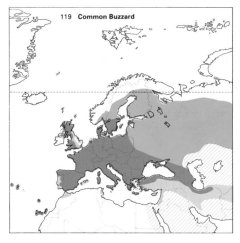

119　**Common Buzzard**

woodland bird occurring in all types of forest where some open ground is present for feeding, extending into parkland, cultivated areas, and heath or moorland where scattered trees are present, and in montane areas with trees up to *c.* 3,000 m. It nests in trees or on rock outcrops. The form occurring in lightly forested steppe has in the past been treated as a separate species. Eastern European birds migrate to Arabia and through eastern Africa to the Cape.

Rough-legged Buzzard　*Buteo lagopus*
(Maps 118, 120)
Migrant; breeding in Arctic to Subarctic zones, and Arctic/Alpine areas of Scandinavia, and wintering in the Temperate zone. It

Common Buzzard

Rough-legged Buzzard

breeds in open country, on bare moist tundra and shrub to forest tundra, on bare upland moors and heathland, and in mountains. It will use open forest at times. It nests on a rock ledge, sometimes on trees. In winter it frequents bare open areas, particularly lowland marshes near water. Migratory movements and nesting limits are controlled and modified in part by the availability of lemmings and voles from year to year.

Long-legged Buzzard   *Buteo rufinus*
(Maps 118, 121)
Resident and migrant; breeding in drier Warm Temperate to Subtropical zones, with a partial southward shift in winter into northern India and East Africa. It occurs mainly in dry steppe, semi-desert and desert edge, and open dry montane areas, up to *c.* 2,500 m in some Asiatic regions. The northern breeding limit is near to the 23°C July isotherm, but other buzzard species do not show obvious temperature correlates. The nest is on a low ledge, bank or tree. Migration occurs across some high mountain ranges.

HONEY BUZZARDS *Pernis* species
(Map 123)

Buzzard-like raptors. Open forest species specialising in feeding on insects and larvae of bee and wasp nests, and also taking a range of small creatures. The nest is in a tree. There are three forms in Eurasia. The European Honey Buzzard occurs in a continuous range to mid-Siberia. A similar eastern species, *Pernis ptilorhynchus* has two distinct and separate populations in Eurasia. The Siberian Honey Buzzard *P. p. orientalis* replaces the western form in similar latitudes, and they may meet or overlap in the region of the upper Ob. It is migratory. The Crested Honey Buzzard *P. p. ruficollis*, with a small pointed crest, occurs in the Indian region. Other forms occur through Indochina, Indonesia and the Philippines and all are sometimes treated as a single species. There is no apparent North American counterpart.

Honey Buzzard   *Pernis apivorus*
(Maps 122, 123)
Migrant; breeding in Boreal to Temperate zones, wintering in Africa south of the Sahara. It occurs in more open or broken forest where

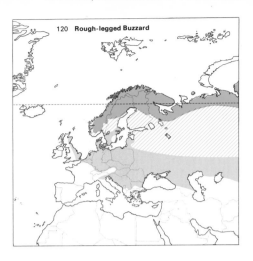
120 Rough-legged Buzzard

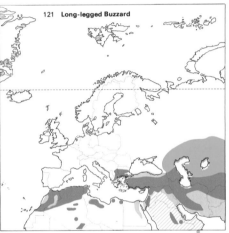
121 Long-legged Buzzard

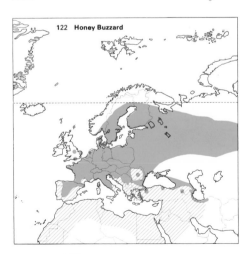
122 Honey Buzzard

Long-legged Buzzard

Upland Buzzard

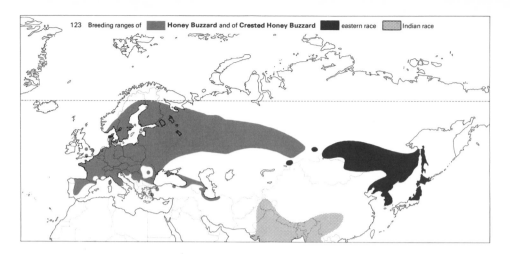

123 Breeding ranges of ▮ **Honey Buzzard** and of **Crested Honey Buzzard** ▮ eastern race ▨ Indian race

small grassy areas are present, and sometimes on forest edges or parkland; more frequently in broadleaf than in pure conifer forest. It tends to keep low among the trees. Its specialised feeding necessitates migration in colder climates.

TYPICAL EAGLEŠ *Hieraaëtus* and *Aquila* species

The *Hieraaëtus* species in the Palaearctic are two actively hunting buzzard-sized eagles of warmer regions. Except in Spain and North Africa the breeding ranges of the two tend to replace each other longitudinally. The larger Bonelli's Eagle occurs through the drier and more montane areas of Old World Warm Temperate to Subtropical zones, from Spain to eastern China, south through India and through Africa south of the Sahara. A smaller migrant species, the Booted Eagle, is a forest species. It has a Warm Temperate to Temperate steppe range, and winters in tropical Africa and southern Asia. Another smallish species, the Rufous-bellied Hawk-eagle *Hieraaëtus kiernerii* occurs through India south of the Himalayas in forests on the lower hill slopes, while Ayre's Hawk-eagle *H. dubius* is present in forested parts of Africa south of the Sahara.

The *Aquila* eagles consist of three larger species that replace each other, and three smaller ones similar in size to *Hieraaëtus* species. Their food ranges from mammals and birds to carrion. Of the first three the Golden Eagle is a bird of more northern, mountain areas, extending across the whole of Eurasia,

and tends to be replaced in warmer lowlands by the Imperial Eagle, while Verreaux's Eagle is a replacement species on higher ground in the Ethiopian region. The Imperial Eagle has two populations, one in Spain and Morocco, the other around the Black Sea and Caspian, the two showing some plumage differences. They may represent two populations separated in the Pleistocene. The Spotted Eagle is a species of moister, lowland forest edges with a mainly boreal distribution from the east China coast across Eurasia into eastern Europe where it overlaps extensively with the Lesser Spotted Eagle. The latter is a bird of forest, usually broadleaf, and more associated with montane forest and not with the presence of water as is the previous species. The Lesser Spotted Eagle has a mainly Temperate to Warm Temperate distribution, and there is a distinct, resident population in India and Pakistan. The two spotted eagle species appear to have converged in Europe from easterly and southerly directions. The Tawny or Steppe Eagle has a widespread distribution through drier open regions of steppes, savannahs and plains, overlapping a little in general distribution with the similar-sized spotted eagles, but ecologically separated. The Eurasian population, extending from the Black Sea to Mongolia and eastern China, has in the past been regarded as a separate species, the Steppe Eagle, and the name Tawny Eagle is used for the forms occurring in Africa north and south of the Sahara, and in India.

Honey Buzzard

Crested Honey Buzzard

Bonelli's Eagle *Hieraaëtus fasciatus*
(Map 124)
Resident; in Warm Temperate to Subtropical
zones. It occurs in open and broken forest of
mountain and hill slopes up to *c.* 2,000–
2,300 m, extending into the hill areas of
sparsely forested grassland, tree steppe and
scrub. It nests on a rock outcrop or tree. The
form in Africa south of the Sahara is more a
bird of lowland savannah, scrub and cultivation where a few trees are present. In Europe
its northern limit is near the 25°C July isotherm. It is a vigorous hunter, taking fairly
large birds and mammals.

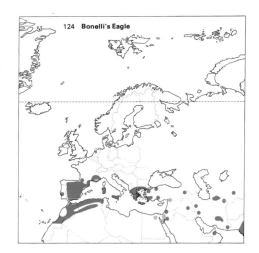

Booted Eagle *Hieraaëtus pennatus*
(Map 125)
Migrant; breeding in a discontinuous range in
the drier parts of the southern Temperate to
Warm Temperate zones, wintering in Subtropical to Tropical zones. It occurs in various
types of forest, from sea level to altitudes of
up to 3,250 m, usually in broadleaf or mixed
forest; and on forest edges. The nest is in a
tree, or sometimes on a rock outcrop. Like the
previous species it is an able hunter.

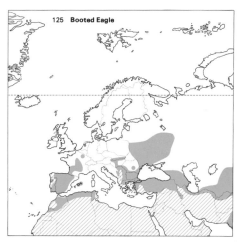

Golden Eagle *Aquila chrysaetos* (Map 126)
Resident, partial migrant and dispersive, in
Boreal to Warm Temperate zones. It occurs in
rocky montane areas with or without trees,
extending in the north to lower and more
varied forest and moorland. It nests on a crag,
rarely in a tree. Its absence in western Europe
is almost certainly due to past extermination
by man.

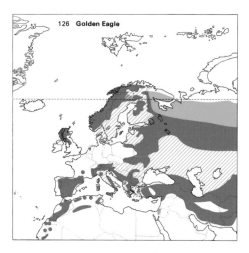

Bonelli's Eagle

Booted Eagle

Golden Eagle

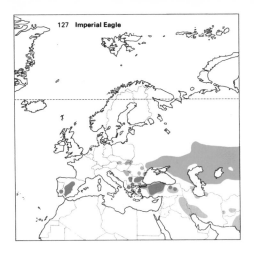

Imperial Eagle   *Aquila heliaca* (Map 127)
Resident and migrant; breeding in Temperate to Warm Temperate zones, wintering in Warm Temperate to Subtropical zones. It occurs generally on lowland areas – forest edges, open forest and parkland, open grassland, steppes, marshes and plains where scattered trees are present, and on partly wooded foothills, but may occur at altitudes of up to *c.* 2,000 m. The nest is in a tree. Its range and numbers are decreasing, particularly in the west, where it nested in the past in Portugal and northern Morocco; and possibly decreasing in the east since its breeding status appears to be in doubt in Afghanistan and Pakistan, although it apparently nested in the past in the Punjab.

Verreaux's Eagle   *Aquila verreauxi*
(Map 128)
Resident; in Subtropical to Tropical zones of Africa, with a small number extending into north-east Africa and the Arabian peninsula where the distribution is uncertain. It breeds in dry open areas, mountains and hills, deserts, dry scrub, and in rocky hills in savannah areas. The nest is on a rock ledge or a tree.

Spotted Eagle   *Aquila clanga* (Map 129)
Mainly migrant, possibly resident in the southern Caspian; breeding in warmer Boreal to Temperate zones, and wintering in the Warm Temperate zone. It occurs in or near open or thick forest, usually in the vicinity of rivers or swampy areas, and usually in lowland, rarely at an altitude. It may occur in forest steppe and more open areas, usually along rivers where trees are present. The nest is in a large tree, rarely on a lower site. It winters in Africa mostly in the north-east on open ground, savannah and cultivation; in India in open lowland by water.

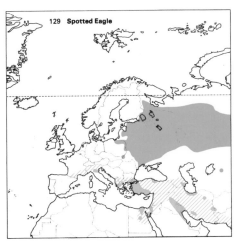

Lesser Spotted Eagle   *Aquila pomarina*
(Map 130)
Migrant in Europe, resident in India; breeding in warmer Boreal to Temperate European zones, wintering in the Temperate zone. When breeding it occurs in forest, usually broken or open, sometimes dense, without the previous species' preference for the vicinity of water; often in montane forest up to *c.* 2,000 m. The

Imperial Eagle

Verreaux's Eagle

nest is in a forest tree. The majority of European birds winter in Africa, south of the Equator, on open savannah, and at this time and on passage occur more often near water.

Tawny or Steppe Eagle *Aquila rapax*
(Map 131)
Resident and partial migrant; in drier Warm Temperate to Subtropical zones. It occurs in open areas, steppe, thin scrub, grassland savannah, open cultivated areas, semi-desert and stony desert. Usually it occurs at low altitudes, rarely above *c.* 1,000 m, but in the southern parts of its range may go up to *c.* 2,500 m. It feeds by piracy and scavenging as well as hunting. The nest is on a tree, shrub or other raised site. Migration and local movements occur in winter, the northern population partly moving into Africa south of the Sahara and into northern India.

――――――――――――――――――――

VULTURES *Neophron, Gypaetus, Torgos, Aegypius* and *Gyps* species
These are carrion-eating raptors, ranging from very large to medium-sized birds. They tend to be far-ranging with limited nest sites and the distribution is difficult to determine accurately. They are decreasing in Europe and other parts of their ranges. Where several species occur together they show a dominance hierarchy at a carcase, depending mainly on size and stoutness of bill, progressing from Black Vulture or Lappet-faced, to Griffon, White-backed and Egyptian Vultures. The Lammergeier specialises in feeding on broken bones left by others. In the complex of larger vultures the very large Black Vulture, which ranges across Eurasia to the east China coast, is replaced in Africa by the equally large Lappet-faced Vulture. The group includes two smaller (but still large) species, the Indian Black Vulture *Sarcogyps calvus* in the Indian region, and the White-headed Vulture *Trigonoceps occipitalis* in Africa south of the Sahara. Among the griffon vultures (map 137) the Eurasian Griffon extends to the western edge of the Tibetan massif. It is replaced in Africa by Rüppell's Griffon *Gyps rüppelli*, with the two apparently overlapping in north eastern Egypt and possibly in Oman. There are two Asiatic species, the smaller Indian Griffon *G. indicus* from Pakistan to Indochina, and a high altitude form, the Himalayan Griffon *G. himalayensis* around the Tibetan massif.

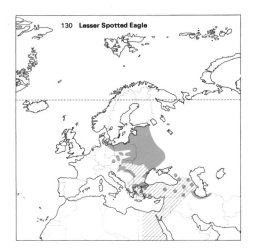

130 Lesser Spotted Eagle

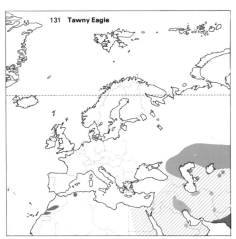

131 Tawny Eagle

The Eurasian species appears to have invaded the area later, overlapping with both species in places but as a breeding species separated from the last by altitudinal differences. There are also a pair of very similar white-backed species; the Indian White-backed Vulture, and the African White-backed Vulture *G. africanus* as a counterpart in Africa south of the Sahara. The Egyptian Vulture which extends through Africa in drier and open areas has a medium-sized counterpart, not closely related, in the Hooded Vulture *Necrosyrtes monachus* which occurs in the wetter forested regions of Africa. Asia east of Tibet appears to lack any smaller vultures. There are no true vultures in the Americas where they are replaced by the New World Cathartid vultures.

Spotted Eagle

Lesser Spotted Eagle

Tawny or
Steppe Eagle

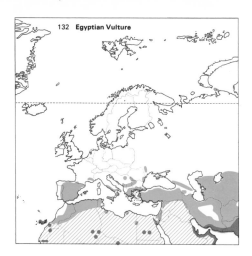

Egyptian Vulture   *Neophron percnopterus*
(Map 132)
Mainly migrant or dispersive; in Warm Temperate to Tropical zones, wintering in Africa north of the equator and in India. The range extends to the west side of Tibet and through India. The Indian lowland population is a distinct form, suggesting some period of isolation in the past. It occurs in the drier and more open areas, frequently associated with man, in cultivated areas, plains, steppe and desert, and at altitudes of 0–*c.* 3,250 m. It nests in a tree or a cavity in rocks or buildings and is generally sociable.

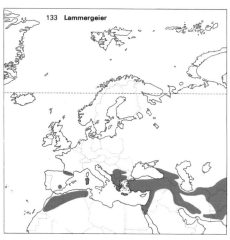

Lammergeier   *Gypaetus barbatus* (Map 133)
Resident; in Warm Temperate to Tropical zones, but in these extending up into Boreal and Arctic/Alpine altitude zones. Distribution is very discontinuous and associated with mountainous areas. The range extends through Tibet to western China, and northwards to the Altai and Sayan; discontinuous in east to south Africa and western Arabia. It occurs in areas of high mountains, foraging at lower altitudes, and in the Himalayas goes up to *c.* 5,000 m, exceptionally up to 8,000 m. Since the mid-nineteenth century it has disappeared from Switzerland, Bavaria, Hungary, Romania, Sardinia and Sicily, and is decreasing in Spain.

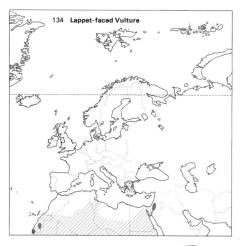

Lappet-faced Vulture   *Torgos tracheliotus*
(Map 134)
Resident and partial migrant; in drier Subtropical to Tropical zones. It occurs in thorn scrub, dry plains, semi-desert and desert. Normally it occurs in lowland but in some regions occurs at up to 5,000 m. The nest is in a solitary tree or on a rock outcrop.

Egyptian Vulture   Lammergeier   Lappet-faced Vulture

Black Vulture *Aegypius monachus*
(Map 135)
Resident and partial migrant; in drier Warm
Temperate zone, but extending up into Temperate, Boreal or Arctic/Alpine zones of altitude. It occurs east to Mongolia and northern
China. In winter it extends into northern
Africa, northern India and southern China. It
occurs in rugged and mountainous country,
foraging at lower altitudes, and also extends
into steppe and desert in the east, and into
colder Asiatic high areas. It occurs at up to
4,000 m and exceptionally to 7,500 m. The
nest is in an isolated tree, rarely on a rock
ledge. It is said to have bred earlier in Morocco, was recently lost in Sicily, Romania
and Bulgaria, and the range is now reduced in
Spain and Yugoslavia.

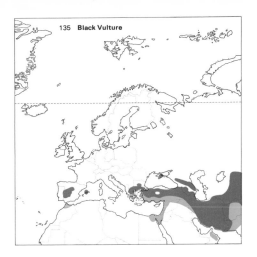

Indian White-backed Vulture *Gyps
bengalensis* (Map 136)
Resident; in Subtropical to Tropical zones.
The range extends through Pakistan, India,
Burma, Indochina and Malaya. It occurs in
cultivated country with trees, and open and
broken forest, particularly in trees bordering
rivers, and is sociable at all times. It nests in
colonies in trees. Usually it is found in lowland
or up to *c.* 1,000 m, but as a non-breeder can
occur up to *c.* 3,000 m.

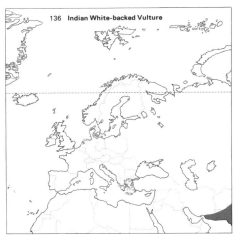

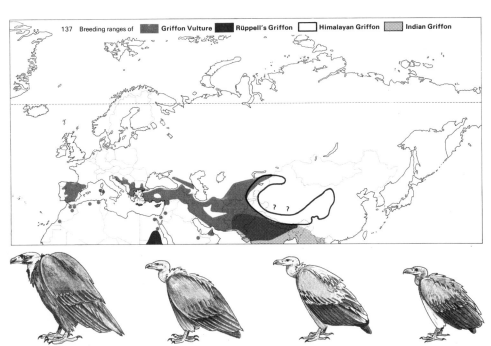

Black Vulture   Indian White-backed Vulture   Himalayan Griffon   Indian Griffon

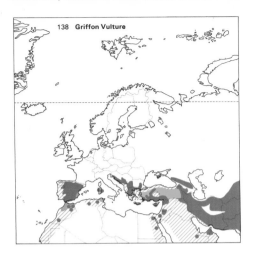

Griffon Vulture *Gyps fulvus* (Maps 137, 138)
Resident, and migrant or dispersive to a limited extent; in Warm Temperate to Subtropical zones, but ascending into Temperate and Boreal altitude zones in mountains. It often forages at lower altitudes. It prefers drier, open areas with trees few or absent, and occurs on upland plateaus and montane steppe; usually below *c.* 2,000 m, occasionally up to *c.* 3,000+ m. Nests are in colonies on rock ledges. Some migration occurs on the west and east edges of North Africa and into India. It has disappeared in the present century from southern France and Corsica.

Rüppell's Griffon *Gyps rüppelli*
(Maps 137, 139)
Resident and dispersive; in Subtropical to Tropical zones. Occurrence in north-east Africa and Arabian peninsula may be due to dispersive non-breeders. It occurs in drier open areas, on savannah, semi-desert, desert and mountainous areas, and nests on rock ledges on rugged or mountain sites.

HARRIERS *Circus* species
Medium-sized, slenderly built raptors, with long wings, tails and legs; hunting by gliding low over the ground and dropping suddenly on small creatures. The nest is on the ground. They nest in scattered pairs but may be sociable when not breeding. The larger Marsh Harrier extends across Eurasia but consists of distinct eastern and western forms, the two meeting around the Altai region of Siberia.

Forms on Indian Ocean islands, in the south Pacific and in Australasia have been regarded as subspecies of this species. There is a very closely related species, the African Marsh Harrier *Circus ranivorus*, in Africa south of the Sahara. The Hen Harrier is a Boreal to Temperate species of drier open grassland through Eurasia, and North and Central America where it is the only Harrier. The

Griffon Vulture

Rüppell's Griffon

Pallid Harrier is a Eurasian steppe species of more limited distribution. Montagu's Harrier is a smaller species of the Temperate zone occurring east to the Altai. From near Lake Baikal to Korea and Manchuria there is a replacement species, the Pied Harrier *C. melanoleucus*. It is suggested that the Black Harrier *C. maurus* of South Africa may form a superspecies with the previous two.

Marsh Harrier   *Circus aeruginosus* (Map 140)

Resident and migrant; in warmer Boreal to Temperate zones, wintering in Warm Temperate to Tropical zones. It occurs in larger swamps and marshes, reedswamps and grassy floodplains with pools or ditches and reedbeds; usually with still or slow-moving water; also on large deltas. Normally it occurs on lowland but may winter at up to *c.* 3,000 m in small swampy areas. The boundary of the migrant/resident zones is close to the 0° C winter isotherm; and birds winter in tropical Africa and India. Drainage and persecution have exterminated it in Ireland and much of England since *c.* 1900.

Hen Harrier   *Circus cyaneus* (Map 141)

Resident and migrant; in Boreal to Temperate zones, wintering in Temperate to Warm Temperate zones. It occurs in open grassy regions, on moorland, montane grassland, coastal plains and steppes, but less frequently on the last than the Pallid Harrier. In drier habitats it tends to use marshy ground for nesting. In North America, where the Marsh Harrier is absent, it occurs more frequently in marshland. It winters in open country, including cultivated areas, further north than the other species.

Pallid Harrier   *Circus macrourus* (Map 142)

Migrant, possibly resident in a few marginal south-west areas; breeding in drier Temperate steppe zones, wintering in Warm Temperate to Tropical zones. It has irrupted west into Europe at times and bred in Sweden and Germany (possibly resembling other steppe species in this respect). It occurs on open grassland, grassy marshland, steppes and extensive grain fields, at 0–4,500 m, occasionally extending briefly into open woodland. It winters in similar country in Africa south to the Cape and in the Indian region.

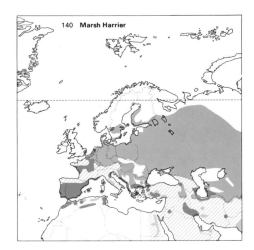

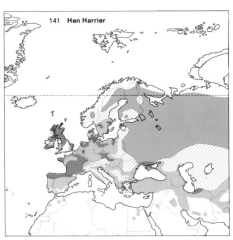

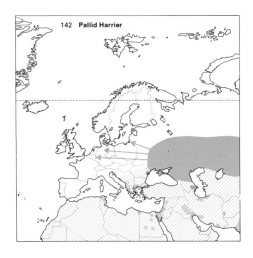

Marsh Harrier

Hen Harrier

Pallid Harrier

143 Montagu's Harrier

Montagu's Harrier *Circus pygargus*
(Map 143)
Migrant; breeding in Temperate to Warm
Temperate zones, wintering in Subtropical to
Tropical zones. A smaller species, occurring
mainly in moister lowlands – marshland,
swamps, moorland, rough grassland and
young conifer plantations, at 0–2,750 m. In
winter it normally occurs on drier open grassland, usually away from marshy areas. The
north-western limits of the range fluctuate
with minor climatic variations.

FALCONS *Falconidae*

These are twelve medium-sized to small raptors. The larger species feed mainly on birds,
usually taken in the air, while the smaller
species include weaker hunters taking small
rodents, reptiles and insects. The species fall
roughly into three types of which at least one
of each may occur in any area. There are
a group of larger, actively hunting forms,
mainly replacing each other (map 144), a
group of two smaller active hunters partly
replacing but with more extensive overlap,
and three less vigorous hunters also partly
replacing and overlapping. Between the first
two groups are two species which specialise on
migrant birds.

The large Arctic/Alpine Gyrfalcon is a circumpolar, Holarctic species with small outlier
populations in the high mountain ranges of
mid-Asia north of Tibet, within the general
range of the Saker Falcon. The Saker Falcon
occurs through more southerly, drier Temperate and montane areas, replaced by the Lanner Falcon in the Mediterranean and Africa
and by the Lagger Falcon *Falco jugger* in
India. The Prairie Falcon *F. mexicanus* is a
representative in western North America.
Much of the remaining area is occupied by the
Peregrine Falcon, a cosmopolitan species that
overlaps in range with these other species.
The very similar Barbary Falcon, regarded by
some as only a race of the Peregrine Falcon,
occurs through drier zones from North Africa
to the Himalayan region, mainly replacing the

Peregrine Falcon in these areas. The specialist
migrant predators are smaller, slimmer birds
breeding late to utilise the autumn migration
passage. They are Eleonora's Falcon in the
Mediterranean and the Sooty Falcon in North
Africa and the Middle East. The two smaller
active hunters overlap extensively but are
separated by ecological preferences, the
more northern Merlin in bare, open habitats,
and the more southerly Hobby in open areas
with scattered trees. The Red-headed Merlin
F. chicquera is a tree-nesting replacement
species in India and also in Africa south of the
Sahara where it overlaps with the African
Hobby *F. cuvieri*. The Oriental Hobby *F. ser-
verus* fills the gap in the Indochina and Malaya
region. The Merlin, but neither Hobby nor
hobby-type replacement species, occurs in
North America. Of the three weaker hunters
the Kestrel has an extensive Boreal to Tropical
distribution over most of Eurasia and Africa,
but is absent from lowland India, Malaysia
and Indochina. There is a replacement species,
the American Kestrel *F. sparverius* in the
Americas and other species in the Indian Ocean
Islands and in Australasia, while in Africa
south of the Sahara a further four kestrel-like
species occur, mainly replacing each other.
The last two smaller species of Eurasia, the
Lesser Kestrel and the Red-footed Falcon,
both have a distribution across Eurasia with
a break at about the level of Lake Baikal. In
the Lesser Kestrel this is of little significance,
but the Red-footed Falcon has a distinct race
with a white underwing in the isolate Chinese

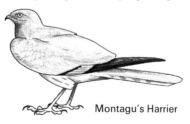

Montagu's Harrier

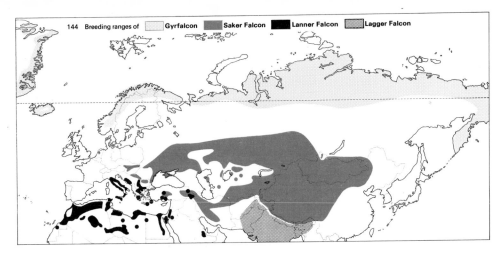

144 Breeding ranges of   Gyrfalcon   Saker Falcon   Lanner Falcon   Lagger Falcon

population. Of the two the Lesser Kestrel is a bird of drier open country, nesting mainly in rock cavities, while the Red-footed Falcon prefers country with some trees, or partly forested, and uses old nests of Rooks and other corvids.

Gyrfalcon *Falco rusticolus* (Maps 144, 145)
Mainly resident, sometimes partial migrant; in Arctic/Alpine zone. It occurs on open areas of tundra, rocky coastlines, barren uplands, and mountains, up to 1,000 m; also extending at times into partially wooded areas. The usual southern limit of breeding is near the 15°C July isotherm on lowland. It nests on a rock outcrop, cliff or bank, rarely in forest tundra trees. In the extreme Arctic it occurs mainly on sea coasts. Southward extension of range and migration may occur when food is scarce.

Saker Falcon *Falco cherrug* (Maps 144, 146)
Migrant and resident; in drier Temperate to Warm Temperate zones, with some wintering in the Subtropical zone. It occurs in open areas, areas with scattered trees, thin riverine forest, open forest on plains, grass and tree steppe and montane plateaus up to *c.* 3,500 m, but rarely in rugged mountain areas. It takes prey from the ground more frequently than the Peregrine Falcon. The nest is on a rock ledge or in a tree. It is not a typical migrant and some birds may winter in breeding areas.

145 Gyrfalcon

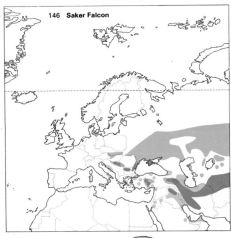

146 Saker Falcon

Gyrfalcon   Saker Falcon   Lagger Falcon

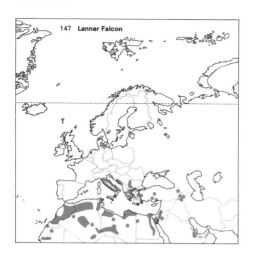

Lanner Falcon *Falco biarmicus*
(Maps 144, 147)
Resident; in Warm Temperate to Tropical zones. Mainly Ethiopian, extending into Arabia and the Mediterranean. It occurs, usually in drier regions, in steppe, savannah, semi-desert, rocky desert, and on rugged mountain and coastal areas, from 0–2,500 m, usually in drier habitats than the Peregrine Falcon. The nest is on a rock ledge, or (rarely) in a tree.

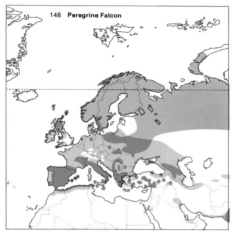

Peregrine Falcon *Falco peregrinus*
(Map 148)
Resident and migrant; in Arctic/Alpine to Tropical zones. It occurs in a wide range of habitats, usually open, from tundra and moorland to steppe and scrub; less frequently in forested areas; and is absent from humid forest and hot desert. It is found from 0–*c*. 3,500 m altitude. The nest is usually on a rock ledge, very rarely in a tree cavity or on the ground. In winter extreme northern birds migrate as far as southern Africa. Although widespread the species has a very sporadic distribution and has been greatly reduced by direct and indirect interference by man in many regions.

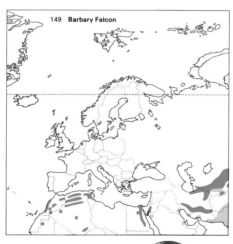

Barbary Falcon *Falco pelegrinoides*
(Map 149)
Resident, or partial migrant in the east of the range; in drier Warm Temperate to Subtropical zones. It occurs in arid semi-desert, desert, dry steppes and rugged montane areas, and nests on a rock ledge.

Sooty Falcon *Falco concolor* (Map 150)
Migrant; breeding in dry Subtropical zone, wintering in Tropical to southern Subtropical zones. It occurs in stony desert, usually with rock outcrops, and on rocky islands around Arabia. The nest is in a cavity or sheltered site, low or at ground level. It winters in savannah areas, often sociably, in East Africa to Madagascar.

Lanner Falcon   Peregrine Falcon   Barbary Falcon

Eleonora's Falcon   *Falco eleonorae*
(Map 151)
Migrant; breeding in the Warm Temperate
zone and wintering in the southern Subtropical zone. It occurs mainly on the rocky sea
coasts of Mediterranean and Atlantic islands;
hunting over various types of local country
from marsh to mountain, nesting in colonies
on ledges and in cavities in cliffs. It nests in
late summer, and migrates via the Red Sea
area to East Africa and Madagascar.

Hobby   *Falco subbuteo* (Map 152)
Migrant; breeding in Boreal to Warm Temperate zones, wintering in Subtropical zone. It
occurs in open areas with some scattered trees,
groups of trees or patches of woodland on
moorland and steppe with trees, parkland,
forest edge, cultivation with trees, broken
forest in montane areas and in the north of the
range in open forest near the tree line. The
nest is in a tree, usually in the old nest of
another bird. It winters mainly in savannah,
scrub and cultivated areas in Africa south of
the Equator, and in northern India and southern China.

Red-headed Merlin   *Falco chicquera*
(Map 153)
Resident; in Subtropical to Tropical zones, in
the Indian region and afrotropical Africa. It
occurs in scattered pairs in open country with
trees, often associated with Borassus palms, in
arid *Acacia* scrub, and into barer areas and
desert if isolated trees occur.

150 Sooty Falcon

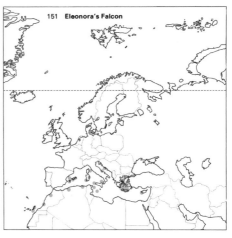

151 Eleonora's Falcon

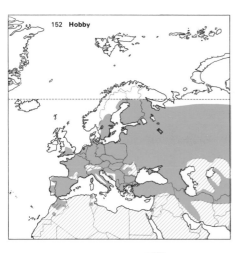

152 Hobby

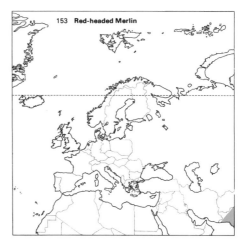

153 Red-headed Merlin

Sooty Falcon   Eleonora's Falcon   Hobby   Red-headed Merlin

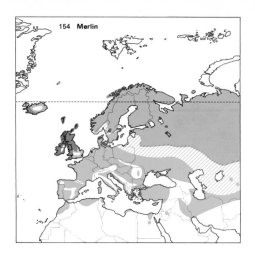

Merlin *Falco columbarius* (Map 154)
Mainly migrant, resident in a few marginal and western areas; breeding in Arctic/Alpine to Boreal zones, wintering in Temperate to Warm Temperate zones. It occurs on open areas, moorland, open montane areas, heathland, grassy dunes, shrub tundra, and open birch and conifer forest. Nests occur usually on the ground, but sometimes in an old tree nest of other birds. It winters on open lowlands, particularly coastal marshland, also grass steppes and semi-desert.

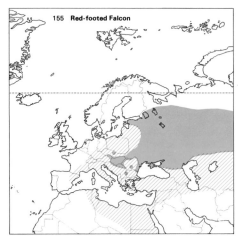

Red-footed Falcon *Falco vespertinus* (Map 155)
Migrant; breeding in warmer Boreal to Temperate zones and wintering in southern Warm Temperate to Subtropical zones. It occurs in drier open areas with scattered trees, groups of trees or patches of woodland, on forest steppes, parkland, cultivation with trees, riverine forest and forest edge. Usually it is highly sociable. Like the Pallid Harrier it only occurs in eastern Europe but has nested irruptively as far west as Sweden, Silesia and Algeria. It nests usually in trees, in old nests of other birds such as Rooks. It winters on savannah and dry grassland of Africa south of the Equator; the Chinese race also migrating to this region.

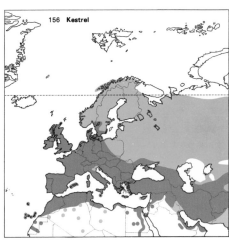

Kestrel *Falco tinnunculus* (Map 156)
Resident and migrant; in Boreal to Tropical zones. It occurs mainly in open country, grassy or cultivated, but has a wide tolerance of habitat provided that there are open spaces for hunting. It is found at altitudes of 0–5,000 m. It will use suburbs and cities, but is absent from large expanses of sand desert, thick tropical forest and cold steppes. The nest is in a cavity in rocks, buildings or trees; exceptionally on the ground. Northern birds winter south to central Africa and the Indian region.

Merlin

Red-footed Falcon

Kestrel

Lesser Kestrel *Falco naumanni* (Map 157)
Mainly migrant, but some birds winter in
Morocco; breeding in Warm Temperate to
Temperate steppe zones, wintering in Tropical
to southern Subtropical zones. It occurs in
drier open country – steppe, semi-desert, desert, open grassland, cultivation and rocky hillsides, usually at low altitudes, sometimes up to
c. 2,750 m. Usually it is highly sociable, and
nests colonially in cliffs, outcrops or old buildings, exceptionally in tree holes. It winters in
savannah and grass plains of East and South
Africa and in India.

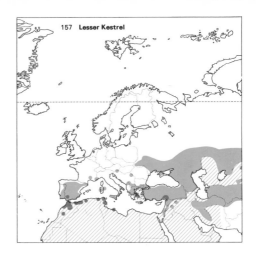

GROUSE   *Tetraonidae*

These are medium to large ground-nesting
birds, mostly of forest and of colder habitats
than the typical gamebirds. They have representatives through various zones, from the
Ptarmigan of open, alpine-arctic habitat, to
the moor to scrub Willow Grouse, the forest
edge Black Grouse, conifer forest Capercaillie
and mixed to broadleaf forest Hazelhen. The
nest is in a sheltered scrape on the ground.

TYPICAL GROUSE *Lagopus* species
There are three forms, of bare open country
and broadleaf scrub, occupying the coldest
zones. The distribution of Ptarmigan and
Willow Grouse overlap, but there is altitudinal separation with the former at higher
altitudes. With post-glacial retreat the Ptarmigan has left relict populations in the Alps
and Pyrenees, but the Willow Grouse does not
have these outlier populations. However, the
Red Grouse, a form occurring in the British
Isles and usually regarded as conspecific with
the Willow Grouse, has been isolated long
enough to have evolved differences.

Ptarmigan *Lagopus mutus* (Map 158)
Resident; in the Arctic, Alpine and Boreal
zones. It survives by burrowing under snow
cover in winter, but may descend to lower
levels or into scrub. It occurs on bare and

rocky moss and lichen tundra, and in similar habitats further south on mountains,
above the tree line; in Scotland usually above
c. 700 m, in the Alpine and Pyrenean regions
at above 2,165 m. It was introduced into
the Faeroes. The populations of Scandinavia,
Britain and montane Europe ("mutus" group
of subspecies) can be separated from other
populations ("rupestris" group) by greyer or
blacker plumages, which may give some indication of the relationship of present subspecies prior to post-glacial separations.

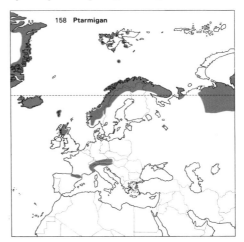

Lesser Kestrel

Ptarmigan

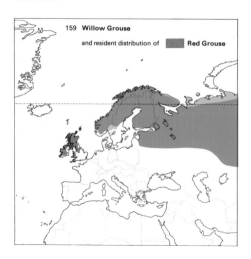

Willow Grouse   *Lagopus lagopus* (Map 159)
Resident, but some irruptive movements in north of range; in Arctic and Boreal zones, and similar zones of mountains. It occurs in swampy scrub tundra, on marshy heathland and on bogs in conifer forest; in birch and willow forest of Boreal zone, and in riverine scrub of steppe. The Red Grouse, *L. l. scoticus* (map 159), is usually regarded as a race of the Willow Grouse, but separation, presumably by the post-glacial opening-up of the North Sea or possibly longer ago if that area was unsuitable habitat, has produced a form that has lost the white plumage and is more adapted to open moorland and bog, especially in areas dominated by heather (*Calluna*).

CAPERCAILLIES *Tetrao* species
Two large forest species, the typical western Capercaillie and the eastern Black-billed Capercallie *T. parvirostris*. There is an overlap of general range in the mid-Siberian region (map 160). They are similar in general appearance but the eastern form occurs usually in broadleaf, mixed or larch forest, and less often in pure evergreen conifer forest. The smaller Black Grouse is a replacement species in open forest and forest edge over a similar but slightly more extensive range without a separate eastern form. There is, however, a distinct isolate species, the Caucasian Black Grouse, in the Caucasian region where a forest area persisted during the Pleistocene glaciations and provided a refuge.

Capercaillie   *Tetrao urogallus* (Map 160)
Resident; in Boreal and Temperate zones. It occurs in conifer and mixed forests; usually in areas with undershrubs, close to small clearings or bogs. The species is closely associated with conifers, although in north-west Spain the winter distribution is linked with holly trees. Distribution is mainly between July isotherms of 13–21°C, with a continuous zone through the conifer forest regions and some isolated populations in montane areas further south. Forest clearing and/or shooting have probably reduced its range. It was lost in Ireland and Scotland in the eighteenth century but reintroduced in the latter in the early nineteenth century.

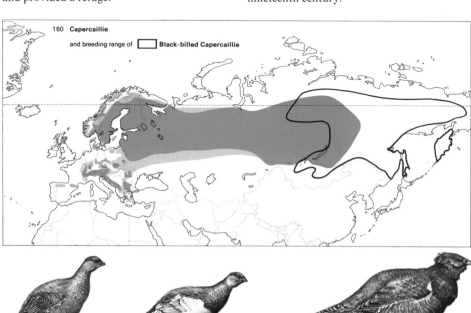

Red Grouse   Willow Grouse   Capercaillie

Black Grouse *Tetrao tetrix* (Map 161)

Resident, in Boreal and Temperate zones. It occurs along forest edge, principally in conifer and birch forest, in open forest and areas of rock and broken woodland scrub, and extending to swampy heathland, moorland and bogs, but usually with some trees. In the north of its range it occurs at low altitudes but in the south in mountains at higher altitudes, up to *c.* 2,000 m. Distribution mainly between 11°C and 21–24°C July isotherms.

Caucasian Black Grouse *Tetrao mlokosiewiczi* (Map 162)

Resident; with some altitudinal movements in hard winters. It occurs in the Caucasus and extreme north-eastern Turkey, with a small population in the Kelibar Mountains of northern Iran; in the upper broadleaf forest and scrub and alpine meadow zones.

HAZELHENS *Tetrastes* species

Hazelhen *Tetrastes bonasia* (Map 163)

Resident; in Boreal and Temperate zones, in a continuous belt across to Sakhalin and the Sea of Okhotsk. A bird of thick forest with undergrowth; occurring in mountain conifer forest, spruce forest with bilberry layer, mixed forest with undershrubs, beech forest and riverine alder forest; but in taiga only where mixed forest occurs around water or swamps. Distribution is mainly between 13°C and 21–22°C July isotherms. Distribution has probably contracted with forest clearing.

GAMEBIRDS *Phasianidae*

Ground-nesting birds of open country, and except for the introduced pheasant grade from large birds in cold zones to small ones in hot zones. In general the large snowcocks occur on Alpine and Subalpine mountain zones; of the medium-sized partridges and francolins the Common Partridge is in the Temperate zone, the *Alectoris* partridges in the Warm Temperate zones, the francolins and guineafowl in the Warm Temperate to dry Subtropical zones, and the small sand partridges in the dry Subtropical zone. The Common Quail is in the Warm Temperate to dry Subtropical zones but as a migrant occupies the Temperate zone in its warm season.

161 Black Grouse

162 Caucasian Black Grouse

163 Hazelhen

Black-billed Capercaillie

Black Grouse

Caucasian Black Grouse

Hazelhen

164 Caucasian Snowcock

165 Caspian Snowcock

SNOWCOCKS *Tetraogallus* species

Five forms, very similar in appearance, on high mountain ranges of Asia. Probably derived from a single parental form which was widespread during the colder glacial periods but became fragmented in the warmer interglacials, leaving isolates at higher, cooler altitudes. The Altai Snowcock *T. altaicus* occurs in the Russian Altai and north-western Mongolia. The Tibetan Snowcock *T. tibetanus* occurs over the Tibetan plateau and Himalayas east of Nepal, replaced in the western Himalayas, Pamirs, and northern edge of the Tibetan plateau by the Himalayan Snowcock *T. himalayensis*. The Caucasian and Caspian Snowcocks are only separated by the narrow barrier of the Kura valley (maps 164, 165).

Caucasian Snowcock   *Tetraogallus caucasicus* (Map 164)
Resident; through the Alpine and Subalpine zones of the Caucasus range at 1,700–4,300 m, descending lower in winter. It is found on rocky slopes and screes, the upper parts of rock outcrops and cliffs and on alpine meadows with sparse growth, up to the snowline.

Caspian Snowcock   *Tetraogallus caspius* (Map 165)
Resident; in similar habitats and at similar altitudes to previous species. Usually on open rocky slopes, but it also uses taller herbage and rhododendron scrub. Has seasonal movements between snows and upper tree limit.

QUAILS *Coturnix* species

A superspecies group of five widespread species, the males differing in the head pattern and colour, the amount of black on breast and underside, and in the calls. One, the Stubble Quail *C. pectoralis*, is in Australia; another, the Harlequin Quail *C. delegorguei*, over the drier parts of Africa south of the Sahara; and a third, the Rain Quail *C. coromandelicus*, in the Indian subregion. The Common Quail extends over most of Eurasia but is replaced in the east by the Japanese Quail *C. japonica* (map 166). Its breeding range overlaps that of the Rain Quail in northern India, and the African race has a similar range to the Harlequin Quail, indicating an extension of range, probably from the North

African/Mediterranean region after speciation. Most of the northern population of the Common Quail, and the Japanese Quail, are migratory, with winter ranges overlapping in part those of the resident Rain and Harlequin Quails and the African race of the Common Quail.

Common Quail   *Coturnix coturnix* (Map 166)
Resident and migrant; a bird mainly of Warm Temperate and dry Subtropical zones, but through migration also able to occupy the Temperate zone during summer. The northern limit of distribution approaches the July 15°C isotherm but is irregular, probably through lack of suitable habitat, and in periods

Caucasian Snowcock   Caspian Snowcock

Common Quail   Japanese Quail

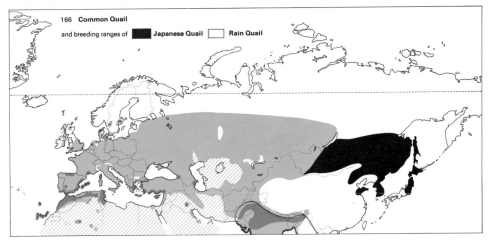

166 **Common Quail** and breeding ranges of **Japanese Quail** □ **Rain Quail**

African race of **Common Quail** breeds in most of Africa south of the Sahara.

of warmer weather it may temporarily extend north of the normal breeding and wintering limits. It occupies grassland and areas of low herbage, preferring well-drained soils in the north of its range; and occurs from desert edge and steppes to warmer alpine meadows (to 3,000 m in the High Atlas). It quickly adapts to extensive cultivation, especially cereal crops, and this has probably aided its European distribution. Winters normally in a zone just south of the Sahara and in India.

TYPICAL PARTRIDGES *Perdix* species

Three similar species with differing head markings. The western Common Partridge and eastern Daurian Partridge *P. dauricae* (previously called *P. barbata*) overlap in distribution (map 167), and mixed flocks, and a few hybrids, are recorded. The Tibetan Partridge *P. hodgsoniae* is isolated on the Tibetan plateau and upper Himalayas.

Common Partridge   *Perdix perdix* (Map 167)
Resident; mainly in the Temperate zone, but extending into both Boreal and Warm Temperate zones, possibly aided to some extent by the extension of cultivation and by encouragement as a gamebird. The Pyrenean and Cantabrian mountain populations are isolated and show slight differences from the typical form. It is a species of moister grasslands, including grass moors, heathlands, borders of

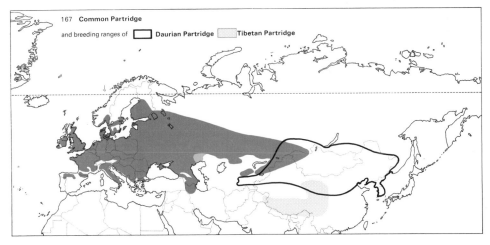

167 **Common Partridge** and breeding ranges of □ **Daurian Partridge** ▨ **Tibetan Partridge**

Rain Quail

Common Partridge

Daurian Partridge

Tibetan Partridge

bog and marshland, steppes, alpine and low-land meadows and open scrub; and also on cultivated areas where some cover is present. Where ranges overlap *Alectoris* partridges replace it in drier places.

RED-LEGGED PARTRIDGE
COMPLEX *Alectoris* species (Map 168)
These are birds of rocky hillsides in warmer drier areas, occupying a zone from the Mediterranean to China. There is a group of seven similar species, differing mainly in the patterns of head, neck and upper breast. They probably arose as isolated populations which differentiated during the Pleistocene glaciations. The sequence consists of Barbary Partridge in North Africa and Sardinia; the Red-legged Partridge in the Iberian Peninsula and southern France, and introduced successfully to southern England; the Rock Partridge in Greece, the Alps, Italy and Sicily; Philby's Partridge *Alectoris philbyi* in a small mountain zone on the east side of the Red Sea, and the Arabian Partridge *A. melanocephala* in southern Arabia. The Chukar Partridge probably evolved in the Himalayan regions, but appears the most adaptable and has spread westwards to Thrace, and eastwards to eastern China and Manchuria, while Przewalski's Rock Partridge *A. magna* occurs in north-east Tibet and nearby north-west China.

The four European species occupy very similar habitats around the Mediterranean. As they have extended their ranges in the past, the Rock and Red-legged Partridges now meet in the south-west Alps, and the former also meets the Chukar Partridge in Thrace. In addition to the head patterns there are marked differences in voice between the Rock Partridge and the other two, helping to maintain the separation, and where they meet there is also some ecological segregation with the Rock Partridge preferring higher altitudes. The Red-legged and Chukar Partridges, which do not normally meet, appear not to have evolved any barrier to hybridisation, and where the latter has been introduced recently into the range of the former in Spain, France and England there has been considerable hybridisation. Philby's Partridge and the Arabian Partridge meet in the Azir Mountains in the south of the former's range, but are usually altitudinally separated, the former normally at over 1,500 m. There appears to be a similar altitudinal separation of the Chukar Partridge and Przewalski's Rock Partridge in the Far East, with the latter at altitudes of over 2,500 m. All species are resident. Nest is a shallow scrape on the ground, usually sheltered by plant tuft or rock.

Rock Partridge *Alectoris graeca* (Map 168)
In Mediterranean zone on mountains, and in Alpine to Subalpine areas. Recorded at 1,000–2,300 m in Greece, 500–2,500 m in Alps. It may descend to lower altitudes in winter. Typically it is found on dry bare rocky hillsides with scattered trees and sparse shrubby vegetation. It may occur in thicker scrub and open woodland and feed in cultivation and olive groves bordering typical habitat, and

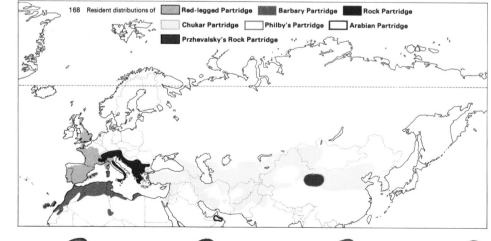

168 Resident distributions of ▦ Red-legged Partridge ▦ Barbary Partridge ■ Rock Partridge
▦ Chukar Partridge □ Philby's Partridge □ Arabian Partridge
▦ Przhevalsky's Rock Partridge

Rock Partridge   Barbary Partridge   Red-legged Partridge   Chukar Partridge

may travel some distance (up to 10 km) for water.

Chukar Partridge *Alectoris chukar*
(Map 168)

Typically in Mediterranean, steppe and desert zones. Although in Europe it is usually found at lower levels than the Rock Partridge, in the Himalayas this species occurs up to 5,000 m. Like the Rock Partridge it typically requires warm dry slopes with rocks, sparse low scrub and thin grasses, but may be found on lowland, level desert and semi-desert, through grass steppes, to bare but cool mountain slopes. It appears tolerant of a range of temperatures and has been extensively introduced into western Europe and North America as a gamebird.

Red-legged Partridge *Alectoris rufa*
(Map 168)

In Mediterranean and Temperate zones. It usually occurs on mountains at lower altitudes than the other species, and also in lowland. In the Iberian Peninsula and southern France it occurs on dry rocky hillside habitats similar to those of the other *Alectoris* partridges. Elsewhere it occurs on dry and well-drained lowland soils on heathland, grassland, vineyards and cultivated fields. In its natural range its northern breeding limit is about the 20°C July isotherm and the limit appears to have shifted during historical times with climatic fluctuations, but it was introduced to Britain *c.* 200 years ago and breeds north to *c.* 15°C July isotherm. It was also introduced to the Azores,

Madeira, and the Canary Islands. The Chukar Partridge has been introduced recently into most of its range, from Spain to Britain, and has hybridised extensively.

Barbary Partridge *Alectoris barbara*
(Map 168)

In Mediterranean, steppe and desert zones. Like the Chukar Partridge it shows a wide range from desert and grass steppe of lowland, to alpine grassland at 3,500 m in the Atlas Mountains. It is more tolerant of a hot climate, nesting within a range with a mean minimum July isotherm of *c.* 24°C, usually on dry, rocky hillsides with sparse scrub and grasses, but also in desert areas in thin scrub and grasses bordering streams or in wadis, within reach of water. It occurs in Sardinia where it has been suggested that it may have been introduced. It has been introduced to some of the Canary Islands and to Porto Santo north-east of Madeira.

––––––––––––––––––––––––––––––––

FRANCOLINS *Francolinus* species

The Double-spurred Francolin is one of a group of African francolins, and the main population is in West Africa, west and south of the Sahara. The Moroccan population is a small isolate presumably cut off in earlier times by the spread of the desert. The spotted-plumaged francolins form a superspecies of three species; males differing in head and breast colour (map 169). The Black Francolin now extends from the Aegean to northern India. In southern India it is replaced by the Painted Francolin *F. pictus* with some hy-

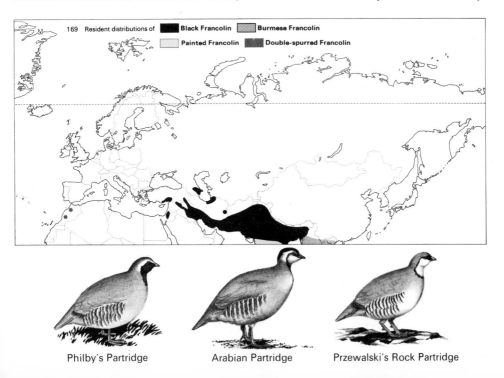

169 Resident distributions of ■ **Black Francolin** ▨ **Burmese Francolin**
▨ **Painted Francolin** ▨ **Double-spurred Francolin**

Philby's Partridge   Arabian Partridge   Przewalski's Rock Partridge

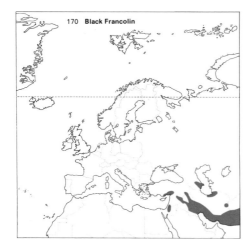

170   Black Francolin

171   Double-spurred Francolin

bridisation where they meet. In Burma and Indochina the Burmese Francolin *F. pinta-deanus* is the replacement species.

Black Francolin   *Francolinus francolinus*
(Maps 169, 170)
Resident; in Warm Temperate to Subtropical zones. Like Common Partridge it prefers moister areas with good growth of vegetation, occupying such habitats within more arid areas. Distribution is mainly in areas above the 26°C July isotherm. It occurs in shrubby thickets bordering watercourses and lakes, extensive areas of scrub or shrubby herbage, lush grasses, marshy areas with tall herbage and grasses, and also extends into forest edge and forest clearings. The range has apparently contracted. In the middle of the nineteenth century it was exterminated in south-eastern Spain and Sicily, and may have occurred in Italy and on some Aegean Islands. As with other gamebirds it is not possible to be certain that early occurrences on islands and elsewhere were not due to human introduction.

Double-spurred Francolin   *Francolinus bicalcaratus* (Maps 169, 171)
Resident; in dry Subtropical zone. It occurs in grassland and open forest areas around the western Sahara, but with a very fragmented northern distribution. The habitat is low cover of thick scrub along streams and gullies, and in open forest; also in more open places in forest clearing, grassland and cultivation.

PHEASANTS *Phasianus* species
These are present in Europe only as introduced species. The Common Pheasant occurs naturally from the Caucasus to China (map 172) but can be divided into a western, brown-rumped form and an eastern blue-grey-rumped form, with a small intermediate population north of Tibet. The Japanese Green Pheasant probably evolved as an isolate of the blue-grey-rumped population. There is no representative in the Indian subcontinent but several other pheasant species occur through the Himalayas.

Common Pheasant   *Phasianus colchicus*
(Map 172)
Resident; distributed through eastern Temperate to Warm Temperate zones, but discontinuous in mainly dry areas due to habitat requirements. The natural habitat is grassland or similar herbage near a source of water, with some cover such as scattered trees or shrubs; also in forest edge and on borders of reedy marshland. Where introduced and deliberately maintained by man in Europe it occurs in a variety of habitats from Boreal to Warm Temperate zones, often in areas of cultivation

Burmese Francolin

Painted Francolin

Black Francolin

Double-spurred Francolin

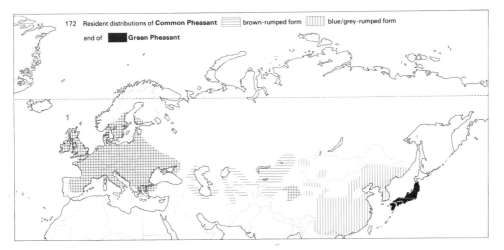

172 Resident distributions of **Common Pheasant** ▭ brown-rumped form ▥ blue/grey-rumped form
and of ■ **Green Pheasant**

with little cover. The natural population can be divided into a western form with brown-rumped males, and an eastern form with blue-grey-rumped males, with a small intermediate population where they meet. The western form subdivides into a group around the Caspian with brown wing-coverts and the remainder with whiter wing-coverts. The introduced European population is an interbreeding mixture of forms.

Green Pheasant   *Phasianus versicolor*
(Map 172)
Resident, occurring naturally in mid- and southern Japan in similar habitats to the Common Pheasant. This species is more tolerant of wetter habitats than the latter and for that reason, although introduced in sporadic scattered populations in Europe, it is more frequent in the moister north-western parts.

SAND PARTRIDGES *Ammoperdix*
species
Two species of small gamebirds, differing mainly in the males' head and breast colours; replacing each other on opposite sides of the Persian Gulf/Mesopotamia gap (map 173). Birds of stony, arid desert edge areas, restricted by a need for a nearby water source.

Sand Partridge   *Ammoperdix heyi* (Map 173)
Resident; in dry Subtropical zone. Distribution and habitat are like those of the next species. Possibly more often found on true desert edge, it also occurs on rocky areas, wadis and hill slopes.

See-see Partridge   *Ammoperdix griseogularis*
(Map 173)
Resident; in dry Subtropical zone. Distribution is controlled overall by presence of arid areas, but mostly within average July temperatures of $+80°$F. The habitat is open, arid areas with very sparse low herbage and rocky or stony but not violently rugged terrain,

where it is found on bare stony areas, stony or gullied and eroded hill slopes, rocky stream banks and ravines, gravels and bare areas with small rocky outcrops. There may be some change of altitude in hills at different seasons.

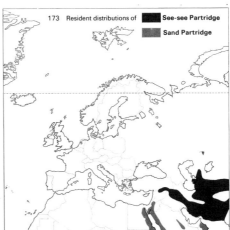

173 Resident distributions of ■ See-see Partridge
▨ Sand Partridge

Common Pheasant   Green Pheasant   Sand Partridge   See-see Partridge

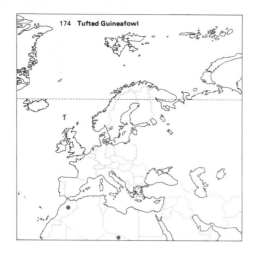

174　Tufted Guineafowl

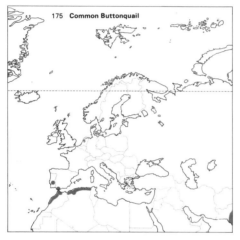

175　Common Buttonquail

GUINEAFOWL *Numida* species
A group of species, sometimes regarded as a single species with well-marked subspecies, in the dry scrub and tree-savannah zones of Africa south of the Sahara.

Tufted Guineafowl *Numida meleagris* (Map 174)
Resident; in dry Subtropical zone. It occurs in savannah and forest edge in an area from Senegal eastwards to Sudan on the southern side of the Sahara, extending north into Ennedi and Tibesti massifs of central Sahara; also in south-west Arabia. A population isolated in north-west Africa sufficiently long to form a distinct subspecies has shrunk in distribution to a limited area of the Moroccan hills. The Moroccan population inhabits dry wooded ravines on hillsides, roosting in trees. The central Saharan birds are in mountain wadis with scrub. It has been introduced into southern France.

BUTTONQUAILS　*Turnicidae*

One species in the present area. Small, quail-like birds living and nesting on the ground in herbage. The main adaptive radiation has occurred in Australasia. Outside the area of the present maps the Common Buttonquail overlaps in distribution with similar species which prefer damper habitats; one in southern Africa and two in Asia.

Common Buttonquail *Turnix sylvatica* (Map 175)
Normally resident; in dry Warm Temperate to Tropical zones. Distribution is within the 21–24°C isotherms of summer temperature; extending through most of Africa south of the Sahara, and through the Indian region and South-east Asia to the Philippines and Indonesia. Superficially its requirements appear similar to those of the quail, and its more limited distribution may be due in part to non-migratory habits. It occurs on dry grassland, steppe, crops and herbage on well-drained soils, also in low dry scrub and dwarf palmetto.

CRANES　*Gruidae*

Large, ground-nesting birds of open spaces. Three species, two of them with wide ranges, the medium-sized Common Crane in the Boreal to Warm Temperate zones, and the smaller Demoiselle Crane overlapping the southern edge of this range and extending further into the Warm Temperate zone. Their limited and broken distribution at the European end of the ranges may be a result of human activities. There is archaeological evidence of a larger species, of similar size to the Sarus Crane *Grus antigone*, existing in Germany, northern France and Britain until the Iron Age, and possibly the ecological

Tufted Guineafowl

Common Buttonquail

counterpart of the larger forms elsewhere. The Siberian Crane is a medium-sized but long-billed species with a discontinuous relict distribution in Siberia and evidence of loss of an earlier wider distribution which is not obviously attributable to human interference.

Common Crane   *Grus grus* (Map 176)
Mainly migrant, resident in limited areas of the Middle East. The breeding range extends from Boreal, through Temperate to Warm Temperate zones. The breeding distribution is between July isotherms of 11–13°C and 28–30°C. For breeding it requires relatively large undisturbed areas. It occurs in large wet meadows, bogs and swamps associated with birch scrub or various types of conifer and mixed forest, also on large marshes and bogs, swampy heathland and wet grassland extending into steppes. It winters in similar areas to south and on more open grassland and cultivation, the winter range extending into Warm Temperate to Subtropical zones of Mediterranean basin, north and east Africa around and south of the Sahara, and southern Asia. Probably it once occurred right across Europe, but was lost as a breeding bird in Britain in the sixteenth century, the early twentieth century in Hungary, and probably more recently in Spain?

Siberian Crane   *Grus leucogeranus* (Map 177)
Migrant; breeding in Boreal zone in west to Arctic tundra zone in east, wintering in Warm Temperate to Subtropical zones. The former range was much more extensive, but is now limited to relict populations in a few larger river basins across Siberia. It occurs in large areas of swamps, on lake or river edges with extensive low herbage. It appears to overlap in distribution with Common Crane but the much longer bill may indicate utilisation of different food resources. In winter it moves to similar habitats further south.

Demoiselle Crane   *Anthropoides virgo* (Map 178)
Migrant; breeding in Boreal, dry Warm Temperate (steppe) and arid Subtropical (desert) zones, wintering in Subtropical to Tropical zones. The distribution is mainly between July isotherms of 22°–23° and 32°C. Usually it occurs in drier and more open habitats than Common Crane, breeding along moister river valleys or grassy plains, and grass and shrub

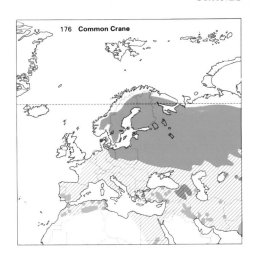

176 Common Crane

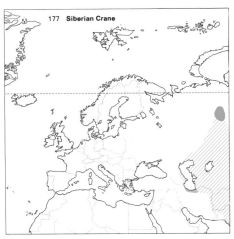

177 Siberian Crane

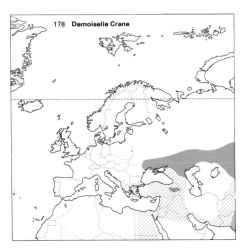

178 Demoiselle Crane

Common Crane

Siberian Crane

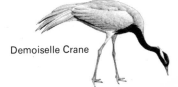

Demoiselle Crane

steppes, and in marshy lowlands. In North Africa it breeds on mountain plateaus where at other times it may feed on wet lowland areas nearby. It mainly winters in eastern Africa and in the Indian region.

RAILS *Rallidae*

Mainly skulking species of waterside and marsh, in Boreal to Subtropical zones; feeding on small creatures and plants, nesting among ground or water vegetation. Two medium-sized species, the coots, are adapted to an aquatic, freshwater habitat; the large Purple Gallinule to reedbeds; and the medium-sized Moorhen to anywhere where water and waterside cover are present. Another medium-sized rail, the Corncrake, is adapted to drier meadows; the three smaller species are all birds of thick waterside vegetation.

COOTS *Fulica* species

Two species occupying similar habitats; the Common Coot *F. atra* in a broad zone across Eurasia into the Oriental and Australasian regions; the Crested Coot *F. cristata* in southern and eastern Africa with a relict population in Morocco and Spain. The latter may have been a form which failed to recolonise western Europe after glaciation, the Common Coot replacing it in most areas. *F. cristata* appears to be gradually losing ground.

Common Coot   *Fulica atra* (Map 179)
Part resident, part migrant; in Boreal to Subtropical zones, where areas of fresh water are large enough to support pairs, deep enough for diving for submerged vegetation, and with thick reeds or waterside vegetation. It migrates from the north-east of its range, and may leave other frozen waters. In winter large numbers may occur on open waters, rivers and sea coasts. It is present across to Japan, also in the Indian region and in Australasia.

Crested Coot   *Fulica cristata* (Map 180)
Part resident, part migrant; in Warm Temperate zone in this area. It formerly extended into Algeria and Tunisia. In similar habitats to the previous species, but more frequently in reed swamps with areas of open water, and not apparently co-existing on the same waters. It may disperse when not breeding, including northwards as far as southern France.

GALLINULES *Porphyrio* and *Gallinula* species

The large Purple Gallinule has a wide distribution with several colour forms: purplish-blue in western Europe and north-west Africa; blue, green-backed in Egypt and afrotropical Africa; and blue-grey-faced in the Middle East and India. A deep blue, black-backed form occurs from Indonesia to Australasia. The flightless, heavy Takahe *Notornis mantelli* of New Zealand is sometimes placed in the genus *Porphyrio*. The Moorhen is present right

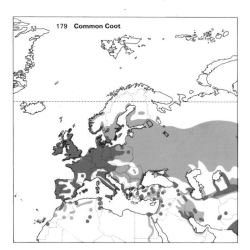

179 Common Coot

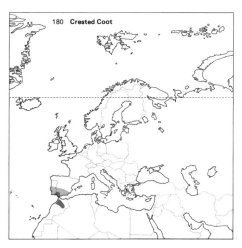

180 Crested Coot

Common Coot

Crested Coot

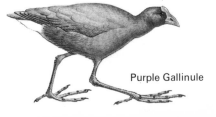
Purple Gallinule

across Eurasia through Indonesia, and in
Africa and the Americas. In Australasia it is
replaced by the possibly conspecific Dusky
Moorhen *G. tenebrosa*. In parts of North
America it is replaced by the similar-sized
American Purple Gallinule *Porphyrula mar-
tinica*.

Purple Gallinule *Porphyrio porphyrio*
(Map 181)
Resident; in Warm Temperate to Subtropical
zones. It occurs in extensive tall marshy vegetation, large reedbeds and overgrown swampy
areas, usually bordering still or slow-moving
fresh waters. The bird is adapted for climbing
in tall reeds with grasping feet.

Moorhen *Gallinula chloropus* (Map 182)
Part resident, part migrant; in Boreal to Subtropical zones. It occurs anywhere where there
is water, from tiny pools and ditches to rivers
and lakes, in waterside vegetation, also feeding by grazing in the open or swimming. Usually it prefers thick waterside vegetation as
cover but can exist in very sparsely vegetated
places and may become tame in urban areas.
In winter it migrates from the north-east of its
range, approximately north of the 0°C January isotherm.

RAILS *Crex* and *Rallus* species
There are two skulking species of similar size,
a short-billed bird of moist grassland and a
long-billed marsh species. The first, the Corncrake, occurs west to Lake Baikal. In eastern
China the Chestnut-breasted Crake *Porzana
paykulli* is a similar bird, nesting in grassland
but only where shrub or tree cover is also
present, and migrating to Malaya and Indonesia. In India the Slaty-legged Banded Rail
Rallina eurizonoides is similar in size and occupies drier habitats with some scrub or forest.
The Water Rail is present in a broad discontinuous distribution right across Eurasia,
apparently replaced in the Indian and Malaysian regions by the similar Blue-breasted Rail
R. striatus; and Voous suggests that the Vir-
ginia Rail *R. limicola* is a replacement species
in North America.

Corncrake *Crex crex* (Map 183)
Migrant, breeding in Boreal to Temperate
zones, wintering in Africa south of the Sahara,

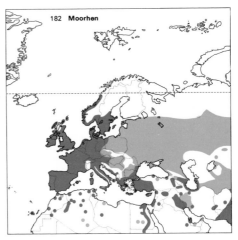
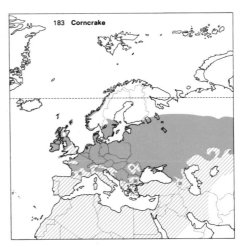

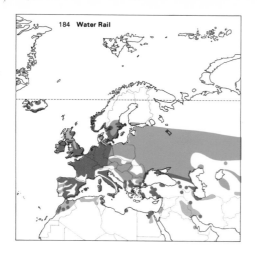

184 Water Rail

and Madagascar. It occurs through natural
and man-made grasslands, including grassy
marshes and meadow clearings in forest. In
some areas, particularly north-western Europe, it has decreased due to disturbance by
farm machinery and destruction of nests and
young by early mowing. Breeding distribution
extends west, north of Tibet, to Lake Baikal,
all apparently migrating to Africa.

Water Rail   *Rallus aquaticus* (Map 184)
Part resident, part migrant, in Boreal to Warm
Temperate zones. It occurs in thick vegetation
bordering waterside, pools, lakes, rivers or
ditches, or in lush vegetation in marshy areas.
It migrates from north-east of range and in
addition may be forced to leave other areas in
winter if the ground is frozen.

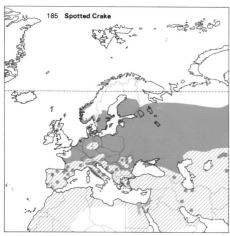

185 Spotted Crake

SMALL CRAKES *Porzana* species
Within this area are three species, two very
small and similar; the third, the Spotted Crake,
a little larger. All are secretive and the distribution is inadequately known, with apparently erratic sporadic breedings in some areas.
The two smaller birds form a species pair,
Baillon's Crake having a wide but mainly easterly distribution, while the Little Crake is
mainly European. Voous has suggested that
the latter may be a European species isolated by glacial changes, while Baillon's Crake
evolved in the east and re-invaded westwards,
the two now overlapping without obvious ecological separation. The Spotted Crake extends
no further east than Mongolia, without an
obvious eastern replacement. To the south
Baillon's Crake nests in northern India, and
elsewhere in this region the smaller rails of
the genus *Amaurornis* appear to replace this
genus.

Spotted Crake   *Porzana porzana* (Map 185)
Mainly migrant, resident in a narrow south-
west zone; breeding in southern Boreal to
Temperate zones. It is widespread in small
numbers in suitable places. It occurs in thick
grassy or sedge vegetation bordering pools,
lakes and slow-moving rivers; and in wet
meadows and marshes with tussock plant
growth. The distribution extends eastwards to
western Mongolia.

Baillon's Crake   *Porzana pusilla* (Map 186)
Migrant; breeding in Temperate to Warm

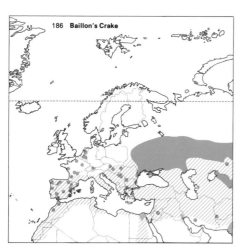

186 Baillon's Crake

Water Rail

Spotted Crake

Baillon's Crake

Little Crake

Temperate zones. Distribution is discontinuous in drier southern part of range. It nests in thick vegetation bordering fresh water of all kinds, including small pools and ditches, and in reedbeds and wet marshland with sedges. Its general distribution extends across Eurasia to Japan; and it is also present in northern India, Australia and Africa.

Little Crake   *Porzana parva* (Map 187)
Migrant; breeding in Temperate zone. It occurs in similar habitats to Baillon's Crake, and distribution extends eastwards to eastern Kazakhstan.

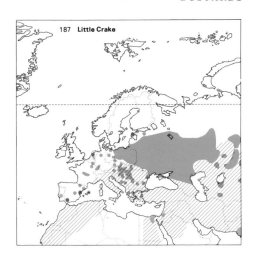

BUSTARDS   *Otididae*

These are large birds of open country, shunning thick or tall cover and nesting on the ground. One large and one small species in Temperate and Warm Temperate zones, larger originally extending into sub-Boreal. Migration slight in larger bird, more marked in smaller. One large species with relict distribution in dry Subtropical zone. One medium-sized species in dry Subtropical to Tropical zones, migrating from north of range. The Great Indian Bustard *Ardeotis nigriceps*, now almost extinct, may be a large ecological replacement species in the Indian region. Several species have contracted, especially from northwest of ranges, due to hunting and disturbance by man, and destruction of open habitat.

Great Bustard   *Otis tarda* (Map 188)
Resident, with some small winter movement; mostly in Temperate to Warm Temperate zones, but extends to open dry heathland in south of Boreal zone near the Baltic; and in recent historic times occurred in Britain, Denmark and south Sweden. Now decreasing in Europe. Eastwards it extends through Kazakhstan, then is discontinuous in an area south and east of Lake Baikal and with a small population north of Vladivostok. Typically a bird of extensive, open and well-drained grassland, short-grass steppe, grassy heathland, also on large open areas of crops, particularly grain.

Little Bustard   *Otis tetrax* (Map 189)
Partly migratory; in Temperate to Warm Temperate zones, migrating from north of most of range during winter. It previously bred further

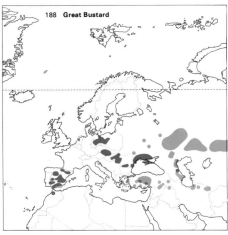

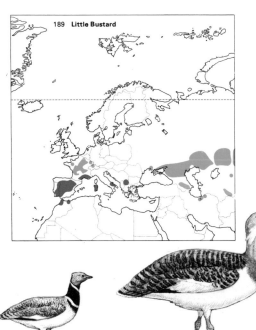

Little Bustard   Great Bustard

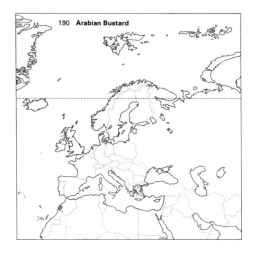

190 Arabian Bustard

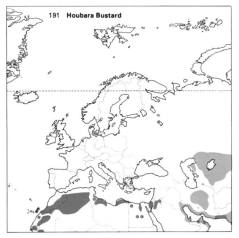

191 Houbara Bustard

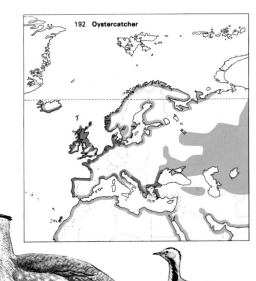

192 Oystercatcher

north in Europe, being lost from southern Germany, Hungary and Czechoslovakia during last hundred years. It occurs in very open grassy country, flat or undulating, and may occupy more hilly country than the Great Bustard; on open fields of low crops and on fallows; on heathland, short-grass steppe, extending at times into open stony, arid areas.

Arabian Bustard *Ardeotis arabs* (Map 190)
Resident; in subtropical dry savannah, scrub and semi-desert on Sahara edge. The distribution extends from western Arabia and eastern Sudan through a zone on the southern and south-western sides of the Sahara, with a small isolate population in Morocco. This is a northern representative of a group of bustard species found through Africa south of the Sahara.

Houbara Bustard *Chlamydotis undulata* (Map 191)
Resident and partly migratory; in dry Subtropical to dry Tropical zones. It occurs on Fuerteventura and Lanzarote in east Canaries and the range also extends north-eastwards to Tuva and north-west Mongolia. It is found in open country, flat or undulating, on arid steppe such as *Artemesia* steppe, or semi-desert and stony desert where some sparse vegetation is present. It is heavily hunted and has been reduced or exterminated in parts of Arabia, around the Gulf, parts of Pakistan and probably elsewhere.

OYSTERCATCHERS
Haematopodidae

Oystercatcher *Haematopus ostralegus* (Map 192)
A cosmopolitan bird with replacement species in most parts of the world, and an additional all-black species in some regions. Resident and migrant; breeding in Subarctic to Warm Temperate zones and wintering in Warm Temperate to Subtropical zones. It occurs on all types of coasts and shores of salt, brackish and fresh waters in open habitats, and on mudflats, saltmarshes, grassland by water including inland river meadows and open lakesides, dunes and sand steppes. Migration is away from frozen waters and may be more in the nature of cold weather movements. It breeds inland but usually winters on coasts.

Arabian Bustard   Houbara Bustard

PLOVERS   *Charadriidae*

Mainly small, plump-bodied waders of bare or short-grass areas, taking surface food and nesting on the ground in scattered pairs. Often sociable when not breeding.

RINGED AND SANDPLOVERS
Charadrius species
Seven species of small plovers in this region (map 193), with some latitudinal replacement, the Ringed Plover having an Arctic to Boreal distribution, with the Semi-palmated Plover as a North American subspecies; the Little Ringed Plover in Warmer Boreal to Tropical zones on inland waters; and the Kentish or Snowy Plover in Temperate to Tropical areas of the Holarctic on mainly coastal areas. The Long-billed Ringed Plover *Charadrius placidus* occurs in eastern China and Japan within Temperate to Subtropical zones, partly overlapping with the Little Ringed Plover. The sandplovers (map 197) occur in drier inland areas. The Caspian Plover breeds on dry saline steppe, wintering on grassy plains, and the Oriental Plover *C. veredus* is an eastern replacement in similar habitats on dry montane areas. The little Kittlitz Sandplover occurs in similar habitats in Africa. The Greater Sandplover utilises saline steppe and drier semi-desert and some upland areas. The Lesser Sandplover is a species of Arctic/Alpine mountain tundra in north-eastern Siberia and the Himalayan-Tibetan region.

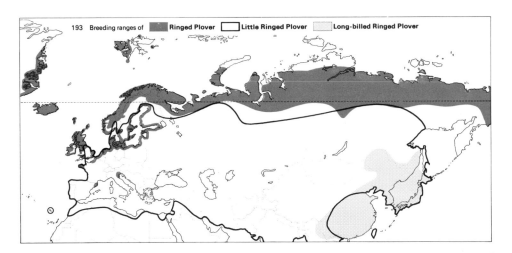

193 Breeding ranges of ■ Ringed Plover □ Little Ringed Plover ▨ Long-billed Ringed Plover

Ringed Plover   *Charadrius hiaticula*
(Maps 193, 194)
Mainly migrant, resident in the south-west of its range; breeding in Arctic to cool Boreal zones, wintering in Warm Temperate to Tropical zones, but in western Europe breeding and wintering in the Temperate zone. It occurs on bare, open shores of mud, sand or stones, by salt, brackish or fresh water; on coasts, estuaries, lakes and occasionally rivers, on moss and shrub tundra, and also on muddy or wet stony plains. It has spread to northern France since 1941, and occasionally pairs may nest further south.

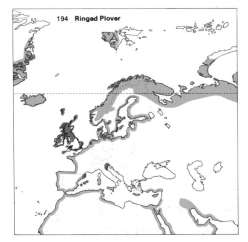

194 Ringed Plover

Oystercatcher   Ringed Plover   Little Ringed Plover

195   Little Ringed Plover

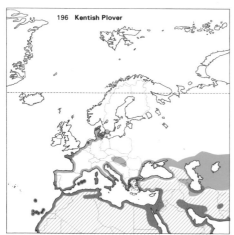

196   Kentish Plover

Little Ringed Plover   *Charadrius dubius*
(Maps 193, 195)
Mainly migrant, resident along southern limit of breeding range within present area; breeding in Boreal to Warm Temperate zones, and to Tropics in the Oriental region, wintering in Tropical zone. It is an inland species usually of fresh waters, on bare shores of rivers, small lakes, gravelpits and reservoirs; on sandbanks, dry river beds, mudflats and occasionally on bare, moist soils and sands, sometimes on estuaries. It winters in similar habitats, mainly north of the Equator. It has spread into England since 1938.

Kentish Plover   *Charadrius alexandrinus*
(Map 196)
Migrant and resident; except on the Atlantic seaboard breeding mainly between the 50° latitudes, migrant in winter from inland Asia and much of Europe but movements are uncertain. It occurs in drier, sandier areas than the Ringed Plover with which it otherwise can compete. It is found on bare sand or mud shores, mainly on coasts and sometimes on rivers, also on dunes, mud or sand plains, sparsely vegetated grass or salt steppes, sand deserts and coral coasts. In the past it has bred on the southern English coast.

Kittlitz Sandplover   *Charadrius pecuarius*
(Maps 197, 198)
Migrant; occurring on open muddy or sandy shores and mud and sand banks of inland waters – rivers, lakes, lagoons – and on mud and sand flats of sea coasts. It also occurs

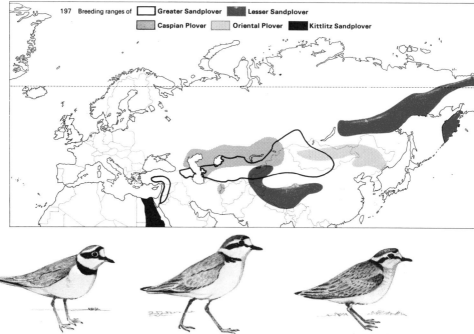

197   Breeding ranges of ☐ Greater Sandplover   ▓ Lesser Sandplover
▨ Caspian Plover   ░ Oriental Plover   ■ Kittlitz Sandplover

Little Ringed Plover   Kentish Plover   Kittlitz Sandplover on dry short-grass areas and bare soils, often at some distance from water. Non-breeding birds may flock. It occurs in suitable habitats in Africa south of the Sahara, extending through north-east Africa to Egypt.

Greater Sandplover   *Charadrius leschenaultii*
(Maps 197, 199)
Migrant; breeding in dry Warm Temperate to steppe zones, wintering in Subtropical to Tropical zones. It breeds on salt steppe or clay plains with sparse vegetation, in stony semi-desert plains, barren stony desert, and on dry or barren montane plateaus. In the west of its range it occurs on high ground, and in the Altai at *c.* 1,200–1,800 m. It winters mainly on bare sandy or muddy sea coasts.

Lesser Sandplover   *Charadrius mongolus*
(Maps 197, 200)
Migrant; breeding in the montane Arctic/Alpine zone, wintering in Subtropical to Tropical zones. In the south-west of its range it breeds in level, stony valleys near water, and in shingle-banks of shallow river sources, at high altitudes in the Upper Himalayas, Tibetan plateau and Pamirs. It winters mainly on bare sandy or muddy coasts.

Caspian Plover   *Charadrius asiaticus*
(Maps 197, 201)
Migrant; breeding in Temperate steppe zone and wintering in Subtropical to Tropical zones. It breeds on salt and *Artemesia* steppes with sparse shrubby vegetation, up to 12 km from water, but with young may occur in wet

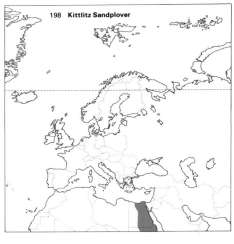

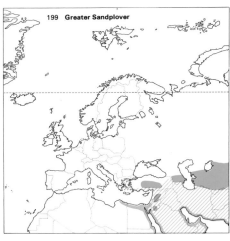

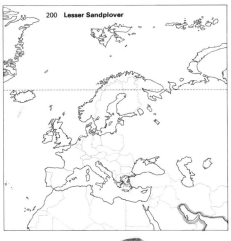

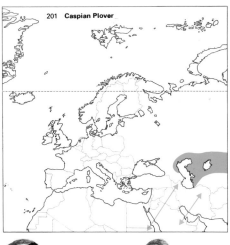

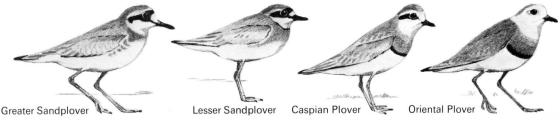

Greater Sandplover   Lesser Sandplover   Caspian Plover   Oriental Plover

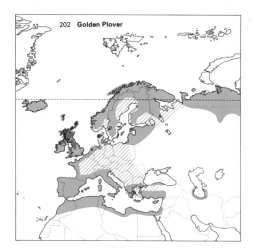

202 Golden Plover

203 Grey Plover

204 Dotterel

grassland or by rivers. It winters in Africa south of the Sahara, on dry grassy plains. Migration appears to be direct with little evidence of any halts on passage.

GOLDEN PLOVERS *Pluvialis* species
Two western species, both nesting on tundra and the Golden Plover extending to Arctic/Alpine areas. The Golden Plover appears to be a north-western isolate species nesting east to the Ob. From the River Ob eastwards through arctic Siberia and in North America it is replaced by the similar Lesser Golden Plover *Pluvialis dominica*.

Golden Plover   *Pluvialis apricaria* (Map 202)
Migrant; breeding in Arctic/Alpine and Subarctic to Arctic zones, wintering in Temperate to Warm Temperate zones. It breeds on grassy areas of low tundra and wetter areas of montane tundra, on lakesides and small islands; and at higher altitudes further south on heather or grass moorland, bogs and heath barrens. It winters on grassy lowlands along the coast or by fresh waters and estuaries, and on cultivated land.

Grey Plover   *Pluvialis squatarola* (Map 203)
Migrant; breeding in the Arctic zone, wintering in Warm Temperate to Tropical zones, and in Temperate areas along the Atlantic seaboard. It breeds on drier, rocky parts of the tundra on lichen, grass or stony moss areas. It winters on muddy and sandy shores of coasts, estuaries and saltmarshes.

DOTTERELS *Eudromias* species

Dotterel   *Eudromias morinellus* (Map 204)
Migrant; breeding in Arctic/Alpine zone and wintering in the Warm Temperate zone. It breeds in the Arctic on open gravelly tundra and elsewhere on a similar tundra equivalent in high mountains. Records suggest erratic use of some areas, and it has bred on newly drained Dutch polders. In southern Europe it occurs at altitudes of *c.* 1,600–2,500 m. It has a fragmentary distribution in a few high-mountain parts of Eurasia as an Arctic/Alpine relic, with a doubtless more continuous distribution in colder glacial periods. It tends to halt at particular places on migration and winters on shores and semi-desert areas of North Africa.

Golden Plover   Grey Plover

Dotterel

LAPWINGS *Vanellus* species

Five species of larger plovers occurring mainly on grassland or open areas near water. The Lapwing has a broad warmer Boreal to Warm Temperate distribution right across Eurasia and is replaced in North America, where none of the genus occurs, by a large species of the ringed plover group, the Killdeer Plover *Charadrius vociferus*. The other lapwings form a complex of six species in southern Eurasia. The Sociable Plover breeds on cooler dry steppes, the White-tailed Plover in wet and vegetated steppe and scrub areas, while on open areas by water the Spur-winged Plover has a divided distribution in the eastern Mediterranean to North Africa and the Himalayas to South-east Asia, while the Grey-headed Plover has a limited distribution in eastern China. In the Indian region there are two species overlapping, the Yellow-wattled Lapwing *Vanellus malabaricus* in drier country of peninsular India and the Red-wattled Lapwing in wetter places and with a more extensive range between the Middle East and South-east Asia.

Lapwing   *Vanellus vanellus* (Map 205)

Migrant, and resident mainly in the southwest of the breeding range; breeding in Warmer Boreal to Warm Temperate zones, wintering in Temperate to Warm Temperate zones. It breeds on open short grassland, and short herbage areas of marsh, heathland, moorland, bogs, saltmarsh, and open cultivated areas. It winters on similar areas where not frozen, and on the edges of fresh waters, estuaries and coasts, and on mud and sandflats.

Spur-winged Plover   *Vanellus spinosus* (Maps 206, 208)

Resident and migrant; in Warm Temperate to Subarctic zones. It breeds by fresh, brackish and salt water on open shores and sandbanks of rivers, lakes, lagoons and swamps. The Mediterranean population winters in Africa where it occurs across the savannah region south of the Sahara and in the north-east.

Red-wattled Lapwing   *Vanellus indicus* (Maps 207, 208)

Mainly resident, migrant in north Afghanistan; in Warm Temperate to Subtropical zones. It occurs in open grassy, swampy or cultivated areas, including forest clearings,

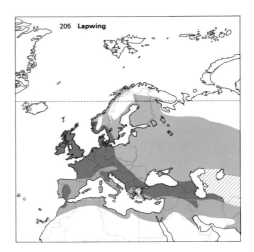

205 Lapwing

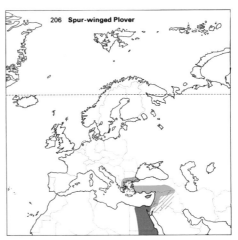

206 Spur-winged Plover

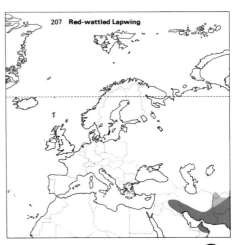

207 Red-wattled Lapwing

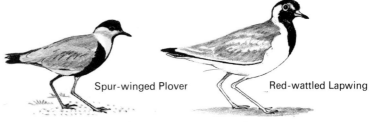

Lapwing   Spur-winged Plover   Red-wattled Lapwing

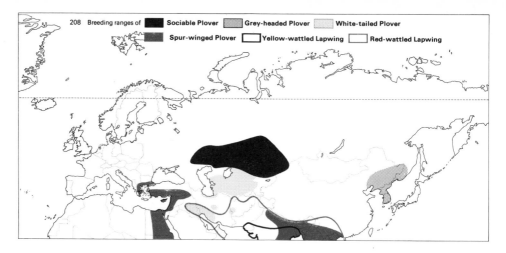

208 Breeding ranges of ■ Sociable Plover ▨ Grey-headed Plover ░ White-tailed Plover
▨ Spur-winged Plover ☐ Yellow-wattled Lapwing ☐ Red-wattled Lapwing

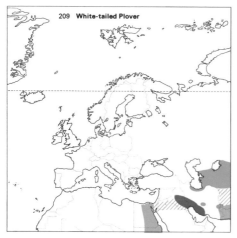

209 White-tailed Plover

where there is some surface water present, from lakes and rivers to ditches and puddles; and on the bare edges of all types of fresh waters.

White-tailed Plover *Vanellus leucurus*
(Maps 208, 209)
Migrant and resident; nesting in Temperate steppe to Warm Temperate zones, wintering in Subtropical zones. It breeds by water, fresh, brackish or salt, in areas with a low plant growth bordering lakes, or on small grassy islands, or in marshy, vegetated areas of drier steppes. It winters in similar habitats.

210 Sociable Plover

Sociable Plover *Vanellus gregarius*
(Map 208, 210)
Migrant; breeding in the Temperate dry steppe zone and wintering in the Subtropical zone. It breeds on dry short-grass steppe with scanty vegetation and on *Artemesia* steppe. It winters on open grassy areas bordering water, on bare cultivation, stubble and on dry wasteland.

Grey-headed Plover

White-tailed Plover

Sociable Plover

Yellow-wattled Lapwing

CRAB PLOVER　*Dromadidae*

Crab Plover　*Dromas ardeola* (Map 211)
Resident and migrant; in Subtropical to
Tropical zones. It occurs on sea coasts and
islands of the northern and western Indian
Ocean. It breeds colonially in sandy areas,
usually on small islands, where unlike other
waders it makes a nest burrow. It feeds on
mud and sand flats and on tidal shorelines.

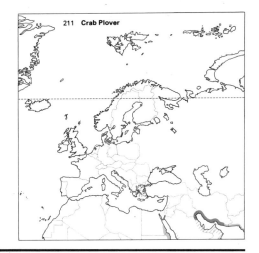

AVOCETS AND STILTS
Recurvirostridae

Moderate-sized waders with long slender legs
and bills. The Avocet is cosmopolitan and
divided into several poorly defined species.
The same is true of the Black-winged Stilt,
but in Australia a second species, the Banded
Stilt *Cladorhynchus leucocephalus*, is present.
An odd, curlew-like bird of the Himalayan-
Tibetan region, the Ibisbill *Ibidorhynchus
struthersi*, is also assigned to this family.

Avocet　*Recurvirostra avosetta* (Map 212)
Mainly migrant and occasionally resident,
breeding in Temperate to Warm Temperate
zones, wintering in Subtropical to Tropical
zones, and into the Temperate zone on the
Atlantic seaboard. It breeds and winters on
the edges of shallow saline, brackish, or alkaline waters of coastal lagoons, saltmarshes
and inland salt or alkaline lakes with bare
shores. It may colonise temporary lakes in
desert or semi-desert regions.

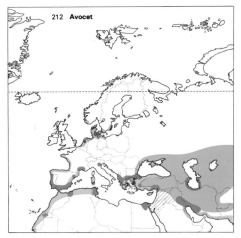

Black-winged Stilt　*Himantopus himantopus*
(Map 213)
Migrant and resident; in Warm Temperate to
Tropical zones. It breeds by shallow waters,
fresh or brackish, and preferably with extensive muddy areas; in swamps, flooded grassland, ricefields, coastal lagoons and sometimes
salt lakes. It occurs erratically on widely
scattered waters and has on occasions nested
in the Netherlands and England.

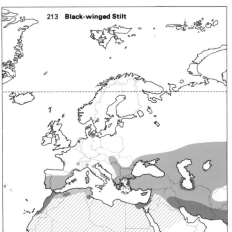

Crab Plover　　　　　　　　　　　　Avocet　　　　Black-winged Stilt

TYPICAL WADERS *Scolopacidae*

A large group of mostly long-legged water birds with slender bills that may be long or short, straight or upcurved or downcurved. With the exception of the Green Sandpiper, which may use old nests in trees, they nest on the ground, often with little or no nest material. They are mostly migratory, fast-flying birds, nesting and feeding by water in high latitudes and wintering on warmer coasts. The variations in bills and body size enable a number of species to exploit a single habitat without competition. A number of subgroups are recognisable.

214 Turnstone

215 Broad-billed Sandpiper

TURNSTONES *Arenaria* species

Small stout, plover-type birds of stony and shingly areas. The common Turnstone occurs around the Holarctic in Arctic to Boreal breeding zones, with a second species, the Black Turnstone *Arenaria melanocephala*, only on the Bering Sea and North Pacific seaboard of North America.

Turnstone *Arenaria interpres* (Map 214)
Migrant; nesting in Arctic to Boreal zones and wintering in Temperate to Tropical zones. It breeds on rocky, stony or pebbly coasts bordering tundra or grassy shores, offshore and estuarine rocky islands, inland on lichen and moss tundra, and in the Baltic occurs on shores of forested islands. It winters on all types of coasts where there is anything resembling rock or stones of some kind, more rarely on sandy shores. In winter it extends to the southern limits of continents and non-breeding birds may summer in wintering areas.

STINT-TYPE SANDPIPERS
Limicola and *Calidris* species
Eight species of small, shore-haunting sandpipers. The Broad-billed Sandpiper is a northwest isolate, breeding in Scandinavia and not proven elsewhere, using inland swamps. Dunlin and Curlew Sandpiper are very similar but (map 218) one is circumpolar as an Arctic breeder and the other is wide-ranging in winter from a limited north Siberian breeding ground. The stints are very small, short-billed birds (map 219). The Little Stint is a coastal Arctic species and Temminck's Stint a more inland Arctic/Alpine species. The Red-necked Stint *Calidris ruficollis* is an eastern Little Stint replacement with a limited distribution at the eastern end of Siberia. The Long-toed Stint *C. subminuta* is a more southerly form, only known from the exteme east but thought to extend to the Ob basin, although the limits of the range are very uncertain. The remaining three western species are maritime Arctic breeders. The Purple Sandpiper is closely linked with rocky shores and can winter furthest north. The Knot winters on slightly more southerly sandy and muddy coasts, and the Sanderling feeds on sandy shores, furthest south of the three. The Knot has a closely related species, the Great Knot *Calidris tenuirostris*, with a limited and poorly known breeding range in extreme eastern Siberia.

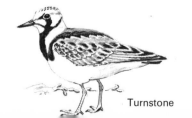

Turnstone

Broad-billed Sandpiper   *Limicola falcinellus*
(Map 215)
Migrant; breeding in the cooler Boreal zone
and wintering in the Subtropical zone. It
breeds in conifer forest areas in bogs, swamps
with wet grassland and in similar sites in
wooded tundra. It migrates in a south-easterly
direction and winters on muddy coasts mainly
in the northern Indian Ocean.

Dunlin   *Calidris alpina* (Maps 216, 218)
Mainly migrant; but resident in much of
north-west Europe; breeding in Arctic/Alpine
and Subarctic zones, extending to Boreal in
north-west Europe, wintering in Temperate to
Subtropical zones. It breeds in swampy areas
or by water in grassy moss tundra, and montane tundra; and further south on moorland
and wet montane heathland, swampy lowland
valleys and coastal saltmarshes. It winters on
muddy shores of sea coasts, estuaries, brackish lagoons and lakes, and freshwater lakes
and rivers, wintering south to *c*. 25° north latitude, and rarely further.

Curlew Sandpiper   *Calidris ferruginea*
(Maps 217, 218)
Migrant; breeding in the Arctic zone, wintering in Warm Temperate to Tropical zones. It
breeds on the drier grassy and shrubby areas
of hilly tundra. It tends to disperse mainly
westwards during migration and large numbers pass through Europe. On passage and in
winter it occurs mainly on muddy shores of
sea coasts and estuaries, and rarely inland.

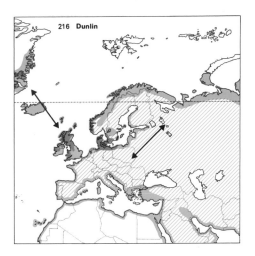

216 Dunlin

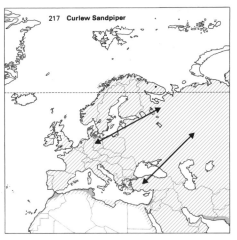

217 Curlew Sandpiper

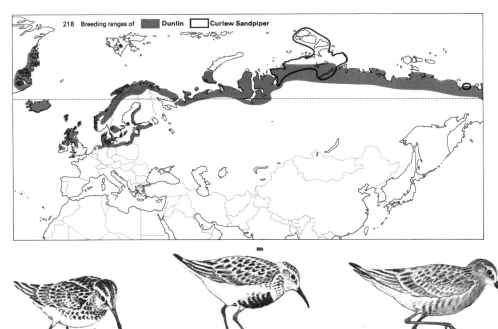

218 Breeding ranges of ▮ Dunlin ☐ Curlew Sandpiper

Broad-billed Sandpiper   Dunlin   Curlew Sandpiper

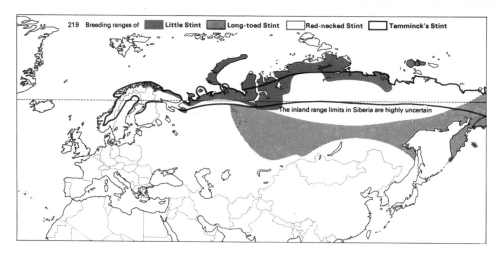

219 Breeding ranges of ▓ Little Stint ▒ Long-toed Stint ☐ Red-necked Stint ☐ Temminck's Stint

The inland range limits in Siberia are highly uncertain

220 Little Stint

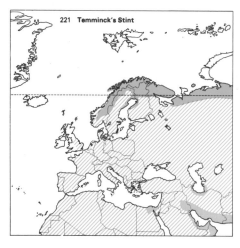

221 Temminck's Stint

Little Stint *Calidris minuta* (Maps 219, 220)
Migrant; breeding in the Arctic zone, and wintering in Warm Temperate to Tropical zones. It breeds on low-lying, wet moss tundra but on the drier raised sites near water, and into willow scrub. It migrates coastally and inland, and on passage and in winter it occurs on sandy or muddy shores of sea coasts, estuaries, rivers and lakes, and on extensive mudflats and sandbanks.

Temminck's Stint *Calidris temminckii* (Maps 219, 221)
Migrant; breeding in Arctic/Alpine to Subarctic zones, and in Scandinavia in cool Boreal zone, wintering in drier Warm Temperate to Subtropical zones. It breeds in montane and swampier areas of shrub tundra and into the birch zone. It has bred occasionally in Britain. On passage and in winter it is usually a freshwater species, migrating inland, and occurring on muddy shores of pools, lakes and rivers, usually where there is some growth of herbage.

Knot *Calidris canutus* (Map 222)
Migrant; breeding in the Arctic zone and wintering in Temperate to Tropical zones. It breeds in a scattered and disintegrated higharctic range, on more level montane stony or lichen tundra, dry but near a swampy food source. It is strongly migratory and winters in flocks on sandy and muddy coasts and estuaries, extending in small numbers well into the southern hemisphere.

Little Stint

Temminck's Stint

Long-toed Stint

Red-necked Stint

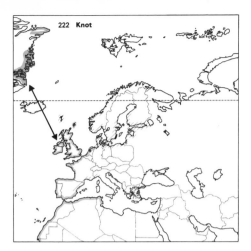

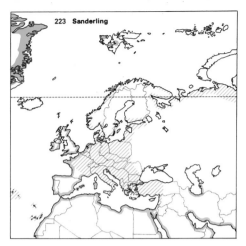

Sanderling   *Calidris alba* (Map 223)
Migrant; breeding in the Arctic zone, wintering in Temperate to Tropical zones. Like the Knot it breeds in a scattered high-arctic range on stony lichen tundra, usually in areas with more herbage than in those used by the Knot. On passage and in winter it mainly occurs on sandy beaches where it feeds at the tide edge. It occurs sporadically on inland waters. As a coastal migrant it occurs through much of the Southern Hemisphere except Antarctica, and non-breeding birds may summer in warmer zones.

Purple Sandpiper   *Calidris maritima* (Map 224)
Mainly migrant; resident in a few areas; breeding in the Arctic/Alpine zone, wintering in Subarctic to Temperate zones. It breeds in swampy areas in moss and lichen tundra, on rocky coastal islands, and in high montane regions on swampy heath and scrub of tundra type with stony areas. On passage and in winter it is a coastal bird, on rocky shores where it feeds in the tidal zone.

LARGER SANDPIPERS *Tringa* and *Philomachus* species
Nine species of moderate-sized to small sandpipers of mainly inland freshwater habitats. The evolutionary origin of the three larger species is more apparent in eastern Eurasia where they show some latitudinal separation. Here the Spotted Redshank occurs in Arctic to Boreal zones, the Greenshank in the Boreal zone and the Redshank mainly in the Temperate zone; but in Scandinavia the three converge and overlap, while retaining their habitat preferences. In North America the Greater Yellowlegs *Tringa melanoleuca* replaces the Greenshank, and Lesser Yellowlegs *T. flavipes* replaces both Common and Spotted Redshanks. In the extreme east of Eurasia Nordmann's Greenshank *T. guttifer* is a similar species to the Greenshank with a very restricted breeding range in the Sakhalin region. Two smaller species also replace each other latitudinally; the Terek Sandpiper in Boreal forest and the Marsh Sandpiper in Temperate steppes. Another two, smaller still, are very similar and overlap extensively, but the Green Sandpiper is a bird of forest swamps while the Wood Sandpiper can utilise more open

Knot   Sanderling   Purple Sandpiper

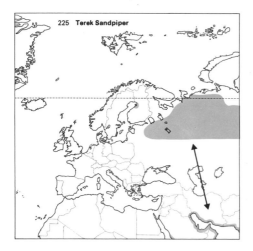

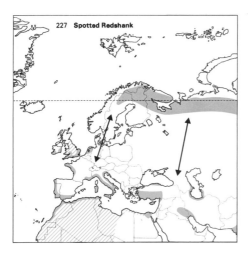

swampy sites and extends further north. In North America they are replaced by a single species, the Solitary Sandpiper *T. solitaria*. The Common Sandpiper has a broad distribution on the margins of freshwater, replaced in North America by the very similar Spotted Sandpiper *T. macularia* which has recently bred once in Scotland. The Ruff is an oddly decorated sandpiper occurring through Boreal and Arctic zones. The Buff-breasted Sandpiper *Tryngites subruficollis* has been suggested as its North American replacement species. All these species extend across Eurasia except for the Marsh Sandpiper which has a mainly steppe distribution to the Altai and a small isolate population in north-east Mongolia, suggesting fairly recent separation.

Terek Sandpiper   *Tringa cinereus* (Map 225)
Migrant; breeding in the Boreal zone, wintering in Subtropical to Tropical zones. It breeds in conifer forest regions on the marshy edges of streams bordered with grass and willow scrub, in flooded forest areas, and extends into shrub tundra and shrub steppe where muddy-edged streams occur. It winters on coastal lagoons, saltmarsh creeks and beaches.

Redshank   *Tringa totanus* (Map 226)
Mainly migrant, but in Europe resident in the extreme west and south of the breeding range; breeding in warmer Boreal to Warm Temperate zones but extending into the Subarctic in areas modified by the North Atlantic Drift current, wintering in Warm Temperate to Tropical zones, and into the Boreal zone on the Atlantic seaboard. It breeds in wet grassy areas over a wide range from coastal saltmarsh and tundra, and freshwater meadows bordering streams, rivers and lakes, to swampy heathland and moorland, and in the east to similar sites in high steppe and subalpine meadow zones at high altitudes up to 4,500 m. It winters mainly on coasts, on the muddy shores of sea coasts, saltmarshes, estuaries and lagoons. In well-inhabited regions it has decreased due to the expansion of drainage and arable cultivation.

Spotted Redshank   *Tringa erythropus* (Map 227)
Migrant; breeding in Subarctic to cooler Boreal zones, wintering in Warm Temperate to Subtropical zones and in the Temperate

Terek Sandpiper   Redshank   Spotted Redshank

zone on the Atlantic seaboard. It breeds in small areas of swamp or heathland near water, within open conifer or birch forest, and in shrub tundra. It winters on shallow muddy shores of both fresh and salt waters.

Greenshank   *Tringa nebularia* (Map 228)

Migrant; breeding in the Boreal zone, wintering in Warm Temperate to Tropical zones and into the Temperate zone on the Atlantic seaboard. It breeds in swampy clearings in conifer and birch forest; and in open marshes and bogs, or on the vegetated shores of lakes, where some trees are present. It winters on muddy shores of coastal lagoons and of inland pools, lakes and slow-moving rivers. It is a strong migrant and occurs over most of the Old World southern hemisphere as far as South Africa and Australia.

Marsh Sandpiper   *Tringa stagnatilis* (Map 229)

Migrant; breeding in the drier steppe Temperate zone and wintering in Subtropical to Tropical zones. It breeds in wet grassy places on the shores of shallow lakes and pools, mainly fresh water, occasionally salt, in grass steppe regions; and also pools and rivers in valleys of more montane regions. It has bred earlier this century in Austria and Hungary around the Neusiedlersee. Like the Greenshank it is strongly migratory, occurring well into the southern hemisphere, and it winters in similar habitats.

Common Sandpiper   *Tringa hypoleucos* (Map 230)

Mainly migrant; resident in a few south-westerly areas; breeding in Subarctic to Warm Temperate zones, wintering in Warm Temperate to Tropical zones, and in the Temperate zone on the Atlantic seaboard. It breeds on the sandy or stony shores of clear fresh waters, from small hill streams and pools to the shores and sandbanks of large slow rivers, lakes and reservoirs. It occurs in open and forest areas and at all altitudes up to tree line; and as a migrant and in winter on the edges of any kind of fresh water. It migrates far into the Southern Hemisphere.

Greenshank

Marsh Sandpiper

Common Sandpiper

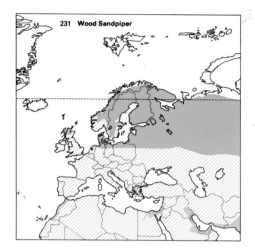

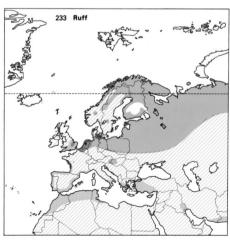

Wood Sandpiper   *Tringa glareola* (Map 231)
Migrant; breeding in Subarctic to Boreal zones, wintering in Subtropical to Tropical zones. It breeds in bogs, open or partly forested swampy heathland, bogs and marshes in shrub tundra and birch or conifer forest. Usually occurs in more open sites than the Green Sandpiper. Distribution has been adversely affected by forest clearance and drainage. It ceased breeding in the Netherlands in 1936, and was lost to Britain between 1853 and 1958. It winters on muddy shores of saline coastal lagoons and saltmarshes, and fresh waters of pools and slow-moving rivers.

Green Sandpiper   *Tringa ochropus* (Map 232)
Migrant; breeding in Boreal to cooler Temperate zones but absent from western Europe, and wintering in Warm Temperate to Tropical zones, and into the Temperate zone on the Atlantic seaboard. It breeds in forest, usually conifer forest, with swampy areas and streams, and in wet alder woods, overgrown forest marshes and wooded river banks, occurring in suitable habitats at high altitudes in eastern and central Eurasia. Peculiar in that it uses old nests in trees. It had bred in Britain. It winters on the edges of freshwater pools, lakes, ditches, streams and rivers. It tends to winter further north than the Wood Sandpiper.

Ruff   *Philomachus pugnax* (Map 233)
Mainly migrant; resident in a few areas of western Europe; breeding in Boreal to Arctic zones, with a few Temperate relict populations, wintering in Warm Temperate to Tropical zones, and into the Temperate zone on the Atlantic seaboard. It breeds on short grass and herbage of grassy marshes in moss and shrub tundra, clearings and slightly wooded areas of the Boreal zone, wet grassland bordering lakes and rivers, sometimes extending into farmland, and on coastal grasslands and saltmarshes. It winters on mudflats and shallow muddy shores of estuaries, lowland lakes and pools. Its need for social display may limit its nesting opportunities and it appears to have decreased in Europe.

CURLEWS AND GODWITS *Numenius* and *Limosa* species
Five larger waders. Among the curlews (map 234) the large Eurasian Curlew has a broad

Wood Sandpiper   Green Sandpiper

Ruff

Boreal to Temperate distribution across to northern China, but the eastern end of the range is occupied by the Eastern Curlew *Numenius madagascariensis* with a poorly known distribution only certain at its eastern coastal limit. In North America the Long-billed Curlew *N. americanus* is a replacement species. The smaller Whimbrel is a Subarctic to Boreal species. It has a Holarctic distribution but on both continents has a separate eastern and western population, and should perhaps be regarded as having Atlantic and Pacific populations with the eastern Siberian birds referable to the latter. In between the two Eurasian populations occurs the very poorly known breeding range of the Little Whimbrel *N. minutus*; as does the Eskimo Curlew *N. borealis* between the two North American populations. The whimbrel-sized Slender-billed Curlew has a Temperate steppe distribution, within the general range of the Eurasian Curlew and partly overlapping that of the Whimbrel. The two godwits replace each other latitudinally, the Black-tailed Godwit breeding on Temperate grassland and the Bar-tailed Godwit on Arctic tundra. Both occur across Eurasia, the former having a small break in distribution in the northern Altai region. In North America the Bar-tailed Godwit nests in Alaska and the Hudsonian Godwit *L. haemastica* appears to replace the Black-tailed Godwit, but breeds in the Arctic, while the larger Marbled Godwit *L. fedoa* breeds on the Temperate northern prairie.

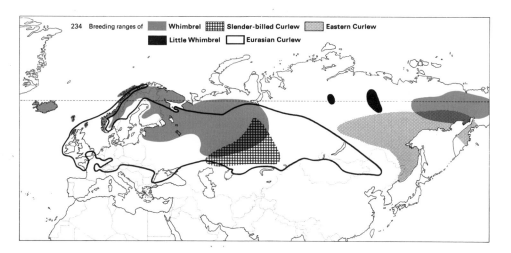

234 Breeding ranges of **Whimbrel** | **Slender-billed Curlew** | **Eastern Curlew** | **Little Whimbrel** | **Eurasian Curlew**

Eurasian Curlew *Numenius arquata*
(Maps 234, 235)

Mainly migrant, resident at the western end of the range; breeding in Boreal to Temperate zones, wintering in Temperate to Warm Temperate zones, and into the Boreal zone on the Atlantic seaboard. It breeds in open grassy areas, the drier parts of marshes, dune grassland, meadows, open arable and low crops, swampy and dry heathland, and moorland, at times with tall heather and trees. It winters on muddy and sandy sea coasts, estuaries and rivers, saltmarshes and coastal lagoons, on coastal grasslands and the shores of freshwater rivers, lakes and marshes.

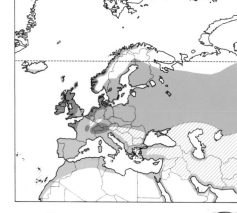

235 Eurasian Curlew

Eastern Curlew

Little Whimbrel

Eurasian Curlew

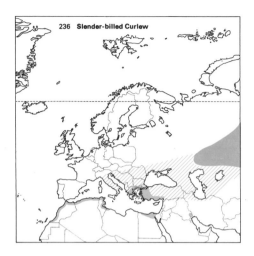

Slender-billed Curlew   *Numenius tenuirostris*
(Maps 234, 236)
Migrant; breeding in the Temperate steppe zones, wintering in the Warm Temperate zone. The breeding is poorly documented and the extent of the area is very uncertain. It has been found breeding in a sedge bog with drier ridges of willow and birch scrub. It winters on Mediterranean coasts. It is a rare and probably decreasing species.

Whimbrel   *Numenius phaeopus*
(Maps 234, 237)
Migrant; breeding in Subarctic/Alpine to Boreal zones but absent from Europe other than Scandinavia, wintering in Warm Temperate to Tropical zones. It breeds in low grassy herbage in marshy areas of moss and shrub tundra, and old burnt forest clearings, and in drier areas with moss and lichen among willow or birch scrub, usually near water. It winters on muddy and sandy coasts and estuaries; wintering south to Tierra del Fuego, South Africa and New Zealand.

Black-tailed Godwit   *Limosa limosa*
(Map 238)
Mainly migrant; resident in small areas of France and England; breeding in the warmer Boreal to cooler Temperate zones, wintering in Temperate to Subtropical zones. It breeds on usually low-lying lush grassland by water – on the shores of lakes, ponds and slow-moving rivers, on wet and dry meadows and grazing land, grassy clearings in forest, and swampy and grassy heathland. It winters on muddy shores of saline and fresh waters in estuaries, rivers and lakes; feeding in shallow water.

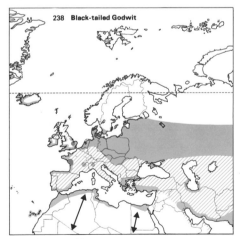

Bar-tailed Godwit   *Limosa lapponica*
(Map 239)
Migrant; breeding in the Arctic zone, wintering in Warm Temperate to Subtropical zones, but into the Tropical zone in Indonesia. It breeds usually in swampy areas of moss and

Slender-billed Curlew

Whimbrel

Black-tailed Godwit

shrub tundra, extending into marshy heathland in willow and birch zones, and reaching the Boreal conifer forest zone. It is strongly migratory and in the east reaches New Zealand.

SNIPE *Scolopax* and *Gallinago* species
The Woodcock is a large species adapted to moist forest conditions, occurring right across Eurasia in Boreal to Temperate zones with an isolate population in the Himalayas. The American Woodcock *Philohela minor* is a replacement species in eastern North America. Of the smaller species the Common Snipe has a broad Holarctic distribution, and the very small Jack Snipe has a trans-Eurasian range. The other Eurasian species (map 244) have smaller and often very poorly known breeding distributions. The Great Snipe and Pintailed Snipe appear mainly to replace each other in the eastern and western parts of the Boreal zone with an overlap in the Ob basin. The Solitary Snipe *G. solitaria* breeds in the mountain regions of the Altai and Manchuria. The Swinhoe's Snipe *G. megala* has a limited range to the north of the Solitary Snipe in the upper basins of the Ob, Yenesei and Amur Rivers. The Wood Snipe *G. nemoricola* occurs in the Himalayas with a poorly known distribution.

Woodcock   *Scolopax rusticola* (Map 240)
Resident and migrant; breeding in warmer Boreal to Temperate zones, wintering in Temperate to Warm Temperate zones, and into the Boreal zone along the Atlantic seaboard. It breeds in moist forest areas with a deep leaf litter; in thick broadleaf and mixed forest, in conifer forest with broadleaf scrub or with ferns and fallen branches, and in swampy overgrown forest with streams. It winters in similar habitats in marshy woodland and scrub with ground cover. The boundary of the migratory zone in the west is close to the 0°C winter isotherm.

Common Snipe   *Gallinago gallinago* (Map 241)
Resident and migrant; breeding in Subarctic to Temperate zones, wintering in Warm Temperate to Subtropical zones, and into the warmer Boreal zone in western Europe. It breeds in marshy areas of all kinds where taller herbage is present, from wet and reedy

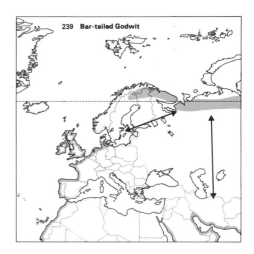
239   Bar-tailed Godwit

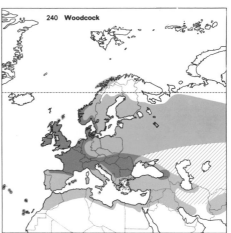
240   Woodcock

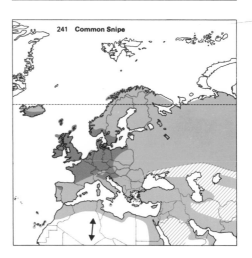
241   Common Snipe

Bar-tailed Godwit

Woodcock

Common Snipe

242 Great Snipe

meadows to swampy shores of lakes and rivers, sedge bogs, marshes and tundra edge; utilising large and small marshy areas in open areas and forest clearings at varying altitudes. It winters in similar habitats. It is usually confined to fresh waters.

Great Snipe   *Gallinago media*
(Maps 242, 244)

Migrant; breeding in the Boreal zone, wintering in Subtropical to Tropical zones. It breeds on marshy and grassy areas in birch and willow forest and scrub, on drier and more wooded sites than the Common Snipe, also in tussock bog and on wet meadows in forest areas. Its northern limit is at the tree line, and in the south of its range it may occur at altitudes up to 1,700 m. It winters in eastern and southern Africa south of the Sahara, on marshy grassland or grassy marshes. It is decreasing and in the past bred in the Netherlands and northern Germany.

243 Pin-tailed Snipe

Pin-tailed Snipe   *Gallinago stenura*
(Maps 243, 244)

Migrant; breeding in eastern Boreal to cooler Temperate zones, wintering in Subtropical to Tropical zones. It breeds in grassy marshes bordering small rivers, lakes and pools, wet meadows and marshy areas in conifer or birch forest, occurring in the south of its range at altitudes of 1,200–2,300 m. It winters in areas with moist herbage, on the marshy edges of lakes and reservoirs, in ricefields and in marshy places in scrub, but usually in drier sites than those used by the Common Snipe.

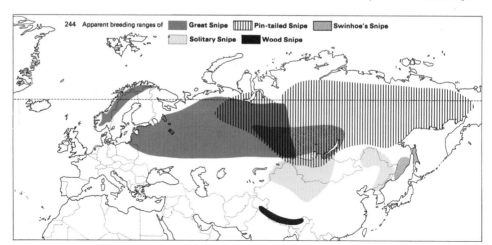

244 Apparent breeding ranges of ▦ Great Snipe ▥ Pin-tailed Snipe ▧ Swinhoe's Snipe ▨ Solitary Snipe ■ Wood Snipe

Great Snipe

Pin-tailed Snipe   Swinhoe's Snipe

Solitary Snipe

Jack Snipe *Limnocryptes minimus* (Map 245)
Migrant; breeding in Subarctic to Boreal zones, but absent from the north-west, wintering in Warm Temperate and Subtropical to western Temperate zones. It breeds in conifer forest in bogs and marshes with grassy and tall herbage, and in wet alder woods and marshy willow scrub, extending north into birch scrub. It winters in more open marshy grassland, on muddy river banks, river floodland, wet meadows and ricefields. It has decreased in range and at an earlier period was said to nest in southern Sweden and on the southern side of the Baltic.

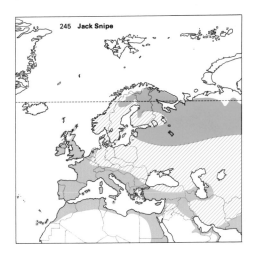

245 Jack Snipe

PAINTED SNIPE *Rostratulidae*

A family of two species, the present one in Africa and through the Oriental region to Australasia; and a second species in South America.

Painted Snipe *Rostratula benghalensis*
(Map 246)
Resident; in Subtropical to Tropical zones. It occurs in overgrown marshy areas bordering small muddy waters, thickly vegetated banks of slow-moving rivers, tussock marshes and ricefields. It is usually a lowland bird but has occurred up to *c.* 1,800 m in the Himalayas. There are some local movements probably controlled by changes in water levels.

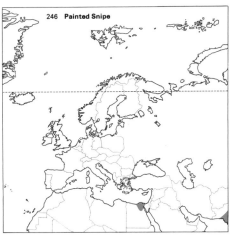

246 Painted Snipe

PHALAROPES *Phalaropodidae*

Small, short-billed waders that spend much of the time swimming, and winter at sea. There are two Holarctic species, nesting in Arctic to Subarctic regions with extensive overlap of general range. In North America the larger, longer-billed Wilson's Phalarope *Phalaropus tricolor* also occurs, breeding in inland Temperate regions.

Grey Phalarope *Phalaropus fulicarius*
(Map 247)
Migrant; breeding in the Arctic zone and wintering in the Subtropical zone. It breeds on the edge of fresh water in low-lying grassy moss tundra south to *c.* 10°C July isotherm limit. It winters at sea off West Africa and southern Arabia in latitudes 10–25° north.

247 Grey Phalarope

Wood Snipe

Jack Snipe

Painted Snipe

Grey Phalarope

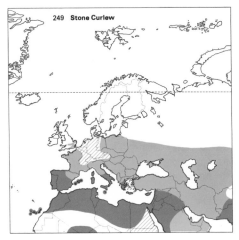

Red-necked Phalarope *Phalaropus lobatus*
(Map 248)
Migrant; breeding in Arctic to Subarctic zones, and extending to the Scandinavian Arctic/Alpine zone, wintering in the Subtropical zone. It breeds on the edges of fresh water in grassy moss tundra, shrub tundra and into the birch zone, in both lowland and montane habitats, to a southern *c.* 17°C July isotherm limit. It winters at sea off West Africa and southern Arabia, in a more northerly limit than the previous species.

STONE CURLEWS *Burhinidae*

Large, short-billed wading birds, crepuscular in habit and usually occurring as running birds on open dry habitats. The Stone Curlew is found from Europe to South-east Asia, but with no replacement in China. There are three species in Africa, two by water, one in dry areas; two in South America, one in grassland the other in desert; and one in scrub in Australia. In addition there are two larger species, the Great Stone Curlew of Indian rivers and coasts, and the Beach Curlew *Esacus magnirostris* of sea coasts from Malaya to Australia.

Stone Curlew *Burhinus oedicnemus*
(Map 249)
Resident and migrant; breeding in Temperate to Subtropical zones, wintering in Warm Temperate to Subtropical zones. It occurs on dry grassland, well-drained arable land, shingle and stony shores of slow rivers, dry mudflats, *Salicornia* heaths, sand dunes, sparsely vegetated *Artemesia* and grass steppe, stony, sand or clay plains, and sand or stony deserts, but requires in such areas some shrubby growth and herbage. It has a poor tolerance of human disturbance and has decreased in western Europe.

Great Stone Curlew *Esacus recurvirostris*
(Map 250)
Resident, with some local movements; in the Subtropical zone. It occurs on bare shores and sandbanks of large, slow-moving rivers, and on bare areas, rocky stretches and dry floodplain zones bordering their lower reaches. Occasionally on estuaries, salt pans and sea coast beaches. It may appear and disappear seasonally in some areas.

Red-necked Phalarope   Stone Curlew   Great Stone Curlew

Senegal Thick-knee   *Burhinus senegalensis*
(Map 251)
Resident; in the Subtropical to Tropical zones.
Its range extends through north-east Africa
and across the southern edge of the Sahara
into West Africa. It occurs in dry places but
is usually found on bare sandy areas on the
edges of large rivers and lakes, and may utilise
smaller wet areas and spread to cultivated
gardens. It is always more closely associated
with water than the Stone Curlew.

251 Senegal Thick-knee

PRATINCOLES AND COURSERS   *Glareolidae*

A small family of two distinct groups of short-
billed waders. The pratincoles, with two
species in the present area, are swallow-like
birds that feed in the air; the coursers, with
three present species, are long-legged running
birds of open places, feeding on the ground.
All lay eggs on the ground with little or no
nest. The three Eurasian pratincoles (map 252)
are sometimes treated as races of a single
species. They differ in the colours of under-
wings, and tail length, and show some overlap
of breeding distribution. The Collared Pratincole has a Warm Temperate distribution,
the Black-winged Pratincole occurs in grassy

steppe regions, and the Eastern Pratincole
Glareola maldivarum in south-eastern Subtropical regions. Within the range of the last
species the smaller Little Pratincole *G. lactea*
occurs, nesting on river sandbanks. The
Cream-coloured Courser is a desert species,
replaced in dry but less desert habitats in India
by the Indian Courser, and by a small group of
species in Africa south of the Sahara. The
Egyptian Plover is an isolate species occurring
only on waterside sands in Africa.

Collared Pratincole   *Glareola pratincola*
(Maps 252, 253)
Migrant; breeding in the Warm Temperate
zone, wintering in Subtropical to Tropical

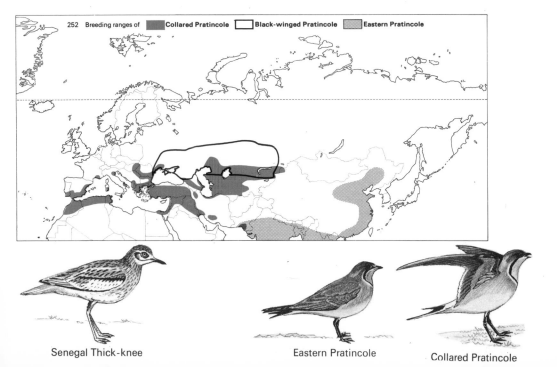

252 Breeding ranges of ▨ Collared Pratincole ☐ Black-winged Pratincole ▨ Eastern Pratincole

Senegal Thick-knee   Eastern Pratincole   Collared Pratincole

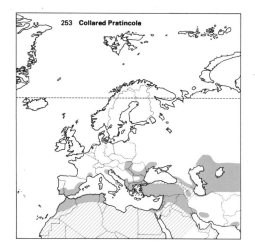

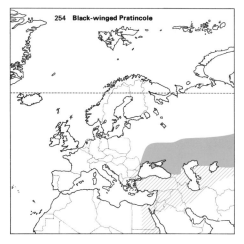

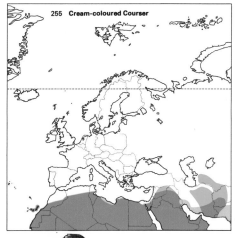

zones. It breeds in open places, usually close to water, on short or sparse grass or herbage, expanses of dry bare mud on shores of shallow lakes or lagoons, fresh or salt, by pools in bare or grassy steppes, or on burnt-over grassland. It is a wide-ranging species and an erratic and irregular nester at some sites. It winters near water in savannah and dry grass areas across Africa south of the Sahara, and on coastal and river mudflats, deltas and lagoons.

Black-winged Pratincole *Glareola nordmanni*
(Maps 252, 254)
Migrant; breeding in the Temperate steppe zone, wintering in Subtropical to Tropical zones. It breeds, like the previous species, on open sites near fresh or brackish water. It occurs on dry mud and salt flats, beaches of inland seas, salt or short-grass steppes, grass meadows and bare cultivated areas, open ground with sparse herbage, damp meadows and grassy marshland. It winters in Africa south of the Sahara, occurring further south than the previous species, on open grassland, bare cleared land and sandy river banks.

Cream-coloured Courser *Cursorius cursor*
(Map 255)
Partly resident, but migrant in some eastern parts of its range; in Subtropical to Tropical zones. It occurs in open arid areas but usually with some scanty vegetation, in clay or sand desert, and semi-desert with sparse scrub. Although it occurs through true desert regions it is absent from areas of extreme desert conditions. It is a strong flier and may occur accidentally at some distance from the normal range.

Indian Courser *Cursorius coromandelicus*
(Map 256)
Resident, with possible local movements; in fairly dry Subtropical zones. It occurs in dry areas, but not the desert areas favoured by the previous species, nesting in dry scrub, sparse vegetation, and in cultivated and grazed areas of an arid type.

Egyptian Plover *Pluvianus aegyptius*
(Map 257)
Resident; in Subtropical to Tropical zones. It occurs through the northern half of afro-tropical Africa on sandy shores and sandbanks of rivers and lakes.

Black-winged Pratincole

Cream-coloured Courser

Indian Courser

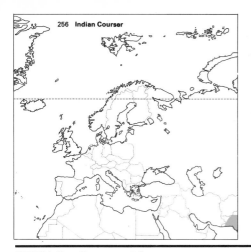

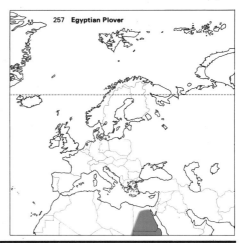

SKUAS *Stercorariidae*

Four species of gull-like seabirds, hunting and also obtaining food by forcing other seabirds to disgorge it; breeding in open places, nesting on the ground, often in groups or colonies, and spending most of the non-breeding period at sea. The largest, the Great Skua, occurs extensively in the Antarctic, where a second closely related species is present, and the very restricted Northern Hemisphere distribution from Britain to Iceland suggests a recent invasion of the north via the Atlantic. The other three are tundra-breeding birds with Holarctic, circumpolar distributions overlapping extensively. Of these, the Pomarine Skua is a slightly larger bird of coastal and inland tundra, and the Great Skua when breeding occupies part of the limited area of the Arctic where the former does not occur. The Arctic Skua breeds in similar habitats and on low rocky coasts and islands, extending further north, while the Long-tailed Skua has a similar distribution to the last but on drier, more montane and less coastal sites.

Great Skua *Stercorarius skua* (Map 258)
Migrant; breeding in Boreal to Subarctic zones, wintering in Temperate to Warm Temperate seas. It occurs by rocky coasts on open moorland and grassland, usually near seabird colonies. When not breeding it is an oceanic, far-ranging species. It has occurred north to Spitzbergen and has bred on Bear Island, and has increased around Scotland and decreased in Iceland during the present century.

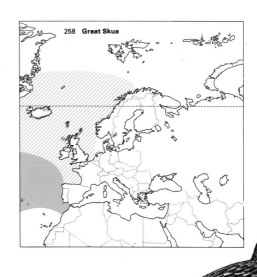

Egyptian Plover

Great Skua

Arctic Skua   *Stercorarius parasiticus*
(Map 259)
Migrant; breeding in the Arctic zone but extending into the Boreal coastland zone in the north-east Atlantic and wintering in southern Warm Temperate to Temperate zones. It breeds on low-lying moist tundra, coasts, and low rocky islands, and in the more southerly part of the range on open moorland. It usually breeds colonially. It migrates frequently along coasts, and winters in the southern ocean at *c*. 30–50° latitudes.

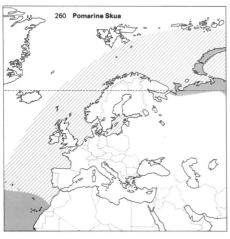

Pomarine Skua   *Stercorarius pomarinus*
(Map 260)
Migrant; breeding in the Arctic zone, wintering in Subtropical to Tropical seas. It breeds in low-lying moist moss tundra on coastal and slightly hilly inland sites. It winters at sea, often far out in oceanic waters.

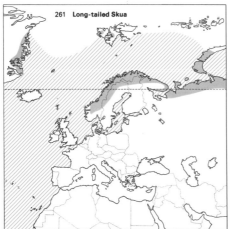

Long-tailed Skua   *Stercorarius longicaudus*
(Map 261)
Migrant; breeding in the Arctic/Alpine zone, and wintering at sea into southern zones. It breeds on drier, higher moss and lichen tundra, and on rocky plateaus, bare high moorland and shrub tundra. The breeding distribution is linked to some extent to the availability of lemmings. In winter it is an ocean wanderer and its movements are very imprecisely known.

Arctic Skua   Pomarine Skua   Long-tailed Skua

GULLS AND TERNS *Laridae*

Large to small scavengers, mainly seabirds; the large ones sometimes predators, the smaller often taking invertebrates. Often colonial breeders; nesting on the ground or on a rock ledge. There is a complex group of mainly medium to small, inland and coastal dark-headed species; a smaller group of mainly coastal and marine larger species; and a residue of more specialised, smaller white-headed birds.

DARK-HEADED GULLS some *Larus* species (Maps 262, 263)

It is not certain that the dark head implies close relationship. The more tern-like Sabine's Gull nests on Arctic shores and winters well south at sea. The Black-headed and Little Gulls occupy a broad Boreal to Temperate zone. In the latter species it is discontinuous and there is an extreme eastern isolate species, the Chinese Little Gull *Larus saundersi*, the breeding ground of which is still unknown. The large Great Black-headed Gull occupies a central steppe zone, very fragmented and extending to western China. The Relict Gull *L. relictus* breeds at Lake Alakul, within the range of the former species, and on some lakes around the north-east Mongolian border. In the south-west the Mediterranean Gull has a limited Warm Temperate distribution; and the Brown-headed Gull *L. brunnicephalus*, sometimes regarded as a close relative of the former,

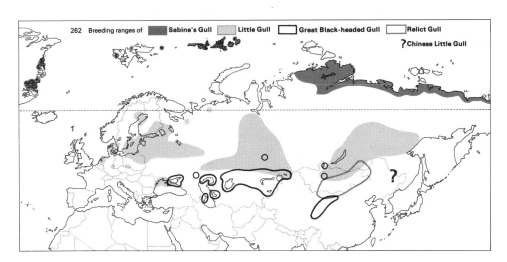

262 Breeding ranges of ■ Sabine's Gull ▨ Little Gull □ Great Black-headed Gull □ Relict Gull
? Chinese Little Gull

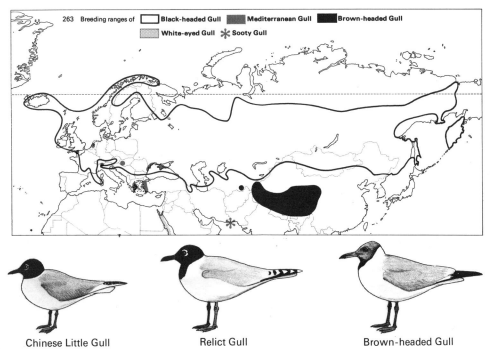

263 Breeding ranges of □ Black-headed Gull ▨ Mediterranean Gull ■ Brown-headed Gull
▨ White-eyed Gull ✳ Sooty Gull

Chinese Little Gull   Relict Gull   Brown-headed Gull

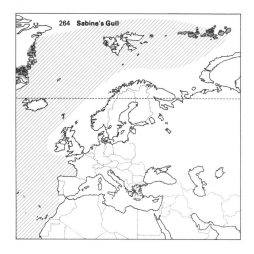

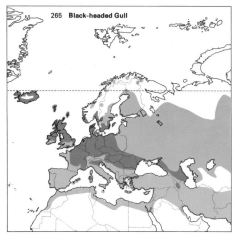

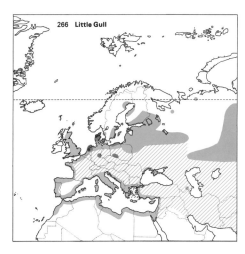

is a species of cool, montane regions, breeding on the Tibetan-Himalayan plateau. In the seas around the Arabian area are two dark-headed forms, the Sooty Gull and the White-eyed Gull. It has been suggested that the last two and the Great Black-headed Gull may be more closely related to the larger White-headed Gulls than to the other dark-headed forms.

Sabine's Gull   *Larus sabini* (Maps 262, 264)
Migrant; breeding in the Arctic zone and wintering at sea in the south. It breeds in swampy areas of low-lying tundra with freshwater pools, sea coasts bordering low tundra and small low coastal islands with grassy or tundra vegetation. In winter it is oceanic, movements not certainly known, but occurring in numbers off the western coast of southern Africa.

Black-headed Gull   *Larus ridibundus*
(Maps 263, 265)
Resident, dispersive and migrant; breeding in Boreal to Temperate zones, wintering in western Temperate to Warm Temperate zones. It breeds, between *c.* 43° and 56° latitudes, on grassy sites in small to large swamps, fens, wet grasslands, saltmarshes, dunes, by fresh and saline pools, lakes and rivers, and occasionally on drier grassland and moorland. It occurs in both open country and forest areas, usually nesting colonially. In winter it occurs around open waters, marshes, coasts, farmland, and increasingly as a scavenger in man-made habitats. It has increased its range, colonising Norway and Iceland in the last hundred years and extending northwards.

Little Gull   *Larus minutus* (Maps 262, 266)
Mainly migrant, with very limited resident zone in north-west Europe; breeding in Boreal to Temperate zones and wintering on coasts in Temperate to Warm Temperate zones. It breeds by freshwater pools and on marshes, fens, bogs and wet grasslands, requiring waters rich in aquatic and emergent vegetation. A rather sporadic and erratic breeder. It winters on coasts, at sea, and to a lesser extent on large inland waters.

Great Black-headed Gull   *Larus ichthyaetus*
(Maps 262, 267)
Migrant, resident in limited area around Crimea; breeding in Warm Temperate steppe and semi-desert zones, wintering in coastal

Sabine's Gull   Black-headed Gull   Little Gull   Great Black-headed Gull

267   Great Black-headed Gull

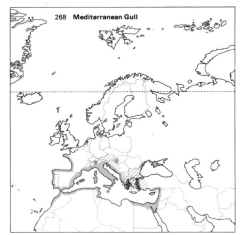

268   Mediterranean Gull

269   Sooty Gull

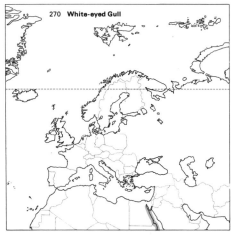

270   White-eyed Gull

Warm Temperate zone. It breeds on shores of low-lying steppe lakes, inland seas and deltas, with a scattered and disruptive distribution across to Mongolia and China. It winters on and near the coasts of warmer seas, and on nearby lakes and marshland.

Mediterranean Gull   *Larus melanocephalus*
(Maps 263, 268)
Migrant; breeding and wintering in the Warm Temperate zone. It breeds in a limited area around the Aegean and Black Seas, with sporadic and scattered breeding of odd pairs further west to between Spain and Britain. The nesting is like that of the Black-headed Gull, with which it sometimes occurs, but with greater use of estuarine saltmarshes. It winters mainly on sea coasts.

Sooty Gull   *Larus hemprichii* (Maps 263, 269)
Migrant, in the Subtropical zone. It breeds on offshore islands from East Africa and the southern Red Sea to the coast of Pakistan; nesting in solitary pairs rather than in colonies. In winter it disperses along the coasts.

White-eyed Gull   *Larus leucophthalmus*
(Maps 263, 270)
Migrant; in the Subtropical zone. Breeding in the Red Sea and dispersing southwards in winter. It breeds in colonies on islands; feeding mainly on fish, caught at sea, and is more marine than the previous species.

Mediterranean Gull   Sooty Gull   White-eyed Gull

LARGER WHITE-HEADED GULLS
some *Larus* species
Of the largest gulls, the Glaucous Gull has a circumpolar Arctic distribution, with the Great Black-backed Gull in the Boreal region of the North Atlantic and a replacement species, the Slaty-backed Gull *Larus schistisagus*, in the North Pacific. The Herring Gull group also has a pale northern Palaearctic form, the Iceland Gull, nesting in Greenland. In Eurasia a yellow-legged form occurs along the northern tundra, with a second population from the Canary Islands and Mediterranean to western China, the two connecting in mid-Siberia. From mid-Siberia eastwards the tundra form becomes increasingly pink-legged. The northern Russian form has a distinctly dark grey back and yellow legs and in Scandinavia a darker-backed form apparently derived from this has become a separate species, the Lesser Black-headed Gull, sharing most of its range with a presumed extension of range of the American pink-legged Herring Gull. As mentioned earlier, it has been suggested that some of the more southerly dark-headed forms may be most closely related to this group.

Glaucous Gull   *Larus hyperboreus* (Map 271)
Dispersive, resident in some areas; breeding in the Arctic zone, some wintering in Subarctic to Boreal zones and exceptionally northern Temperate zone. It breeds on rocky coasts and islands, usually on cliffs and stacks, nesting in colonies. It winters on coasts. It underwent a slight northward shift in the earlier part of the century.

Great Black-backed Gull   *Larus marinus* (Map 272)
Resident and dispersive; breeding in Subarctic to northern Temperate zones, some wintering in coastal Temperate to Warm Temperate zones. It breeds on rocky coasts and small islands, usually in scattered pairs, rarely colonially. It winters on coasts and estuaries, and may use inland feeding sites. It has increased and spread north-west in the present century, its shift matching that of the Glaucous Gull, both probably in response to climatic changes.

Glaucous Gull

Great Black-backed Gull

Iceland Gull   *Larus glaucoides* (Map 273)
Dispersive and resident; in the Arctic zone, wintering in Subarctic to Boreal zones. It occurs on rocky coasts, usually nesting colonially on cliff sites. Winters on coasts.

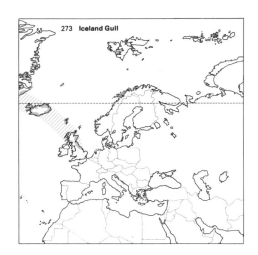

Herring Gull   *Larus argentatus* (Map 274)
Resident and dispersive; breeding in Subarctic to Warm Temperate zones and wintering in Temperate to Warm Temperate zones. It breeds colonially on all types of coasts, on estuaries, rivers and the beaches of fresh and saline inland lakes; using islands, rock ledges, dunes, beaches and moorland sites, and occasionally roofs of buildings. It winters on coasts and inland waters, on cultivated areas, and as a scavenger of refuse on coasts and inland. Like other large gulls it has spread northwards in the present century and has considerably increased in numbers in recent years.

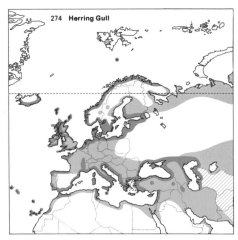

Lesser Black-backed Gull   *Larus fuscus* (Map 275)
Migrant and resident; breeding in Subarctic to northern Temperate zones, wintering in western Temperate to Subtropical zones. It breeds on rocky islands, on coasts and inland lakes, on dunes, moorland, and swampy grassland; nesting in colonies. Where it occurs with Herring Gulls it tends to prefer more level sites. It winters on coastal areas, along rivers and on inland lakes; some moving as far as West and East Africa. It is increasing in Britain, and has colonised Denmark, the Netherlands and Iceland since 1920.

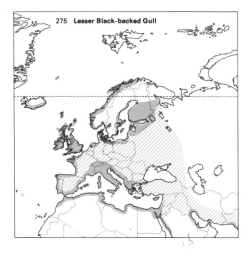

Iceland Gull

Herring Gull

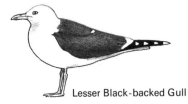

Lesser Black-backed Gull

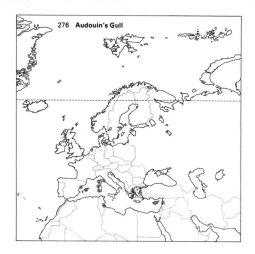

276 Audouin's Gull

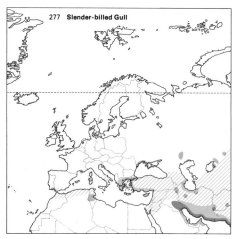

277 Slender-billed Gull

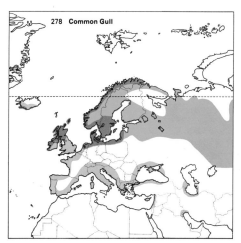

278 Common Gull

SMALLER WHITE-HEADED GULLS some *Larus* species, *Rissa* and *Pagophila* species

These smaller gulls are a heterogeneous group of five unrelated species. There are two southern species of a relict type. Audouin's Gull is a marine type, nesting mainly on islands and occurring in the Mediterranean. The Slender-billed Gull is a more inland species breeding around lagoons and shallow waters of the Mediterranean and steppe regions. It may be most closely related to the dark-headed gulls. The Common Gull is a mainly Subarctic to Boreal species, its breeding range extending right across Eurasia and into western North America. The Ring-billed Gull *Larus dela-warensis* appears to be a North American replacement species. These are inland to coastal species. The Kittiwake is a marine species with a discontinuous circumpolar breeding range on Arctic to Boreal coasts. In the North Pacific a second species, the Red-legged Kittiwake *Rissa brevirostris*, is also present. The Ivory Gull is a purely Arctic species, breeding in the Arctic regions and wintering along the edge of the polar ice.

Audouin's Gull   *Larus audouinii* (Map 276)
Resident; in the Warm Temperate zone. It breeds mainly on islands, sometimes on coasts, on both sand and rocks; nesting colonially. It feeds mainly at sea. It appears to be decreasing in numbers.

Slender-billed Gull   *Larus genei* (Map 277)
Migrant and resident; breeding in Temperate steppe to Warm Temperate zones, wintering in the Warm Temperate zone. It breeds in a very discontinuous range, east to the upper basin of the Ob; occurring on fresh and brackish lagoons and temporary waters in drier steppe and semi-desert regions, on small coastal islands, on large deltas and coastal grasslands, inland wide valleys and swampy grasslands with open water. It usually breeds in small colonies. It winters mainly along coasts.

Common Gull   *Larus canus* (Map 278)
Migrant and resident; breeding in Subarctic to northern Temperate zones, wintering in coastal Boreal to Warm Temperate zones. It breeds inland on low-lying and montane lakes and on wider rivers, in both open areas and

Audouin's Gull   Slender-billed Gull

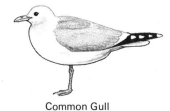

Common Gull

forest, and on all types of coasts; nesting in colonies or scattered pairs. It winters on and near coasts and on inland waters, often feeding on cultivation or wet grasslands. It has increased in the present century, colonising the Faeroes *c*. 1890, the Netherlands in 1908, and Iceland *c*. 1950.

Kittiwake   *Rissa tridactyla* (Map 279)
Dispersive and migrant; breeding in Arctic to Subarctic zones, extending into Boreal and Temperate zones on the Atlantic seaboard, and wintering at sea in Boreal to Warm Temperate zones. It breeds in colonies, usually on steep rock faces, on cliffs, stacks, rocky islands and occasionally on buildings. Except when breeding it occurs at sea, extending right across the ocean. It has been increasing in numbers for some decades, probably after an earlier decrease.

Ivory Gull   *Pagophila eburnea* (Map 280)
Migrant; breeding and wintering in the Arctic zone. It breeds on flat and rugged coasts and on stony coastal plains, nesting in groups of scattered pairs. It winters on open seas along the edge of the pack ice, and exceptionally single individuals straggle further south.

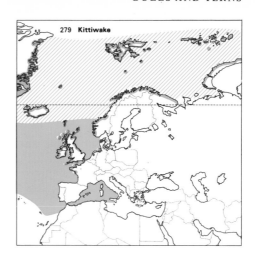

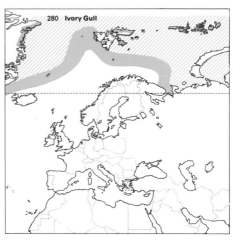

GULL-BILLED TERNS   *Gelochelidon* species

Gull-billed Tern   *Gelochelidon nilotica* (Map 281)
Mainly migrant, resident in part of the Persian Gulf; breeding in this area mainly in Warm Temperate and steppe zones, and wintering in Warm Temperate to Subtropical zones, but also occurring discontinuously in widely scattered parts of the world. In Europe it has bred occasionally in Britain, the Netherlands, and Italy. It is a more terrestrial, more insect-feeding species than other typical terns. It breeds on shallow saline lakes in steppes, and on fresh and saline lagoons bordered by sand, mud or grassland, or on saltmarsh, or on rivers with stony or sandy shores, on deltas and on river flood-zones. It winters on sea coasts and large lakes.

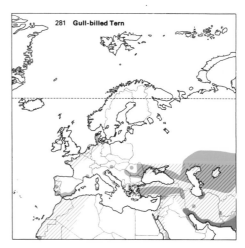

Kittiwake

Ivory Gull

Gull-billed Tern

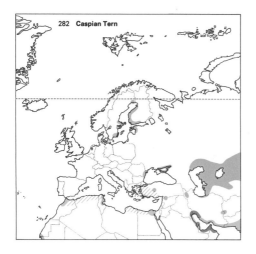

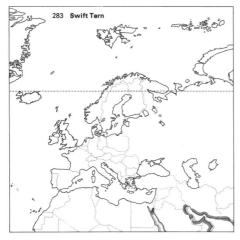

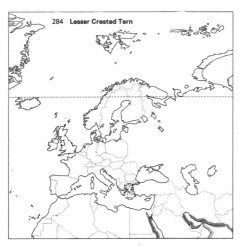

CRESTED SEA TERNS *Hydroprogne* and some *Sterna* species

Four species of generally larger sea terns with shaggy crests and stouter or longer bills. They nest on the ground in close colonies. Of these only the Caspian Tern has an extensive inland distribution, in the steppe region, and like the Gull-billed Tern and other steppe species it has bred in scattered parts of western Europe on occasions. Like other terns it has a generally widely scattered and highly discontinuous distribution in various parts of the world. The other three are coastal terns, but the Sandwich Tern extends to the coasts of inland seas in Eurasia and is otherwise confined to sea coasts of mid- and north Atlantic. The Swift and Lesser Crested Terns differ in size and occupy similar overall ranges on sea coasts of the Indo-Pacific Oceans, south to Australia. A third species, the Chinese Crested Tern *Sterna zimmermanni*, has a very restricted breeding range around the Gulf of Chihli in eastern China.

Caspian Tern *Hydroprogne tschegrava* (Map 282)

Mainly migrant, resident at the head of the Persian Gulf; occurring in widely scattered localities in Boreal to Tropical zones, wintering from the southern edge of the Warm Temperate zone to Tropical zones. It breeds on the bare shores of fresh and saline lakes and inland seas, river flood-zones, estuaries, coastal lagoons and shallow sea coasts. It had bred at various times in north Germany, the Netherlands, Sardinia and Yugoslavia. It winters on large freshwater lakes and coastal lagoons.

Swift Tern *Sterna bergi* (Map 283)

Resident and dispersive; in Subtropical to Tropical zones. It breeds on islands and sea coasts, on sand, rock or coral. It feeds at sea and rarely occurs inland.

Lesser Crested Tern *Sterna bengalensis* (Map 284)

Resident and dispersive; in Subtropical to Tropical zones. It breeds on islands and sea coasts; and in preferences and behaviour is very similar to the previous species.

Caspian Tern   Swift Tern   Lesser Crested Tern

Sandwich Tern   *Sterna sandvicensis*
(Map 285)
Migrant; breeding in Temperate to Subtropical zones, wintering in Subtropical to Tropical zones. It breeds on open or partly vegetated areas of beaches, dunes and grassy areas by sea coasts or lake shores, or on deltas or offshore islands. It winters mainly on sea coasts, the western European population moving to West African waters, between the 20° latitudes but mainly north of the Equator.

TYPICAL SEA TERNS   some *Sterna* species
Seven species, smaller than the previous ones, but like them mostly occurring on sea coasts and nesting on the ground in close colonies. There is some latitudinal replacement. The Arctic Tern is circumpolar at high latitudes, and the Common Tern replaces it in Boreal to Temperate zones, with some coastal overlap. The latter has a broad Holarctic distribution, except in western North America where Forster's Tern *S. forsteri* replaces it. In the Bering Sea area the Aleutian Tern *S. aleutica*, possibly an isolate of this group, breeds in parts of coastal Alaska and eastern Siberia. In the Indian and South-east Asian region there are two apparent replacement species occurring inland, the Indian River Tern *S. aurantia* on the larger rivers, estuaries and lakes, and the slightly smaller Black-bellied Tern *S. acuticauda* on a variety of smaller waters. The remaining species are coastal; the White-cheeked Tern on northern Indian Ocean sea coasts and both the Roseate and Bridled Terns with widely scattered coastal colonies, mostly in warmer regions, while the Little Tern is smaller than the others and overlaps them in a wide discontinuous distribution, Temperate to Tropical. On the northeast African to Indian sea coasts it is replaced by the very similar Black-shafted Tern.

Arctic Tern   *Sterna paradisaea* (Map 286)
Migrant; breeding in Arctic to Subarctic zones and into north Temperate zones on the Atlantic seaboard, and wintering in the Antarctic seas. It breeds on beaches and bare shores of coasts and rivers, on low rocky islands, bare rocky or rock and grass shores, coastal salt-marshes, coastal tundra and inland wet tundra with pools and lakes. Where it overlaps with the Common Tern it is more of a seabird and utilises the barer breeding sites. It winters at sea, making a journey between the two polar regions.

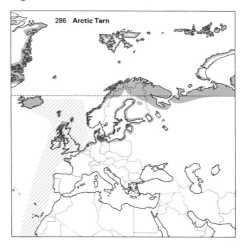

Sandwich Tern

Arctic Tern

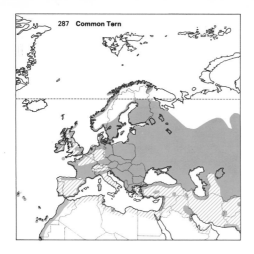

287   Common Tern

Common Tern   *Sterna hirundo* (Map 287)
Migrant; breeding in Boreal to Warm Temperate zones, and into the Subarctic zone on the Atlantic seaboard, wintering in Tropical seas. Where there is water it breeds inland as well as coastally; on beaches and bare shores of sea coasts, estuaries, rivers, lagoons, gravelpits and lakes, on sand dunes, salt and fresh marshes, and on islands off rocky coasts. It prefers shallow waters. The European population winters mainly off West Africa between the 20° latitudes but mainly north of the Equator.

Roseate Tern   *Sterna dougallii* (Map 288)
Migrant; with an odd, scattered distribution, in the western Palaearctic along Temperate coasts affected by the North Atlantic Drift current, in the western Mediterranean, and in the Red Sea. It breeds on beaches and islands of sandy and rocky coasts, feeding at sea and nesting in scattered and fluctuating colonies. The European population migrates to the seas off West Africa between *c.* 0–10°C north latitudes.

288   Roseate Tern

White-cheeked Tern   *Sterna repressa*
(Map 289)
Migrant and dispersive, in Subtropical to Tropical zones. It breeds on rocky and sandy offshore islands, and when not breeding occurs at sea.

Little Tern   *Sterna albifrons* (Map 290)
Migrant; breeding in Temperate to Warm Temperate zones, wintering in the Tropi-

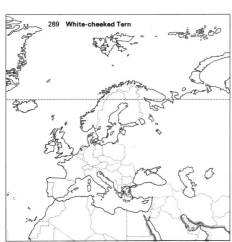

289   White-cheeked Tern

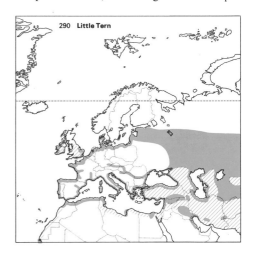

290   Little Tern

Common Tern

Roseate Tern

White-cheeked Tern

Little Tern

cal zone. It breeds on bare shores and sand, shingle, and mud banks of shallow sea coasts, estuaries and the larger rivers, and on rocky shores; usually in small colonies or scattered pairs. It winters on Subtropical to Tropical sea coasts.

Black-shafted Tern   *Sterna saundersi* (Map 291)
Dispersive; in Subtropical to Tropical zones. It breeds on sea coasts in similar fashion to the Little Tern, and is sometimes regarded as a race of the latter.

Bridled Tern   *Sterna anaethetus* (Map 292)
Dispersive, possibly migrant; in Subtropical to Tropical zones. It breeds on islands and sea coasts, on sandy and rocky areas, at times with shrubby vegetation. It is an oceanic species, using deeper sea waters than some other species, and when not breeding may occur well out at sea.

––––––––––––––––––––––––––––––––

MARSH TERNS *Chlidonias* species
Three species of inland, mainly insect-eating terns, nesting in colonies on floating vegetation or marshy ground. The Whiskered Tern occurs over much of the Old World between the 50° latitudes. The White-winged Black Tern occurs from eastern China and Siberia across to eastern Europe in Temperate to Warm Temperate zones, with a break in distribution in the Siberian Altai region. The Black Tern occurs through North America and from the west coast of Europe across to the Altai in similar zones. It is possible that the latter has a North American or Atlantic coast evolutionary origin and that the White-winged Black Tern is of more eastern origin.

Black Tern   *Chlidonias niger* (Map 293)
Migrant; breeding in southern Boreal to Warm Temperate zones and wintering in Subtropical to Tropical zones. It breeds on large freshwater marshes with open water and reedy growth, on large lakes bordered with reeds or swampy grasses, and slow-moving rivers. There may be sporadic extensions of breeding on the north-west edge of its range. On passage and in winter it occurs on coastal waters, as well as inland lakes. It winters in central Africa and northern Africa south and east of the Sahara.

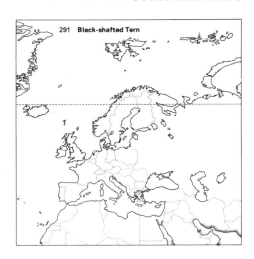

291   Black-shafted Tern

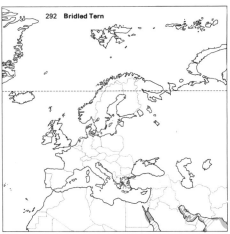

292   Bridled Tern

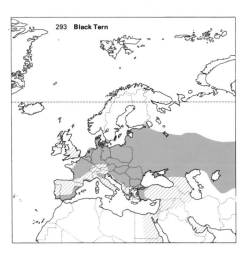

293   Black Tern

Black-shafted Tern

Bridled Tern

Black Tern

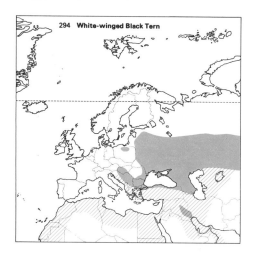

294   White-winged Black Tern

White-winged Black Tern *Chlidonias leucopterus* (Map 294)
Migrant; breeding in southern Boreal to Warm Temperate zones and wintering in Subtropical to Tropical zones. It usually breeds in similar habitats to the Black Tern, but can utilise drier marshlands. It shows a greater tendency to sporadic nesting to the west of its range, and has nested in Belgium, Germany, Austria, southern France and Corsica, and in the last century in North Africa. It winters in Africa south of the Sahara and in India, South-east Asia and southern China, but unlike the Black Tern does not usually occur on sea coasts.

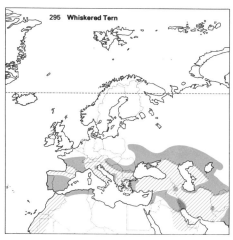

295   Whiskered Tern

Whiskered Tern *Chlidonias hybrida* (Map 295)
Migrant; breeding in southern Temperate to Warm Temperate zones, wintering in Subtropical to Tropical zones. It breeds mainly on the dense aquatic vegetation of usually freshwater marshes and reedy lakes. Like the other species it breeds sporadically in the north-west and has bred in the Netherlands, Belgium and Switzerland. It winters in the northern half of Africa south of the Sahara and in India where it is resident; occurring on fresh waters and on saline lagoons.

AUKS   *Alcidae*

Six species of diving seabird, medium-sized to small, catching food underwater, living mainly at sea and nesting on coasts. They occur on both shores of the North Atlantic and two have Bering Sea–North Pacific populations. The latter region has a larger and more complex auk population than the North Atlantic. The Guillemot and Brünnich's Guillemot nest on open ledges of cliffs, the former in Warm Temperate to Subarctic zones, the latter in the Arctic zone; but in the Bering Sea there is considerable overlap. The Razorbill occupies a similar habitat from northern Temperate to Subarctic zones, nesting in deeper cliff crevices

and cavities. The Puffin nests in Temperate to Arctic zones of the Atlantic with the closely related Horned Puffin *Fratercula corniculata* replacing it in the Bering Sea and North Pacific. It breeds mainly in burrows on clifftop turf. The Black Guillemot is a North Atlantic and Arctic Sea species from the northern Temperate zone northwards. In the North Pacific a very similar species, the Pigeon Guillemot *Cepphus columba*, occurs; while a third species, the Dusky Guillemot *Cepphus carbo*, is present in a limited area of the eastern seaboard of Eurasia. These are species of more sheltered waters, nesting in cavities and crevices. The Little Auk is a very small species breeding between west Greenland and Sever-

White-winged Black Tern

Whiskered Tern

naya Zemlya. It nests in rock falls and small crevices. In addition, in the North Pacific region there is a complex of nine other small auk species.

Razorbill   *Alca torda* (Map 296)
Dispersive and migrant; breeding in Subarctic to cooler Temperate zones in the region of the North Atlantic Drift current, and in the Baltic, in seas with surface temperatures of $c. 0°–10°C$ in summer, wintering in Arctic to Warm Temperate Atlantic waters. It breeds colonially in scattered pairs in recesses and crevices of cliffs, and among boulders, on rocky coasts and offshore islands. It feeds and winters in shallow coastal seas.

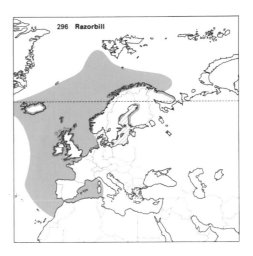

Guillemot   *Uria aalge* (Map 297)
Dispersive and migrant; in Arctic to Warm Temperate zones, in the region of the North Atlantic Drift current in areas with summer temperatures of $c.0°–15°C$. It breeds usually in close colonies on rock ledges of cliffs, or on rock stacks. It feeds and winters at sea, often occurring in deeper waters than the Razorbill.

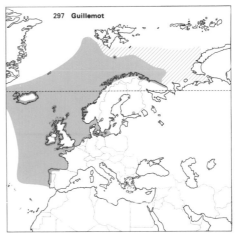

Brünnich's Guillemot   *Uria lomvia* (Map 298)
Migrant; breeding in Arctic to Subarctic zones and wintering mainly in Arctic to Boreal seas of the north-west Atlantic. It breeds on very similar sites to the Guillemot, mainly in more northerly areas but with a zone of overlap. In winter it is a more oceanic species than the previous two, and may dive deeply for fish.

Razorbill   Guillemot   Brunnich's Guillemot

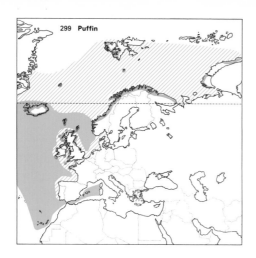

Puffin   *Fratercula arctica* (Map 299)
Migrant and dispersive; breeding in Arctic to cooler Temperate zones in the region of the North Atlantic Drift current with summer sea temperatures of *c.* 0°–17°C, wintering in Boreal to Warm Temperate seas. It breeds mainly in burrows on rocky coasts, sometimes in rock crevices, on coasts and offshore islands. It winters at sea, usually well away from land.

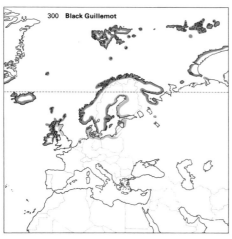

Black Guillemot   *Cepphus grylle* (Map 300)
Resident and migrant; in Arctic to Boreal zones, in the region of the North Atlantic Drift current and in seas with a summer temperature of *c.* 0°–15°C. It breeds in colonies of scattered pairs in cavities and crevices of fallen boulders, talus slopes at cliff bases and on low rocky coasts and islands. It tends to winter mainly in the shallow sheltered waters – bays, inlets and creeks – near the nest colony but with some migration in the Baltic and North Sea areas.

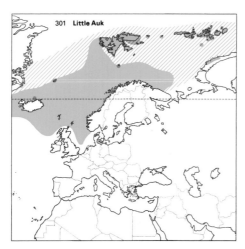

Little Auk   *Alle alle* (Map 301)
Migrant and dispersive; in the Arctic zone in seas with summer surface temperatures of *c.* 0°–5°C, wintering south into Boreal seas. It breeds in colonies in rocky crevices, talus slopes, and in holes and clefts in more level ground; usually on high ground and at times well inland. It winters in cool seas, often well out in the ocean.

Puffin   Black Guillemot   Little Auk

SANDGROUSE   *Pteroclididae*

Squat, pigeon-like desert birds, feeding and
nesting on open ground. They fly strongly and
although living in desert places fly long distances daily to water. Of the eight species, six
are typical desert *Pterocles* species in habitats
that show slight variation. The Spotted and
Crowned Sandgrouse occur through the main
desert regions, the former using sandy areas
and preferring fresh drinking water, the latter
avoiding sand and utilising saline sources.
Lichtenstein's and the Chestnut-bellied Sandgrouse occupy the sparsely vegetated desert
edges with the former in more montane rocky
sites, while the Black-bellied and Pin-tailed
Sandgrouse occupy the cooler Warm Temperate zone, and are migratory to some extent;
with the former tending to occur in more open
sandy areas and avoiding hilly habitats. The
two *Syrrhaptes* species (map 308) occur in
cooler Asian steppe zones, with Pallas's Sandgrouse on lowland steppe and the Tibetan
Sandgrouse in high-altitude areas. The former
is the most irruptive of all steppe species, having occurred at times across most of Europe.

Spotted Sandgrouse   *Pterocles senegallus*
(Map 302)
Mainly resident, but partly migrant in the
east; occurring in the desert Subtropical zone.
It occurs in sandy or rocky desert regions, or
on dry marsh and salt-flats on semi-desert;
and tends not to use highly saline water.

Crowned Sandgrouse   *Pterocles coronatus*
(Map 303)
Resident, with some local movement; occurring in the desert Subtropical zone. It occurs
on level and montane stony desert, and areas
of very sparse grasses. It can utilise saline
water.

Lichtenstein's Sandgrouse   *Pterocles*
lichtensteinii (Map 304)
Resident; in the Subtropical zone. It occurs in
desert areas which are rocky or gravelly with
sparse scrub, in sparse *Acacia* scrub in Africa,
on rocky foothills or dry gullies. In India it
also occurs in bare, burnt areas of savannah or
forest. Where necessary it may descend wells
for water.

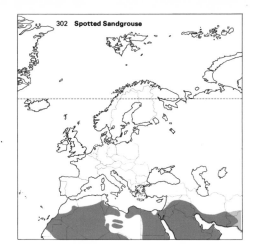

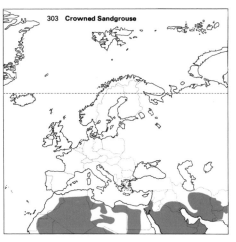

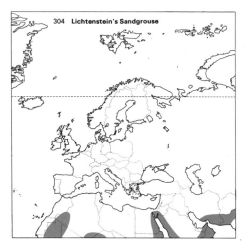

Spotted Sandgrouse

Crowned Sandgrouse

Lichtenstein's Sandgrouse

305 Pin-tailed Sandgrouse

Pin-tailed Sandgrouse *Pterocles alchata* (Map 305)

Resident in the west, and migrant in part of the eastern range; in the Warm Temperate zone. It occurs in arid, desert-type stony or sandy open areas, usually with some sparse vegetation, avoiding total desert, on clay desert with sand ridges, sandy zones bordering rivers, sparsely vegetated sandy steppes, *Salicornia* flats, and exceptionally in dry areas of cultivated crops.

Chestnut-bellied Sandgrouse *Pterocles exustus* (Map 306)

Resident, with some local movements; occurring in the Subtropical zone. It has a very discontinuous distribution, occurring in usually stony semi-desert areas, level or hilly, with thin scrub, and on arid ploughland, fallow and stubbles.

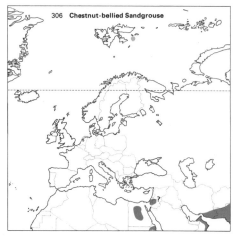

306 Chestnut-bellied Sandgrouse

Black-bellied Sandgrouse *Pterocles orientalis* (Map 307)

Resident and migrant; occurring in Warm Temperate to Temperate steppe zones. It occurs in steppe and montane areas with clay or gravel soils and some grass or sparse *Artemisia* growth, open stony hills, moister plains with herbage, and the borders of cultivated areas. It has been recorded at altitudes of up to 800 m. Where migrant it winters on dry plains, salt-flats and around cultivated land.

Pallas's Sandgrouse *Syrrhaptes paradoxus* (Map 308)

Resident and irruptive; in Temperate steppe zones. It occurs on level or montane grass or *Artemisia* steppes on stabilised soils, and in suitable habitats at altitudes up to 2,500 or exceptionally 3,250 m but usually lower. The species is notorious for periodic and often long-distance irruptions, during which birds may breed well away from the normal range. The movements are usually westerly, and the species has occurred at times over most of Europe, nesting as far afield as Britain, but not establishing itself. On such occasions it occurs on steppe-like short-grass areas, or grassy dunes or beaches.

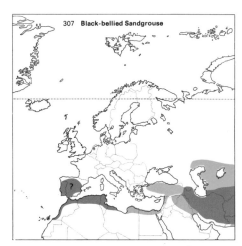

307 Black-bellied Sandgrouse

Tibetan Sandgrouse *Syrrhaptes tibetanus* (Map 308)

Resident; in Arctic/Alpine high altitude zone.

Pin-tailed Sandgrouse   Chestnut-bellied Sandgrouse   Black-bellied Sandgrouse

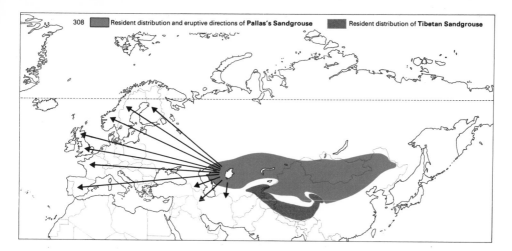

308 ▨ Resident distribution and eruptive directions of **Pallas's Sandgrouse** ▨ Resident distribution of **Tibetan Sandgrouse**

It occurs at high altitudes in the mountains of Tibet, Pamirs and Altai, at 4,400–6,000 m, sometimes down to 3,615 m, on gravelly areas of river valleys and lake depressions, desert plateaus, dune and sand areas, and bare stretches bordering snow-fields. This and the previous species replace each other at different altitudes where the ranges meet.

PIGEONS *Columbidae*

There are twelve medium-sized to small species in the region. Two groups can be recognised, six medium-sized *Columba* species, and six smaller Turtle Dove type birds of mainly warmer regions.

TYPICAL PIGEONS *Columba* species
Of the first group the domesticated form of the Rock Dove has been introduced by man into every part of the world and muddled the distributional picture. As wild birds the ledge and hole-nesters are absent from North America. The rock doves of Eurasia show a triple pattern (map 309) with the wild Rock Dove in the west, east to the Altai; replaced in eastern Eurasia, with a small area of overlap, by the Eastern Rock Dove *Columba rupestris* with similar habitat and temperature range. The Snow Pigeon *C. leuconota* is a replacement species at high altitudes in the Himalayas and Tibet. The hole-nesting Stock Dove has a more limited distribution with a small separate population between Lake Balkhash and Afghanistan, where scattered areas of forest are present. The latter area is also the breeding range of the Eastern Stock Dove, the two oc-

curring together (map 310). The tree-nesting, mainly European Wood Pigeon also has an isolate population in this area. In addition it occurs to a varying degree in the western Himalayas. In the eastern Himalayas there are three tree-nesting *Columba* species – the Purple Wood Pigeon *C. punicea* at lower altitudes, extending into Indochina, the Ashy Wood Pigeon *C. pulchricollis* at higher altitudes from Nepal to northern Thailand, and the Speckled Woodpigeon *C. hodgsonii* at highest altitudes of forest from Kashmir into Burma and western China. These tree-nesters are oddly absent from most of eastern Eurasia. In North America the Band-tailed Pigeon *C. fasciata* may be a partial Wood Pigeon replacement, and the extinct Passenger Pigeon *Ectopistes migratorius* may have been another in the past. On the Atlantic islands early invasions by birds of wood pigeon type may have given rise to the endemic Long-toed and Laurel Pigeons.

Rock Dove *Columba livia* (Map 309)
Resident; as a wild bird in Warm Temperate to Subtropical zones extending to the Temperate zone on the Atlantic seaboard. As a feral bird it may occur in almost any zone. It nests

Pallas's Sandgrouse

Tibetan Sandgrouse

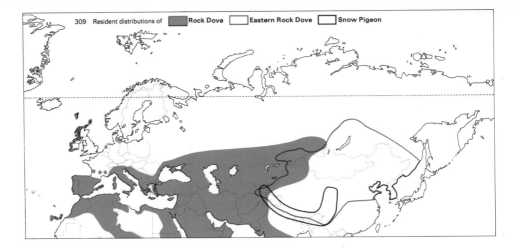

309   Resident distributions of ▊ Rock Dove ☐ Eastern Rock Dove ☐ Snow Pigeon

in caves and crevices, on ledges and in cavities of buildings. It is basically a bird of rocky areas with nearby open space. The last may be bare, stony or with low herbage, and the bird occurs on rocky coasts and islands, in mountains and any areas with rocky outcrops or equivalent sites in open grassland, cultivation or steppe.

Stock Dove   *Columba oenas* (Map 310)

Resident and migrant; in warmer Boreal to Warm Temperate zones. It breeds in cavities in trees or in cliffs, quarries or old buildings, and occasionally will use burrows in the ground or cavities under thick shrubs. It occurs in forest, mainly in more open mixed or broadleaf forest, in broken forest, or on forest edge, open land with small woods, parkland or open cultivated areas with nest sites. In winter it occurs in more open wasteland and cultivated areas. It has been suggested that it has only spread through western Europe – the Netherlands, Britain, France and Spain – in the last hundred years.

Eastern Stock Dove   *Columba eversmanni* (Map 310)

Migrant; breeding in the Warm Temperate steppe zone and wintering in the Subtropical zone. It breeds mainly in lowland, nesting in colonies in holes in cliffs and sometimes in trees. It occurs mainly in lowland open riverine forest and parkland on river plains, in old orchards and less frequently in mountain

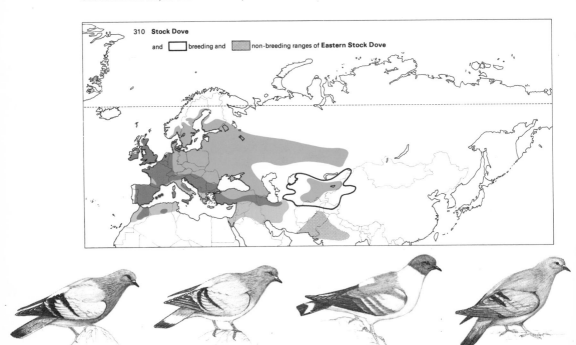

310 **Stock Dove**
and ☐ breeding and ▨ non-breeding ranges of **Eastern Stock Dove**

Rock Dove   Eastern Rock Dove   Snow Pigeon   Stock Dove woodland, usually near water. In winter it occurs on open cultivation with scattered trees or groves.

Wood Pigeon *Columba palumbus* (Map 311)
Resident and migrant; in Boreal to Warm Temperate zones. It builds a nest in a tree or shrub, rarely on a ledge, very exceptionally on the ground. It occurs in forest, particularly broadleaf forest, on forest edge, in parkland, and has adapted itself to farmland and cultivation and more recently to urban areas, utilising anywhere that trees are present. During the last hundred years there has been some northward expansion of the range.

Long-toed Pigeon *Columba trocaz*
(Map 312)
Resident. Sometimes regarded as two species. The typical Trocaz pigeon occurs on Madeira in laurel forest, nesting on cliff ledges or in trees. Its existence is threatened by shooting and deforestation. The other form, Boll's Pigeon *C. t. bollei*, occurs on the Canary Islands in montane laurel forest and like the Madeiran bird is threatened with extinction.

Laurel Pigeon *Columba junoniae* (Map 313)
Resident. Occurs only on the Canary Islands of Palma and Gomera. It occurs in mixed forest or scrub on mountain slopes and may visit open cultivated areas. It is rare and may be extinct on Gomera.

SMALLER DOVES *Streptopelia* and *Oena* species
There are six species. In North America the Mourning Dove *Zenaida macroura* and Ground Dove *Columbagallina passerina* may be equivalent species. The two turtle doves are the most widespread and are mainly migrant, with the typical species in the west, replaced with some overlap by the Eastern Turtle Dove in eastern Eurasia (map 316). The Collared Dove extends in a discontinuous distribution across Eurasia, replaced in the south Sahara and Red Sea region by the African Collared Dove. In India and South-east Asia it overlaps extensively with the Spotted Dove *Streptopelia chinensis*. The Collared Dove has spread through Europe in recent times, in areas of human habitation and cultivation. The Palm Dove is a smaller species, mainly of warm areas, and like the Collared Dove often associ-

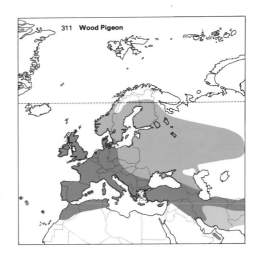

311 Wood Pigeon

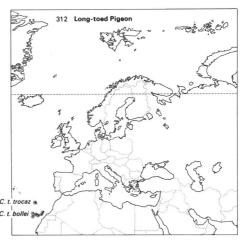

312 Long-toed Pigeon

C. t. trocaz
C. t. bollei

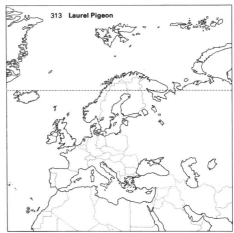

313 Laurel Pigeon

Eastern Stock Dove   Wood Pigeon   Long-toed Pigeon   Laurel Pigeon

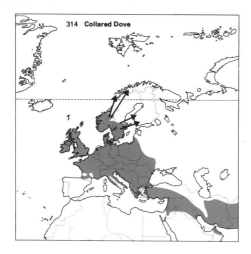

314 Collared Dove

315 African Collared Dove

ated with man. In India it overlaps with the similar-sized Red Collared Dove *S. tranquebarica* which occurs from India through southern China and South-east Asia. The tiny Namaqua Dove *Oena capensis* is one of the small spot-wing doves confined to Africa.

Collared Dove *Streptopelia decaocto* (Map 314)
Resident; in the east in Warm Temperate to Subtropical zones and in Europe spreading into Temperature and warmer Boreal zones. It occurs in drier open areas with scrub or trees and elsewhere has spread through cultivated country in association with grain cultivation and human habitation. This species has spread from Turkey right through Europe, most of this taking place in the present century. There has also been some small spread into Turkmenistan and Japan.

African Collared Dove *Streptopelia roseogrisea* (Map 315)
Resident; in the desert Subtropical zone. In arid desert regions and semi-desert where some scrub is present; thorn or *Acacia* scrub or scattered trees or palm groves.

Turtle Dove *Streptopelia turtur* (Map 316)
Mainly migrant, possibly resident in parts of Africa; breeding in Temperate to Subtropical zones, wintering in Subtropical to Tropical zones. It occurs mainly in open country with scattered trees and scrub, in open forest, riverine forest, parkland with shrubs, cultivated and grassland areas with scattered trees or tall

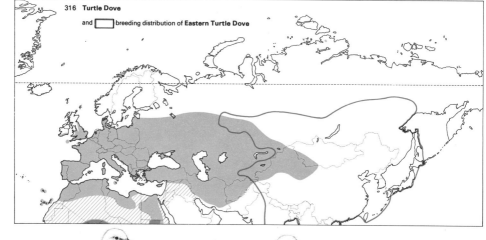

316 Turtle Dove
and ☐ breeding distribution of **Eastern Turtle Dove**

Collared Dove

African Collared Dove

Turtle Dove

hedgerows and scrub, orchards, garden areas, date groves, and sparse growth of trees and shrubs along rivers and around wells in arid open country. In the south of its range it occurs at altitudes of up to 2,500 m. It winters mainly in Africa south of the Sahara and north of the Equator.

Eastern Turtle Dove *Streptopelia orientalis* (Map 316)
Mainly migrant, resident in parts of India and South-east Asia; breeding in Temperate to Subtropical zones, wintering in Subtropical to Tropical zones. It occurs in conifer and broadleaf forest where open spaces are present, in open or broken forest and forest edge, usually near cultivation, in parkland, steppe forest, mountain forest, scrub and cultivation with trees.

Palm Dove *Streptopelia senegalensis* (Map 317)
Mainly resident; in Warm Temperate to Tropical zones. It occurs in areas of dry scrub and thorn scrub but has adapted to man-modified habitats and occurs in cultivated areas, farms, orchards, palm groves, gardens and towns. In Asia it occurs at altitudes of up to 1,600 m.

Namaqua Dove *Oena capensis* (Map 318)
Resident; in Subtropical to Tropical zones. It occurs in arid open country with some scrub, in dry open woodland, cultivated areas and gardens. It has recently spread in central Arabia.

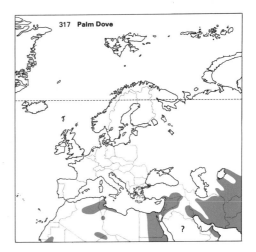

CUCKOOS *Cuculidae*

Medium to small birds of widely varying appearance, ranging from brood parasites of passerine-like appearance to large, aberrant, fast-moving terrestrial forms. There are four species in the present area, three of them parasitic. The Great Spotted Cuckoo is one of a small genus of African, Oriental and Australasian species. It is mainly African but also occurs in the Mediterranean region, parasitising birds of the crow family. The Eurasian Cuckoo occurs throughout Eurasia in a wide variety of habitats, and is replaced in Africa, where it winters, by the similar Red-chested Cuckoo *Cuculus solitarius*. The Eurasian Cuckoo may be of western origin, since the very similar Oriental Cuckoo appears to have evolved in eastern parts, where it occurs in thicker forest which is less used by the other species. The Oriental Cuckoo extends through eastern China into the Himalayas (map 321) and overlaps extensively with the Indian Cuckoo *C. micropterus*, another similar species occurring in India and South-east Asia (where the Eurasian Cuckoo is absent) but in most of the northerly half of its range overlapping with the Oriental Cuckoo. All three species parasitise small songbirds. The situation in southern Asia is complicated by the presence of a number of other smaller and fairly similar species with similar ranges. The last species is the large, skulking and non-parasitic Senegal Coucal, an Africa savannah species with

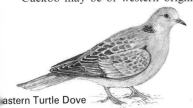

Eastern Turtle Dove

Palm Dove

Namaqua Dove

319 Great Spotted Cuckoo

an outlying population in the Nile Delta region. In North America parasitic cuckoos are absent. There are three slender woodland *Coccyzus* species, and the large, rapid terrestrial Roadrunner *Geococcyx californianus*.

Great Spotted Cuckoo   *Clamator glandarius*
(Map 319)
In Europe mainly migrant; breeding in Warm Temperate to Tropical zones, wintering in Subtropical to Tropical zones. It parasitises birds of the crow family, and occurs in dry savannah with some scrub, scrub with scattered trees, dry parkland, olive groves, open and broken conifer and broadleaf forest, riverine forest and forest edge. The Mediterranean population winters within the range of the species in Africa south of the Sahara.

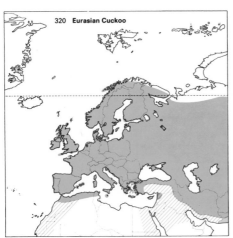

320 Eurasian Cuckoo

Eurasian Cuckoo   *Cuculus canorus*
(Map 320)
Migrant; breeding in Subarctic to Warm Temperate zones and wintering in Subtropical to Tropical zones. It occurs through a great variety of zones from shrub tundra and high, open moorland, through all types of scrub and open or broken forest, parkland, cultivation and gardens, swamps and reedbeds. It is usually absent from the thicker forest, particularly thick conifer forest where it is replaced in the east by the next species. It winters in Africa south of the Sahara and in southern Asia.

Oriental Cuckoo   *Cuculus saturatus*
(Map 321)
Migrant; breeding in Boreal to Temperate

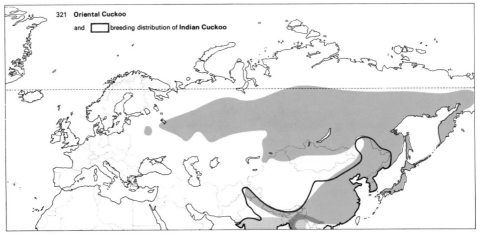

321 Oriental Cuckoo
and ☐ breeding distribution of **Indian Cuckoo**

Great Spotted Cuckoo   Eurasian Cuckoo   Oriental Cuckoo   Indian Cuckoo

zones, and in South-east Asia into the Sub-tropical zone, and wintering in Subtropical to Tropical zones. It occurs in conifer forest including thick forest in lowland and mountains, and in mountain valleys, usually at lower altitudes than the Eurasian Cuckoo but ascending to *c.* 3,000 m in the Himalayas. It extends into mixed forest in the south and into birch and willow scrub in places.

Senegal Coucal   *Centropus senegalensis* (Map 322)

Resident; in Subtropical to Tropical zones. It occurs across Africa south of the Sahara, extending into the Sudan, and with an isolated population in the Nile Delta region. It occurs in thick low vegetation bordering streams and swamps, and in woodland with thick, low shrubs or tall grasses.

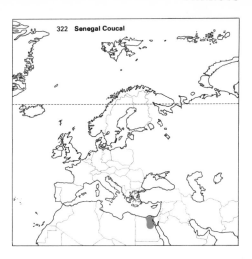

PARROTS   *Psittacidae*

Heavy-billed, mainly arboreal birds of warmer regions, feeding mainly on seeds and fruit, and on nectar in some species.

Ring-necked Parakeet   *Psittacula krameri* (Map 323)

Resident; in the Subtropical region. It occurs in open moist or dry deciduous forest, and has adapted to orchards, gardens, and cultivated areas with trees. It nests in holes in trees or buildings, and is sociable in general behaviour. It has been introduced into Iraq, and to various other places, and in the past into Lower Egypt, and recently in small numbers into southern England where there is no evidence that it is successfully established.

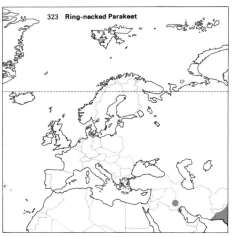

BARN OWLS   *Tytonidae*

A very small family of moderate-sized nocturnal owls: one successful cosmopolitan species, and endemic ones in some warmer regions.

Barn Owl   *Tyto alba* (Map 324)

Resident; in Temperate to Tropical zones. It occurs mainly in more open areas where cavities in rocks, houses or trees are present as nest sites; in marshland, grassland, moorland, parkland and open woodland, scrub, culti-

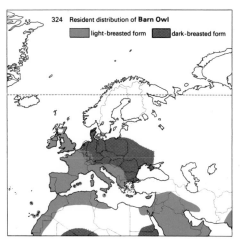

324   Resident distribution of **Barn Owl**
light-breasted form   dark-breasted form

Senegal Coucal   Ring-necked Parakeet   Barn Owl

vated areas and towns. There are a number of populations, suggesting differentiation in isolated units in the past, with light-breasted forms now present in western and southern Europe and the Middle East, and dark-breasted forms in eastern Europe and Africa.

TYPICAL OWLS *Strigidae*

Large to small raptors, mainly nocturnal. Three groups can be recognised – the six larger birds, usually with ear-tufts; six small owls; and five large to medium forest owls.

LARGER OWLS, MAINLY WITH EAR-TUFTS *Nyctea, Bubo, Ketupa* and *Asio* species

Six large to medium-sized owls. Of the three biggest forms the Snowy Owl occurs in the Arctic. The Eagle Owl occupies the main range from Subarctic to Subtropical zones, but in the past separation and temporary isolation have produced a number of forms (map 327). A smaller, paler form of the African desert and Middle East is sometimes separated as a species *Bubo ascalaphus*, and a small dark Indian form as *B. bengalensis*. Tropical speciation has been complex and there are two other eagle owl species in India, and six in Africa. The Brown Fish Owl is a riverine species occurring discontinuously from the Mediterranean to western Siberia (map 326), the isolated north China to Siberia form sometimes regarded as a separate species *Ketupa blakistoni*. In South-east Asia its range overlaps those of two others, the Malaysian Fish Owl *K. ketupa* of wetter and often more coastal regions, and the montane Tawny Fish Owl *K. flavipes*. Of the three *Asio* species, the Long-eared and Short-eared Owls show extensive overlap of general range which tends to conceal the fact that the first is a bird of forest and the other of bare open spaces. The African Marsh Owl is a close relative of the Short-eared Owl, replacing it in the marshy areas of Africa. Snowy, Long-eared and Short-eared Owls all occur also in North America, where the Eagle Owl is replaced by the Great Horned Owl *Bubo virginianus*. The marsh and fish owls are not represented there.

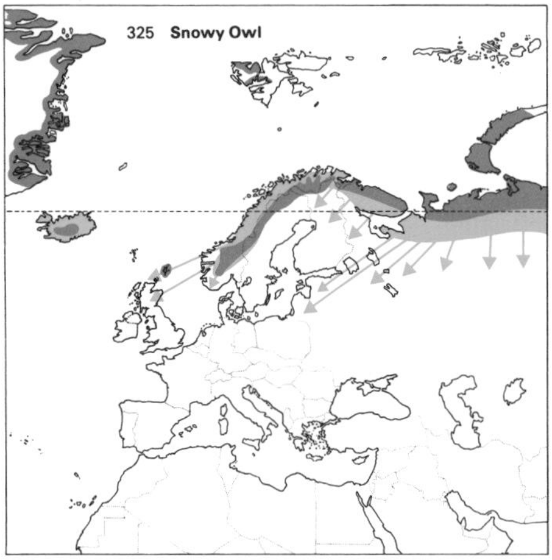
325 Snowy Owl

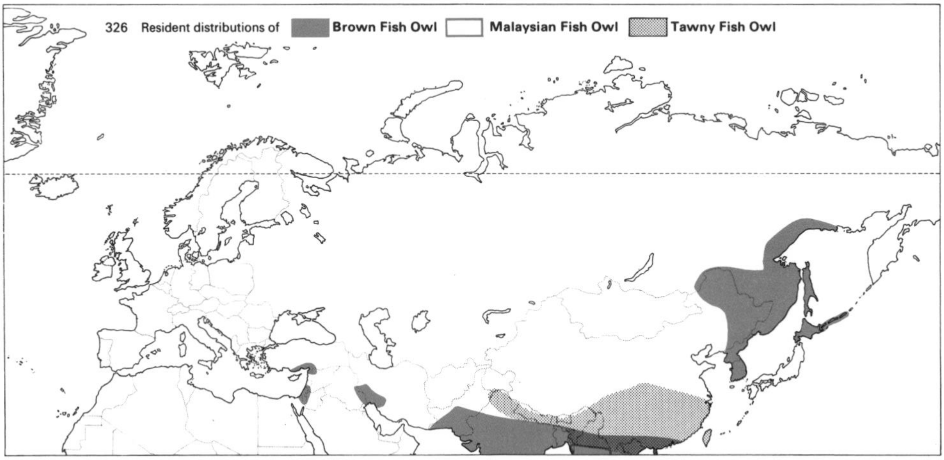
326 Resident distributions of
Brown Fish Owl
Malaysian Fish Owl
Tawny Fish Owl

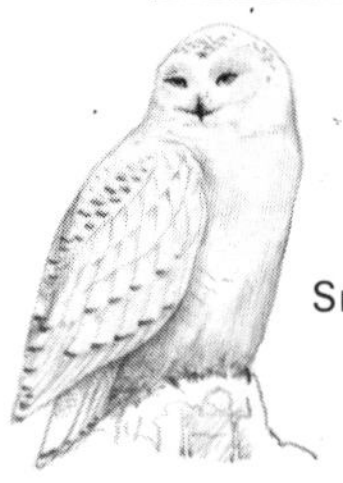
Snowy Owl

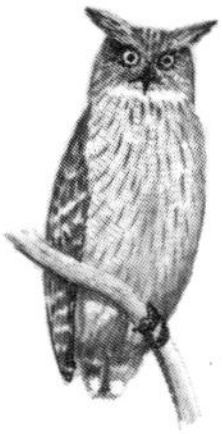
Brown Fish Owl

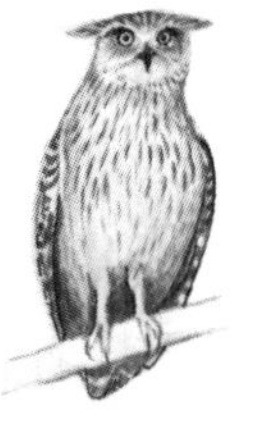
Malaysian Fish Owl

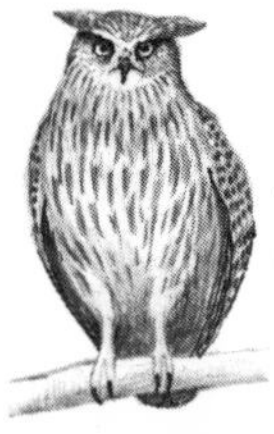
Tawny Fish Owl

Snowy Owl   *Nyctea scandiaca* (Map 325)
Usually resident, with dispersive irruptions southwards in periods of food scarcity; occurring in the Arctic zone and extending to the Alpine zone in Scandinavia. It occurs on uneven or hilly dry tundra, rocky offshore islands, rocky outcrops in icefields, and on high stony or mossy moorland of dry tundra type. It nests on the ground. Individuals may stray widely during irruptions.

Brown Fish Owl   *Ketupa zeylonensis* (Map 326)
Resident; in the Subtropical zone. It feeds mainly on fish taken from the water and occurs by slow-moving or still waters where trees are present, typically along the edges of streams, rivers, lakes and pools, particularly where these occur in forest; but also where only a few trees are present, and by reservoirs or flooded ricefields. It may also occur in coastal forest or mangroves. It nests on a ledge or in a cleft, or uses an old nest in a tree.

Eagle Owl   *Bubo bubo* (Map 327)
Resident; in Subarctic to Subtropical zones. Because of persecution it is absent from most cultivated and well-inhabited areas but otherwise occurs in all types of rocky or wooded areas, from mountains and forests to low rocky outcrops in grassland or semi-desert, and from dense forest to bare areas with groups of trees. It nests in cavities, on ledges or in old nests of large birds. It has decreased in northern and western Europe.

Long-eared Owl   *Asio otus* (Map 328)
Resident and migrant; breeding from mid-Boreal to Warm Temperate zones, wintering in warmer Boreal to Warm Temperate zones. It occurs in coniferous, mixed or broadleaf forest, but is not present in the northern parts of the Boreal forest zone north of about the 15°C July isotherm limit in Europe and further south in eastern regions. It is also present in broken forest, parkland, and scattered groups, lines or plantations of trees in moorland, grassland or cultivation. It usually uses old nests of other birds for breeding. The migratory movements are often erratic, depending on food and weather conditions.

Short-eared Owl   *Asio flammeus* (Map 329)
Resident and migrant; breeding in Subarctic

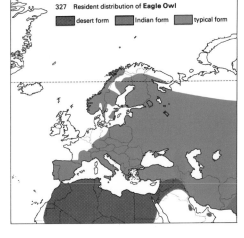
327 Resident distribution of **Eagle Owl**
desert form   Indian form   typical form

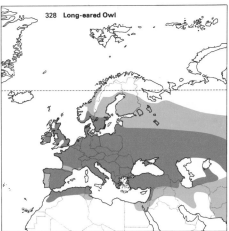
328 Long-eared Owl

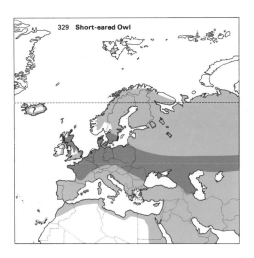
329 Short-eared Owl

Eagle Owl

Long-eared Owl

Short-eared Owl

330   African Marsh Owl

to Temperate zones, wintering in Temperate to Subtropical zones. It is an open country species, resting and nesting on the ground. It occurs, frequently in swampy sites, in moss tundra, saltmarshes and coastal grasslands, dunes, low moorland, open marshes and bogs, moist and dry grassland, grass and scrub steppes and savannahs, and open forest clearings and river floodplains. In winter it also occurs in arid desert regions and open cultivated areas. Its occurrence is locally erratic, depending on small rodent populations.

African Marsh Owl   *Asio capensis*
(Map 330)
Resident; in Subtropical to Tropical zones. Its main distribution is in Africa south of the Sahara with an isolated population in Morocco. It occurs in open swampy areas with tall, lush herbage.

SMALL OWLS *Otus, Glaucidium, Athene* and *Aegolius* species
The small ear-tufted owls of the genus *Otus* occur through most warm parts of the world. The typical Scops Owl occurs through lightly forested areas across southern Eurasia to the Altai, and in Africa south of the Sahara. The Striated Scops Owl occurs from the Middle East to the Pamirs, overlapping with the other in Iran and Afghanistan, while the Oriental Scops Owl *O. surnia* replaces these from India to Japan and eastern Siberia. The Spotted Scops Owl *O. spilocephalus*, a species of thick forest, and the larger Collared Scops Owl *O. bakkamoena* also occur through the general

range of the Oriental Scops Owl. Another two species of the genus occur in North America. The pygmy owls (map 334) are forest species with the typical species across Eurasia in Boreal forest, with a similar American Pygmy Owl *Glaucidium gnoma* in North America. There are two southern Asian species, the Jungle Owlet *G. radiatum* in India (map 334) and the Collared Owlet *G. brodiei* in the Himalayas, south China and Indochina. The intervening Temperate to Warm Temperate area is occupied in the more open places mainly by the Little Owl. The Spotted Little Owl replaces the latter in India and Burma, and within its range in north India a third species, the Forest Little Owl *Athene blewetti*, occurs in thick forest. The Little Owl is a partially terrestrial species and this genus has probably given rise in North America to the long-legged terrestrial Burrowing Owl *Speotyto cunicularis*. Like the Pygmy Owl the Tengmalm's Owl, a larger species, occurs through Boreal forest; and also extends through North America, where the smaller Saw-Whet Owl *Aegolius acadicus* has an overlapping but more extensive and southerly distribution.

Scops Owl   *Otus scops* (Map 331)
Mainly migrant, resident in a few circum-Mediterranean areas; breeding in drier Temperate to Warm Temperate zones, wintering in central Africa. It occurs in lightly forested regions, in open or broken forest, riverine

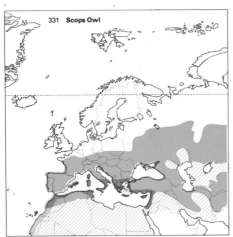

331   Scops Owl

African Marsh Owl

Scops Owl

Striated Scops Owl

forest, parkland or areas with scattered trees. It is usually in drier broadleaf forest, avoiding thick conifer forest and wet areas. It also occurs in orchards, olive groves and cultivation with scattered trees. It nests in cavities in trees, rocks or buildings. On passage it may occur in more open desert areas.

Striated Scops Owl *Otus brucei* (Map 332)
Resident and migrant; in dry Warm Temperate to Subtropical zones. It occurs in drier to arid open country, semi-desert, open cultivated areas and dry stony hillsides, where some scattered trees, groves or riverine forest are present. The nest is in a cavity, or old nest of another bird.

Little Owl *Athene noctua* (Maps 333, 334)
Resident; in Temperate to Warm Temperate zones, and into the Subtropical zone in Africa and Arabia. It is a more terrestrial bird, found in a wide range of more open country, from open and broken forest, orchards and groves, to cultivated areas with scattered trees or scrub, and into rocky arid areas, steppes and semi-desert. In the south it may occur high in dry rocky mountains. It nests in a cavity in a tree, among rocks or in the ground. It was introduced into England and has established itself over the last century.

Pygmy Owl *Glaucidium passerinum* (Map 334)
Resident; in the Boreal zone but extending into the more boreal altitudinal zones in the Temperate areas of middle Europe. It occurs

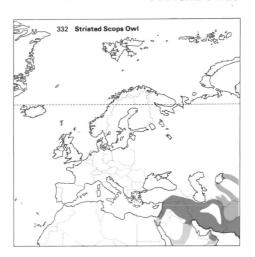

332 Striated Scops Owl

333 Little Owl

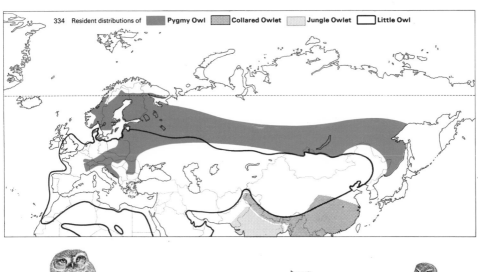

334 Resident distributions of ▓ Pygmy Owl ▒ Collared Owlet ░ Jungle Owlet □ Little Owl

Little Owl

Pygmy Owl

Collared Owlet

Jungle Owlet

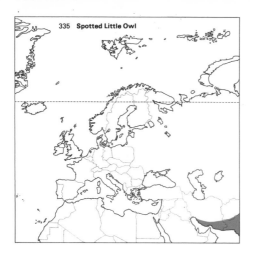

335 Spotted Little Owl

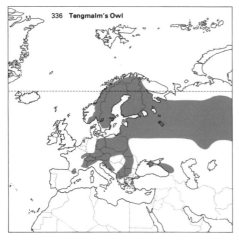

336 Tengmalm's Owl

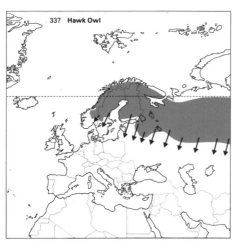

337 Hawk Owl

in conifer forest, often in lighter or more open types of climax forest, or in mixed conifer forest with birch and poplar. It nests in a tree hole.

Spotted Little Owl   *Athene brama* (Map 335)
Resident; in Subtropical to Tropical zones of India. It is a replacement species for the Little Owl in the Indian region, occupying a similar range of habitats, most frequently in scattered trees and groves in cultivated areas but also occurring in dry rocky areas.

Tengmalm's Owl   *Aegolius funereus* (Map 336)
Usually resident, exceptionally some dispersal or irruption; in the Boreal zone, extending into montane Boreal-type forest areas of Temperate Europe, and some lowland temperate pinewoods. It occurs mainly in conifer forest, including thick forest, and into mixed forest. It nests in holes in trees.

———————————————————————

FOREST OWLS *Surnia* and *Strix* species
Of these round-headed forest owls the Hawk Owl has become modified for a diurnal falcon-like existence in more open Boreal forest through the Holarctic. The large Great Grey Owl has a similar distribution, but the Ural Owl, a slightly smaller species also in Boreal forest, occurs only through Eurasia and this and the Tawny Owl are replaced in North America by two other intermediate-sized *Strix* owls. The Tawny Owl occurs across Temperate Eurasia with a break in distribution in northern Iran, and is replaced in the Middle East by Hume's Tawny Owl, which is adapted to hot, rocky regions.

Hawk Owl   *Surnia ulula* (Map 337)
Resident, but erratically irruptive when food is scarce; in the Boreal zone. It occurs in conifer forest, preferring lighter, more open forest, and in mixed forest with birch, poplar and willow; often around clearings and burnt areas. Its range extends to some degree into forest tundra, and wooded steppe.

Tawny Owl   *Strix aluco* (Map 338)
Resident; in warmer Boreal to Warm Temperate zones. It occurs mainly in broadleaf and mixed forests, often in open or broken forest, parkland, cultivation and urban areas

Spotted Little Owl   Tengmalm's Owl

Hawk Owl

Tawny Owl

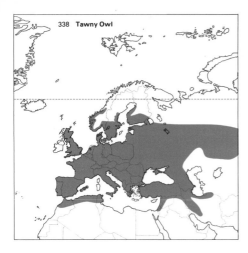

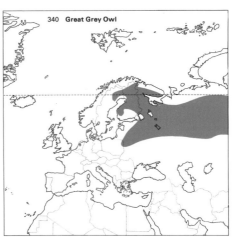

with scattered trees or groups of trees. In the southern part of its range it occurs in mountain conifer forest. It usually frequents mature trees and nests in tree cavities, more rarely in old nests or among rocks.

Hume's Tawny Owl   *Strix butleri* (Map 339)
Resident; in the Subtropical zone. It occurs in drier and more open areas than the previous species, frequenting rocky ravines and wadis of arid semi-desert and desert, and in groves or scattered trees near rocks. It nests in a cavity in a rocky outcrop. It is still a little-known species.

Great Grey Owl   *Strix nebulosa* (Map 340)
Resident; in the Boreal zone. It occurs usually in thick conifer forest but in the east of its range may be found in broadleaf forest. It also extends into the more open northern edge of the conifer zone. It nests in the old nests of other large birds. Exceptionally it may irrupt southwards in times of food scarcity.

Ural Owl   *Strix uralensis* (Map 341)
Resident, but irruptive in periods of food scarcity; in the Boreal zone, with isolated populations in Boreal altitudinal zones in Temperate Europe. It occurs in thick, mixed forest, and in conifer forest to a lesser degree and occasionally in mountain beechwood. It has also spread into more open and varied conifer forest habitats. It nests in cavities, usually in trees, sometimes in old nests or rock crevices. The northern European population has increased in recent years.

Hume's Tawny Owl   Ural Owl   Great Grey Owl

NIGHTJARS   *Caprimulgidae*

Nocturnal birds, feeding in the air, resting on the ground, or sometimes on a branch; and nesting on a bare site on the ground. Five similar species occur in the region. Three tend to replace each other (map 343). The European Nightjar breeds in warmer Boreal to Warm Temperate zones east to Mongolia; replaced from India to Japan and eastern Siberia by the Jungle Nightjar *Caprimulgus indicus*; and in some desert areas by the Egyptian Nightjar which has a discontinuous distribution; while the Nubian Nightjar occupies the area along the Red Sea from north-east Africa. Vaurie's Nightjar *C. centralasicus*, known only from a single specimen, appears to occupy a space between the first two, occurring in Sinkiang. The Red-necked Nightjar occurs within the south-western corner of the European Nightjar's range, and may indicate earlier separation and a later westward spread of the latter. Further east Sykes's Nightjar shares the eastern Iranian region with both the European and Egyptian Nightjars; where both the first and the last are desert species. In North America there are two other *Caprimulgus* species and another three similar nightjars of the genera *Phalaenoptilus* and *Chordeiles*.

European Nightjar   *Caprimulgus europaeus*
(Maps 342, 343)

Migrant; breeding in warmer Boreal to Warm Temperate zones, wintering in Subtropical to Tropical zones. It breeds among trees and undergrowth in areas of dryish, open ground covered with dead leaves and twigs or similar debris; most often on well-drained sandy soils. It occurs in open or broken broadleaf, mixed or conifer forest, on forest edge and in clearings, in birch and poplar scrub, on heathland, grassland, and grass steppe with scattered trees and groves, on shrub steppe and semi-desert with scrub. It is a trans-Saharan migrant, wintering in Africa south of the Sahara, and in western India.

Red-necked Nightjar   *Caprimulgus ruficollis*
(Map 344)

Migrant; breeding in the Warm Temperate zone, wintering in the Tropical zone. It breeds in similar habitats to the European Nightjar

342   European Nightjar

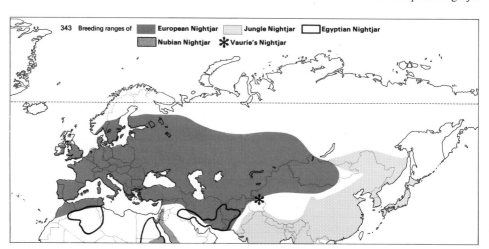

343   Breeding ranges of ▨ European Nightjar ░ Jungle Nightjar ☐ Egyptian Nightjar ▨ Nubian Nightjar ✳ Vaurie's Nightjar

European Nightjar

Red-necked Nightjar

Jungle Nightjar

but usually in drier, hotter and stonier sites. It occurs in arid, open localities with scattered trees, in dry oak scrub, and semi-desert with some scrub. It winters further south in Africa.

Egyptian Nightjar *Caprimulgus aegyptius*
(Maps 343, 345)
Migrant and resident; in the dry Subtropical zone. It occurs in lowland sandy desert or semi-desert, but usually not far from some source of water, on areas of bare sand with some very sparse grass, scrub or trees. It winters in the Sudan region and probably elsewhere, but its movements and winter occurrence are poorly known.

Sykes's Nightjar *Caprimulgus mahrattensis*
(Map 346)
Mainly resident; in the dry Subtropical zone. It occurs in semi-desert with sparse vegetation or bordering cultivation, in stony dry torrent beds, and in semi-desert with sparse scrub growth and possibly within reach of moister areas where feeding may occur. There is some southward movement into the Indian peninsula in winter, when it may occur in areas of tussock grass on the dry margins of pools.

Nubian Nightjar *Caprimulgus nubicus*
(Maps 343, 347)
Resident; in the dry Subtropical zone. It occurs in rocky, often montane, regions of desert and desert edge, usually within reach of water, and where some low scrub such as thorn or tamarisk is present. Its main distribution is in north-east Africa as far south as Kenya.

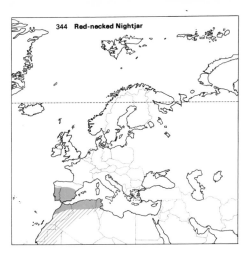

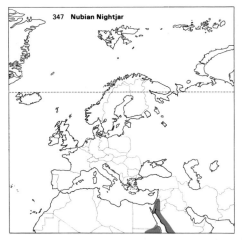

Egyptian Nightjar

Nubian Nightjar

Vaurie's Nightjar

Sykes's Nightjar

SWIFTS *Apodidae*

Small birds, leading an entirely aerial existence except when at the nest. They feed on insects caught in the air and their distribution is determined by weather conditions rather than ground habitats. They may move well beyond their normal ranges during exceptional weather conditions. The nests are of sparse material glued together, and to the site, with saliva. They usually nest in cavities or crevices, or with a round structure stuck to the site in the Little Swift, while the White-rumped Swift uses swallow nests as its cavities. The Common Swift extends across Eurasia, probably from the more westerly end, and in the east only reaches the sea in a limited range. It is partly replaced by the Large White-rumped Swift *Apus pacificus* which occurs in the Himalayas and through much of eastern Eurasia west to Lake Balkhash and the eastern Ob basin. In the Mediterranean the Pallid Swift is the local species, overlapping with the southern distribution of the Common Swift; while the Plain Swift is the Atlantic island form, overlapping with the Pallid Swift in this area. This suggests that the Common Swift might in the past have had a more easterly, Middle East origin. These species are absent from lowland India where the Little Swift may be a partial replacement, but this species occurs across most of southern Asia and much of Africa. The large Alpine Swift occurs east to the Pamirs and is in India. It is absent further east where the equally large Needle-tailed Swift *Hirundapus caudacutus* may be a partial replacement. In North America two hollow-tree- and chimney-nesting *Chaetura* species occur extensively, while two larger, cliff-nesting species in the genera *Cypseloides* and *Aeronautes* are found in the western mountains.

348 Swift

Common Swift *Apus apus* (Map 348)
Migrant; breeding in Boreal to Warm Temperate zones, wintering in the Tropical zone. It breeds in cavities and crevices on buildings and in rock faces and cliffs, on ledges in crevices and caves, and less frequently in cavities in old trees, or in woodpecker holes. Where suitable sites are present it occurs in a variety of habitats from sea cliffs, mountains and rock walls to all types of buildings, towns, rock outcrops in steppes and desert, and old trees in mixed forest and forest edge. It usually nests in colonies. It is possible that except when nesting it spends the entire time flying.

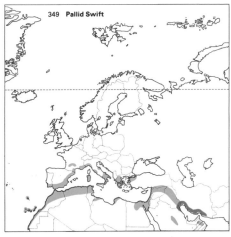

349 Pallid Swift

Pallid Swift *Apus pallidus* (Map 349)
Mainly migrant, resident around the Persian Gulf; breeding in Warm Temperate to Subtropical zones, wintering in Subtropical to Tropical zones. It breeds in similar sites to the Common Swift, sometimes sharing the same colony, but more frequently on cliffs and steep rock walls of coasts and rocky islands. It occurs in mountains and rocky hills in desert regions. The nest may be in a more open site against a rock surface. In general it shows a preference for hotter and more arid areas than the previous species.

Common Swift

Pallid Swift

Plain Swift *Apus unicolor* (Map 350)
Mainly migrant? Breeding in the Warm Temperate zone, wintering in the dry Subtropical zone. It breeds only on some Atlantic islands, nesting in cavities high in the face of tall rocky cliffs. It winters further south around Cape Verde but some birds may be resident.

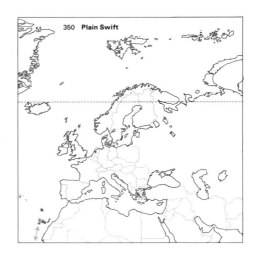

White-rumped Swift *Apus caffer* (Map 351)
Migrant; breeding in Subtropical to Tropical zones, wintering in the Tropical zone. Unlike other swifts it re-lines the elongated, retort-shaped nests of some swallows. In the Western Palaearctic it uses those of the Red-rumped Swallow *Hirundo daurica* and its distribution is tied to some parts of the south-western range of the swallow. It is more widespread further south in Africa beyond the Sahara, and it appears to be spreading north, only recently invading southern Spain.

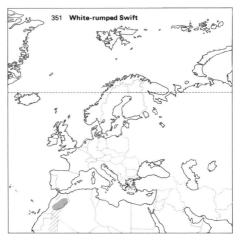

Alpine Swift *Apus melba* (Map 352)
Migrant; breeding in the Warm Tropical zone and the warmer edge of the Temperate zone, but may occupy Temperate to Boreal altitude zones in these areas. It winters in the Tropical zone. It breeds in arid mountain and cliff areas and occurs mainly on rocky coasts with high cliffs, and high in mountains, nesting in colonies in small cavities and holes of high rock faces, and in cavities or on small ledges in the roofs of high buildings. It winters in tropical Africa and southern Asia.

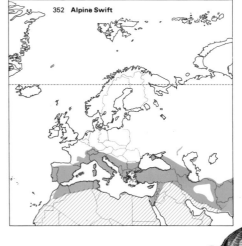

Plain Swift

White-rumped Swift

Alpine Swift

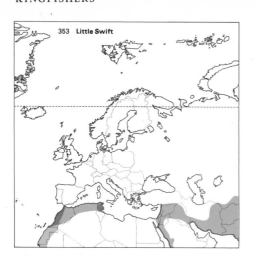

353 Little Swift

Little Swift   *Apus affinis* (Map 353)
Mainly migrant, resident in some parts of its range; in Warm Temperate to Tropical zones (to *c.* 10° south latitude), migrants wintering in Subtropical to Tropical zones. It breeds in colonies, the rounded nests being fixed to sheltered walls, eaves, and each other. It usually nests on buildings but uses similar slightly overhung sites on inland cliffs or rock faces, and may use old nests of other hirundines.

KINGFISHERS   *Alcedinidae*

Small birds feeding by suddenly swooping or plunging on fish or other living prey. Within our region there are three species, a small and a larger species which plunge-dive for fish, and a larger species of the forest kingfisher type which takes most of its prey from the ground. They nest in tunnels bored in earth banks. The small Common Kingfisher occurs right through the warmer Eurasian region, Africa and the Oriental region, where water is present. In the Oriental region, where it occurs in more open habitats, the similar but darker Deep Blue Kingfisher *Alcedo meninting* replaces it in forest habitats, while in the Him-alayan foothills the similar but larger Blyth's Kingfisher *A. hercules* also occurs on forest streams. The Lesser Pied Kingfisher is widespread from the Mediterranean through southern Asia to China, and in Africa. It will utilise still and stagnant waters while the Large Pied Kingfisher *Ceryle lugubris* occurs on running waters from India to Japan. The Smyrna Kingfisher is a bird of land as well as water, ranging from the Mediterranean through southern Asia to China, but not in Africa. From India into China its range overlaps that of the similar Black-capped Kingfisher *Halcyon pileata*, which feeds mainly by fishing and occurs more in forested areas.

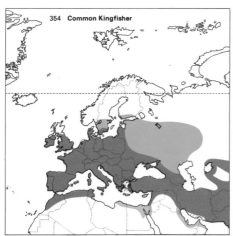

354 Common Kingfisher

Common Kingfisher   *Alcedo atthis* (Map 354)
Resident, dispersing and migrating if waters freeze; breeding in warmer Boreal to Warm Temperate zones, mainly wintering in Temperate to Subtropical zones. It occurs on still or flowing water, but not violent or fast-flowing waters. It uses fresh waters when breeding but at other times may occur on brackish or salt waters. It occurs on streams, larger ditches and rivers, usually with some waterside shrubs or trees, and on ponds, lakes, reservoirs, and flooded ricefields. It is mainly a lowland bird, occurring at times at higher altitudes, up to 2,000 m in parts of its range, but not usually above the tree line. In winter it may occur on estuaries, brackish lagoons and sheltered coasts.

Little Swift

Common Kingfisher

Smyrna Kingfisher *Halcyon smyrnensis*
(Map 355)
Resident; in eastern Warm Temperate to
Tropical zones. It frequently occurs by water,
sometimes larger lakes or rivers, but usually
small pools, ditches, streams and canals, and
also occurs in wet ricefields, mangrove swamps
and on sea coasts. In addition it frequents
drier broadleaf forest well away from water,
usually in clearings, broken forest or forest
edge, and in orchards, gardens and urban parkland in some places. It occurs at altitudes of
0–c. 1,800 m. It feeds mainly by taking creatures from the ground, less often by fishing.

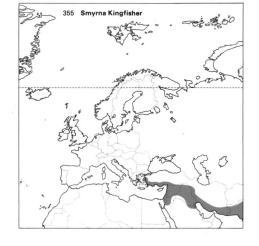

355 Smyrna Kingfisher

Lesser Pied Kingfisher *Ceryle rudis*
(Map 356)
Resident; in eastern Warm Temperate to
Tropical zones. It occurs on all kinds of still
or slow-moving waters; usually on fresh water
in fairly open country, with some shore vegetation. It is found on pools, lakes, lagoons,
reservoirs, ditches, canals and slow streams
and rivers; exceptionally on salt tidal creeks
and coastal rock pools. It occurs at altitudes of
0–c. 1,800 m. It tends to hunt by hovering and
then plunge-diving.

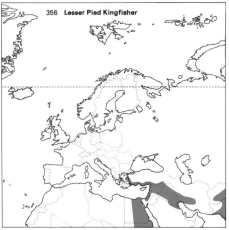

356 Lesser Pied Kingfisher

BEE-EATERS *Meropidae*

Smallish, slender-billed perching birds, catching insects by hawking on the wing or flying
out from a perch; and requiring open perches
with good visibility. They nest in tunnels bored
into banks or level ground, and are usually
sociable and colonial nesters. The need for
bee-sized flying insects restricts their range to
warmer regions. There are three species in the
area. The European Bee-eater nests in Temperate to Warm Temperate regions east to the
Altai and Tibetan highlands. It has no eastern
replacement, but the Chestnut-headed Bee-
eater *Merops leschenaultii* from southern India
and China to Java appears to be closely re-

lated and of similar habits. The Blue-cheeked
Bee-eater has a more southerly range and extends into north-west India where it is replaced,
with slight overlap, by the Blue-tailed Bee-
eater *M. philippinus*, so similar that it has been
regarded as a subspecies. The latter occurs
into south-east China and south through
Malaysia. The Little Green Bee-eater has
a still more southerly range, mainly on the
southern edge of the Sahara, through southern Asia and across and through India and
Indochina, but is replaced in extreme south-
east China and Indonesia by the larger Blue-
throated Bee-eater *M. viridis*. There are none
in North America.

Smyrna Kingfisher

Lesser Pied Kingfisher

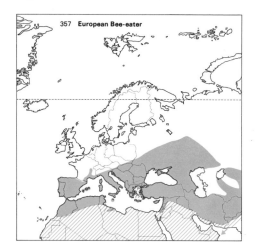

357 European Bee-eater

European Bee-eater *Merops apiaster*
(Map 357)
Migrant; breeding in drier Temperate to Warm
Temperate zones, wintering in Subtropical to
Tropical zones. It occurs usually in open areas
with scattered trees or clumps of shrubby
growth with high, open perching sites, often
near water, in sheltered valleys, low hills and
open steppes. In bare open places it may utilise
man-made perches such as telegraph or fence
poles and wires. It winters in savannah regions
of Africa south of the Sahara. In warm springs
it may overshoot the usual breeding range and
breed further north, in northern France, and
more exceptionally it has bred in Belgium,
southern England and Denmark.

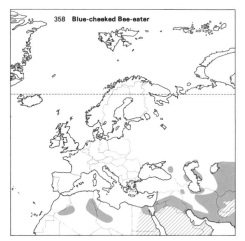

358 Blue-cheeked Bee-eater

Blue-cheeked Bee-eater *Merops superciliosus*
(Map 358)
Migrant; breeding in eastern Warm Temperate to dry Subtropical zones, wintering in
Subtropical to Tropical zones. In habitat and
requirements it is similar to the previous
species, but is limited to warmer regions. It
occurs in open areas, usually with vegetation
or scrub of some kind, or scattered trees, and
frequently near water. In steppe regions it usually occurs in river valleys, deltas and oases, or
on the sandy margins of lakes; in semi-desert
and desert areas it is found in broken hilly
country or dry creek areas with sparse vegetation, but not at high altitudes. It winters in
savannah areas of Africa south of the Sahara.

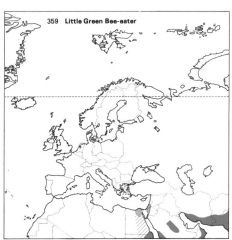

359 Little Green Bee-eater

Little Green Bee-eater *Merops orientalis*
(Map 359)
Resident, but migrant in the south-east Mediterranean; in the dry Subtropical to Tropical
zones. Occurs in open country often in or near
cultivated areas, usually with some woodland,
scrub or scattered trees. It tends to prefer
sandy areas, at times in rocky semi-desert edge
or on sandy sea coasts. It occurs at up to
2,000 m in hilly country in India. It is more
tolerant of arid conditions than the other
species.

European Bee-eater   Blue-cheeked Bee-eater   Little Green Bee-eater

ROLLERS   *Coraciidae*

Stout, large-billed perching birds, usually watching from an open perch for large insect prey, or hawking it in the air, and like the bee-eaters are largely limited to warmer regions. They breed in holes in trees, banks or buildings. They are not normally sociable in their behaviour. There are three species in the region. The European Roller is absent from Atlantic Europe and breeds from eastern and southern Europe eastwards to the Altai. The Abyssinian Roller, similar except for two long tail feathers, replaces it in Africa on the south side of the Sahara; and the Indian Roller does so in India and across to Indochina. The broad-billed Roller *Eurystomus orientalis* occurs in the south-east of Eurasia from Japan to eastern India and through the Oriental region to Australasia, but is a forest species. There are none in North America.

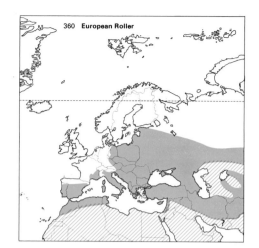

European Roller   *Coracias garrulus*
(Map 360)
Migrant; in drier Temperate to Warm Temperate zones, wintering in Subtropical to Tropical zones. It occurs in more open mature broadleaf forest, parkland, forest steppe, riverine forest, cultivated areas and grass steppe with scattered trees, groves and plantations, thorn scrub, foothill slopes with vegetation or rocky outcrops, and open steppe in areas of broken ground. A mainly lowland bird, found to *c.* 2,300 m in the south of its breeding range. It winters in savannah regions of eastern Africa south of the Sahara.

Abyssinian Roller   *Coracias abyssinicus*
(Map 361)
Resident; in dry Subtropical to Tropical zones. It occurs in savannah grassland and cultivation where scattered trees are present, and in thin scrub and open scrubby forest. It is present in north-east Africa and in the Savannah zone on the southern side of the Sahara.

Indian Roller   *Coracias benghalensis*
(Map 362)
Resident; in the Subtropical zone. It occurs in light broadleaf forest, in open forest and clearings, forest edge with and without scrub, scrub and open cultivated areas with groves or scattered trees. It is usually in lowland but occurs at up to 1,300 m.

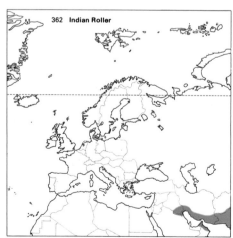

European Roller

Abyssinian Roller

Indian Roller

HOOPOES   *Upupidae*

Long-billed, broad-winged, ground-probing birds, feeding on insects and other small creatures; and nesting in a hole in tree, bank or building. Only one species, present through Eurasia and south to Ceylon and Sumatra, in Arabia and most of Africa and Madagascar. The southern African form, with a large white wing patch, is sometimes separated as a species *Upupa africanus*.

Hoopoe   *Upupa epops* (Map 363)
Migrant, resident in the south of its range; breeding in warmer Boreal to Tropical zones, wintering in Subtropical to Tropical zones. It occurs in warm, dry areas and requires partly

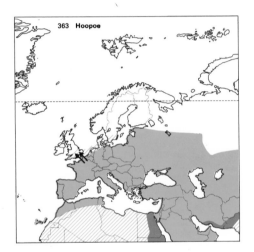

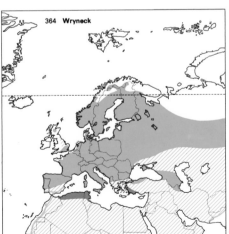

Hoopoe

bare, dry soil in which to probe. Where these conditions occur it is found in forest clearings and forest edge, parkland and forest steppes, orchards, vineyards, groves and gardens, open arable land, grass steppes, cliffs and rockfalls, and broken rocky areas of semi-desert. In some areas it nests at up to *c.* 2,000 m. The northern populations winter in Africa south of the Sahara and in southern Asia. In periods of warmer drier summers it nests further north at the north-west edge of its range. It occasionally nests in southern England and has nested in Denmark.

WOODPECKERS   *Picidae*

Large to small arboreal birds, usually clinging upright to trunks and branches of trees, and obtaining food and making nests and roost holes by hacking into wood. Several sub-groups can be recognised – wrynecks, Black Woodpecker, Three-toed Woodpecker, green woodpeckers, pied, and large and small barred woodpeckers. Within these groups these forest species produce a complex of forms speciating in isolated forest refuges in past ice ages. The green woodpeckers have a North African species but otherwise the pied woodpecker group shows the most complex pattern, with species in mid-Europe, the Balkans, Arabia, Iran and the sparse eastern steppe forests. In each group an eastern Eurasian species extends across, usually to overlap with western species of more limited distribution. In the south-east the pattern is more complex (fig. 3, p. 32), most groups having a western Himalayan species, two species of probably eastern origin extending west through the Himalayas as well, and in some groups species are also present in peninsular India and Japan. The main Eurasian species overlap with these to varying degrees.

WRYNECKS *Jynx* species
Only two species, of small birds, one right through Eurasia, and the Red-breasted Wryneck *Jynx ruficollis* in Africa south of the Sahara. They are sometimes regarded as a single species. They are more like typical passerines and less like woodpeckers than most species. They feed mainly on ants, often on the ground, and nest in natural cavities in trees or among rocks. There is no North American equivalent.

Wryneck

Wryneck *Jynx torquilla* (Map 364)
Migrant, resident in a few places on the southern edge of the breeding range; breeding in Boreal to Temperate zones, wintering in Subtropical to Tropical zones. It occurs in broadleaf and mixed forest on forest edge and broken forest areas and clearings, in riverine forest, parkland, orchards, gardens, open land with plantations, groves or scattered trees, and scrubby tree growth in rocky areas. Occurs mainly in lowland or on warm montane slopes. It winters in central Africa and southern Asia, in areas of broadleaf scrub, thorn scrub, semi-desert and cultivation.

BLACK WOODPECKERS *Dryocopus*
species
The large Black Woodpecker occurs right through Eurasia, replaced in montane forest in peninsular India and east and southwards through the Oriental region by the White-bellied Black Woodpecker *Dryocopus javensis*. The two are separated by the Great Slaty Woodpecker *Mulleripicus pulverulentus* which occurs through the Himalayan forests. In North America the Pileated Woodpecker is a replacement species, with several others in Central and South America.

Black Woodpecker *Dryocopus martius*
(Map 365)
Resident; in Boreal to Warm Temperate zones. It occurs in climax forest, more frequently in conifer forest with pines, but also in mixed forest and climax beech forest. In winter it may also occur in more open forest or partial clearings with dead timber. In the south of the range it is mainly in mountain forest. It feeds on or near the ground. It has a relict distribution in south-west Europe and an isolated population in western China bordering the Tibetan massif.

THREE-TOED WOODPECKERS
Picoides species
Only two species in the genus. One in Boreal conifer forest through Eurasia and also in North America, but absent from the middle region. The Black-backed Three-toed Woodpecker *Picoides arcticus* is present in similar habitats in mid-North America and also extends across it within the range of the other species, which may have been a secondary invader in North America.

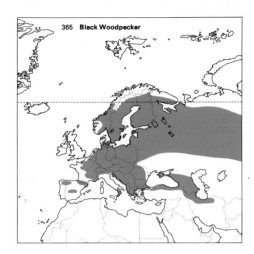

365 Black Woodpecker

366 Three-toed Woodpecker

Three-toed Woodpecker *Picoides tridactylus*
(Map 366)
Resident, with seasonal movements within the range; in the Boreal zone, with southern isolates in the Temperate zone in Boreal altitudinal zones. It occurs in thick damp conifer forest with plentiful dead wood, but rarely in pure pine. In northern areas it is often in thick burnt or cut-over forest areas, in the south usually in mountain forest, and in all types of habitat often in damper areas. It occurs at times in Boreal willow or birch forest, forest tundra, and in the east of its range in mixed forest.

Black Woodpecker   Three-toed Woodpecker

PIED WOODPECKERS some
Dendrocopos species

This is a group of moderate-sized black-and-white patched woodpeckers with a complex distribution pattern (map 367). The Middle Spotted Woodpecker is probably of south central European origin and the Syrian Woodpecker of Middle Eastern origin; the two now overlapping. The Arabian Woodpecker is isolated in south-west Arabia, and the White-winged Woodpecker in the eastern wooded steppe region. Further east the Sind Pied Woodpecker occupies the Pakistan mountains, while beyond our area (fig. 3, p. 32) the Himalayan Pied Woodpecker *Dendrocopos himalayensis* occupies the western Himalayas, and the Darjeeling Pied Woodpecker *D. darjellensis* and Lesser Pied Woodpecker *D. cathpharius* occur together through the eastern Himalayas, the former extending into northern Indochina, the latter to south-west China. The Great Spotted Woodpecker, by analogy probably spreading back from eastern Eurasia, occurs right across it to western Europe, and south into Japan, China and the eastern end of the Himalayas. Its North African form, with red across the breast-band, might be an isolate relic of an earlier spread rather than part of the present range. In North America the wide-

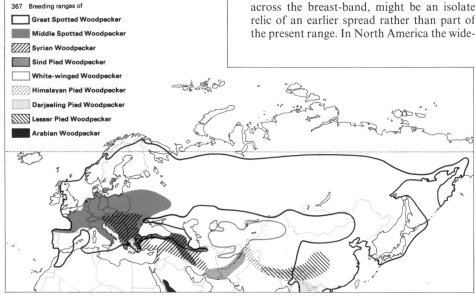

367   Breeding ranges of
☐ Great Spotted Woodpecker
■ Middle Spotted Woodpecker
▨ Syrian Woodpecker
■ Sind Pied Woodpecker
☐ White-winged Woodpecker
▨ Himalayan Pied Woodpecker
▨ Darjeeling Pied Woodpecker
▨ Lesser Pied Woodpecker
■ Arabian Woodpecker

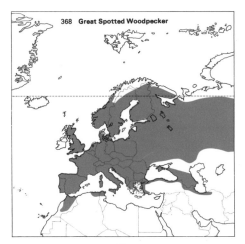

368   Great Spotted Woodpecker

spread Hairy Woodpecker *D. villosus* and localised Arizona Woodpecker *D. arizonae* are replacement species.

Great Spotted Woodpecker   *Dendrocopos major* (Maps 367, 368)
Resident; in Boreal to Warm Temperate zones, with some seasonal movements within the range. It occurs in a wide range of forest, broadleaf, mixed and conifer, wet and dry, and from lowland to mountains; extending to tundra and mountain tree lines and steppe and desert borders. In the south of its range it is more typically a bird of mountain forest, at altitudes of up to *c*. 2,500 m. It is found in closed, open and riverine forest, parkland, gardens and cultivated areas with lines and

Great Spotted Woodpecker   Middle Spotted Woodpecker   Syrian Woodpecker

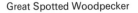

groves of trees, but usually requires forest with more mature trees for nesting. In winter it may move into more open habitats.

Middle Spotted Woodpecker *Dendrocopos medius* (Maps 367, 369)

Resident; in western Temperate to Warm Temperate zones. It occurs mainly in mature broadleaf forest, preferring hornbeam (*Carpinus*), with which its northern range may be linked, and oak forest. It also occurs in mixed forest and beech forest in some parts of its range, and in parkland, orchards and gardens with mature trees. Its specific preferences give it a more limited range.

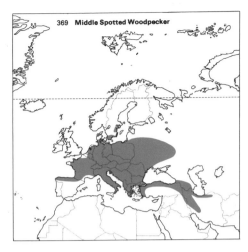

Syrian Woodpecker *Dendrocopos syriacus* (Maps 367, 370)

Resident; in the Middle East Warm Temperate zone. It has spread through the Temperate zone of Europe north of Turkey since 1890, in areas where the Great Spotted Woodpecker is mainly a mountain species. Where the range does not overlap that of the latter it occurs in broadleaf mountain forest, but elsewhere occurs in more lowland habitats, in open broadleaf forest, riverine forest, parkland, orchards and trees in gardens and cultivated areas; confining itself to marginal and less forested habitats than the Great Spotted Woodpecker. It has been recorded feeding in reedbeds. In the south of its range it occurs at altitudes of up to *c*. 2,200 m.

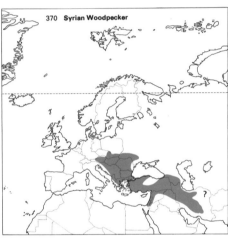

Arabian Woodpecker *Dendrocopos dorae* (Maps 367, 371)

Resident; in the dry Subtropical zone. It occurs in the arid hilly areas of western Arabia where it is found in the trees of sparsely wooded wadis and montane valleys where juniper, acacia and other broadleaf trees occur, and extends into nearby scrub. It is usually found in hills between 450 and 2,300 m, but also occurs at lower altitudes where suitable vegetation is present.

Arabian Woodpecker

Darjeeling Pied Woodpecker

Lesser Pied Woodpecker

Himalayan Pied Woodpecker

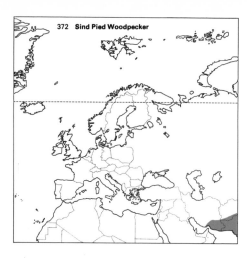

Sind Pied Woodpecker *Dendrocopos assimilis* (Maps 367, 372)

Resident; in the dry Subtropical zone. It is a bird of more open areas. It occurs in trees and plantations along canals and irrigation on desert borders, in semi-desert regions in thin scrub and euphorbias, and in riverine forest or scrub, including that through dune areas bordering rivers. It usually occurs in lowland areas, but in drier hill areas has occurred at up to *c.* 2,200 m.

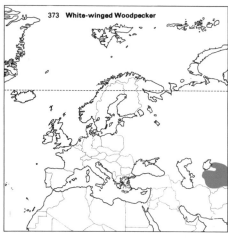

White-winged Woodpecker *Dendrocopos leucopterus* (Maps 367, 373)

Resident, with some local seasonal movements; in the eastern steppe Warm Temperate zone. It occurs in broadleaf, or mainly broadleaf forest of lower mountain slopes, riverine broadleaf forest and valley bottom forest, juniper and willow scrub and sparse woodland or scrub of desert regions. Occasionally it occurs in orchards, gardens and groves in cultivated areas.

BARRED WOODPECKERS some *Dendrocopos* species

In the large and the small barred woodpeckers only a single species of each group extends into Europe. Among the large species the White-backed Woodpecker occurs right across Eurasia into eastern Europe, and also to Japan and China. Isolate populations in the Pyrenees, central Italy and in southern China suggest either relics of an earlier invasion prior to the present spread, or a northward shift of the present population leaving relict mountain isolates. The species does not overlap in range with those of the south-eastern complex (fig. 3, p. 32) in which the Brown-fronted Woodpecker *Dendrocopos auriceps* occurs in the western Himalayas, with the Rufous-bellied Woodpecker *D. hyperythrus* and lowland-tolerant Fulvous-fronted Woodpecker *D. macei* extending from the east through most of the Himalayas. The Yellow-fronted Woodpecker *D. mahrattensis* of peninsular India is probably related to this group. The small barred woodpeckers show a simpler pattern (fig. 3, p. 32). The Lesser Spotted Woodpecker extends right across Eurasia and also south into Japan and north-east China, in both areas overlapping with the Japanese Pygmy Woodpecker *D. kizuki*. A single species, the Grey-headed Pygmy Woodpecker *D. canicapillus*, is present through the Himalayas; and in peninsular India the Brown-headed Pygmy Wood-

Sind Pied Woodpecker

White-winged Woodpecker

pecker *D. nanus*, extending through northern Indochina and eastern China to meet the ranges of the Lesser Spotted and Japanese Pygmy Woodpeckers in the north-east. In North America there is a complex of six larger barred Woodpeckers of this genus, and the small Downy Woodpecker replaces the Lesser Spotted Woodpecker.

White-backed Woodpecker   *Dendrocopos leucotis* (Map 374)

Resident; in warmer Boreal and in Temperate zone montane areas. It occurs in mature forest with abundant large dead trees, usually in mixed or broadleaf forest, occasionally in climax conifer forest, and in broadleaf forest in valleys, floodplains and along rivers and streams. In the south of its range it occurs in mountain beech and fir forest. In winter it may move into more open areas of forest edge or forest mixed with cultivated areas.

Lesser Spotted Woodpecker   *Dendrocopos minor* (Map 375)

Resident, with some seasonal movements within the range; in Subarctic to Warm Temperate zones. It feeds on smaller branches of trees than do other woodpeckers and can utilise younger or smaller tree growth. It occurs in broadleaf or mixed forest, rarely in conifers, often in lower scrub growth with scattered mature trees, in light or open forest, willows, aspens or birches in conifer regions, riverine forest, parkland, and areas with scattered and isolated groves and plantations. It extends into tundra birch scrub, wooded steppes and old orchards. In winter it may pass through areas with sparse and shrubby tree growth, and urban areas.

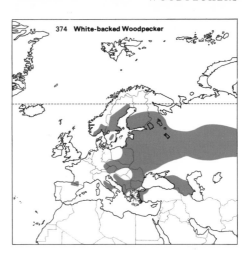

374   White-backed Woodpecker

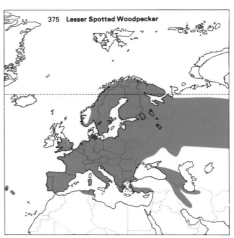

375   Lesser Spotted Woodpecker

GREEN WOODPECKERS   *Picus* species

The green woodpeckers show a similar distribution pattern to the previous groups (fig. 3, p. 32). Levaillant's Woodpecker occurs in North Africa, and the Green Woodpecker through most of Europe. The Grey-headed Woodpecker is the eastern Eurasian species which extends across into Europe and overlaps extensively with the Green Woodpecker. In the east it extends into northern Japan, but is replaced in southern Japan by the Japanese Green Woodpecker *Picus awokera*. The Grey-

headed Woodpecker extends south into Indonesia and through the Himalayas where it overlaps with species of the south-eastern complex. The Scaly-bellied Woodpecker occurs from Iran through the western Himalayas. A pair of species differing in size, the Yellow-naped Woodpecker *P. flavinucha* and the Small Yellow-naped Woodpecker *P. chlorolophus*, occur through the Himalayas also, while the Little Scaly-bellied Woodpecker *P. myrmecophoneus*, another small species, occurs in most of peninsular India, and in the lower Himalayas and Burma. In parts of this

White-backed Woodpecker

Lesser Spotted Woodpecker

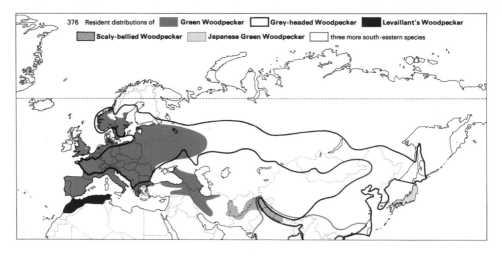

376   Resident distributions of �enGreenWoodpecker   □ Grey-headed Woodpecker   ■ Levaillant's Woodpecker
Scaly-bellied Woodpecker   Japanese Green Woodpecker   □ three more south-eastern species

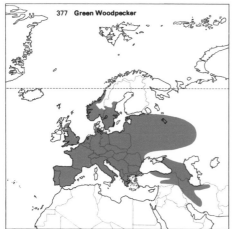

377   Green Woodpecker

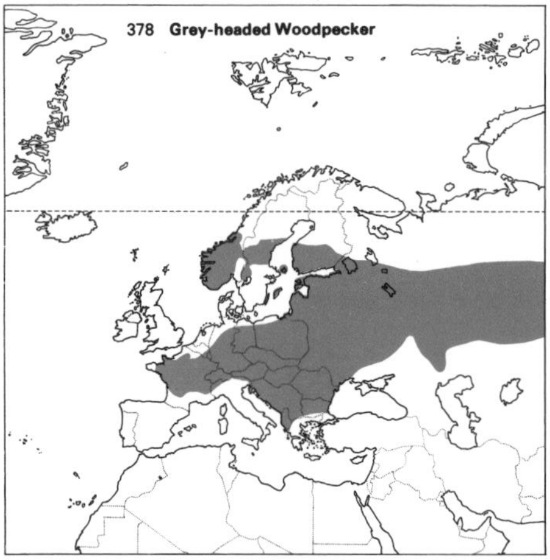

378   Grey-headed Woodpecker

area, therefore, the ranges of four or five species within this group overlap, the birds being separated in the field by size and differences of habitat preference. In general the green woodpeckers are birds of more open country, feeding frequently on the ground, taking ants and termites. In North America they are replaced by the ground-frequenting flickers, *Colaptes* species.

Green Woodpecker   *Picus viridis*
(Maps 376, 377)
Resident, with seasonal movements within the range; in European warmer Boreal to Warm Temperate zones. It occurs in light, open or broken broadleaf or mixed forest with grassy clearings, in parkland, riverine forest, orchards, groves and gardens, and cultivated areas with scattered trees or groups of trees. In the north of its range it may occur in conifer forest with broadleaf shrub layers. In winter it may move to more open areas and occur in scrub, or heathland and cultivation with scrub or overgrown hedgerows. Hard weather movements may occur when ground is frozen. It is more of a lowland species than the Grey-headed Woodpecker and in the areas of overlap the latter is more a bird of forests.

Grey-headed Woodpecker   *Picus canus*
(Maps 376, 378)
Resident, with seasonal movements within the range; in warmer Boreal to Temperate zones. It occurs usually in light or open mixed or broadleaf forest, usually with grassy clearings, but in the east of its range may occur in conifer

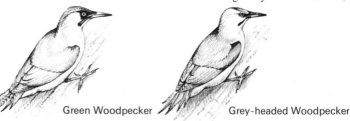

Green Woodpecker   Grey-headed Woodpecker

forest with clearings. Its range of habitats is similar to those of the Green Woodpecker but in regions where both occur it tends to occur more in mixed or predominantly conifer stands and in forest clearings and rides. It also occurs in more montane habitats than the Green Woodpecker. In Europe there is still some evidence of a westward spread.

Levaillant's Woodpecker   *Picus vaillanti*
(Maps 376, 379)
Resident; in the Warm Temperate montane zone. It occurs in open forest or scattered trees on hilly slopes, in oaks, poplar, cedar and pine. It is found up to the tree limit and at altitudes of up to *c.* 2,100 m. It will move away from trees and beyond the tree line to forage on the ground on rocky slopes. It does not occur in the coastal lowland areas.

Scaly-bellied Woodpecker   *Picus squamatus*
(Maps 376, 380)
Resident, with some seasonal altitudinal movements; in Temperate altitudinal zone. It occurs in broadleaf or mixed forest, in open forest or bordering clearings, on forested mountain slopes at 1,000–3,300 m. In the north-west of its range it occurs in broadleaf riverine and valley bottom forest. It feeds extensively on the ground as well as in trees. In winter it may also occur in orchards and around cultivated areas.

379   Levaillant's Woodpecker

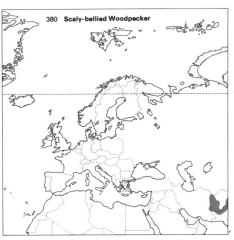

380   Scaly-bellied Woodpecker

Levaillant's Woodpecker

Scaly-bellied Woodpecker

Japanese Woodpecker

LARKS　*Alaudidae*

A group of 22 ground-frequenting songbirds, usually in very open places, and mainly in warm dry regions. They feed on insects, seeds and plants. They nest on the ground and mostly have loud songs usually delivered in flight. There are several subgroups, the stout-billed larks, crested larks, small-billed desert larks, long-billed desert larks and horned larks. Of the last the Shore Lark is a tundra species, the only lark to invade North America, with another species in the northern Afro-Arabian desert area. The crested larks are mainly in Boreal and Temperate grasslands, with wide ranges. The stout-billed larks are in Warm Temperate to Cool Temperate steppe

zones as a number of species with more limited ranges. The others are birds of semi-desert and desert. In these, as in the sandgrouse, some species occur in pairs with similar wide ranges and small differences of habitat preference.

STOUT-BILLED LARKS
Melanocorypha and *Rhamphocorys* species
There are five species within the area (map 382). These are heavily built stout-billed birds of steppe and stony semi-desert, with seven species occurring through these habitats from North Africa and Spain to Mongolia and northern China. The Thick-billed Lark, which may not be closely related to the others, occurs on stony desert borders in the northern Afro-Arabian deserts. The Calandra Lark occurs in dry grasslands and grass steppes, replaced in the east on higher ground by the Bimaculated Lark. On the Temperate steppes there are a pair of similar species, the Black and the White-winged Larks, the latter occupying drier and barer sites. In the Tibetan region the Long-billed Calandra Lark *Melanocorypha maxima* is a replacement species, and further north-east the Mongolian Lark *M. mongolica* occupies the Gobi desert and adjacent China.

Thick-billed Lark　*Rhamphocorys clotbey*
(Maps 381, 382)
Mainly resident, but with some seasonal movement; in the dry Subtropical to Tropical zones. It occurs on open, stony hammada-type desert, and at times in stony semi-desert areas, where some sparse vegetation is present. In winter it may move out of its normal

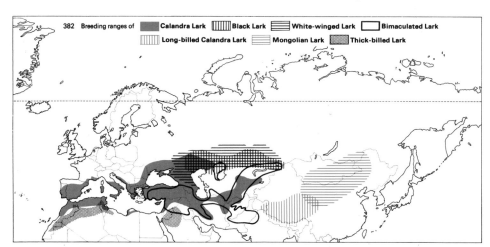

381　Thick-billed Lark

382　Breeding ranges of　Calandra Lark　Black Lark　White-winged Lark　Bimaculated Lark
Long-billed Calandra Lark　Mongolian Lark　Thick-billed Lark

Thick-billed Lark　　　Calandra Lark　　　White-winged Lark

range and occur as a migrant between the two breeding areas and to the south.

Calandra Lark   *Melanocorypha calandra* (Maps 382, 383)

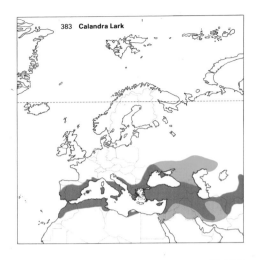

Resident and migrant; in Warm Temperate to Temperate steppe zones. It is typically a bird of drier, warmer grass steppes in lowland areas, but may occur to the west in a variety of places where similar conditions are present. It occurs on grass steppes with some tall herbage and often shrubby growth, on feathergrass and short *Artemesia* steppe, and on large level areas of arable ground. It tends to avoid stony places. Its preference for grassier areas separates it from related species.

Bimaculated Lark   *Melanocorypha bimaculata* (Maps 382, 384)

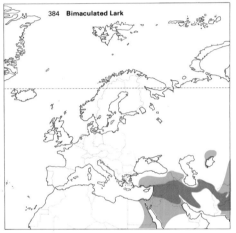

Resident and migrant; in the eastern Warm Temperate dry zone, wintering into the Subtropical zone. It occurs on higher ground, in more montane and rocky areas than the last species. It breeds in dry heath and maquis-type vegetation, usually on the borders of cultivation, on montane steppes with stony soils and some shrub growth, and in rocky and semi-desert areas, at altitudes of 1,200–2,000 m. In winter it occurs on open cultivated areas, bare semi-desert and dry areas of lake margins and tidal mudflats.

White-winged Lark   *Melanocorypha leucoptera* (Maps 382, 385)

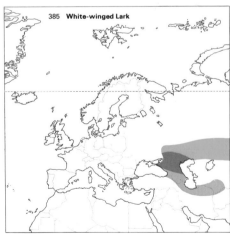

Migrant and resident; breeding in the Temperate zone and wintering in the warmer Temperate zone. It occurs on areas of short, sparse herbage with patches of open soil, on dry, short-grass steppes where bare open soil is present, steppes with sparse feathergrass or *Artemesia* on gravels, arable areas in steppes, and stony semi-desert. In winter it moves southwards and may occur in both open and forest steppes. It also strays westwards and has occurred a number of times in southern and western Europe as far as southern England.

Bimaculated Lark

Long-billed Calandra Lark

Mongolian Lark

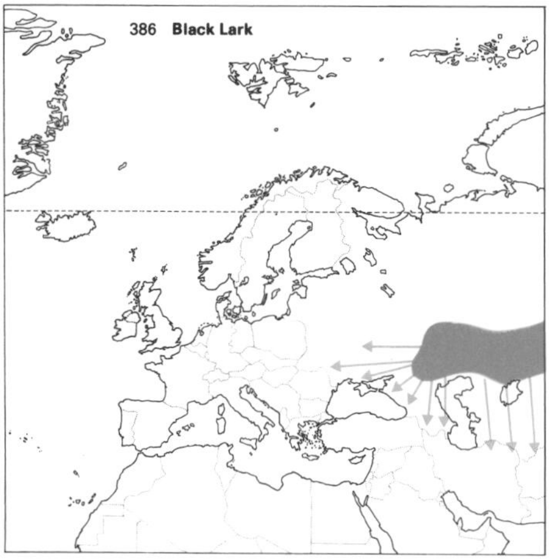

Black Lark *Melanocorypha yeltoniensis* (Maps 382, 386)
Resident and partly migrant; in the Temperate steppe zone. It occurs in dry grass steppes and *Artemesia* steppes, usually near water, and generally in less arid situations than the last species. Winter movements are irregular and in response to bad weather conditions. There is a general south and west shift with erratic occurrence in south and west Europe as far as southern England.

CRESTED LARKS *Alauda, Lullula* and *Galerida* species
Four species occur in the area, with another marginally. With the exception of the Woodlark the typical pattern appears to be one of presence across Eurasia with replacement species in the Indian region. The Skylark occurs in open moist grassland in a wide band across Eurasia (map 387) and the Small Skylark replaces it in India and South-east Asia and extends north-west into the steppe regions, in the equivalent type of habitat. The Woodlark is a purely European species of well-drained areas of sparse herbage with some shrubs or trees. The Crested Lark replaces these species in drier, stonier and less vegetated regions, extending across Eurasia and through Africa on both edges of the Sahara. It is one of a species pair, the other being the Thekla Lark. The latter has a more restricted and broken distribution, usually on more montane and rocky ground. The Crested Lark extends into India but is replaced there in part by Sykes's Crested Lark *Galerida devi*, while the Malabar Crested Lark *G. malabarica* appears to be a counterpart of the Thekla Lark in peninsular India.

Skylark *Alauda arvensis* (Maps 387, 388)
Resident and migrant; in Boreal to Warm Temperate zones, wintering in western Temperate to Subtropical zones. It occurs in open

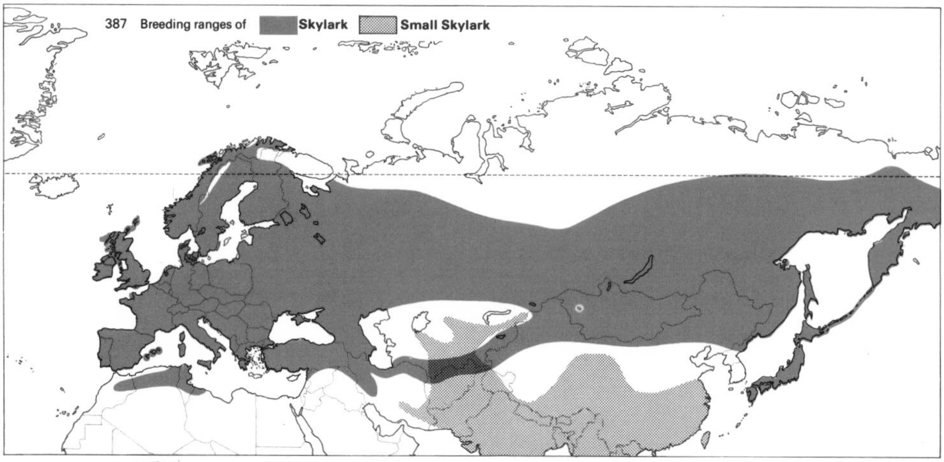

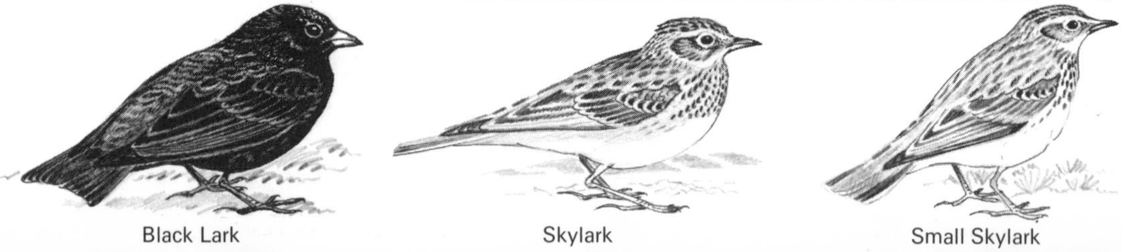

Black Lark Skylark Small Skylark

grassland areas, mostly away from shrub or tree growth, and also in open areas of arable cultivation, valley and waterside meadows and cultivated grassland, moist steppes, saltmarsh and shore grassland, grassy heathland and moorland and upland and alpine meadows. It has increased with the spread of cultivation.

Small Skylark   *Alauda gulgula* (Map 387)
Resident, with some seasonal movements; in the Subtropical to Tropical zones and into Temperate altitudinal zones. It occurs on open areas of cultivation, damp grassland and thick herbage bordering water or cultivation, dry ricefields, montane grazing and open grassland of all types, and in hill cultivation and alpine meadows at up to *c.* 4,500 m in the Himalayas and Tibet.

Woodlark   *Lullula arborea* (Map 389)
Resident and migrant; breeding in European warmer Boreal to Warm Temperate zones, wintering in Warm Temperate to western Temperate zones. It usually occurs on drier, well-drained short or sparse grassland, often on hill slopes, with sparse scattered trees or shrubs. It occurs in thin and open birch or oak forest, parkland, golfcourses, heathland with scattered trees or bordering forest, particularly in burnt-over areas, dunes with trees or shrubs, dry hill slopes, alpine meadows with junipers, well-drained arable land with trees or hedgerows, and olive groves and orchards. It is sensitive to small climatic changes and its northern limit is variable.

Crested Lark   *Galerida cristata* (Map 390)
Resident; in Temperate to Subtropical zones. It occurs, usually in lowland, in drier, less vegetated areas than the previous species, in sandy areas of steppes, semi-desert or desert, sandy coasts and dunes, areas with sparse tufted vegetation and bare sandy or stony soils, and usually with scattered shrubs, on the borders of cultivation, dry hillsides, river banks, open cultivated areas, cleared or fallow sites around human habitation, desert edge with scrub and desert oases.

388 Skylark

389 Woodlark

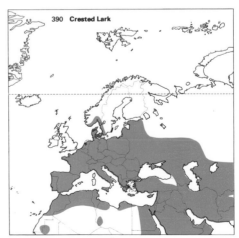

390 Crested Lark

Woodlark

Crested Lark

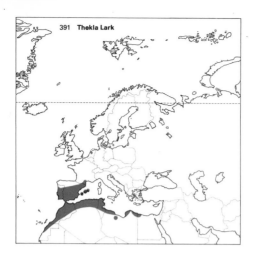

Thekla Lark *Galerida theklae* (Map 391)
Resident; in the western Warm Temperate to Subtropical zones. It occurs in similar habitats to the Crested Lark, but is more rarely a bird of lowland, occurring more frequently on rocky montane sites, which may have more shrub vegetation. It is found in montane or mountainous desert areas, rocky outcrops or arid areas, dry hillsides and rocky places with xerophytic and succulent shrubs, stony stretches of cultivation, and exceptionally in sandy desert. There is a southern population in the highlands of north-east Africa.

SMALL-BILLED DESERT LARKS
Eremopteryx, Calandrella and *Ammomanes* species
There are seven species in the area, two of them marginal. They are small, mainly seed-eating birds, occurring from dry stony and sandy areas to true desert. The Black-crowned Finch Lark has a discontinuous desert range across to Pakistan and western India. In the last region there is partial overlap with an Indian species, the Ashy-crowned Finch Lark *Eremopteryx grisea* which occurs in less arid habitats, and in the south Sahara it overlaps with the Chestnut-backed Finch Lark *E. leucotis* which mainly inhabits more marginal desert areas. Both short-toed and desert larks have species pairs with extensively overlapping ranges, one of each in stonier and more vegetated areas within the range, the other in more desert places. The short-toed larks occur right across southern Eurasia with similar general ranges. Within the ranges there is a mountain species, Hume's Short-toed Lark, in Afghanistan and the Pamirs and Tibetan highlands, while the Indian Sand Lark is a replacement species in dry open areas around rivers and coasts in lowland India and into Iran. The desert larks, *Ammomanes* species, occur through the desert regions from the western Sahara to Pakistan. The Bar-tailed Desert Lark also has a form in peninsular India which occurs in less arid open areas and is here regarded as a separate species, the Rufous-tailed Desert Lark *A. phoenicurus*.

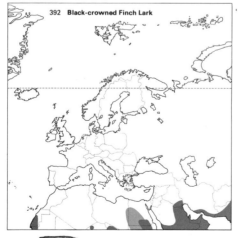

Black-crowned Finch Lark *Eremopteryx nigriceps* (Map 392)
Resident, with some local migratory movements; in the dry Subtropical to Tropical zones. It occurs across the southern part of the Afro-Arabian deserts and into Pakistan. It is found in arid, open and sandy areas, and arid stretches with sparse dry herbage or shrubs, and on the borders of irrigated desert cultivation. Outside the breeding season some migratory shift occurs, northwards in the Sahara, southwards in India.

Thekla Lark   Black-crowned Finch Lark   Hume's Short-toed Lark

Hume's Short-toed Lark   *Calandrella acutirostris* (Map 393)
Migrant; breeding in dry Temperate altitudinal zones, and wintering in the Subtropical to Tropical zones. It occurs at altitudes of *c.* 1,000–4,000 m on dry hillsides with sparse herbage or shrubby growth, or rocky montane steppe areas with sparse herbage on gravelly soils, dry stream-beds and small cultivated areas in such regions, and on bare hill ridges. It winters in lowland India in open semi-desert and stubbles, and low rocky hillsides with sparse vegetation.

Indian Sand Lark   *Calandrella raytal* (Map 394)
Resident; in the Subtropical zone. It occurs on sandy banks and islands of rivers and streams, saltpans and dry areas of coastal tidal mudflats with scanty vegetation. It extends through Pakistan, the northern parts of India and into Burma.

Short-toed Lark   *Calandrella cinerea* (Map 395)
Migrant; breeding in Warm Temperate to Subtropical zones, wintering in Subtropical to Tropical zones. It occurs on open steppes, usually with sparse and stunted vegetation and areas of bare soil, on sand, stones, gravel and clay; on short-grass steppes, salt steppes, on bare dry river banks and dry channels, open stony areas of cultivation, semi-desert with shrubs, rocky desert, and exceptionally in grassy areas of cultivation or on dunes. It winters on grassy steppe-like areas and semi-desert in Africa south of the Sahara.

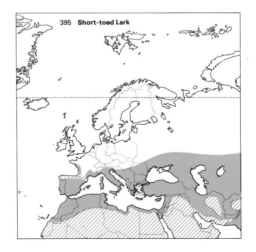

Indian Sand Lark

Short-toed Lark

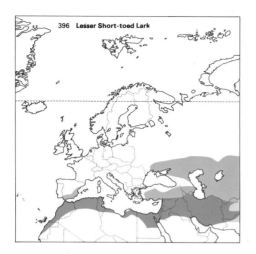

Lesser Short-toed Lark   *Calandrella rufescens* (Map 396)
Migrant and resident; breeding in Warm Temperate and Temperate steppe zones, wintering in Warm Temperate to Subtropical zones. It may occur in similar habitats to the Short-toed Lark, but in general prefers barer, drier habitats. It is found in stony, gravel and clay steppes, more bare and arid salt steppes, semi-desert and desert areas with sparse, stunted vegetation, dunes, bare or sparsely grassed areas of cultivation and grazing, areas of bare dry earth and dry mud of saline lake shores. In winter it may occur on more sandy semi-desert areas.

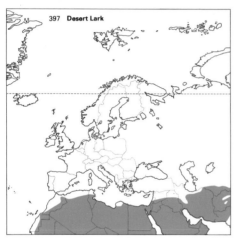

Desert Lark   *Ammomanes deserti* (Map 397)
Resident; in dry Subtropical to Tropical zones. It occurs in stony desert and semi-desert, areas with rocky outcrops with some sparse vegetation, and on rocky hillsides and dry ravines with scattered shrubs and trees.

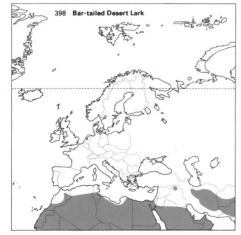

Bar-tailed Desert Lark   *Ammomanes cincturus* (Map 398)
Resident; in dry Subtropical to Tropical zones. It occurs on more level stony and sandy desert and semi-desert than does the previous species; and on stony montane plateaus and areas of thin scrub. At times on bare cultivation and around the borders of cultivation in arid areas.

Lesser Short-toed Lark

Desert Lark

Bar-tailed Desert Lark

LONG-BILLED DESERT LARKS
Chersophilus, Eremalauda and *Alaemon*
species

There are only three species in the area, with ranges mainly in North Africa. They occupy the Afro-Arabian desert region. Dupont's Lark has a narrow range on the northern edge in Africa, Dunn's Lark along the southern edge of the Sahara and into Arabia, while the Hoopoe Lark has a broad central range from the western Sahara to northern India. They are typically probers in loose soil.

Dupont's Lark *Chersophilus duponti*
(Map 399)
Mainly resident; in dry Subtropical to Tropical zones. It occurs mainly in arid scrub, and *Artemisia* and grass steppes. It may occur erratically outside its normal range, and occurs at times in sand or stony desert and semi-desert, but normally prefers areas with sufficient ground vegetation for concealment.

Dunn's Lark *Eremalauda dunni* (Map 400)
Resident; in dry Subtropical to Tropical zones. It occurs in open grassy arid areas on the Saharan desert border; and in Arabia in sandy desert and in arid areas with sparse *Acacia* scrub.

Hoopoe Lark *Alaemon alaudipes* (Map 401)
Resident; in dry Subtropical to Tropical zones. A desert species and one of the few which appears to utilise loose sands. It occurs in arid semi-desert with some herbage, open desert areas with irregular sand-drifts or low dunes and sparse salt shrubs, sand desert with dry grasses, or bare and dry salt mud areas. It also occurs less frequently in gravel or stony desert, and may be found on coastal dunes and shores, most often in winter.

HORNED LARKS *Eremophila* species
There are only two species. The Shore Lark is an Arctic/Alpine bird with two Eurasian populations, one in the northern tundra regions, the other through the southern regions of Eurasia in mountain areas. It is the only species of lark to have invaded North America where, in the absence of other species, it oc-

399 Dupont's Lark

400 Dunn's Lark

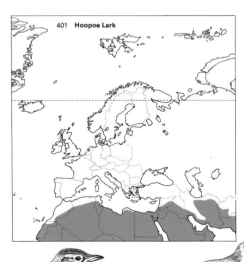

401 Hoopoe Lark

Dupont's Lark

Dunn's Lark

Hoopoe Lark

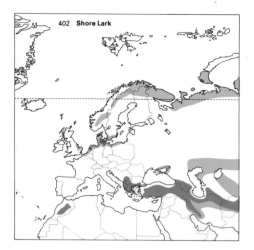

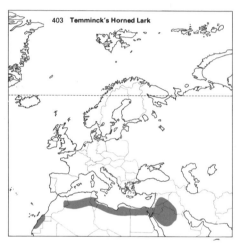

curs in all open habitats from tundra to desert. Temminck's Horned Lark has a restricted distribution along the northern edge of the Afro-Arabian desert region, where it occupies hot lowland areas.

Shore Lark   *Eremophila alpestris* (Map 402)
Migrant and resident; breeding in the northern Arctic/Alpine zone, and in Boreal to Alpine altitudinal zones further south, wintering in Warm Temperate to Temperate lowland and coastal zones. It occurs in drier, stony areas of lichen tundra, barren stony steppes with sparse grass, alpine and subalpine meadows, high rocky areas, moraines, and gravels near the snowline with very sparse herbage and scrub, and sometimes in more grassy sites in mountain valleys. In the south it breeds at altitudes of *c.* 1,600–2,000 m in southern Europe, 2,500–3,500 m further east, and in Tibet up to 5,500 m. In winter it occurs at lower altitudes on open areas with sparse plant growth, arable cultivation, beaches and dunes with some vegetation, and snow-free steppes. Its spread from the tundra to Scandinavian mountains has occurred in the last two hundred years, and in more recent cold years it has bred in northern Scotland.

Temminck's Horned Lark   *Eremophila bilopha* (Map 403)
Resident; in the dry Subtropical zone. It occurs on areas of stony ground, or on sandy desert areas with stony or rocky patches and some sparse plant growth, in lowland regions.

SWALLOWS AND MARTINS
Hirundinidae

Small birds, spending most of their time in the air feeding on insects caught on the wing, and therefore restricted to migrant species in most of the European range. The nests are mostly of mud, stuck to rock faces or buildings, or resting on a ledge, or a tunnel bored in a bank of sand or earth. The family is mainly Tropical in distribution with three widespread Eurasian species. Of these the Swallow and Sand Martin also occur in North America. The House Martin is absent from North America but the cavity-nesting Tree Swallow *Iridoprocne bicolor* might be a partial replacement. The Swallow has a wide Eurasian range but is absent as a breeding species from India and is there replaced in some areas by the Pacific Swallow *Hirundo tahitica* of the Oriental region. The Red-rumped Swallow occurs through Warm Temperate regions across Eurasia, the southeast Asian form being sometimes separated as the Striated Swallow *H. striolata*. The Wire-tailed Swallow is a still more southerly species, breeding through Africa south of the Sahara, in the Indian subcontinent and parts of Southeast Asia. The crag martins also show some latitudinal replacement, the common Crag Martin occurring through the Warm Temperate zone with two species on its southern side, the Pale Crag Martin through the Afro-Arabian deserts and into western Pakistan, and the Dusky Crag Martin from India into

Shore Lark   Temminck's Horned Lark

Indochina. As breeding birds house martins are restricted to Eurasia. The common House Martin extends right across, with the duller easternmost form sometimes treated as a separate species, the Asiatic House Martin *Delichon dasypus*. There is another species, the Nepal House Martin *D. nipalensis*, with blackish throat and square tail, in the Himalayas, north Burma and north Vietnam. The Sand Martin is another species with a wide Eurasian distribution. The Plain Sand Martin occurs widely through much of Africa south of the Sahara to northern Sudan, just below our map, and the Moroccan population is an outlier of this. The species also occurs from Afghanistan to southern China.

Crag Martin *Hirundo rupestris* (Map 404)
Migrant and resident; breeding in the Warm Temperate zone, wintering mainly (possibly wholly?) in North Africa. It occurs in hills with rocky outcrops or cliffs, coastal cliffs, rocky ravines and drier mountain slopes. The cup nest is stuck to a vertical surface, on a rock under a slight overhang, or on an old building. It often nests in small colonies. It occurs in drier mountain areas at varying altitudes, up to *c.* 2,200 m in the Alps, *c.* 3,000 m in North Africa and up to 5,000 m in the Himalayas.

Dusky Crag Martin *Hirundo concolor* (Map 405)
Resident; in Subtropical to Tropical zones, from India to Burma and north Thailand. It occurs in open country and hills up to *c.* 1,800 m; usually around hills with rock outcrops or old buildings and fortifications, on isolated buildings and in towns. The cup nest is stuck to a vertical surface, a rock or wall, usually under an overhang, sometimes in a cave or building.

Pale Crag Martin *Hirundo obsoleta* (Map 406)
Mainly resident; migrant in parts of Iran and Afghanistan, and seasonal movements within the range elsewhere; in Subtropical to Tropical zones. It occurs in basically similar types of country to the Crag Martin, but in more arid areas, frequenting desert rock outcrops, ravines and bare foothills with crags and cliffs. Its nesting habits are like those of the Crag Martin.

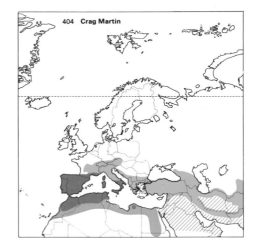

404 Crag Martin

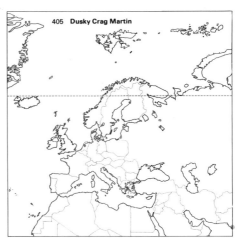

405 Dusky Crag Martin

406 Pale Crag Martin

Crag Martin

Dusky Crag Martin

Pale Crag Martin

407 Swallow

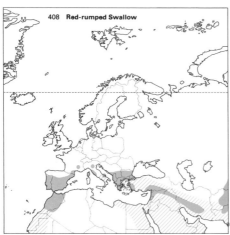
408 Red-rumped Swallow

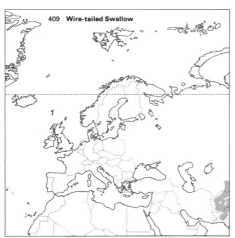
409 Wire-tailed Swallow

Swallow *Hirundo rustica* (Map 407)
Migrant, resident in the Nile region; breeding in Boreal to Warm Temperate zones, wintering in Subtropical to Tropical zones. It occurs in open country. The nest is a mud cup on a ledge, usually in a building or on a man-made structure, exceptionally on a rock face, bank or tree branch. The bird occurs most frequently over grassy areas near water, mainly in lowlands and valleys, but also in most types of cultivated areas, open areas with grass or low scrub growth, parkland but not forest, and in mountain areas near water. In the south of its range it occurs at up to *c.* 2,500–3,000 m. It winters in Africa south of the Sahara, India and South-east Asia.

Red-rumped Swallow *Hirundo daurica* (Map 408)
Migrant; breeding in the Warm Temperate zone, wintering in Subtropical to Tropical zones. Like the Swallow it occurs in open country, but not necessarily near water, on dry sea coasts, rocky hills and grassy mountain slopes, but often around cultivated areas. The nest is an elongated structure stuck to the underside of a surface – a large rock overhang, on the ceiling of a cave or room of a building, the upper side of a hole or cleft in buildings or rocks, the underside of a bridge or culvert (sometimes quite low) or under a balcony or veranda. It is less dependent on man-made structures than the Swallow. It may occur at altitudes of up to *c.* 3,300 m in the Himalayas. Migrants winter in Africa south of the Sahara, in India and in South-east Asia, often within the range of resident races. It winters in open grassland or cultivated country or clearings in light forest.

Wire-tailed Swallow *Hirundo smithii* (Map 409)
Migrant; breeding in the Warm Temperate zone, but outside the area it is resident in Subtropical to Tropical zones of India (where the migrants winter) and Africa south of the Sahara. Its occurrence is closely linked with the presence of rivers, canals, lakes or reservoirs, and it feeds over open grassland or cultivation nearby. The cup nest is stuck to a vertical surface – a rock, cave, bridge, culvert, wall, rafter, or steep rocky or stony bank;

Swallow　　　　　Red-rumped Swallow　　　　　Wire-tailed Swallow

normally over water. It usually breeds at altitudes of up to *c.* 1,500 m but has been recorded at up to *c.* 2,700 m.

House Martin *Delichon urbica* (Map 410)
Migrant; breeding in Boreal to Warm Temperate zones, wintering in Subtropical to Tropical zones. It occurs in open country, in similar habitats to those of the Swallow, but extends into more mountainous, bare and rocky areas. The deep cup nest is stuck to a vertical surface immediately below an overhang, on cliff or rock wall, steep rocky bank, and below the eaves or a ledge on walls of buildings but not inside caves or buildings. It often nests in colonies. It winters in Africa south of the Sahara, India and South-east Asia.

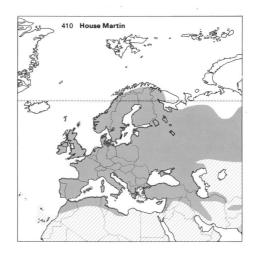

Sand Martin *Riparia riparia* (Map 411)
Migrant; breeding in Subarctic to Warm Temperate zones, wintering in Subtropical to Tropical zones. It occurs mainly in lowland and distribution is largely limited by availability of nest sites. It nests in colonies in tunnels bored into a firm sand, gravel or clay bank; usually in the vertical bank of a river or stream, in man-made quarries and pits, in softer seams of rock faces or in sandy estuaries and sea coast banks at times. In the far north it may occur on very small and low banks and earth heaps. In the south of its range, in north India, it may nest at altitudes of up to *c.* 4,500 m. Outside the breeding season it usually occurs near water. It winters in Africa south of the Sahara and in northern India.

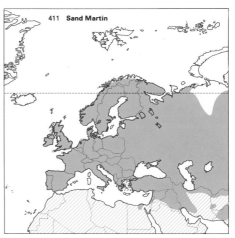

Plain Sand Martin *Riparia paludicola* (Map 412)
Resident; in the Subtropical to Tropical zones. It occurs in similar situations to the previous species, nesting in colonies in tunnels bored into river banks and alluvial cliffs, but in hotter, drier areas.

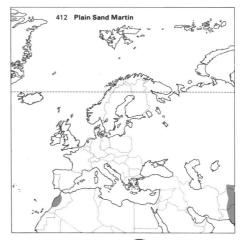

House Martin   Sand Martin   Plain Sand Martin

PIPITS AND WAGTAILS
Motacillidae

Small, slender, long-legged insect-eaters, mainly terrestrial, nesting on the ground. There are two groups, the drab brown pipits (nine species) and the more brightly coloured wagtails (four species).

GRASSLAND PIPITS some *Anthus* species

This genus may be subdivided into those species which prefer an open, treeless habitat, and those usually associated with trees. Of the first group (map 413) the best-known is the Meadow Pipit, occurring in Boreal and Temperate grasslands. The Red-throated Pipit occurs through open tundra in the east and overlaps with the Meadow Pipit in the west. Richard's Pipit is a larger species of open grassy areas in eastern Eurasia. It also occurs as a resident and local migrant in Africa south of the Sahara and in the Oriental region south to Australasia. In spite of this distribution it occurs regularly in western Europe during migration periods. Where Richard's Pipit is absent in the Tibetan region the Rosy Pipit *Anthus roseatus* occurs. The drier, warmer zones of southern Europe are occupied by the Tawny Pipit, another larger species which overlaps with the Meadow Pipit in the north, and with Richard's Pipit in the east. The easternmost form of the Tawny Pipit, in Mongolia and China, is sometimes separated as a species, Blyth's Pipit *Anthus godlewskii*. It is almost indistinguishable from Richard's Pipit with

which it co-exists in this region, but shows behavioural differences. The Long-billed Pipit replaces the Tawny Pipit in some more southerly south-eastern areas. Berthelot's Pipit is an isolate endemic to the Atlantic islands. In the cool, rocky coastal regions of the north and the high Alpine zones further south the Rock/Water Pipit replaces these other species, showing a well-defined subdivision of an Arctic/Alpine distribution. The Rock Pipit also occurs in North America where it occupies a broader range of open habitats in the absence of most other species. Only one other pipit occurs there, Sprague's Pipit *A. spraguei*, in a limited central prairie region.

Meadow Pipit   *Anthus pratensis*
(Maps 413, 414)
Resident and migrant; breeding in Arctic to Temperate zones, wintering in Warm Temperate and western Temperate zones. It occurs mainly in open grassland, from tundra to grassy high moorland and heathland, coastal, waterside and hillside meadows, saltmarshes and dunes. Where the Tree Pipit is absent it may occur in parkland, very open forest and forest and shrub tundra. In winter it occurs frequently on open cultivated areas. In the southern part of its range it utilises mountain meadows where it may occur with the Rock/Water Pipit.

Red-throated Pipit   *Anthus cervinus*
(Maps 413, 415)
Migrant; breeding in the Arctic zone, wintering in Warm Temperate to Tropical zones. It

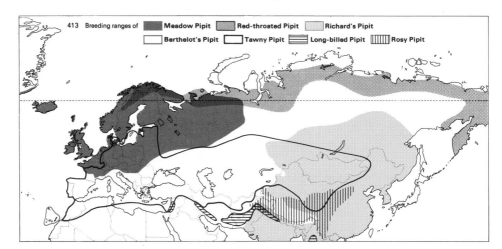

413 Breeding ranges of ▨ Meadow Pipit ▨ Red-throated Pipit ▨ Richard's Pipit ▢ Berthelot's Pipit ▢ Tawny Pipit ▤ Long-billed Pipit ▥ Rosy Pipit

Meadow Pipit   Red-throated Pipit   Richard's Pipit

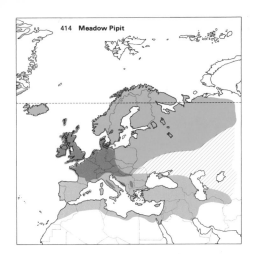

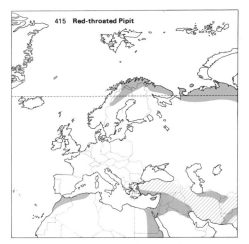

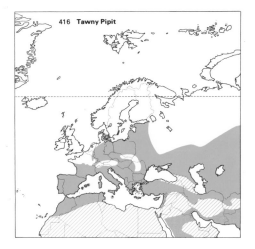

breeds in swampy areas of moss and shrub tundra, and in open parts of coasts and river and lake edges. In the west in Scandinavia it occurs in birch and willow scrub, on high ground. It winters on open grassland and cultivated areas.

Richard's Pipit   *Anthus novaeseelandiae*
(Map 413)
This is a species of moist, low-lying grasslands, and occurs in Europe as a migrant on open grasslands, marshes or cultivated areas.

Tawny Pipit   *Anthus campestris*
(Maps 413, 416)
Migrant; breeding in drier Temperate to Warm Temperate zones, and wintering in dry Subtropical zones. It occurs in dry open areas with scanty vegetation, on sandy or lime soils with sparse herbage, dry heathland, dunes, sand or clay steppes with grass or shrubs and areas of bare soil, or salt steppes, on dry hill slopes and mountains with sparse plant growth, on sandy areas of cultivation and on similar sites extending at one extreme into desert edges and at the other into large clearings and open forest edges. It winters in savannah areas and arid zones bordering desert in Africa south of the Sahara, Arabia and India.

Long-billed Pipit   *Anthus similis*
(Maps 413, 417)
Resident and partly migratory; in the Warm Temperate zone. A similar species to the Tawny Pipit, but occurring in warmer regions, nesting on dry grassy and stony hillslopes

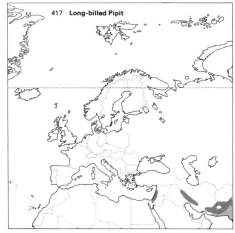

Tawny Pipit   Long-billed Pipit   Rosy Pipit

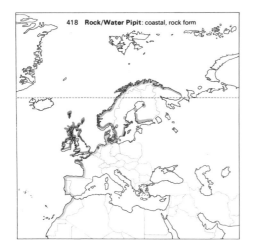

418 **Rock/Water Pipit**: coastal, rock form

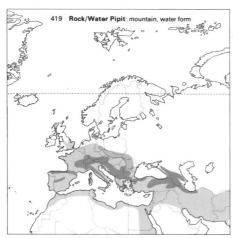

419 **Rock/Water Pipit**: mountain, water form

420 **Tree Pipit**

where thin vegetation is mixed with stones, boulders and screes, at altitudes of *c.* 500–3,000 m. It winters at lower altitudes in grassy areas, low scrub, dry sandy areas and cultivation.

Berthelot's Pipit   *Anthus berthelotii*
(Map 413)
Resident; in Warm Temperate Atlantic zone. It occurs in open dry areas of scanty vegetation, semi-desert areas of volcanic rock and more restricted open places such as tracks.

Rock/Water Pipit   *Anthus spinoletta*
(Maps 418, 419)
Resident and migrant; breeding in coastal Arctic to Temperate zones, and montane Temperate to Warm Temperate zones at Arctic to cool Temperate altitudes, and wintering in Temperate to Warm Temperate zones. It occurs as the Rock Pipit on rocky sea coasts and coastal islands, coasts with low earth cliffs and a few rocks, and on grassy and rocky moss tundra, and shrub tundra. The southern montane Water Pipit occurs on marshy meadows in mountains and high valleys, and on high plateaus, in alpine scrub and up to the snowline, usually in broken habitats with a mixture of grasses, boggy areas and rocks; at altitudes of from *c.* 320 m, although usually higher, to *c.* 3,150 m. The winter movements are dispersals rather than migration, with birds appearing on mud and sandy coasts, and in marshy areas and wet meadows at low altitudes.

————————————————————

TREE PIPITS some *Anthus* species
(Map 421)
The typical Tree Pipit occurs in areas of open and scattered trees and shrubs with which it is closely linked. In eastern Eurasia the Olive-backed Pipit replaces it but there is a large area of overlap where the latter appears to prefer taller and thicker forest than the other species. The Pechora Pipit appears to replace both in the shrub tundra region, but with an imprecisely known range. In the extreme south-east the Upland Pipit *Anthus sylvanus* occurs in open forest and scrub on mountain slopes. This group does not occur in North America.

Tree Pipit   *Anthus trivialis* (Maps 420, 421)
Migrant; breeding in Boreal to Temperate zones, wintering in Subtropical to Tropical

Rock Pipit   Water Pipit   Berthelot's Pipit

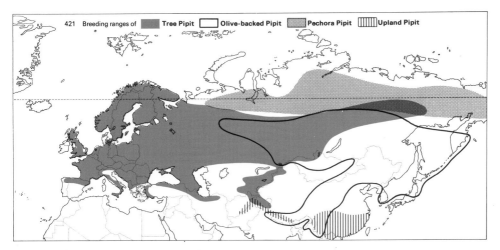

421 Breeding ranges of [ ] Tree Pipit [ ] Olive-backed Pipit [ ] Pechora Pipit [ ] Upland Pipit

zones. It occurs in areas of herbage with scattered trees on drier hill and mountain slopes, parkland and lowland heath with scattered trees, forest edge and more open broadleaf and conifer forest with mixed young and old trees, large clearings and burnt areas in forest, the upper tree limit and scattered trees at higher altitudes, and on forest steppe. In the southern part of the range it occurs at *c.* 2,000–2,600 m. It winters in similar areas, parkland, savannah, grassland and cultivation where scattered trees or groves are present.

Olive-backed Pipit   *Anthus hodgsoni* (Map 421)

Migrant; breeding in Boreal to Warm Temperate eastern zones, wintering in Subtropical to Tropical zones. It occurs in similar habitats to the Tree Pipit but in the region of overlapping ranges appears to utilise thicker forest areas. In general it occurs in the more open areas, clearings, watersides, and sparser growth of forest edges and altitude zones; mainly in conifers, sometimes in broadleaf forest. It may extend into low sparse high-mountain scrub. In the south of its range it breeds at up to *c.* 4,000 m. It winters at lower altitudes in mainly broadleaf forest and patches of trees, and in cultivation with scattered trees.

Pechora Pipit   *Anthus gustavi* (Map 421)

Migrant; breeding in Subarctic to cooler Boreal zones, wintering in the Tropical zone. The extent and boundaries of the breeding range are very uncertain. It occurs in shrub tundra, and forest bordering shrub tundra, in willow scrub along rivers and open marshy areas with dead trees in the Boreal conifer forest. It winters in tropical Oriental regions.

WAGTAILS *Motacilla* species

There are four species with widely overlapping general distributions; two of them, the Pied/White and Yellow/Blue-headed Wagtails, extending just into North America in Alaska. The Citrine Wagtail has the smallest distribution from Russia and Iran to eastern China. The other species extend right through Eurasia, limited locally by habitat requirements, the Grey Wagtail usually occurring by running water and having the more limited distribution, the Yellow/Blue-headed Wagtail in lowland valley grasslands, and the Pied/White Wagtail in a wider range of moist habitats. The Grey Wagtail shows little variation through its range, but has a species group in Africa south of the Sahara – the Mountain Wagtail *M. clara*, the Cape Wagtail *M. capensis* and the Madagascan Wagtail *M. flaviventris* – with the black throat replaced by a white throat with black border, and a decreasing amount of yellow colour. In the Himalayas its place appears to be taken by the wagtail-like *Enicurus* thrushes. The last two Eurasian species have a number of very distinct forms, probably arising during glacial isolation. In

Tree Pipit   Olive-backed Pipit   Pechora Pipit   Upland Pipit

the Pied/White Wagtail complex (map 393) grey-mantled birds have a wide distribution, but in Britain and in the south-east in China, Mongolia, extreme south-east Siberia and Japan the males are black-backed, and in the south-east there is an increase of white on the wings. There are three closely related species with blacker plumage peripheral to this range, the Japanese Wagtail *M. grandis* partly overlapping with a pied wagtail, the Large Pied Wagtail *M. madaraspatensis* in the Indian peninsula, and in Africa the widespread African Pied Wagtail *M. aguimp* occurring as far north as upper Egypt.

The Yellow/Blue-headed Wagtails present an even more complex picture. Some fourteen subspecies are usually recognised, differing mainly in head colouring which seems especially prone to rapid variation in response to selective pressures. I have tried to find an underlying pattern in these (map 424) and there appears to be evidence of a chain of isolates from east to west, occurring in small areas and, as in other species and species-groups, some of these spread through suitable habitats more rapidly than others. I suspect that some of the finer differences recognised in the subspecies may have arisen since the final spread, and there has also been interbreeding between otherwise distinct forms in some areas. From east to west I have recognised nine forms. (1) The eastern Blue-headed Wagtail *M. f. simillima* of Kamchatka, with which *M. f. alascens* may perhaps be linked. (2) The Kurile Yellow Wagtail *M. f. taivana*, with dark head and yellow eyestripe and chin in

Sakhalin and nearby Siberia. (3) The Grey-headed Wagtail *M. f. thunbergi* in eastern Eurasia overlaps in range with the last form and appears to have spread to southern Scandinavia where it interbreeds with *M. f. flava*. (4) The White-headed Wagtail *M. f. leucocephala* occurs in a limited area of western Mongolia. (5) The Yellow-headed Wagtail *M. f. lutea* occurs in the northern steppes. It appears to be a distinct form with a limited habitat but its status as a subspecies has been questioned because it now shares its range with either the blue-headed or black-headed forms. (6) The Black-headed Wagtails *M. f. feldegg* and *M. f. melanogrisea*, becoming slightly less black and with white on the chin in the latter, occurring from the Balkans and Middle East into Iran and the southern steppes and interbreeding with *M. f. flava* in the northern Balkans. (7) The Ashy-headed Wagtail *M. f. cinereocapilla* around the Adriatic and Italy, extending into Tunisia. (8) The Blue-headed Wagtails, *M. f. iberiae, M. f. flava* and *M. f. beema*, showing a gradual increase of white on the head from west to east and occurring from North Africa through Spain and right through temperate Eurasia to the northern Altai and Lake Baikal. The Egyptian Blue-headed Wagtail *M. f. pygmaea* might be part of this, or a similar but distinct isolate population like the Eastern Blue-headed Wagtail. (9) The Yellow Wagtail *M. f. flavissima* of the British Isles. This array of forms may indicate the potential for the production of new forms in a bird nesting in moist valley or lowland meadows.

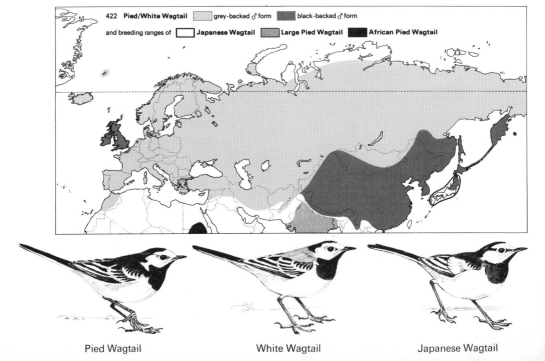

422 **Pied/White Wagtail** [ ] grey-backed ♂ form   [ ] black-backed ♂ form

and breeding ranges of [ ] **Japanese Wagtail**   [ ] **Large Pied Wagtail**   [ ] **African Pied Wagtail**

Pied Wagtail   White Wagtail   Japanese Wagtail

Pied/White Wagtail *Motacilla alba*
(Maps 422, 423)
Resident and migrant; breeding in Arctic to
Warm Temperate zones, wintering in Warm
Temperate to Tropical zones, and in the western Temperate zone. It occurs on open areas,
particularly grassland and most often by
water; but less closely associated with water
than other species. It is found on waterside
grassland, open parkland and lawns, urban
parks and gardens, farms and cultivated land,
forest edge and clearings. From open tundra,
cooler steppes, alpine grassland and rocky
open areas in mountain forest, to Warm Temperate lowland areas. It winters in a wide
range of habitats in Africa, India and the
northern Oriental region.

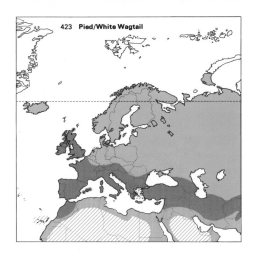

423 Pied/White Wagtail

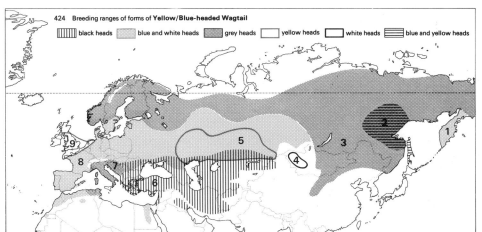

424 Breeding ranges of forms of **Yellow/Blue-headed Wagtail**

||||| black heads   blue and white heads   grey heads   yellow heads   white heads   blue and yellow heads

Yellow/Blue-headed Wagtail *Motacilla flava*
(Maps 424, 425)
Mainly migrant, resident in a few southern
Mediterranean areas; breeding in Subarctic to
Warm Temperate zones, wintering in Subtropical to Tropical zones. It occurs generally
in moist grassy areas, near water and usually
with lush herbage. It is found in grassy tundra,
marshes and bogs, grassland with tall herbage,
open cultivation, grassland by fresh or salt
waters, moist areas in grass and shrub steppes
and forest clearings. Mainly a lowland bird,
but in southern mountains it breeds at up to
c. 2,500 m. It winters mainly in Africa south of
the Sahara, India and South-east Asia.

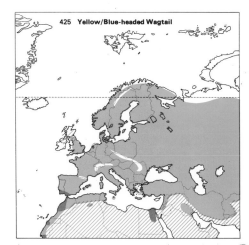

425 Yellow/Blue-headed Wagtail

Large Pied Wagtail   African Pied Wagtail   Yellow/Blue-headed Wagtail

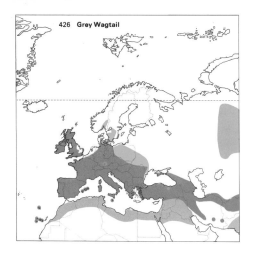

426 Grey Wagtail

Grey Wagtail *Motacilla cinerea* (Map 426)
Resident and migrant; breeding in western Temperate to Warm Temperate zones, and eastern Boreal to Temperate zones, wintering in Africa south of the Sahara, India and South-east Asia, and western Temperate to Warm Temperate zones. It occurs usually by flowing water with rocks and stones, very typically by hill and mountain streams and rivers, but occurring in lowland on short stretches of faster-flowing streams or small waterfalls. These requirements limit its distribution mainly to hilly and mountain regions. It occurs at up to *c.* 2,200 m in the Alps, *c.* 3,000 m in the Caucasus and 4,300 m in the Himalayas. In winter it occurs in a wider range of habitats, but usually by flowing water.

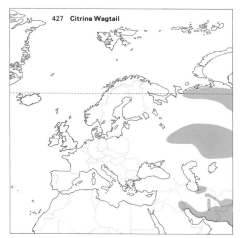

427 Citrine Wagtail

Citrine Wagtail *Motacilla citreola* (Map 427)
Migrant in Subarctic to Warm Temperate zones, wintering in Warm Temperate to Subtropical zones. It occurs in wet tundra willow scrub, mountain tundra and meadows with tussock-grass marsh and willow scrub, sedge marshes and hummocky peat bogs, water-meadows, marshy edges of rivers and streams, and at higher altitudes on swampy patches in mountain meadows and marshy river banks. In the south it breeds mainly in mountains at altitudes of 1,500–4,600 m in the Himalayan region. It winters in the Indian region and South-east Asia, in moist herbage of marsh and swamps, marshy lake and pond borders, ricefields and river and stream banks.

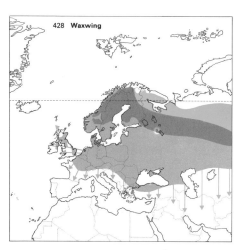

428 Waxwing

WAXWINGS AND HYPOCOLIUS
Bombycillidae

There are three very similar waxwing species, the smaller Cedar Waxwing *Bombycilla cedrorum* of eastern North America, and the typical or Bohemian Waxwing extending right across Eurasia and into western North America. The Japanese Waxwing *B. japonica* breeds in a limited area of extreme eastern Siberia and winters south to Manchuria and Japan. The Grey Hypocolius occurs only in and around the Arabian region.

Waxwing *Bombycilla garrulus* (Map 428)
Resident, migrant and irruptive; breeding in Subarctic to cool Boreal zones, wintering and

| Grey Wagtail | Citrine Wagtail | Waxwing | Grey Hypocolius |

irruptive in Boreal to Temperate zones. It breeds in thick conifer or mixed forest with a berry-bearing shrub layer, on forest edge and river banks, and on forest tundra. In winter it occurs usually in areas with forest or scattered trees, but especially with berry-bearing trees or shrubs. The winter limits are difficult to define and erratic because of frequent irruptive movements.

Grey Hypocolius   *Hypocolius ampelinus*
(Map 429)
Resident and migrant in the Subtropical to Tropical zones. It occurs in desert and semi-desert with patchy or thin scrub, open broad-leaf scrub, groups of trees, irrigated areas with vegetative cover, gardens and palm groves. It is a summer visitor in some areas but in almost all winter areas it seems to be reported as a casual vagrant, and winter movements are im-

429   Grey Hypocolius

perfectly known. During movements it may occur in more desert areas.

BULBULS   *Pycnonotidae*

Small, mainly fruit-eating birds, arboreal and occurring mainly in Subtropical to Tropical zones. The nest is a cup in a tree or bush. The Common Bulbul occurs through Africa south of the Sahara, with an isolated population in north-west Africa and an extension northwards up the Nile. The Arabian population is a distinct form with yellow undertail coverts. It is a hill species in this region and where it meets the lowland White-eared Bulbul in west Oman the two are ecologically separated. Red-vented Bulbuls *Pycnonotus cafer*, escaped cage

birds in this area, have hybridised with both, breaking down the ecological separation and producing a potential nucleus for a hybrid population.

In Afghanistan and Pakistan (map 430) the White-eared Bulbul meets the montane White-cheeked Bulbul *P. leucogenys* and a hybrid zone is present. The latter species occurs through the Himalayas. The Red-vented Bulbul is present through lowland India and Burma. The Golden-vented Bulbul *P. aurigaster* is a southern China and Indochinese species which in eastern Burma hybridises with the Red-vented Bulbul.

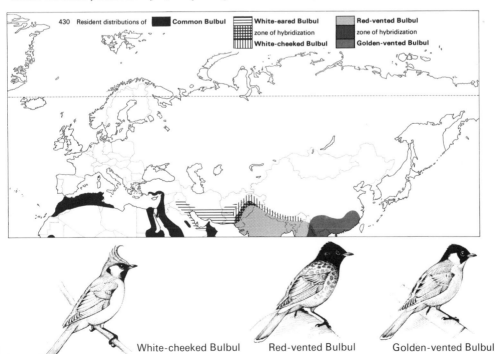

430   Resident distributions of   Common Bulbul   White-eared Bulbul / zone of hybridization / White-cheeked Bulbul   Red-vented Bulbul / zone of hybridization / Golden-vented Bulbul

White-cheeked Bulbul   Red-vented Bulbul   Golden-vented Bulbul

Common Bulbul   *Pycnonotus barbatus*
(Map 430)
Resident; in Subtropical to Tropical zones. It
occurs widely in low bushes and scrub or open
forest in valleys and wadis of arid hilly and
desert areas, and in trees and shrubs of orchards, gardens and palm groves.

White-eared Bulbul   *Pycnonotus leucotis*
(Map 430)
Resident, with some local altitudinal movement in the east of its range; in the Subtropical
zone. It occurs in lowland in semi-desert scrub,
low scrub tree growth, cultivated areas with
shrubs and trees, gardens, palm groves and
coastal mangroves. In Pakistan it occurs at
altitudes of up to 1,800 m in the breeding
season, moving to lower altitudes later.

SHRIKES   *Laniidae*

Small raptorial songbirds, feeding on insects
and various small creatures. Arboreal, usually
in fairly open areas, with a cup nest in a tree or
shrub. There are eight species in the area. The
largest of these, the Great Grey Shrike, is
widespread across Eurasia, northern Africa
and Arabia and through North America. In
eastern Eurasia the range continues through
eastern Siberia but to the south in China it is
replaced by the still larger Chinese Great Grey
Shrike *Lanius sphenocercus*. The Old World
population of the Great Grey Shrike can be
divided into a northern and a southern form
with small consistent plumage differences.
A series of smaller species occur across the
region in open country with the Woodchat
Shrike in western Europe and the Mediterranean region, and the Lesser Grey Shrike in
central Eurasia from eastern France to the
Altai region, the two overlapping, with the
Lesser Grey Shrike in areas with taller trees.
The red-backed shrike group (map 431) also

occurs right across Eurasia but with a complex
of three forms which have been regarded as
one to three species in various combinations.
They are here regarded as two. The Red-backed
Shrike with black and white tail extends to
mid-Siberia, and is then replaced in eastern
Eurasia by the similar Brown Shrike *L. cristatus*. A rufous-tailed form of the Red-backed
Shrike occurs to the south of these in central
Eurasia from Iran to eastern Mongolia. Both
forms of the Red-backed Shrike winter mainly
in Africa. There is a third species in the group,
the Thick-billed Shrike *L. tigrinus* occurring in
south-eastern China and into Japan. It occurs
within the range of the Brown Shrike but uses
forest habitats more than the other species.
Another series of more slender, long-tailed
shrikes occur to the south of these. Beginning
possibly with the Masked Shrike in the eastern
Mediterranean it includes the Bay-backed
Shrike in Iran and the Indian region, and the
Burmese Shrike *L. colluroides* in Burma and
Indochina; together with two larger species,
the Grey-backed Shrike *L. tephronotus* of the

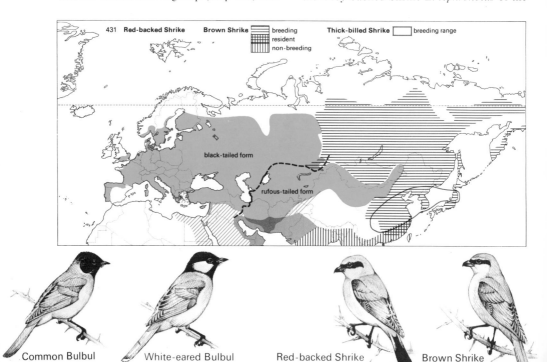

Common Bulbul   White-eared Bulbul   Red-backed Shrike   Brown Shrike

Himalayas and Rufous-backed Shrike *L. schach* from Afghanistan through the Indian and Indochinese regions. The remaining two species are of African origin extending northwards, the Black-headed Bush Shrike isolated on the west side of the Sahara and the Rosy-patched Shrike in north-east Africa adjoining the Red Sea.

Red-backed Shrike   *Lanius collurio*
(Map 431)
Migrant; breeding in warmer Boreal to Temperate zones, wintering in Subtropical to Tropical zones. It often utilises lower shrub growth than other shrikes, and occurs in open thorny scrub on drier soils, heathland with shrubs, shrubby hedgerows, forest edge or clearings and open forest with a thorny shrub layer, riverine scrub, orchards, parklands and tree groves in open country, and shrubby steppe and semi-desert. In the south of its breeding range it extends into mountain junipers up to *c.* 3,000 m. It winters in Africa, the Persian Gulf and north-west India.

Woodchat Shrike   *Lanius senator* (Map 432)
Migrant; breeding in Warm Temperate and dry western Temperate zones, wintering in Subtropical to Tropical zones. It occurs in maquis scrub on dry hillsides, open ground or heathland with scattered shrubs or trees, olive groves, orchards, gardens, forest edge and clearings, desert oases and cultivation with scattered trees. It prefers higher scrub and tree growth for observation perches than does the Red-backed Shrike. It winters in Africa south of the Sahara and north of the Equator.

Masked Shrike   *Lanius nubicus* (Map 433)
Migrant; breeding in the eastern Mediterranean Warm Temperate zone, wintering in Subtropical to Tropical zones. It is more arboreal in habit than other species, occurring in light forest with thorny undergrowth but usually with thick leafy treetops, scrub with scattered large trees, orchards, olive groves, vineyards and gardens. It winters in north-east Africa and Arabia and westwards on the southern side of the Sahara.

Bay-backed Shrike   *Lanius vittatus*
(Map 434)
Mainly resident, migrant in northern mountains; in the Subtropical zone. It occurs in

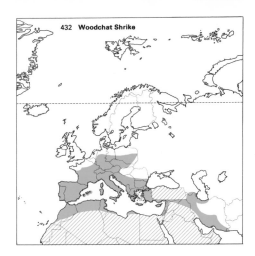
432 Woodchat Shrike

433   Masked Shrike

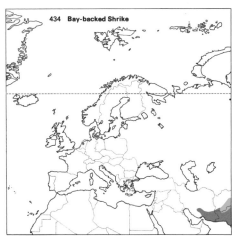
434   Bay-backed Shrike

Thick-billed Shrike

Woodchat Shrike

Masked Shrike

Bay-backed Shrike

435   Lesser Grey Shrike

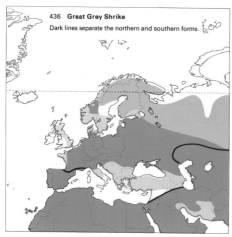

436   Great Grey Shrike
Dark lines separate the northern and southern forms.

open scrub in hills and lowland, and overgrown areas bordering cultivation, and in
semi-desert. It inhabits drier habitats than
the Grey-backed and Rufous-backed Shrikes
which share part of its range. It occurs at
altitudes of up to 1,600 m.

Lesser Grey Shrike   *Lanius minor* (Map 435)
Migrant; breeding in the drier Temperate zone,
wintering in Subtropical to Tropical zones. It
occurs more consistently in grassy areas than
the other two species, with more tall trees, and
in more forested areas than the Great Grey
Shrike. It is found on forest edge, in groves,
shelterbelts and rows of trees in grassland
areas, on dry grass steppe and cultivation with
scattered trees, riverine forest with grassy
areas, forest steppes, parkland and orchards.
It winters in Africa south of the Sahara, mainly
in savannah areas.

Great Grey Shrike   *Lanius excubitor*
(Map 436)
Migrant and resident; breeding in drier Subarctic to Tropical zones and wintering in Temperate to Tropical zones. It is a bird of partly
open areas with scattered trees, tall shrubs or
posts from which to watch for prey. It occurs
in scrub and forest tundra, willow and birch
scrub, more open areas of conifer, mixed and
broadleaf forest, on forest edge and scattered
trees on heathland, moorland or valley grassland, swamp edges, riverine thickets, thorn
scrub on dry hillsides, forest steppes, semi-
desert or desert with thorn scrub, *Acacia* or
cactus and in desert oases.

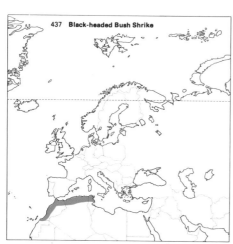

437   **Black-headed Bush Shrike**

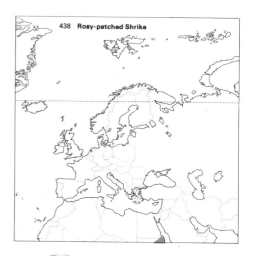

438   **Rosy-patched Shrike**

Lesser Grey Shrike

Great Grey Shrike

Black-headed Bush Shrike   *Tchagra senegala*
(Map 437)
Resident; in thick shrubby growth of arid desert areas, in thorny scrub, and scattered low trees, dry open forest, plantations and gardens. Its main distribution is through Africa south of the Sahara where it is absent from thick wet forest and open desert.

Rosy-patched Shrike   *Rhodophoneus cruentus*
(Map 438)
Resident; occurring in thorn scrub and also bush in arid areas.

DUNNOCKS   *Prunellidae*

Small, furtive, ground-feeding birds, taking insects and seed, and nesting in shrubs or on the ground. Usually in or near shrub or forest growth. The family only occurs in Eurasia, Arabia and North Africa. It is centred on the Himalayan/Tibetan region where seven species occur. In the genus as a whole there are two large montane species, three dull-coloured species, and a group usually with rufous breast and pale eyestripe. The first two occur on rocky mountain slopes at similar altitudes, but are absent from mountains of southern Iran and Afghanistan. Of the dull-coloured birds two very similar species occur at opposite ends of Eurasia, suggesting earlier separation (map 439). These are the European Dunnock in Europe east to the Urals, and the Japanese Dunnock *Prunella rubida*, a slightly browner bird of Japanese mountains. The third of these is the Maroon-backed Dunnock *P. immaculata* of thick forest of the eastern Himalayas and western China. The mid-Eurasia region is occupied by the third group. Of these the Siberian Dunnock occurs in northern forest scrub (map 439), the Black-throated Dunnock in higher birch forest and scrub on forest edges, overlapping in distribution with the previous species in the northern Urals, and the Brown Dunnock in central Asia in scrub in arid and rocky regions, meeting the Siberian Dunnock in the north and extensively overlapping the Black-throated Dunnock in the west. Its range also encompasses that of Koslov's Dunnock *P. koslowi* which occurs on arid Mongolian mountains with thin scrub and sparse grass. In the Himalayas and western China the Rufous-breasted Dunnock *P. strophiata* occurs in scrub at the upper forest limit, and the Robin Dunnock *P. rubeculoides* on the Tibetan plateau in high altitude scrub and moist meadows, while east and south of the Caspian Radde's Dunnock occupies a high alpine mountain zone. A form present in the mountains of southern Arabia is sometimes regarded as a race of the last species or treated as a separate species, *P. fagani*.

Siberian Dunnock   *Prunella montanella*
(Map 439)
Migrant; in the Boreal zone, wintering in the

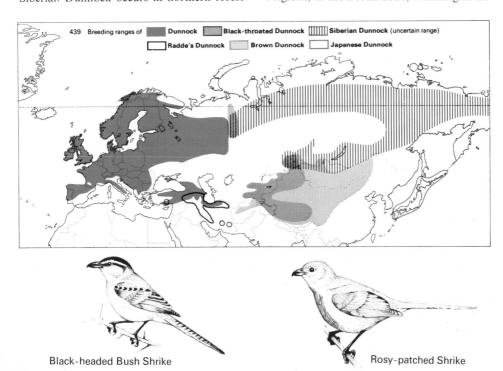

439   Breeding ranges of   Dunnock   Black-throated Dunnock   Siberian Dunnock (uncertain range)
Radde's Dunnock   Brown Dunnock   Japanese Dunnock

Black-headed Bush Shrike   Rosy-patched Shrike

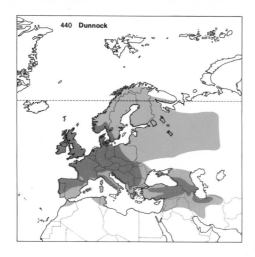

440 Dunnock

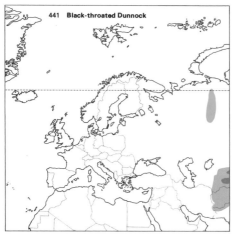

441 Black-throated Dunnock

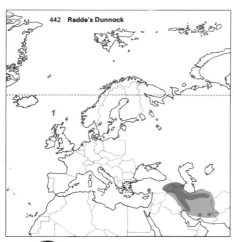

442 Radde's Dunnock

eastern Temperate zone. It has a very imprecisely known range in montane areas on the edge of conifer forest in broadleaf trees and stunted conifers, in riverside shrubs and in willow and alder scrub. In winter it occurs in scrub or long herbage, particularly along watercourses, in northern China.

Brown Dunnock *Prunella fulvescens*
(Map 439)
Resident, with some seasonal altitudinal movements; in the mountain ranges of eastern Temperate to Warm Temperate zones. It breeds on high, arid and stony mountain slopes with grass and scrub, scree and boulders in grass, or dwarf juniper thickets, and stony ridges with sparse herbage in open regions. It is found at altitudes of *c*. 2,500–3,000 m in the north of its range to *c*. 3,500–4,600 m in the south. In winter it descends into mountain valleys.

European Dunnock *Prunella modularis*
(Maps 439, 440)
Resident and migrant; breeding in Boreal to Temperate zones, wintering in the Temperate zone. It occurs in thick scrub and forest with young trees or a shrub layer, usually near an open space; in conifer, mixed and broadleaf forest, forest edge and glades, parkland with shrubby growth, hillside scrub, low bushes with bracken or heather, cultivation with shrub and tree growth and urban gardens. In the south of the breeding range it occurs up to *c*. 2,500 m in mountain and tree-line scrub. In winter it occurs in lowland, frequently in thickets by water, or bordering cultivation.

Black-throated Dunnock *Prunella atrogularis*
(Maps 439, 441)
Resident and migrant; breeding in Boreal and montane Temperate zones, wintering at lower altitudes in the Temperate zone. It occurs in the north in stunted subalpine conifer forest, elsewhere in conifer forest or scrub with juniper. In winter it occurs in more lowland areas, in forest, plantations, orchards, lowland semi-arid or arid scrub, and in shrubby thickets, reedbeds or tall grass stands by water.

Radde's Dunnock *Prunella ocularis*
(Maps 439, 442)
Resident and migrant; breeding in the Warm Temperate zone in Alpine altitudinal zones and wintering at lower altitudes. It occurs in

Siberian Dunnock   Brown Dunnock   Japanese Dunnock   Dunnock

shrubs such as junipers, and in thickets on dry, stony mountain slopes, occurring at altitudes of 2,500–3,000 m. In winter it usually occurs at lower altitudes in shrubby growth bordering mountain streams.

Alpine Dunnock *Prunella collaris* (Map 443)
Resident and partial migrant, with some seasonal altitudinal movements; in Temperate and Warm Temperate zones in Arctic/Alpine altitude zones. It occurs in mountain and high plateau areas between the upper tree limit and snowline, on open rocky slopes, alpine meadows with rocks, and areas of rocks with sparse herbage or small shrubs. It occurs at the highest altitudes in the south-east of its range, reaching *c*. 2,150–3,000 m in the Caucasus, 3,600–5,500 m in the Himalayas. In winter it descends to rocky lower slopes and foothills.

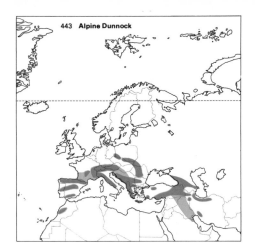

WARBLERS *Sylviidae*

Small, mainly arboreal insect-eating birds, occurring in most types of vegetation and showing a wide range of adaptation from the subarctic to hot deserts, and from tall grasses to tall trees. It is a large group of over fifty species, species often overlapping in range but separated by small differences in habitat preference within the vegetation zones. At least seven subgroups can be recognised – grass warblers (*Locustella* species), marsh warblers (*Acrocephalus* species), bush warblers (*Cettia, Cisticola, Prinia* and *Scotocerca* species), tree warblers (*Hippolais* species), typical *Sylvia* warblers, leaf warblers (*Phylloscopus* species) and Goldcrests.

GRASS WARBLERS *Locustella* species
Skulking species, usually in low wet or waterside vegetation. The cup nest is built low on or near the ground. There are five species in the present area and two more in the east (maps 445–447). Middendorf's Warbler *Locustella ochotensis* is an extreme eastern form with a limited range, and is sometimes regarded as a race of Pallas's Grasshopper Warbler. The others fall into a pattern of three western and three eastern species forming three pairs. In view of the overall similarity of the species the groupings on the maps are a little arbitrary, but appear to provide pairs similar in size and plumage. It has been suggested, however, that

the Western Grasshopper Warbler replaces both Pallas's Grasshopper Warbler and the Lanceolated Warbler.

The Large Grasshopper Warbler *L. fasciolata* appears to replace Savi's Warbler in general distribution and has been mapped accordingly, but it is much more a bird of tall grasses rather than swamps and reedbeds, and has a less insect-like song.

Western Grasshopper Warbler *Locustella naevia* (Maps 444, 445)
Migrant, breeding in warmer Boreal to Temperate zones, wintering in Subtropical to Tropical zones. It occurs in areas of tall her-

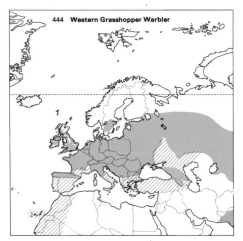

Black-throated Dunnock   Radde's Dunnock   Alpine Dunnock

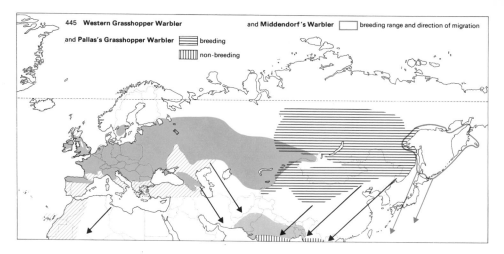

baceous growth mixed with shrubs or young trees, or in waterside plants mixed with reeds and low bushes. It is found around swamps, marshes and pools, along watercourses in young plantations, in swampy forest clearings, low forest edge growth, young secondary forest growth, swampy heathland with low trees, shrubby areas on grassy uplands and coasts, riverine thickets in grass and shrub steppes, and tall crops in cultivated areas. It winters in Africa south of the Sahara and in northern India in areas of tall moist herbage, usually near water or in swamps.

Pallas's Grasshopper Warbler *Locustella certhiola* (Map 445)
Migrant; breeding in eastern warmer Boreal to Temperate zones, wintering in Subtropical to Tropical zones. It occurs in bogs, marshes and wet meadows with tall herbage and reeds bordering scrub, swampy thickets and overgrown borders of streams. Migrant strays occur repeatedly but sporadically in Europe during migration periods. It winters from India and southern China south through the Oriental region.

Savi's Warbler *Locustella luscinioides* (Map 446)
Migrant; breeding in Temperate to Warm Temperate zones, wintering in Subtropical to Tropical zones. It occurs in tall herbaceous growth – reeds, rushes, sedges and other vegetation – growing in shallow fresh or brackish

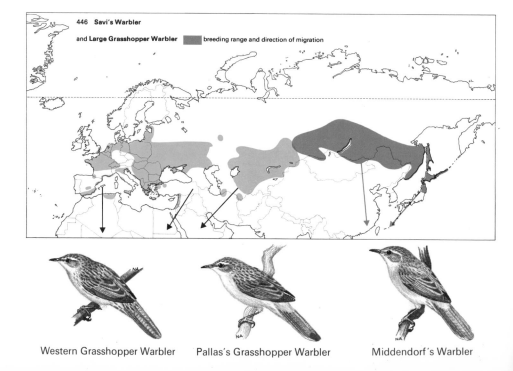

Western Grasshopper Warbler   Pallas's Grasshopper Warbler   Middendorf's Warbler

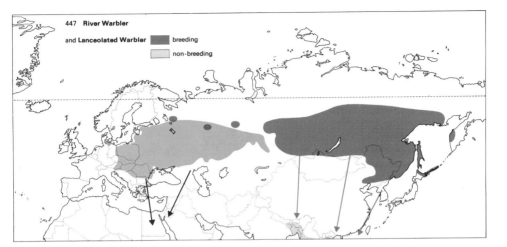

447 River Warbler
and **Lanceolated Warbler**   breeding
non-breeding

water, or on the edges of fresh waters with tall herbage or open reedbeds and scattered shrubs and trees. It winters in East Africa south of the Sahara and north of the Equator.

River Warbler   *Locustella fluviatilis*
(Map 447)
Migrant; breeding in the continental warmer Boreal to Temperate zones, wintering in Subtropical to Tropical zones. It occurs in low broadleaf forest growth with tall herbage bordering freshwater rivers and lakes, in sedge marshes and bogs with low shrubs and trees, in lowland meadows, mixed or conifer forest in moist areas with a thick shrub layer, in bogs, scrub and open riverine forest in steppe areas, and in overgrown orchards, gardens and plantations. On migration it may occur in

tall crops and bushes away from water. It winters through much of East Africa.

Lanceolated Warbler   *Locustella lanceolata*
(Map 447)
Migrant; breeding in eastern warmer Boreal to Temperate zones, wintering in Subtropical to Tropical zones. It occurs in tall herbage – grasses, sedges or reeds – mixed with shrubs on the edges of open, still fresh waters, along ditches, bordering marshes and in forest clearings, and also occurs in open tussock grass marshes and moist grassy areas of open montane forest. It winters in north-eastern India, Indochina and Malaysia in thick scrub with tall grass and sometimes in ricefields, sugarcane or open grassland.

MARSH WARBLERS *Acrocephalus* species
A genus with seven small warblers and two larger species in the present region, occurring as skulking birds in low vegetation growing mainly in or around water. The larger species mainly replace each other geographically (map 449). In Eurasia the Great Reed Warbler occurs in the west and the Eastern Great Reed Warbler in the east, the two narrowly separated in the Altai region, and with the Clamorous Reed Warbler to the south of them. The Thick-billed Warbler *Phragmiticola aedon* is another large warbler sometimes included in the genus *Acrocephalus* but in some respects is similar to *Locustella* species. Its range mainly coincides with the Chinese range of the East-

ern Great Reed Warbler b..t also extends further west to the upper Ob. Among the smaller warblers the four dull brown species form a complex with two pairs, the Reed and Paddyfield Warblers occurring in wetter habitats (map 450) and the Marsh and Blyth's Reed Warblers in drier places (map 453). The ranges of the first two overlap extensively in the steppe area, but they are basically an east and west pair with the Paddyfield Warbler extending in discontinuous range to northern China, and the Blunt-winged Paddyfield Warbler *A. concinens* with a more discontinuous range to the south of it. In China at the head of the Gulf of Chihli there is a small gap in breeding distributions between the two Paddyfield Warblers and in this the limited breeding

Savi's Warbler

Large Grasshopper Warbler

River Warbler   Lanceolated Warbler

ground of the rare Speckled Reed Warbler *A. sorghophilus* occurs. The Marsh Warbler is European in distribution, and Blyth's Reed Warbler occurs further east in forest areas, with some overlap with the previous species. The Black-browed Reed Warbler *A. bistigiceps* is limited to eastern China and might be a counterpart, but in view of the bold pale and blackish brow stripes it may be closer to the Moustached and Sedge Warblers. In this case the forest and scrub species would lack an eastern replacement species within the genus, but in the large and complex warbler family, species from other genera might fill this niche. Of the three species with striped plumage, the Sedge and Moustached Warblers form a pair with the former more northerly and strongly

migratory, the latter more southerly and more resident. The Aquatic Warbler has a limited, mainly eastern European range, and the other two extend only to the lower Yenesei and northern Altai.

Great Reed Warbler   *Acrocephalus arundinaceus* (Maps 448, 449)
Migrant; breeding in Temperate to Warm Temperate zones, wintering in Subtropical to Tropical zones. It occurs mainly in extensive reed marshes bordering fresh waters, from large lakes and slow-moving rivers to streams and ditches, and occasionally in willow scrub bordering water or reedbeds. It usually occurs in lowland areas but has occurred in suitable habitats at 2,000 m in Asian mountains. It winters in Africa south of the Sahara, mainly in reedbeds and tall savannah grasses, but also in moist forest and scrub.

Clamorous Reed Warbler   *Acrocephalus stentorius* (Map 449)
Mainly migrant, resident in a few southern areas; breeding in Warm Temperate to Subtropical zones. It occurs in similar habitats to the previous species but there may be some separation in places. In the Jordan valley where both occur this species is said to prefer papyrus swamps to reeds, but no such differences have been observed in the U.S.S.R. It also utilises small reed clumps in mountain valleys. Migrants winter in India and Southeast Asia in typical habitats, but also in mangrove swamps and pandanus; and on passage occurs in dry scrub and crops.

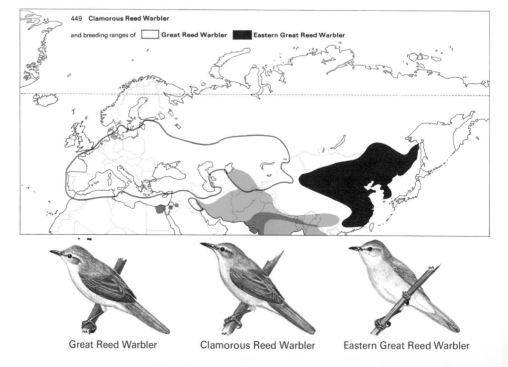

Great Reed Warbler   Clamorous Reed Warbler   Eastern Great Reed Warbler

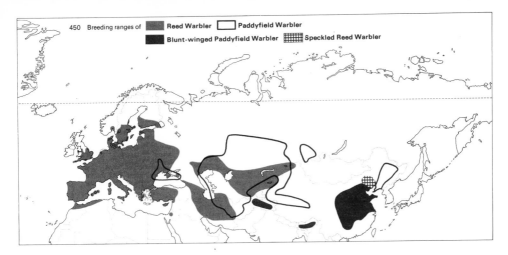

451 Reed Warbler

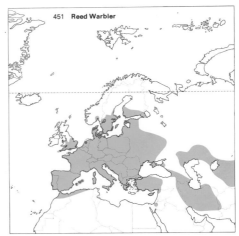

452 Paddyfield Warbler

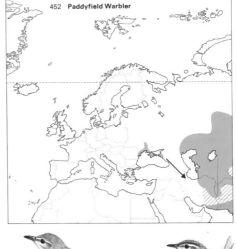

Reed Warbler *Acrocephalus scirpaceus*
(Maps 450, 451)

Migrant; in warmer Boreal to Warm Temperate zones, wintering in Subtropical to Tropical zones. It occurs in reedbeds and similar tall herbaceous growth growing usually in water on the edge of still or slow-moving fresh and brackish waters, from lakes and rivers to ditches, and utilising small or scattered reed patches as well as large areas. Exceptionally it may occur in grainfields or bushes. It winters in Africa south of the Sahara, in reeds and in moist or arid grasslands.

Paddyfield Warbler *Acrocephalus agricola*
(Maps 450, 452)

Migrant; breeding in drier Temperate zone, wintering in Subtropical to Tropical zones. It occurs in the more mixed herbage and shrubs bordering fresh and brackish lakes, pools and irrigation canals in mountain and lowland valleys, forest steppes, grass steppes, semi-desert and desert. It uses small areas of reeds, edges of large reedbeds, grassy swamps and marshy scrub. It occurs at high altitudes in places where waterside vegetation is present. It winters in the Indian region and parts of Southeast Asia, in reeds, ricefields, sugarcane and tall grasses.

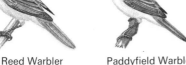

Reed Warbler   Paddyfield Warbler   Blunt-winged Paddyfield Warbler   Speckled Reed Warbler

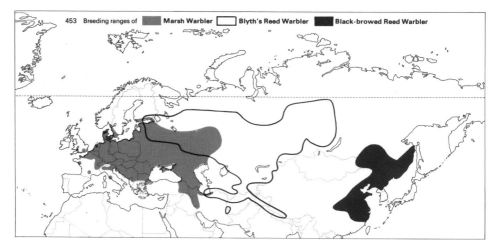

453   Breeding ranges of   ▨ Marsh Warbler   ▢ Blyth's Reed Warbler   ▮ Black-browed Reed Warbler

454   Marsh Warbler

Marsh Warbler   *Acrocephalus palustris*
(Maps 453, 454)

Migrant; breeding in the Temperate zones, wintering in Subtropical to Tropical zones. It occurs in willow and other shrubby thickets bordered by tall herbaceous growth, in damp riverine scrub, drier scrubby mounds in swamps, bushy areas and scattered shrubs in grassland, undergrowth in open forest; cultivation, gardens, old orchards and parkland where these are bordered by or overgrown with shrubs and tall herbage, and similar shrubby and herbaceous growth on steep mountain slopes and bordering subalpine meadows. It occurs at up to *c.* 3,000 m in south-eastern mountains. It winters in the eastern half of Africa south of the Sahara, down to the Cape, in savannah areas.

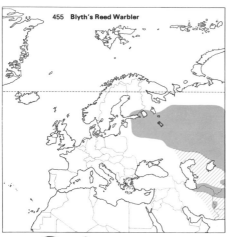

455   Blyth's Reed Warbler

Blyth's Reed Warbler   *Acrocephalus dumetorum* (Maps 453, 455)

Migrant; breeding in warmer Boreal to cool Temperate zones and in higher altitudes of Asiatic Warm Temperate zone, wintering in Subtropical to Tropical zones. It occurs in a wide range of habitats, often in shrubby growth, or mixed shrubs and herbage in swamps or bordering waters of all kinds, in riverine forest, young forest with tall herbage and scrub, overgrown or tall-grassed glades and clearings in conifer, mixed or broadleaf forest; in birch scrub or forest steppes, overgrown farmland or orchards, shrubby growth on hill and mountain slopes and along mountain streams at altitudes of up to *c.* 1,200 m. It

Marsh Warbler   Blyth's Reed Warbler   Black-browed Reed Warbler

winters in the Indian region and in Burma, in shrubby growth, bamboos and grass and grain.

Sedge Warbler *Acrocephalus schoenobaenus* (Map 456)

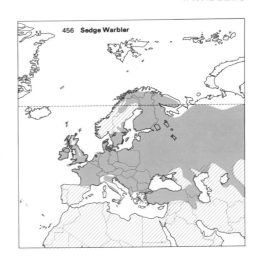

Migrant; breeding in Subarctic to Temperate zones, wintering in Subtropical to Tropical zones. It occurs in tall herbaceous vegetation mixed with shrubs on the edge of still or slow-moving fresh waters – lakes or pools, rivers or ditches – in reed and sedge beds with shrubs or small trees, willow thickets, marshes with reeds and shrubs; and sometimes in boggy grassland, ricefields, grainfields and hedge-rows bordering marshland. On migration it may occur in drier habitats.

Moustached Warbler *Acrocephalus melanopogon* (Map 457)

Resident and migrant; breeding in warmer Temperate to Warm Temperate zones, wintering in the Warm Temperate zone. It occurs in stands of reeds, sedges or reed-mace border-ing fresh or brackish waters, both still and flowing, and at times in small patches of veg-etation. It is present from lowlands to high altitude streams, up to *c.* 1,950 m in the Cau-casus; wintering at lower altitudes.

Aquatic Warbler *Acrocephalus paludicola* (Map 458)

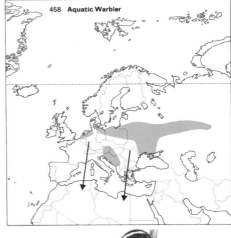

Migrant; breeding in the Temperate zone, wintering in Subtropical to Tropical zones. It occurs mainly in lower vegetation than other species, in sedge and tall grass marshes bor-dering fresh water, in tussock sedge or reeds and reed-mace, usually with a few low scat-tered shrubs. It winters in Africa south of the Sahara.

Sedge Warbler

Moustached Warbler

Aquatic Warbler

BUSH WARBLERS *Cisticola, Cettia,*
Prinia and *Scotocerca*
This is a heterogeneous group of birds in which,
with the exception of the isolate Scrub Warbler, there are single species extending into the
western Eurasian region from large and complex genera of warmer climates. The Fan-tailed
Warbler is a grassland bird occurring through
the Mediterranean region and parts of the
Middle East, and through the Indian region to
South-east Asia. In the last two areas it overlaps with the Yellow-headed Grass Warbler
Cisticola exilis which extends from northern
India south to Australasia. The typical Fan-
tailed Warbler also occurs through much of
Africa south of the Sahara, and within this
region the genus has radiated and adapted to

produce no less than thirty-six other species.
Cetti's Warbler has a more typical distribution through Europe and across to the Altai
in Temperate to Warm Temperate zones. It
is replaced in eastern China by the Chinese
Bush Warbler *Cettia diphone* (map 460). A
third species, the Scaly-headed Bush Warbler
C. squamiceps, occurs in a small part of the
latter's range, and within the Himalaya/South-
east Asia area enclosed by a dark line on the
map there are a further six *Cettia* species. The
genus is absent from Africa. The Graceful
Warbler occurs in scrub and grass areas from
the Middle East and Egypt to northern India.
In the Indian region a further eleven *Prinia*
species occur, and twelve others in Africa. The
Striated Scrub Warbler is a bird of desert and
desert edge with no close relatives.

Fan-tailed Warbler   *Cisticola juncidis*
(Map 459)
Resident; in Warm Temperate to Tropical
zones. It occurs mainly in moist, open places
with tall grassy growth; on the edges of marshes
or swampy areas, wet parts of meadows with
rush clumps, swampy margins of cultivation
or roadsides, marshy places in grassland,
savannah and grass steppes, well-grown grainfields, ricefields, and overgrown grassy fallows. The nest is suspended in grasses or
rushes. As a resident it is vulnerable to cold
winters and its northern limit is variable. Its
recent spread in western Europe north to the
Channel coast with sporadic occurrence beyond may be the temporary result of milder
winters.

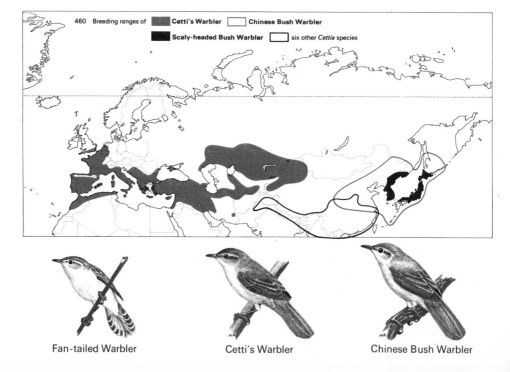

459   Fan-tailed Warbler

460   Breeding ranges of   ▮ Cetti's Warbler   ☐ Chinese Bush Warbler
▮ Scaly-headed Bush Warbler   ☐ six other *Cettia* species

Fan-tailed Warbler   Cetti's Warbler   Chinese Bush Warbler

Cetti's Warbler *Cettia cetti* (Maps 460, 461)
Mainly resident in the Warm Temperate and parts of the Temperate zones, but migrant in its north-easterly range, wintering into Subtropical zones. It occurs in dense shrubby growth with tall herbage bordering fresh waters – pools, streams and rivers – and in similar vegetation in marshy areas and on the edges of reedbeds. It also occurs in wet forest clearings, and in more arid areas in thickets in small marshy sites. It is mainly in lowlands in the north but in the south of its range also occurs in mountain valleys up to *c.* 1,700 m. The nest is a cup low in dense shrubby growth. Like the Fan-tailed Warbler this species has spread north in western Europe in recent years, probably for a similar reason, and now occurs in southern England.

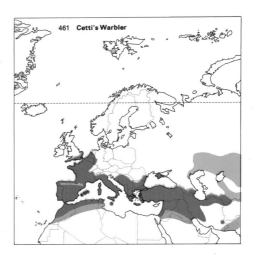

Graceful Warbler *Prinia gracilis* (Map 462)
Resident; in eastern warmer Warm Temperate to Subtropical zones. It occurs in shrubby and grassy areas of swamps, bordering cultivation or on the edges of arid regions. It also occurs in overgrown grassy areas. sometimes by water, and in cultivation, plantations and gardens where shrubs are present. The domed nest is built low in a shrub or tangled grasses.

Striated Scrub Warbler *Scotocerca inquieta* (Map 463)
Resident, in dry Subtropical to Tropical zones. It occurs through the northern part of the Sahara desert, around the Red Sea and southern Arabia and through Iran and Afghanistan. It is found in rocky and stony semi-desert and desert where some sparse shrubby or tufted plant growth is present, often on dry hillsides or in ravines or wadis. In the east of its range it often occurs in hilly areas up to *c.* 3,000 m, descending to lower slopes in winter.

Scaly-headed Bush Warbler

Graceful Warbler

Striated Scrub Warbler

TREE WARBLERS *Hippolais* species
A genus of six species confined to the western Eurasian region, extending only to the Altai region (map 467). They are mainly in warmer zones and show evidence of a single replacement pattern, with the Melodious Warbler in Iberia and North Africa, replaced through most of Europe by the Icterine Warbler which may have had an eastern European or Caucasian origin. The Olive-tree Warbler breeds around the Aegean, Upcher's Warbler in the Middle East and the Booted Warbler mainly further east from Iran and the Indus northwards. The Olivaceous Warbler occurs through North Africa and the Middle East. These are tree- and shrub-haunting species, building a cup nest in a tree or bush.

Icterine Warbler *Hippolais icterina*
(Maps 464, 467)
Migrant; breeding in warmer Boreal to Temperate zones, wintering in Subtropical to Tropical zones. It occurs usually in areas with open ground, well-grown broadleaf trees and tall shrubs; being found on the edges and in clearings of broadleaf forest; open broadleaf, mixed or conifer forest with a tall shrub layer; in riverine forest lowlands and hill and mountain valleys, forest steppes, forest belts in cultivated areas; parklands, orchards, plantations, gardens, rows of trees and shrubs in cultivated areas and bordering lakes. It winters in Africa south of the Sahara in forest savannah.

Melodious Warbler *Hippolais polyglotta*
(Maps 465, 467)
Migrant; breeding in western Warm Temperate zone, wintering in Subtropical to Tropical zones. It occurs in similar habitats to the previous species, but may occur in areas of lower and more dense shrubs and scrub. There is no obvious ecological separation of the two species. It winters in West Africa in forest and shrub savannah.

Olive-tree Warbler *Hippolais olivetorum*
(Maps 466, 467)
Migrant; breeding in Warm Temperate zone, wintering in Subtropical and Tropical zones. It occurs in areas of broadleaf trees – oak forest, orchards, olive groves, gardens and in areas of more scattered mature trees. It winters in East Africa, south of the Sahara, in open forest savannah and arid scrub.

Icterine Warbler   Melodious Warbler   Olive-tree Warbler

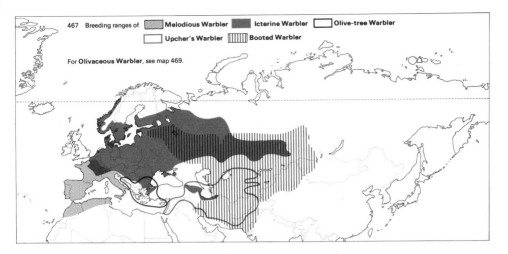

467   Breeding ranges of [Melodious Warbler] [Icterine Warbler] [Olive-tree Warbler]
[Upcher's Warbler] [Booted Warbler]

For **Olivaceous Warbler**, see map 469.

Upcher's Warbler   *Hippolais languida*
(Maps 467, 468)

Migrant; breeding in the dry Warm Temperate zone, wintering in the Subtropical zone. It occurs in arid areas in shrubby growth or small trees, including gardens, vineyards, orchards, open forest; and in scrub on dunes, or bordering large rivers and lakes, and in semidesert and desert areas at varying altitudes up to *c.* 1,600 m. It winters in East Africa and southern Arabia.

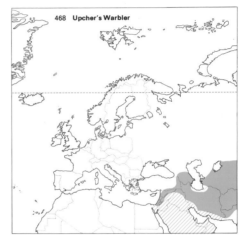

468   Upcher's Warbler

Olivaceous Warbler   *Hippolais pallida*
(Map 469)

Mainly migrant, but resident in the lower Nile region; breeding in Warm Temperate to Subtropical zones, wintering in the Subtropical zone. It occurs in a wide range of dry habitats where trees or shrubs are present, often near water. It is found in shrubby growth on dunes and coasts, scattered trees and shrubs on dry hillsides; plantations, orchards; palm, olive and oak groves, oases, and in sparse riverine trees and shrubs and tamarisk thickets. It winters in Africa south of the Sahara but north of the Equator, in savannah and shrub steppes.

469   Olivaceous Warbler

Upcher's Warbler

Olivaceous Warbler

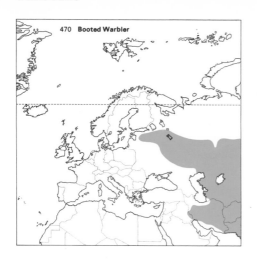

470 Booted Warbler

Booted Warbler *Hippolais caligata*
(Maps 467, 470)
Migrant; breeding in eastern warmer Boreal to Warm Temperate zones, wintering in Subtropical to Tropical zones. It is a bird of shrubby and tall herbaceous growth, often by water or in swampy places. It is found in thickets of all kinds from conifer and broadleaf forest clearings and edges to semi-desert scrub, and shrubs mixed with tall herbage in open grassland and cultivation. It occurs on shrubby slopes and in mountain valleys up to *c.* 1,800 m, in cane brakes, gardens, reedbeds and bushes bordering fresh and saline lakes, scrub and hedgerows bordering cultivation, and in fields of growing grain. It winters in the Indian region, in broadleaf scrub, shrubby growth in cultivated areas and tall grasses.

TYPICAL WARBLERS *Sylvia* species
This is a large genus of 18 species, like the *Hippolais* warblers mainly confined to the western Eurasian region as far east as the Altai with a few species extending to Sinkiang and Mongolia. Five of them, Barred Warbler, Garden Warbler, Blackcap, and Common and Lesser Whitethroats cover most of Europe, but the remainder are confined mainly to the Mediterranean and Warm Temperate zone. They can be divided into subgroups of larger warblers, Sardinian warblers, whitethroats and Dartford warblers.

Of the four larger species the Barred Warbler occupies a broad Boreal to Temperate zone, absent from western Europe but extending from mid-Europe east to the Altai region. The Orphean Warbler replaces it to the south from the Mediterranean to the Himalayas. The other two slightly smaller species share a similar range, with the Garden Warbler preferring shrubs to trees and occurring further north and less far south than the Blackcap. Both occur east to the northern Altai.

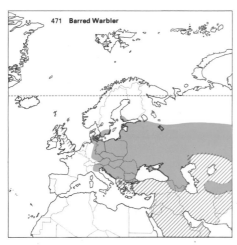

471 Barred Warbler

Barred Warbler *Sylvia nisoria* (Map 471)
Migrant; breeding in the drier Temperate zone, wintering in Subtropical to Tropical zones. It occurs in areas of shrubs, usually thorny and well-grown, on the edge of mixed or broadleaf forest, or in clearings, undergrowth of open forest, riverine forest, parklands, orchards, hedgerows, shelterbelts, or in overgrown marshy or moist areas and the shrubby borders of lakes and rivers. It winters in northeast Africa and southern Arabia in thorn scrub.

Booted Warbler

Barred Warbler

Orphean Warbler   *Sylvia hortensis*
(Map 472)
Migrant; breeding in the Warm Temperate zones, wintering in the Subtropical zone. It occurs in lower trees and taller shrubs; in open conifer or broadleaf forest; scattered trees and tall scrub on hill slopes; orange, cork and olive groves, orchards, parkland and gardens. It winters in Africa on the southern edge of the Sahara and in India; in *Acacia* scrub, palm groves, and sparse scrub and trees in stony and semi-arid areas.

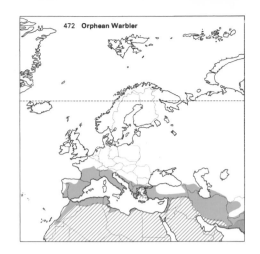

472   Orphean Warbler

Garden Warbler   *Sylvia borin* (Map 473)
Migrant; breeding in Subarctic to Temperate zones, wintering in Subtropical to Tropical zones. It occurs mainly in shrubby under-growth in and on the edge of mixed and broadleaf forest, in clearings, in conifer forest with broadleaf undergrowth, birch scrub, shrubby parkland and gardens. In the south of its breeding range it is mainly a bird of moun-tain forests. It winters in Africa south of the Sahara, in forest savannah, on forest edge and in open forest and secondary growth.

473   Garden Warbler

Blackcap   *Sylvia atricapilla* (Map 474)
Migrant; breeding in warmer Boreal to Warm Temperate zones, wintering in Warm Tem-perate to Subtropical zones, and the Temper-ate zone in the extreme west. It occurs in forest with tall rather than thick undergrowth; and under these conditions in conifer, mixed and broadleaf forest, riverine forest, parkland and well-grown orchards and gardens, shelterbelts and wooded steppes. In the south of its breed-ing range it occurs in forest up to the tree line at altitudes of up to *c.* 2,000 m. In winter it extends to thicker forest, savannah and desert oases, its northern limit depending on the severity of the winter weather.

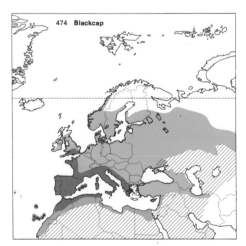

474   Blackcap

Orphean Warbler   Garden Warbler   Blackcap

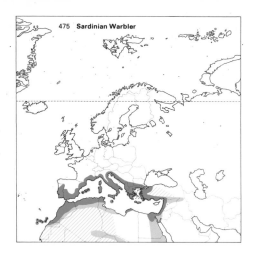

475   Sardinian Warbler

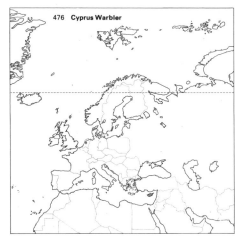

476   Cyprus Warbler

477   Arabian Warbler

SARDINIAN-TYPE WARBLERS
Sylvia species

The four Sardinian-type warblers occur in low scrub of Warm Temperate regions. The Sardinian Warbler occurs right around the Mediterranean, with Rüppell's Warbler in the Aegean and Turkey, the Cyprus Warbler confined to that island, and Ménétries's Warbler from the eastern Mediterranean to Afghanistan. The larger Arabian Warbler appears to belong to this group but occurs in subtropical semi-desert dry scrub in the Red Sea area and north to the Dead Sea.

Sardinian Warbler   *Sylvia melanocephala* (Map 475)

Resident and partial migrant; breeding in the Warm Temperate zone, wintering in Warm Temperate and Subtropical zones. It occurs in dense but taller thorn scrub and maquis with taller trees, often in arid areas; in open oakwood, thickets of tamarisk, euphorbia or cactus; orange and olive groves, parkland with shrubby cover and in gardens. There is some southward shift to desert scrub in winter.

Cyprus Warbler   *Sylvia melanothorax* (Map 476)

Resident on Cyprus in the Warm Tropical zone, occasionally straying to nearer eastern Mediterranean coasts. It occurs in similar habitats to the Sardinian Warbler, which it replaces in Cyprus, and it is sometimes regarded as a race of that species.

Arabian or Red Sea Warbler   *Sylvia leucomelaena* (Map 477)

Resident; in dry Subtropical zone. It occurs in semi-desert areas in *Acacia* trees and scrub and in dry thorn scrub in valleys and wadis, and on hillsides. It occurs on both sides of the southern Red Sea, and on the eastern side, possibly discontinuously, north to just south of the Dead Sea.

Rüppell's Warbler   *Sylvia rüppelli* (Map 478)

Migrant; breeding in part of the Warm Temperate zone, wintering in the Subtropical zone. It occurs at up to *c.* 1,700 m on hill and mountain slopes with arid thorny scrub, in similar growth in narrow valleys, ravines and rock clefts, or in shrubby growth in open oak or cypress forest. It winters in north-east Africa in shrub steppe and arid savannah.

Sardinian Warbler   Cyprus Warbler

Arabian or
Red Sea Warbler

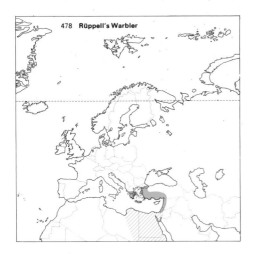

Ménétries's Warbler *Sylvia mystacea*
(Map 479)
Migrant; breeding in the Warm Temperate
zone, wintering in the dry Subtropical zone. It
occurs in taller scrub along rivers and ravines,
in tamarisk scrub, and the scrub, scattered
trees or open forest on lower mountain slopes.
It also occurs in young plantations, shelterbelts and orchards. A mainly lowland species,
it has been recorded at up to *c.* 1,350 m. It
winters in north-east Africa in dry scrub,
shrubby borders of cultivation and in gardens.

WHITETHROATS *Sylvia* species
The seven whitethroats are birds of mainly
low bushy growth, with several species preferring arid areas. The Common Whitethroat
extends from Europe across to the Altai and
northern Mongolia while the smaller Lesser
Whitethroat extends a little further, to the
borders of northern China; the former species
in more open bushy areas, the latter in overgrown areas of taller bushes. The Lesser
Whitethroat has two closely related species in
the south-east, sometimes regarded as races
of it but overlapping in distribution. One of
them, the Desert Lesser Whitethroat, breeds
in drier areas from eastern Iran to the Gobi
Desert, and the other, Hume's Lesser Whitethroat, in montane regions from eastern Iran
to the western Himalayas. Further south the
Spectacled and Subalpine Warblers breed
mainly around the western Mediterranean,
with slight habitat differences, the first in
lower drier scrub than the second; while the
Desert Warbler occurs in sparse desert plant
growth in North Africa and from Iran to
Mongolia and western China.

Desert Warbler *Sylvia nana* (Map 480)
Resident, and migrant in the east; breeding in
dry Warm Temperate to Tropical zones. Wintering in Subtropical to Tropical zones. It occurs in sparse, usually shrubby vegetation in
arid areas, being found in sandy or stony desert with thorn scrub or tamarisk, on sand
dunes, eastern clay or sand desert and steppes
with sparse *Artemesia* and scrub, and sands
with sparse grass and shrubby herbage. It
extends at times on to dry saltflats with *Salicornia*, and stony hillsides and mountain foothills with thin scrub.

Rüppell's Warbler   Ménétries's Warbler   Desert Warbler

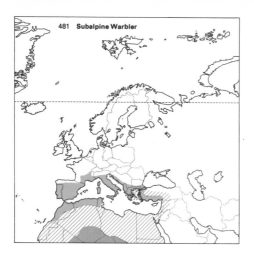

Subalpine Warbler   *Sylvia cantillans*
(Map 481)

Migrant; breeding in the Warm Temperate zone, wintering in dry Subtropical to Tropical zones. It occurs usually in less arid and more overgrown habitats than the Spectacled and Sardinian Warblers, often at higher altitudes. It is found in thorny hillside scrub, frequently with low oak trees, thick shrubby growth in open forest, and in hedgerows and well grown bushy sites in cultivated areas. It has been recorded at altitudes of up to *c.* 2,150 m in the south of its range. It winters in the central and southern Sahara in arid thorn and *Acacia* scrub.

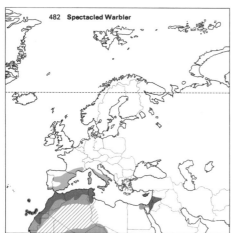

Spectacled Warbler   *Sylvia conspicillata*
(Map 482)

Migrant and resident; in the Warm Temperate zone, some wintering in the dry Subtropical zone. It occurs typically in less dense, low scrub without trees in open arid areas; on dry hillsides and lowland plains, and in semi-desert; occasionally in *Salicornia* on dry salt-flats of coasts and desert edges. In the Canaries it may occur in thicker mountain vegetation. In winter it occurs in desert scrub and oases.

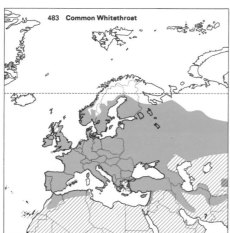

Common Whitethroat   *Sylvia communis*
(Map 483)

Migrant; breeding in Boreal to Warm Temperate zones, wintering in Subtropical to Tropical zones. It occurs in a wide variety of habitats but typically in low shrubby growth of open, well-drained areas; in small areas of scrub on heathland, bordering cultivation or grassland, on forest edge, swamp edge, bordering roads and along river banks, and in young plantations and shelterbelts. It occurs from shrub steppe to dry subalpine mountain shrubs, and extends exceptionally into open woodland or areas of tall shrubby herbage in grasslands. It winters in Africa south of the Sahara and in the Yemen, in thorn scrub and savannah.

Subalpine Warbler   Spectacled Warbler   Common Whitethroat

Lesser Whitethroat *Sylvia curruca*
(Map 484)

Migrant; breeding in Boreal to Temperate zones, wintering in the Subtropical zone. It occurs in taller shrubby growth than the last species, and in small trees, usually bordering an open space; being found in shrubby growth on the edge of conifer, mixed or broadleaf forest, in forest clearings, undergrowth in open forest and in young regenerating forest, tall scrub and overgrown hedgerows, and scrub with scattered trees. It occurs in more shrubby growth on mountains, at times up to *c.* 2,000 m; and into lower thorny scrub in arid areas. It winters in tall *Acacia* scrub and palm groves of arid areas, and trees and tall scrub of semi-desert, in Africa south of the Sahara and through the Indian region.

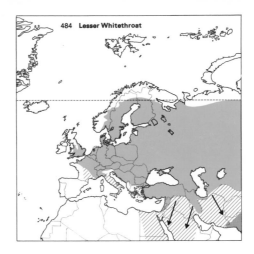

Desert Lesser Whitethroat *Sylvia minula*
(Map 485)

Resident and migrant in arid Warm Temperate to Subtropical zones. It occurs in desert and semi-desert, in thorn scrub and shrubby growth, and in similar vegetation in ravines and along watercourses and rivers. It occurs in orchards and gardens of cultivated areas. It winters in the northern Indian region in semi-desert thorn scrub, and sparse bushes of dune areas.

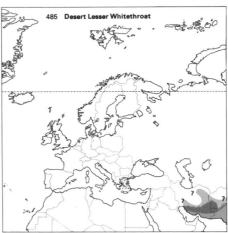

Hume's Lesser Whitethroat *Sylvia althaea*
(Map 486)

Resident and migrant in the montane Subtropical zone, wintering in Subtropical to Tropical zones. It occurs in montane areas at altitudes of up to *c.* 3,600 m, being found in a range of habitats from broadleaf forest in ravines and foothills, to sparse shrub growth on steep stony slopes, and often in shrubs and trees along streams. In winter it occurs through the Indian region on lower hill slopes in *Acacia* scrub and shrubby cover.

THE DARTFORD WARBLER GROUP *Sylvia* species

The Dartford Warbler group consists of three closely related species confined to the western European region. Tristram's Warbler is an arid country species of the North African desert border. Marmora's Warbler occurs on the western Mediterranean islands where it probably evolved, but extends to the Spanish coast and to North Africa in winter. The Dartford

Lesser Whitethroat

Desert
Lesser Whitethroat

Hume's
Lesser Whitethroat

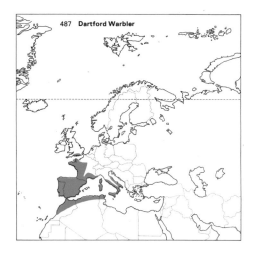

487 Dartford Warbler

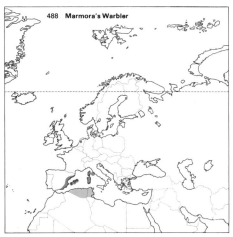

488 Marmora's Warbler

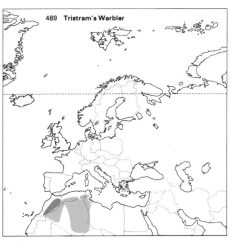

489 Tristram's Warbler

Warbler may have evolved in the Iberian Peninsula, but now extends north to southern England and south to North Africa, overlapping the range of Marmora's Warbler and meeting that of Tristram's Warbler.

Dartford Warbler *Sylvia undata* (Map 487)
Resident; in the western Warm Temperate zone and the Temperate zone of the Atlantic seaboard. It occurs in low thick scrub, in the north of its range usually in gorse and tall heather, further south in dry thick thorny scrub and maquis, often low and discontinuous, on hillsides, and at times in shrubby *Salicornia* on dry saltflats.

Marmora's Warbler *Sylvia sarda* (Map 488)
Resident and partial migrant; in the western Warm Temperate zone. It occurs in rather similar habitats to the previous species, but often in thinner and more open scrub vegetation at lower altitudes, and in maquis mixed with small trees. There is some southward and westward movement in winter.

Tristram's Warbler *Sylvia deserticola* (Map 489)
Resident and migrant: it occurs on dry hillsides and mountains in *Cistus* and similar scrub, and shrubby growth in open forest, moving to desert scrub in winter.

LEAF WARBLERS *Phylloscopus* species
A large genus with nine species in the area and three regular strays. They are small arboreal species, feeding in trees or tall shrubs, taking insects. The nest is a domed structure on or near the ground. In view of the overall similarities, frequent overlap of ranges and small ecological differences, it is difficult to identify potential counterparts and replacements in different areas. In the west there is the climax forest Wood Warbler confined to Europe; the mainly Mediterranean and montane Bonelli's Warbler; another southern species, the Plain Willow Warbler, in montane Iran and Afghanistan; and the lower forest- and scrub-haunting Willow Warbler, extending through the northern forest zone to eastern Siberia, but from its winter range a western immigrant. Two other species appear to have moved in the opposite direction. The Arctic and Greenish Warblers both extend from eastern Eurasia across through the forest zone to

Dartford Warbler

Marmora's Warbler

Tristram's Warbler

Scandinavia, the former the more northerly of the two. They are still gradually extending westwards, but winter in South-east Asia. The Greenish Warbler (map 495) has a counterpart, the Green Warbler (map 496), in the Caucasus and northern Iran. Potential further westward movement can be seen in the four species which occur frequently on passage in western Europe but originate in the east (maps 498–501). The Dusky Warbler and Radde's Warbler are atypical of the genus in being mainly birds of low scrub, while Pallas's Warbler is almost small enough to be a Firecrest replacement and behaves like one (maps 501, 502). All breed in eastern Eurasia and winter in South-east Asia, but while the Yellow-browed Warbler shows a similar eastern range, in the north of its range it extends westwards, reaching the Pechora River. In the centre of Eurasia several species, although nearer the west, do not occur as regular vagrants. The Green Warbler has already been mentioned. The Olivaceous Willow Warbler *Phylloscopus griseolus* occurs in mountains from the Altai to India where it winters (map 500), and the Crowned Willow Warbler *P. occipitalis* has a discontinuous breeding distribution from eastern Afghanistan to eastern China. In the area comprising the Himalayas, southern China and South-east Asia there are a further twelve *Phylloscopus* species. In this pattern of speciation *Phylloscopus* resembles several other warbler genera.

Unlike the other species the Chiffchaff has a more complex distribution pattern. It has a broad range across to eastern Siberia, and isolate populations in the Caucasus to northern Iran and in the western Himalayas. There are two distinct subspecies in the Canary Islands, one in the west, the other in the eastern islands. In the Caucasus region there is a distinct and more resident subspecies *P. c. lorenzii* at higher altitudes which should perhaps be regarded as a distinct species, with a second form at lower altitudes in the same area (map 493). In the area around the Sea of Japan occurs the Pale-legged Willow Warbler *P. tenellipes* which might be another isolate of the Chiffchaff complex.

Bonelli's Warbler   *Phylloscopus bonelli*
(Map 490)
Migrant; breeding in western Warm Temperate and the warmer parts of the western Tem-

perate zones, wintering in the Subtropical zone. It occurs mainly in drier and more open forest on hill slopes, in well-grown conifer, mixed and broadleaf forest. In much of its range it appears to replace the Wood Warbler but in the present century has extended northwards in central Europe and shows some overlap of range with the latter species.

Arctic Warbler   *Phylloscopus borealis*
(Map 491)
Migrant; breeding in Subarctic to cooler Boreal zones, wintering in the Tropical zone. It occurs mainly in broadleaf forest bordering or mixed with northern conifer forest. It is found in tundra birch scrub, subarctic birch forest with a low thick shrub layer, broadleaf

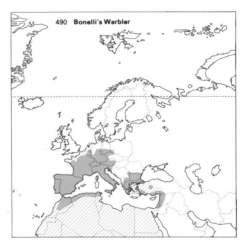

Bonelli's Warbler   Arctic Warbler

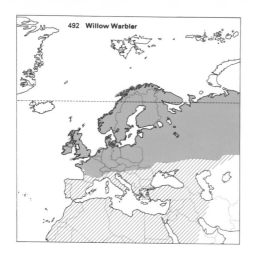

492   Willow Warbler

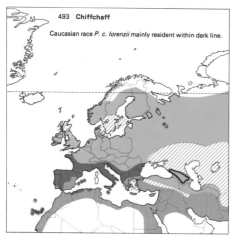

493   Chiffchaff

Caucasian race *P. c. lorenzii* mainly resident within dark line.

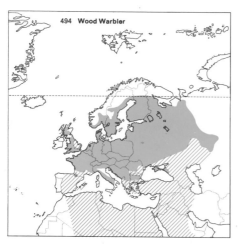

494   Wood Warbler

trees along rivers and streams in conifer forest, damp mixed forest and mixed subalpine forest above *c.* 1,500 m up to the tree line. It winters in southern South-east Asia in forest, tall scrub, plantations and mangrove swamps.

Willow Warbler   *Phylloscopus trochilus*
(Map 492)
Migrant; breeding in Subarctic to Temperate zones, wintering in Subtropical to Tropical zones. It occurs in more open tree growth, with small trees and tall shrubs, and extends into scrub land. It is found mainly in open or broken forest, or on forest edge, mainly in broadleaf or mixed forest, and in broadleaf trees of conifer forest. It occurs in parkland; birch, willow and hawthorn scrub; waterside and riverine thickets in forest or open areas; subarctic birch forest, shrub tundra and forest steppes. It is a mainly lowland species, occurring at times up to 1,500 m. It winters through Africa south of the Sahara in savannah, and riverine and montane forest.

Chiffchaff   *Phylloscopus collybita* (Map 493)
Migrant; breeding in Boreal to Warm Temperate zones, wintering in Warm Temperate to Subtropical zones. It occurs in open, well-grown forest – conifer, mixed and broadleaf – and in more open areas of parkland and scattered large trees, also in shelterbelts and lines of trees bordering roads and cultivation. It occurs in mountain forest, and bushy mountain scrub up to the tree limit, occurring at times up to *c.* 3,150 m in the south-east of its range. It winters in southern Europe, around the Sahara and in the Middle East and northern India, and will frequent lower, more shrubby thickets, reedbeds, tall grass and crops as well as trees.
The Caucasian Chiffchaff *P. c. lorenzii*, possibly a species, occurs in forest, shrub thickets, scrub and tall grasses at altitudes of *c.* 1,000–3,000 m. It appears to winter within, or close to, the breeding range, on lower slopes.

Wood Warbler   *Phylloscopus sibilatrix*
(Map 494)
Migrant; breeding in Boreal to Temperate zones, wintering in Subtropical to Tropical zones. It is typically a bird of all types of climax forest with tall trees and continuous canopy, open at ground level with sparse shrubs. It occurs in all types of forest, particu-

Willow Warbler

Chiffchaff

Caucasian Chiffchaff

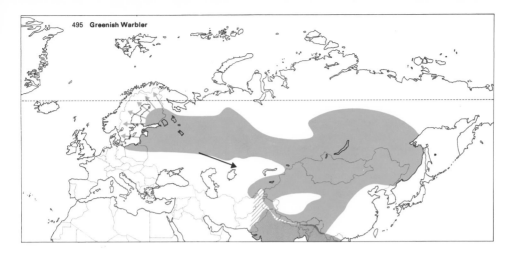

495 Greenish Warbler

larly beech and oak forest, and occasionally in large plantations or orchards. It extends into mountain forest, particularly in the south of its range. It winters in Africa on the southern side of the Sahara in forest and savannah.

Greenish Warbler *Phylloscopus trochiloides*
(Map 495)
Migrant; breeding in warmer Boreal to cooler Temperate zones, wintering in Subtropical to Tropical zones. It occurs in the more open parts of forest, in sparse, open and broken forest, clearings and forest edge, broadleaf areas of mixed forest, and birch scrub. It is found through mountain forest up to the tree line and in dwarf montane forest and scrub, small trees and shrubs along mountain

streams, at altitudes of up to 2,000 m. It winters in the Indian region and South-east Asia, occurring in orchards, groves and gardens as well as open forest. In northern Europe and Scandinavia it has been extending its range westwards during the present century.

Green Warbler *Phylloscopus nitidus*
(Map 496)
Migrant; breeding in the Warm Temperate zone, wintering in the Tropical zone. It occurs in all types of mountain forest and in more shrubby growth on steep slopes and gullies, along rivers and bordering subalpine meadows. It may occur in lowland forest but more usually at altitudes of *c.* 900–3,000 m. It winters in southern India and Sri Lanka in

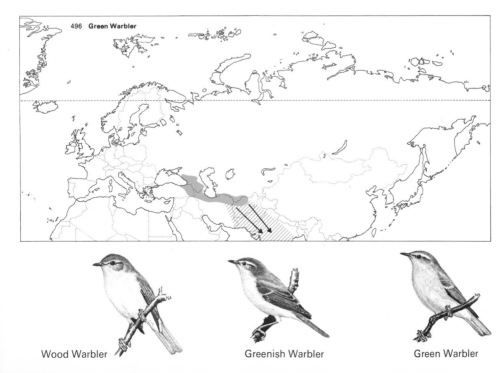

496 Green Warbler

Wood Warbler   Greenish Warbler   Green Warbler

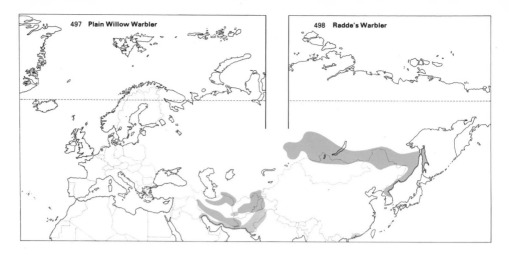

thick forest, orchards, gardens and around cultivation.

Plain Willow Warbler   *Phylloscopus neglectus* (Map 497)
Migrant; breeding in the Warm Temperate zone, wintering in the Subtropical zone. There is little information on this species. It occurs in juniper thickets and shrubby growth on mountain slopes and in gorges at altitudes of *c.* 2,000 – 3,000 m. In winter it occurs at lower altitudes in more open tree growth, in tamarisk and *Acacia* groves and similar growth, particularly in areas of irrigation.

Radde's Warbler   *Phylloscopus schwarzi* (Map 498)
Migrant; breeding in warmer Boreal zone, wintering in Subtropical to Tropical zones. It occurs in shrubby growth and tall herbage in open and burnt forest, forest edge, and hillside and waterside thickets, from lowland up to *c.* 1,000 m. It winters in South-east Asia in low thick scrub.

Dusky Warbler   *Phylloscopus fuscatus* (Map 499)
Migrant; breeding in the eastern warmer Boreal to Temperate zones, wintering in Subtropical to Tropical zones. It occurs in shrubs and willow and birch thickets along mountain watercourses, and the lower growth in open woodland and woodland edge and into high mountain areas. It winters in north-east India and South-east Asia in low scrub, tall herbage, reedbeds and crops in wetter areas.

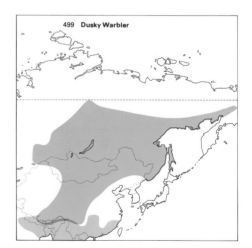

Plain Willow Warbler   Dusky Warbler   Radde's Warbler   Yellow-browed Warbler

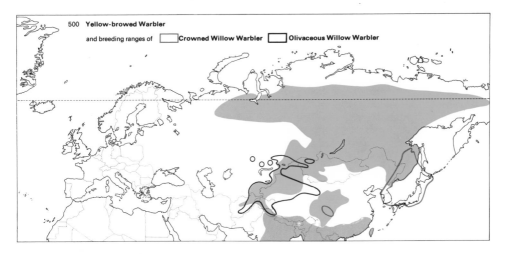

500   Yellow-browed Warbler

and breeding ranges of ☐ Crowned Willow Warbler ☐ Olivaceous Willow Warbler

Yellow-browed Warbler   *Phylloscopus inornatus* (Map 500)

Migrant; breeding in eastern Boreal to Temperate zones, wintering in Subtropical to Tropical zones. It occurs in low tree growth and shrubs, being found in birch and willow scrub, low conifers, and low and open riverine and montane forest, open, mixed and conifer forest and clearings, burnt forest, evergreen and alpine shrub growth on mountains and juniper scrub. In the south of its range it occurs at altitudes of up to 3,500 m. It winters in northern India and South-east Asia in open broadleaf forest, scrub, orchards, groves and gardens.

Pallas's Warbler   *Phylloscopus proregulus* (Map 501)

Migrant; breeding in the eastern Temperate zone, wintering in the Subtropical zone. It occurs mainly in tall conifer forest with a dense shrub layer, but also in mixed conifer and birch forest, and mountain forest with oak and evergreen shrubs. It is typically a bird of mountain forest, particularly in the south of its range where it breeds at altitudes of *c.* 2,000–3,300 m. It winters in the Himalayan foothills, in southern China and northern South-east Asia, in forest and shrubs on hillsides.

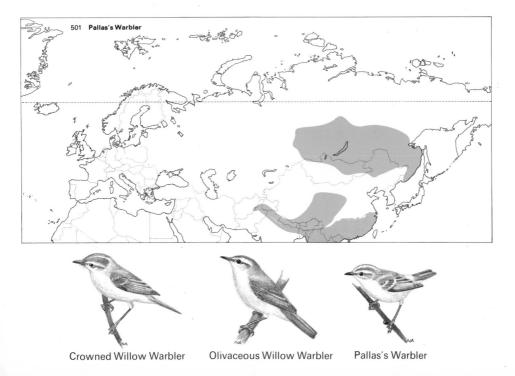

501   Pallas's Warbler

Crowned Willow Warbler   Olivaceous Willow Warbler   Pallas's Warbler

GOLDCRESTS *Regulus* species

A genus of tiny warblers with two species in the region. The Goldcrest occurs across Eurasia mainly in conifer forest. Its distribution is highly discontinuous and populations in the east of its range and in the Azores have been isolated long enough to form distinct subspecies. The Firecrest occurs only in Europe but a firecrest-like species, *Regulus satrapa*, occurs through North America and is sometimes regarded as conspecific. The two European species differ in head markings and the Firecrest has distinct forms on the Canary Islands and on Madeira which also differ in head colour. The two species in Europe overlap in breeding but in most of this region the Goldcrest prefers conifer forest and higher altitudes, separating it from the other. At the other end of Eurasia the Taiwan Firecrest *R. goodfellowi* occurs only on that island. In North America there is a second species, the Ruby-crowned Kinglet *R. calendula*, which like the Goldcrest has a more northerly range.

Firecrest *Regulus ignicapillus* (Map 502)
Resident and migrant; breeding and wintering in Temperate to Warm Temperate zones. It occurs mainly in lowland broadleaf forest, but where it is the only species it occurs in mixed and conifer forest, including mountain conifer zones. It is also found in dry evergreen oak and tree heath in the Mediterranean region. In winter it wanders and often occurs in lower shrubby growth rather than high trees.

Goldcrest *Regulus regulus* (Map 503)
Resident and migrant; breeding and wintering in Boreal to Temperate zones. It is typically a bird of conifer forest, and over much of its range a bird of montane areas. Where the Firecrest is absent it also occurs in mixed and broadleaf forest such as oak and beech. It ascends in mountain conifer zones to *c.* 2,000 m in the Caucasus, *c.* 3,700 m in the Himalayas, *c.* 4,800 m in eastern Tibet. It is an irregular migrant and wanderer, wintering in more open and lowland habitats.

FLYCATCHERS *Muscicapidae*

A large family of small arboreal birds, feeding on insects which are mainly taken in the air.

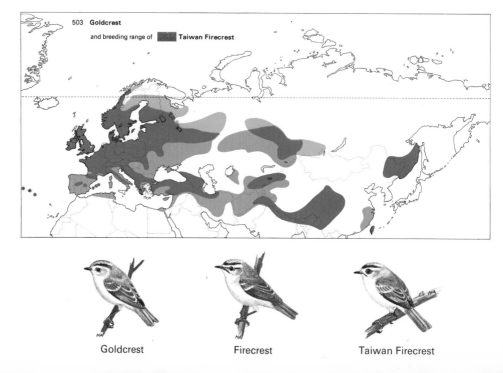

502 Firecrest

503 Goldcrest
and breeding range of Taiwan Firecrest

Goldcrest   Firecrest   Taiwan Firecrest

The cup nest is on a branch, ledge or in a cavity. There are numerous species in the Old World tropics, but few penetrate the Palaearctic. Of these only three appear to originate at the western end. At the eastern end in an area centred around northern China, Manchuria and Japan there are nine of which three extend westwards to meet their counterparts, and one, the Red-breasted Flycatcher, appears to extend across in a single range but has distinct eastern and western forms within it. As with the warblers a large complex of species occupy the Himalayas and Indochinese region, some extending into southern China, and the Indian region has thirty-five typical flycatcher species. The Blue and White Flycatcher *Cyanoptila cyanomelana* of the eastern region is the only representative of its genus in Eurasia, and a southern invader is the Paradise Flycatcher *Terpsiphone paradisi* which occurs from central Afghanistan through India and Indochina and northwards through eastern China to Manchuria with another species, the Black Paradise Flycatcher *T. atrocaudata*, replacing it in Japan. Within the European region two groups of species can be recognised, the pied flycatchers and the brown flycatchers.

PIED FLYCATCHERS *Ficedula* species

The genus *Ficedula* has three species in Europe. They might be regarded as four since the black and white flycatchers produce three distinct forms (map 504): the Pied, Collared (*albicollis*) and Half-collared (*semitorquata*) Flycatchers, each with a discrete range, but the last two generally treated as a single species. Historically these appear to have occurred at some time with the Half-collared in the Middle East, the Collared in southern central Europe and the Pied in south-west Europe. The two western forms moved north and east with the Pied extending furthest, to meet the eastern Mugimaki Flycatcher *F. mugimaki* north of the Altai region (map 504). The latter species is a bird of conifer forest. Also in this eastern region is the Korean Flycatcher *F. zanthopygia* of eastern China, and the Narcissus Flycatcher *F. narcissina* of Japan with a Chinese isolate population. Both of these are birds of more montane forest, usually near water. All these species are boldly coloured birds, the males combining black with white, yellow and red. The Red-breasted Flycatcher (map 507) appears not to have a counterpart species, but has two distinct forms differing in throat and breast colouring and indicating a western population (*F. p. parva*) based on eastern Europe, and an eastern population (*F. p. albicilla*) extending from eastern China to meet it in the region of the Urals. The Kashmir Red-breasted Flycatcher *F. subrubra* occurs in a limited area of the western Himalayas (map 507) and was at one time regarded as another form of *F. parva*. It winters south of the latter, in Ceylon.

Pied Flycatcher   *Ficedula hypoleuca*
(Maps 504, 505)
Migrant; breeding in the Temperate and western Boreal to Warm Temperate zones, wintering in the Subtropical zone. Its breeding

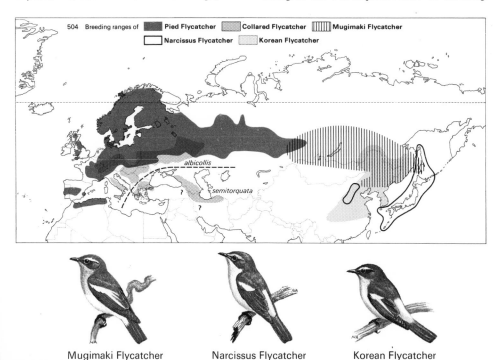

504 Breeding ranges of ▨ Pied Flycatcher ▨ Collared Flycatcher ▥ Mugimaki Flycatcher □ Narcissus Flycatcher ▨ Korean Flycatcher

albicollis

semitorquata

Mugimaki Flycatcher   Narcissus Flycatcher   Korean Flycatcher

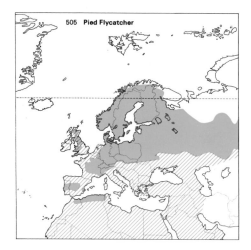

505 Pied Flycatcher

occurrence is limited by the availability of older broadleaf trees providing nest holes, but it may utilise nest boxes. It occurs mainly in broadleaf forest, particularly beech and oak. In the north it occurs in more open sites in tall conifer forest where broadleaf trees occur, and in birch and poplar forest of the Boreal zone. Its breeding sites are often near water. It utilises parkland, orchards, gardens, and groups of trees in cultivation. It tends to feed lower than the next species where both occur. It may have lost ground during forest clearance but has extended north and west in Europe during the present century. It winters in Africa on the southern side of the Sahara in savannah forest.

Collared Flycatcher *Ficedula albicollis*
(Maps 504, 506)

Migrant; breeding in Temperate and Warm Temperate zones, wintering in Subtropical to Tropical zones. It occurs, like the Pied Flycatcher, in forest with trees large enough to provide nest cavities, but in the area of range-overlap usually lives and feeds at higher levels in trees than the former. It occurs mainly in mature beech, oak and hornbeam forest, and only exceptionally in conifer forest. The southern Half-collared form, *semitorquata* (map 504), is more a bird of mountain forest, requiring similar conditions, but occurs in most types of forest, including conifers, up to the treeline, and also in parkland and orchards. It winters in Africa south of the Sahara, in savannah forest; the eastern form extending further south in eastern Africa.

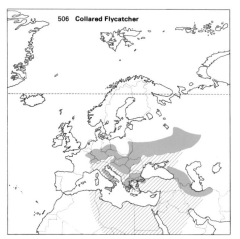

506 Collared Flycatcher

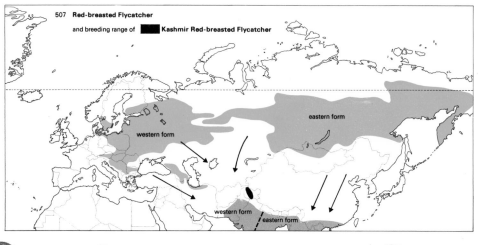

507 Red-breasted Flycatcher

and breeding range of ▮ Kashmir Red-breasted Flycatcher

western form

eastern form

western form

eastern form

Pied Flycatcher

Collared Flycatcher   Red-breasted Flycatcher

Kashmir Red-breasted Flycatcher

Red-breasted Flycatcher   *Ficedula parva*
(Map 507)
Migrant; breeding in warmer Boreal to Temperate zones; wintering in Subtropical to Tropical zones. It occurs in tall forest, often near a break or clearing of some kind. In the north it is found in conifer forest, and further south in mixed and broadleaf forest; often of more open type with thick undergrowth, but with mature trees. It occurs in mountain forest, in the south of its breeding range at up to *c*. 2,350 m, but also uses orchards and vineyards. The western form (*parva*) winters in western India, the eastern form (*albicilla*) in eastern India to Indochina. In winter it occurs in scrub, groves and orchards, plantations and gardens, as well as forest.

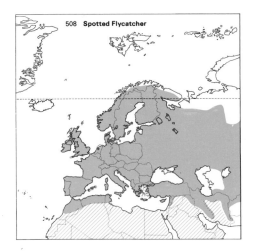

508   Spotted Flycatcher

BROWN FLYCATCHERS *Muscicapa*
species
Only one species of these dull brown typical flycatchers occurs in the European region with three others reaching its eastern border. The Spotted Flycatcher is a bird of forest edge of all types, replaced in the east by two species (map 509), both with a northern and Indian population. The Brown Flycatcher *Muscicapa latirostris* is typically a bird of open and lowland broadleaf forest but extending into larch forest; while the Sooty Flycatcher *M. siberica* is a very similar species preferring the more open parts of conifer forest and for much of its range occurring in the conifer zones of mountains, up to high altitudes in the south. The Brown Flycatcher has occurred as a vagrant in Europe, but the Sooty Flycatcher does not appear to stray westwards. Both species overlap the extreme eastern range of the Spotted Flycatcher in the regions around Lake Baikal. A fourth species, the Grey-spotted Flycatcher *M. griseisticta*, occurs with the other two in north China, Manchuria and Japan, in similar habitats, but does not extend westwards. The Rufous-tailed Flycatcher *M. ruficauda* is one of the Indian species, a mountain forest bird extending from the Himalayas into Afghanistan and the Pamir region.

Spotted Flycatcher   *Muscicapa striata*
(Maps 508, 509)
Migrant; breeding in the Boreal to Warm Temperate zones, wintering in Subtropical to Tropical zones. It occurs on forest edge, forest clearing edges, and in broken forest, and tall

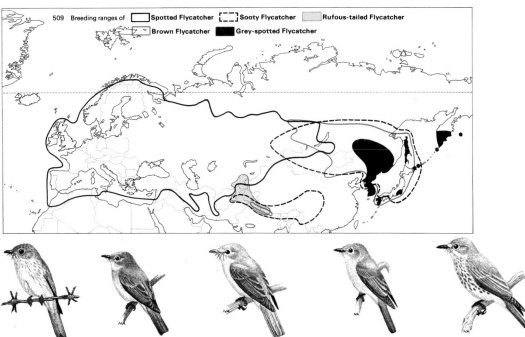

509   Breeding ranges of □ Spotted Flycatcher [¯¯] Sooty Flycatcher ▨ Rufous-tailed Flycatcher
□ Brown Flycatcher   ■ Grey-spotted Flycatcher

Spotted Flycatcher   Sooty Flycatcher   Rufous-tailed Flycatcher   Brown Flycatcher   Grey-spotted Flycatcher

forest with an open or sparsely branched canopy. It is mainly in broadleaf or mixed forest, more rarely in pure conifers. It is also found in northern birch scrub, in riverine

forest, forest steppes, parkland, orchards, groves and gardens. It winters through Africa south of the Sahara in forest areas.

THRUSHES, CHATS, WHEATEARS AND ROBINS   *Turdidae*

A large family of insect- and fruit-eating birds, of small to moderate size, feeding mainly on the ground, and occurring in forest to open and bare rocky habitats. The European region has over forty species representing a number of different subgroups, including chats (*Saxicola* species), bushchats (*Cercotrichas* species), rock thrushes (*Monticola* species), wheatears (*Oenanthe* species), redstarts (*Phoenicurus* and

Cercomela species), robins and nightingales (*Erithacus, Luscinia, Tarsiger, Irania* species) and thrushes (*Turdus* and *Zoothera* species).

CHATS *Saxicola* species (Maps 510–515)
Birds of low scrub, with a cup nest on or near the ground. The Stonechat has a broad distribution across Eurasia, but a darker European form meets a paler eastern form and there are others in Africa. Two closely related species are the Canary Islands Chat and the White-tailed Stonechat *Saxicola leucura* of the Himalayan foothills. The Whinchat is a more European species, and in its central position appears to fill the northern gap between the two stonechat forms. Hodgson's Stonechat *S. insignis* has a discontinuous distribution in Mongolia and the borders of the Altai region. The remaining four species all occur in India. The Pied Stonechat is found breeding from eastern Iran to Indochina: the Grey Stonechat *S. ferrea* overlaps part of its range in the Himalayas, Burma and Indochina, and also occurs in southern China. Stoliczka's Whinchat *S. macrorhyncha* is a bird of arid plains with shrubby cover, now largely confined to the Indus region, and Jerdon's Stonechat *S. jerdoni* is a bird of moist grassy lowland in eastern India and Burma.

Whinchat *Saxicola rubetra* (Maps 510, 512)
Migrant; breeding in Boreal to Temperate zones, wintering in Subtropical to Tropical zones. It occurs in areas with less scrub and more herbage than does the Stonechat, and in moister areas. It is found in moist grassland with taller plants, waterside grassland, moist heath and moorland, grassy forest clearings, and roadside grasses; usually in areas with scattered taller plants or shrubs. It extends into shrub steppes, and onto high moorland and subalpine meadows, occurring in the south at altitudes of *c.* 2,230 m. It winters in Africa south of the Sahara, in scrub, savannah and steppe-type grassland.

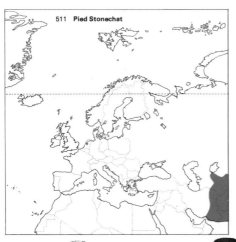

Whinchat   Pied Stonechat   Stoliczka's Whinchat

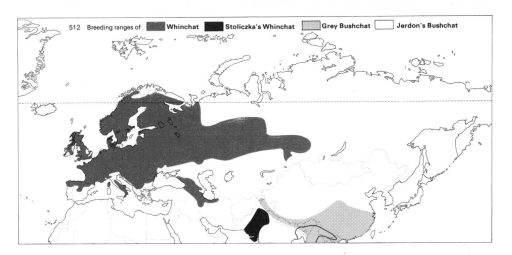

512 Breeding ranges of Whinchat   Stoliczka's Whinchat   Grey Bushchat   Jerdon's Bushchat

Pied Stonechat   *Saxicola caprata*
(Maps 511, 514)
Resident and partial migrant; in Subtropical to Tropical zones. It occurs in similar types of vegetation to other chats, in damp grassland, herbage bordering cultivation, tall herbage by open water or irrigation, tamarisk scrub, and in the south on grassy or sparsely vegetated hillsides with scattered shrubs or trees, shrubby savannah, and at times in open secondary growth forest.

Common Stonechat   *Saxicola torquata*
(Maps 513, 514)
Resident and migrant; breeding in Boreal to Warm Temperate zones in the east, and Temperate to Warm Temperate zones in Europe,

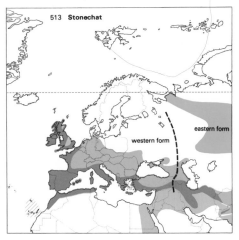

513 Stonechat

eastern form

western form

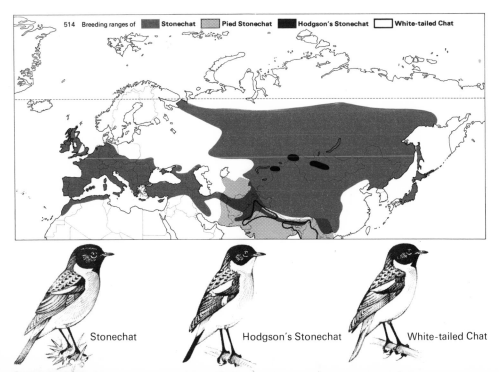

514 Breeding ranges of Stonechat   Pied Stonechat   Hodgson's Stonechat   White-tailed Chat

Stonechat   Hodgson's Stonechat   White-tailed Chat

515 Canary Islands Chat

wintering in Warm Temperate to Subtropical zones. It occurs in open grassy areas, but usually with scattered small shrubs or trees, and often in drier sites than the Whinchat. It is found in all types of hill and lowland grasses, heathland, moorland, grassy areas in forest, reedbed edges, dry steppes, and mountain slopes with low scrub, subalpine scrub and alpine meadows, occurring in the south of its range at up to 4,000–5,000 m. In winter it may occur in arid, semi-desert scrub.

Canary Islands Chat *Saxicola dacotiae*
(Map 515)
Resident; in the Warm Temperate zone. It occurs in arid rocky places, in sparse shrubby vegetation of ravines and gullies; and on lava and rock of small dry islands with very sparse ground vegetation and *Euphorbia* scrub.

BUSHCHATS *Cercotrichas* species
An African genus of ten species, occurring in open and forest scrub and thickets. The nest is a cup in shrub or tree. Most species occur south of the Sahara, but the Rufous Bushchat occurs through the Mediterranean region to Afghanistan, and through the southern Sahara where it occupies a similar range to the Black Bushchat.

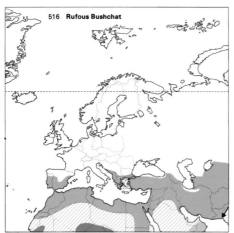

516 Rufous Bushchat

Rufous Bushchat *Cercotrichas galactotes*
(Maps 516, 517)
Migrant and resident; breeding in dry Warm Temperate to Subtropical zones, wintering in Subtropical to Tropical zones. It occurs in arid areas and on dry hillsides with scattered

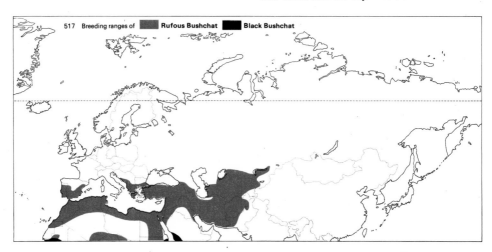

517 Breeding ranges of ▓ **Rufous Bushchat** █ **Black Bushchat**

Canary Islands Chat   Grey Stonechat   Jerdon's Stonechat   Rufous Bushchat

shrubs; in open woodland, thin scrub in desert and sparsely grassed areas, thinly vegetated or shrubby dry steppes, sparse or open maquis, vegetated wadis, oases, cactus hedges, vineyards, orchards and gardens. Migrant birds may winter in dry scrub. In suitable habitats it has occurred at altitudes of up to *c.* 1,950 m.

ROCK THRUSHES *Monticola* species
(Maps 518–520)

A genus of larger chats occurring in open mountainous country and rocky places, the cup nests hidden in rock crevices. The Rufous-tailed Rock Thrush and Blue Rock Thrush overlap through much of their breeding range, but the latter is larger, and prefers warmer and more rugged habitats and sea coasts. The Rufous-tailed Rock Thrush occurs from the Mediterranean to Mongolia and northern China but migrates south-west to Africa. In north-east China it is replaced by the White-throated Rock Thrush *Monticola gularis*, a species with a greater preference for forest habitats, and in the Himalayas by the Blue-headed Rock Thrush *M. cinclorhynchus*. A further six species occur in Africa south of the Sahara. There are two similar larger species. The Blue Rock Thrush is mainly resident in a similar range to the Rufous-tailed, but has a more southerly distribution in the east. Its most easterly race, in north-east China and Japan (map 520), differs from the rest in having the underside chestnut instead of blue. The other large species, the Chestnut-bellied Rock Thrush *M. rufiventris*, occurs within the eastern range of the Blue Rock Thrush, but in the

Black Bushchat   *Cercotrichas podobe*
(Map 517)

Resident; in the Subtropical dry zone. It occurs in desert areas in oases, palm groves, and where thorn scrub or any shrubby growth is present.

----

areas where it occurs the latter is the blue-bellied form.

Rufous-tailed Rock Thrush   *Monticola saxatilis* (Maps 518, 519)

Migrant; breeding in the Warm Temperate zone, wintering in Subtropical to Tropical zones. It occurs on mainly dry, open hill and mountain slopes with rocks, screes and

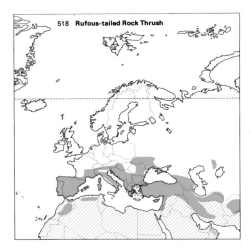

518 Rufous-tailed Rock Thrush

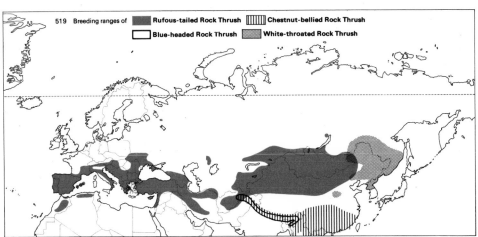

519 Breeding ranges of ■ Rufous-tailed Rock Thrush ▨ Chestnut-bellied Rock Thrush □ Blue-headed Rock Thrush ▦ White-throated Rock Thrush

Black Bushchat   Chestnut-bellied Rock Thrush   Blue-headed Rock Thrush   White-throated Rock Thrush

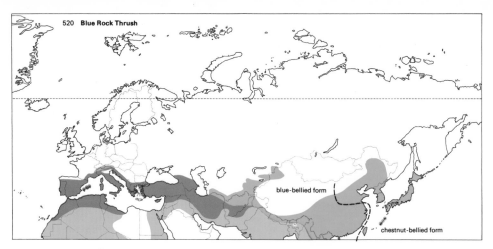

boulders, patches of herbage, and sparse shrubs or trees. In the south it occurs at altitudes of up to *c*. 3,800 m. Occasionally it occurs in arid, stony lowland areas. It is found in more level, less rugged areas than the Blue Rock Thrush. It winters in Africa south of the Sahara in stony savannah and steppe areas.

Blue Rock Thrush   *Monticola solitarius*
(Map 520)
Partial migrant, mainly migratory in the east; in the Warm Temperate zone, wintering in the

Warm Temperate to dry Subtropical zones. It occurs in rocky habitats, usually in warmer areas than the Rufous-tailed Rock Thrush, often in very rugged precipitous areas, mountain gorges and gullies, coastal cliffs and rocks, and rocky outcrops in more level areas. It also utilises buildings and in some parts occurs in towns. In the south of its range it ascends to similar altitudes to the previous species. In winter it extends into rocky areas of dry savannah, shrub steppes and semi-desert.

WHEATEARS *Oenanthe* species
A genus of mainly western Eurasian species, with another eight species in Africa south of the Sahara. The wheatears are birds of bare open country, usually dry, and varying from short or sparse herbage to bare rock. The nest is a cup in a rock crevice or hole. There are fourteen species in the present area.

The species occur as a number of distributionally overlapping subgroups within the genus. The first is a group of four of which the Eurasian Wheatear is the most widespread, extending through Eurasia into Alaska, and in a westerly direction into Greenland and north-east North America, but with the retention of the ancestral migration route to Africa. The northern Eurasian Wheatear overlaps with the Mediterranean Black-eared Wheatear, with some altitudinal separation, the former at higher altitudes. The latter is replaced to the south and east by the Desert Wheatear, and in the north-east by the Pied Wheatear. There are a pair of darker species,

with Finsch's Wheatear occurring eastwards from the northern Middle East and the Mourning Wheatear through North Africa and the southern Middle East; and a pair of rufous-rumped species with the Red-rumped Wheatear in the northern Afro-Arabian deserts and the Red-tailed Wheatear from Iran to the Himalayas. The Isabelline Wheatear resembles a female of the Eurasian Wheatear but otherwise appears to stand alone, occurring from the eastern Mediterranean to northern China in steppes and drier regions. The remaining species occur in the more barren, arid and rocky parts. The Hooded Wheatear is a desert species which provides a link with the last group of large and mainly black-plumaged birds. The Black Wheatear occurs around the western Mediterranean, the White-crowned Black Wheatear replaces it to the south in the Afro-Arabian deserts, Hume's Wheatear occurs in southern Iran and Afghanistan, and the Eastern Pied Wheatear from northern Iran to the Pamirs.

Rufous-tailed Rock Thrush   Blue Rock Thrush   Isabelline Wheatear

Isabelline Wheatear   *Oenanthe isabellina*
(Map 521)
Mainly migrant; resident in a limited area, breeding in dry Warm Temperate to Subtropical zones, wintering in Subtropical zone. It occurs mainly in level open areas of sparse vegetation, preferring dry sand, gravel and clay, on dry steppes and areas of closely grazed grasses, semi-desert and level plains, at up to *c.* 3,500 m. It winters in north-east Africa in dry open areas.

Hooded Wheatear   *Oenanthe monacha*
(Map 522)
Resident; in dry areas of the Subtropical zone. It occurs like the Mourning Wheatear in barren rocky desert ravines and wadis.

Eurasian Wheatear   *Oenanthe oenanthe*
(Map 523)
Migrant; breeding in Arctic to Warm Temperate zones, wintering in Subtropical to Tropical zones. In open, well-drained areas with short grasses, herbage or low scrub, dry lowland to alpine meadows, grassy slopes with rocks, screes, rocky and shrub tundra, stony and shrub steppes, heath, moorland and the borders of cultivation, at altitudes of up to 3,500 m. A montane species in southern parts of its range. It winters in Africa south of the Sahara on dry savannah and steppes.

Black-eared Wheatear   *Oenanthe hispanica*
(Map 524)
Migrant; breeding in the western Warm Temperate zone, wintering in the Subtropical zone.

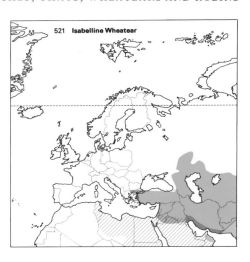

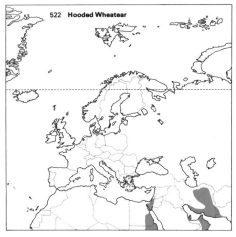

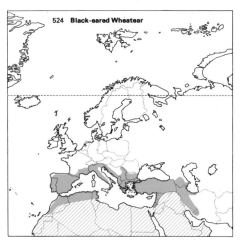

Hooded Wheatear

Eurasian Wheatear

Black-eared Wheatear

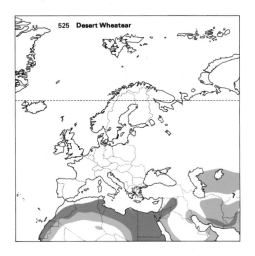

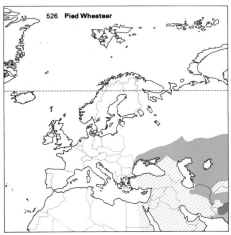

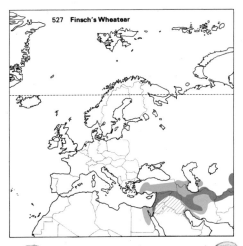

It occurs in warm dry lowland areas where the Eurasian Wheatear is a montane species. It is found on stony plains and dry foothills with low or sparse scrub, dry grasslands and heathland, and cultivated areas and vineyards with scattered rocks or stone walls. It winters in Africa along the southern border of the Sahara in steppes and semi-desert.

Desert Wheatear   *Oenanthe deserti*
(Map 525)
Resident and migrant; breeding in arid Warm Temperate to Subtropical zones, wintering in the Subtropical zone. It occupies a wide range of habitats, more arid but otherwise similar to those of the Eurasian Wheatear. It occurs on irregular and broken but not steep hill terrain, and rarely in level areas unless ruins or gullies are present. It is found in stony, rocky or sandy areas, usually with some sparse vegetation, or arid hill slopes, steppes and dunes, and in the dry south-eastern regions may occur at up to *c.* 5,000 m. It also occupies bare cultivated and irrigated desert areas.

Pied Wheatear   *Oenanthe pleschanka*
(Map 526)
Migrant and resident; breeding in dry Temperate to Warm Temperate zones, wintering in the Subtropical zone. It appears to replace the Black-eared Wheatear in the east, but also occurs in more rugged and hilly areas; on broken terrain in stony and wooded steppes, steep river banks, earth cliffs and rocky slopes and outcrops, usually where shrubs and small trees are present. It winters in north-east Africa and southern Arabia on grassy and stony steppes and arid mountain areas.

Finsch's Wheatear   *Oenanthe finschii*
(Map 527)
Migrant and resident; breeding in the dry Warm Temperate zone, wintering in Warm Temperate to Subtropical zones. It occurs in stony areas, on dry hillsides and mountain slopes up to *c.* 1,800 m, narrow valleys and ravines with sparse scrub, and rocky steppes; and in winter often in level stony desert or semi-desert areas, sometimes bordering on, or within, cultivation.

Mourning Wheatear   *Oenanthe lugens*
(Map 528)
Partial migrant, more migratory in the east; in

Desert Wheatear

Pied Wheatear

Finsch's Wheatear

the Subtropical zone. It occurs in arid, desert regions with broken terrain; in rocky ravines and wadis, and on rocky hill slopes. It does not normally occur in level country.

Red-rumped Wheatear   *Oenanthe moesta*
(Map 529)
Resident; in the Subtropical zone. It occurs in the northern part of the Afro-Arabian desert area, in level, arid and sometimes saline desert or desert edge, where shrubby growth is present. It does not normally occur in bare desert.

Red-tailed Wheatear   *Oenanthe xanthoprymna* (Map 530)
Migrant; breeding in the dry eastern Warm Temperate zone, wintering in the dry Subtropical zone. It breeds on dry rocky hill slopes, often with very scanty vegetation, but usually near a perennial water source, at altitudes of *c.* 1,200–3,300 m. It winters usually at lower altitudes, on the edge of rocky foothills; or on more level stony or sandy semi-desert with sparse shrubs, or dunes of desert edges, often in similar habitats to the Eastern Pied Wheatear.

Black Wheatear   *Oenanthe leucura*
(Map 531)
Resident; in the western Warm Temperate zone. A bird of the western Mediterranean, it occurs in rugged rocky places; bare rock slopes, screes, steep rock faces, cliffs, rocky coasts, quarries, and smaller rock outcrops and ruined buildings in more level areas. In North Africa it occurs at up to *c.* 2,000 m.

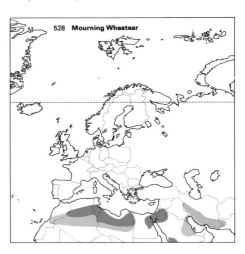

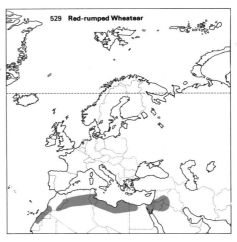

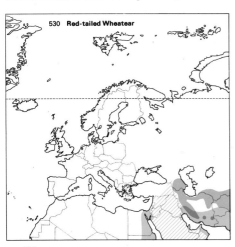

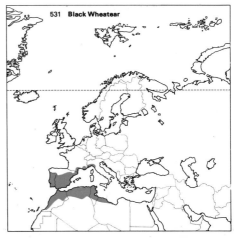

Mourning Wheatear

Red-rumped Wheatear

Red-tailed Wheatear

Black Wheatear

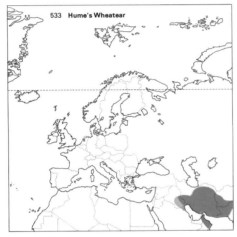

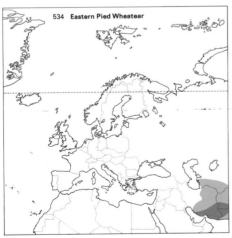

White-crowned Black Wheatear   *Oenanthe leucopyga* (Map 532)
Resident; in dry Subtropical to Tropical zones. It occurs in desert areas of very sparse herbage, where broken terrain occurs, on rocky outcrops, talus slopes, and in wadis and hill ravines. It also uses ruins and buildings, and occurs in desert villages.

Hume's Wheatear   *Oenanthe alboniger* (Map 533)
Mainly resident, with slight winter movements; in the Subtropical zone. It occurs in arid hill areas, on bare or almost bare rocky lower slopes, and the stony sides of ravines. In the east of its range it breeds at *c.* 1,500–1,600 m, but may descend to lower altitudes in winter.

Eastern Pied Wheatear   *Oenanthe picata* (Map 534)
Migrant and resident; breeding in eastern dry Warm Temperate to Subtropical zones, wintering in the Subtropical zone. It breeds in mainly montane country, on rocky slopes with very scanty vegetation, on the stony banks of ravines and rivers, open ground with sparse herbage, ruins and the borders of villages, ranging in altitude from *c.* 600–3,300 m. It winters in Pakistan and north-western India in stony desert and semi-desert with sparse shrubby growth, ravines, and on the borders of cultivation and human habitation; mainly at 0–1,200 m, rarely higher.

REDSTARTS AND BLACKSTART
Phoenicurus and *Cercomela* species
(Maps 535–538)
Small insect-eating birds of woodland or rocky habitats. The nest is a cup in a hole or crevice. Of the two typical European species the Common Redstart is a mainly forest species and the Black Redstart a bird of rocks and ruins. Although their ranges overlap in Europe they diverge in eastern Eurasia with the Common Redstart extending eastwards to Lake Baikal while the Black Redstart extends south-east into China and Mongolia. The Daurian Redstart *Phoenicurus auroreus* (map 535) appears to replace the Common Redstart in the east. There are a series of species with more limited southerly distributions, mostly occurring on rocky hillside habitats. Moussier's Redstart occurs in North Africa. Güldenstädt's Red-

White-crowned Black Wheatear   Hume's Wheatear   Eastern Pied Wheatear

start is a mountain bird, occurring in the Caucasus and through the Himalayan/Tibetan/Mongolian highlands. Eversmann's Redstart occurs in the east of this area, through the Altai, and has an isolate population in central China that is sometimes treated as a separate species, the Alashan Redstart *P. alaschanicus*. The Blue-headed Redstart *P. caeruleocephalus* (map 537) also occurs through the Altai and along the Himalayas; while three other species of the genus also occur in the Himalayas and into western China. The genus *Cercomela* is mainly African, with three species in southern Africa and the Blackstart linking them with a single species in India. The Blackstart has a range mainly to the south of the present area, across the Afro-Arabian deserts.

tropical zones. It breeds in sparse or very open forest, on dry rocky slopes and screes; on forest edge, and in areas of small trees and tall shrubs. It is found up to the tree limit, at altitudes of *c*. 1,800–5,400 m, and in winter at lower levels in scrub, groves and orchards, and areas with scattered trees.

Güldenstädt's Redstart   *Phoenicurus erythrogaster* (Map 537)
Resident, with some local movement; in the Alpine altitudinal zone of Temperate to Warm Temperate zones, and at lower altitudes in winter. Usually near water, on rocky slopes and screes, rocky river beds and ravines, moraines, often in barren areas; in the north of its range at *c*. 2,000–3,000 m and in the

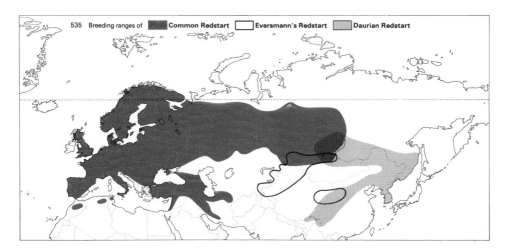

535 Breeding ranges of ■ Common Redstart □ Eversmann's Redstart ▨ Daurian Redstart

Common Redstart   *Phoenicurus phoenicurus* (Maps 535, 536)
Migrant; breeding in Boreal to Warm Temperate zones, wintering in the Subtropical zone. In open forest, forest clearings and forest edge of all kinds, although mainly in broadleaf forest. It occurs from arctic birch forest to the southern mountain tree lines, and in parkland, heathland and cultivation with scattered groups of trees, orchards, groves and gardens. It winters in the southern Sahara in savannah and scrub.

Eversmann's Redstart   *Phoenicurus erythronotus* (Map 535)
Migrant; breeding in the Temperate zone, wintering in the Warm Temperate to Sub-

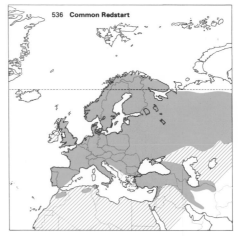

536 Common Redstart

Common Redstart   Eversmann's Redstart   Daurian Redstart

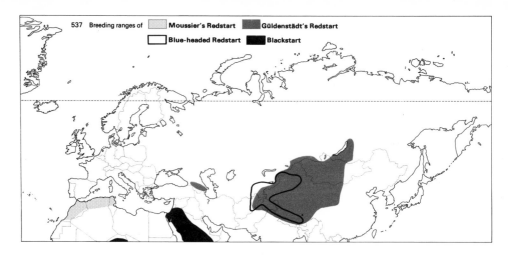

537　Breeding ranges of　□ Moussier's Redstart　■ Güldenstädt's Redstart
□ Blue-headed Redstart　■ Blackstart

Tibetan region at 3,500–5,500 m, but in winter down to *c.* 1,500 or *c.* 700 m in similar habitats but also in low scrub in river valleys.

Moussier's Redstart　*Phoenicurus moussieri*
(Map 537)
Mainly resident, but partially migrant; in the dry Subtropical zone. It occurs on broken or rocky dry hillsides, up to *c.* 3,000 m; being found in open forest, clearings and forest edge, scrub and grassy slopes, and bare montane areas. In winter it occurs at lower altitudes and into more desert regions.

Black Redstart　*Phoenicurus ochruros*
(Map 538)
Migrant and resident; breeding in Warm Tem-

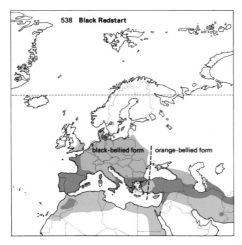

538　Black Redstart

black-bellied form | orange-bellied form

perate and western Temperate zones, wintering in Warm Temperate to Subtropical zones. It occurs on warm rocky slopes, dry hillsides, cliffs, quarries, rock outcrops, and stony and rocky areas from sea level to mountain tops. It frequently occurs on ruins and buildings, and is found in vegetated areas, including mountain scrub, and in orchards and groves where stone walls or rocks are present. It winters in similar places, but often at lower altitudes, in north and north-east Africa, the Middle East and the northern Indian region. During the last century it has extended its range in northwest Europe into Sweden and England.

Blackstart　*Cercomela melanura* (Map 537)
Mainly resident, with some local movement; in dry Subtropical to Tropical zones. It occurs in arid broken desert country, on rocky slopes, ravines and wadis, particularly where some thorn scrub is present.

━━━━━━━━━━━━━━━━━━━━━━

ROBINS, BLUETHROATS, RUBYTHROATS AND NIGHTINGALES *Erithacus, Luscinia, Tarsiger* and *Irania* species

Small insect-eating birds, mainly species of low thick cover, with the nest usually on or near the ground, sometimes in a cavity. The Robin is mainly a forest bird, extending into western Siberia (map 539) with two representatives in the extreme east, the Japanese Robin *Erithacus akahige*, and Ryukyu Robin *E. komadori*. The intervening area appears to be occupied by the Siberian Rubythroat in the northern forest zone, while the Himalayan

Moussier's Redstart　　　Güldenstädt's Redstart　　　Blue-headed Redstart　　　Black Redstart　　　Blackstart

Rubythroat *Luscinia pectoralis* replaces it in the mountain forest around the Tibetan massif. The Siberian Rubythroat has a relict population within the range of the last species in western China. The Bluethroat occurs across most of Eurasia in moist or montane thickets, and also extends into Alaska. It has several colour phases (map 541). The European birds mostly have a white breast spot, and in two southern isolate populations, in Spain and in the Caucasus, the spot is almost absent. Eastern birds have a chestnut spot, and these extend westwards into northern Scandinavia, with a small population in the Austrian mountains. Where the white and chestnut-spotted populations meet in Russia, and also in the Kashmir region, intermediate populations occur. The nightingales show an apparent replacement series of three species from west to east, but the most westerly Nightingale extends south of the second species eastwards through the steppes to the Altai. The Sprosser replaces it in Russia with an overlap of range in eastern Europe (map 543). In the east it appears to be replaced in turn in similar habitats by Swinhoe's Red-tailed Robin *Luscinia sibilans*. Another *Luscinia* species, the Indian Blue Chat *L. brunneus*, occurs through the Himalayas. The Red-flanked Bluetail appears to be of eastern origin, extending through the forest zone into Scandinavia, and migrating eastwards. It has a second population in the Himalayas and western China. The Siberian Blue Robin *Tarsiger cyane* has a similar eastern distribution in the northern forest zone, but only extends to the upper Ob River (map 544). Three other *Tarsiger* species occur in the Himalayan and south China regions. The White-throated Robin is an isolated species extending through dry areas from Turkey to southern Turkestan.

Birds of this group are not present generally in North America, where their counterparts are probably the larger Parulid warblers and the small thrush species.

Robin *Erithacus rubecula* (Map 539)
Resident and migrant; breeding in Boreal to Warm Temperate zones, wintering in Warm Temperate to Subtropical zones, and in the western Temperate zone. It occurs in thick forest with shrubby undergrowth, both broadleaf and conifer; and in the west has moved into more open forest edge, parkland, roadside trees with shrubs, orchards and gardens where shrubby cover is present. In the southern part of its range it is a bird of mountain forest. In winter in the south it may occur in sparser cover in groves, oases and low scrub.

Siberian Rubythroat *Luscinia calliope* (Maps 539, 540)
Migrant; breeding in eastern Boreal to cool Temperate zones, wintering in Subtropical to Tropical zones. It occurs in mixed and conifer forest, where thick undergrowth is present; in marshy areas or the borders of streams and freshwaters, in clearings and forest edge with shrubs and tall herbage, and in stunted conifers and birch zones in mountains. It is mainly a lowland species. It winters in South-east Asia.

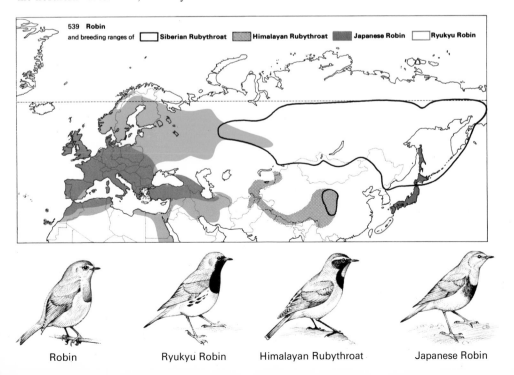

539 Robin
and breeding ranges of ☐ Siberian Rubythroat ▨ Himalayan Rubythroat ▧ Japanese Robin ☐ Ryukyu Robin

Robin   Ryukyu Robin   Himalayan Rubythroat   Japanese Robin

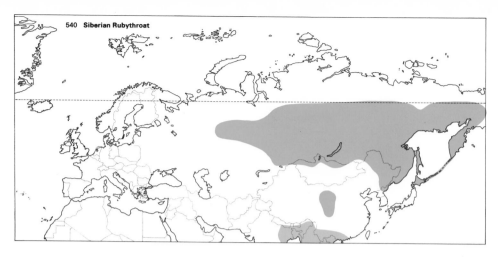

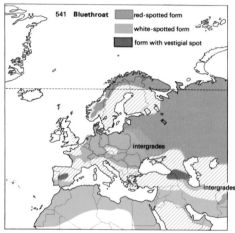

Bluethroat *Luscinia svecica* (Map 541)
Migrant, breeding in Arctic/Alpine to cool Temperate zones, in similar altitudinal zones in the Warm Temperate zone, and wintering in Warm Temperate to Subtropical zones. It occurs in marshy places with low, thick and usually shrubby vegetation, usually in lowland in the north of the breeding range and at higher altitudes in the south. It is found in low willow scrub on marshy tundra areas in the north, and similar sites in alpine meadows; in wet forest with undergrowth, scrub bordering fresh waters and in marshland, and wet grassland with tall herbage and shrubs. In mountains it also occurs in shrubby growth along watercourses. In the south of its breeding range it is found at altitudes of *c.* 1,500–4,200 m. It winters from North Africa to South-east Asia, in thick waterside vegetation.

Nightingale *Luscinia megarhynchos*
(Maps 542, 543)
Migrant; breeding in Temperate to Warm Temperate zones, wintering in Subtropical to Tropical zones. It occurs in light mixed or broadleaf forest, usually in drier areas than those used by the Sprosser, and where thick low bushy undergrowth and herbage is present. It is also found in lower shrubby scrub in lowland areas and on hills, and in more open parkland, hedgerows, orchards and gardens, provided low cover is present. In the Mediterranean it occurs in drier hillside habitats, but usually below *c.* 2,600 m. It winters in Africa south of the Sahara and mainly north of the Equator, in the thick scrub of rivers, ravines

Siberian Rubythroat   Bluethroat   Nightingale   Sprosser

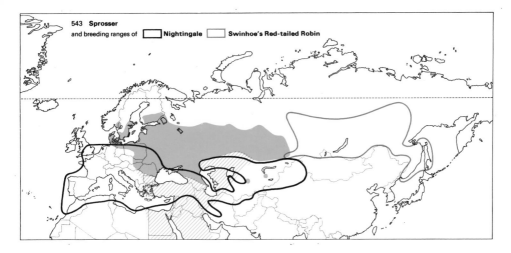

543 Sprosser
and breeding ranges of ☐ Nightingale ☐ Swinhoe's Red-tailed Robin

and on coasts; and in thick shrubby growth along savannah watercourses.

Sprosser *Luscinia luscinia* (Map 543)

Migrant; breeding in warmer Boreal to cooler Temperate continental zones, wintering in Subtropical to Tropical zones. It occurs usually in wetter places than the previous species, occurring in marshy forest and flood zones with dense shrub and herbage growth, and in tree and shrub thickets in marshy places, including small areas in open cultivation or steppes. Usually it occurs in broadleaf forest. It is also found in moister areas of secondary sapling growth, coppice, parkland and orchards, but less frequently than the Nightingale. It winters in eastern Africa south of the

Sahara, in similar habitats to the previous species.

Red-flanked Bluetail *Tarsiger cyanurus* (Map 544)

Migrant; breeding in the Boreal zone, or its altitudinal equivalent, wintering in the Subtropical zone. It occurs in thick, mossy conifer forest with sparse undergrowth, or in more open forest of birch or oak with thick shrubby cover, and in similar shrubby growth on forest edge. In northern areas it occurs in lowland up to *c.* 1,500 m but the southern form breeds at altitudes of *c.* 3,000–4,400 m and winters at *c.* 1,500–2,100 m. It winters in the Himalayan foothills, and southern China, in conifer and mixed forest with undergrowth. It appears to

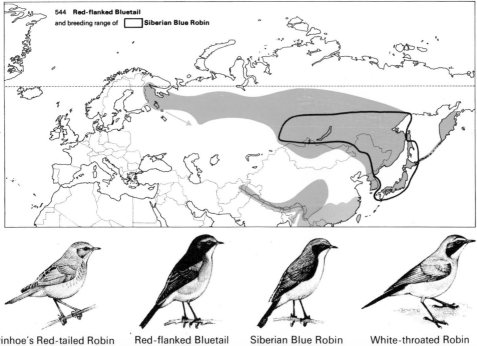

544 Red-flanked Bluetail
and breeding range of ☐ Siberian Blue Robin

Swinhoe's Red-tailed Robin   Red-flanked Bluetail   Siberian Blue Robin   White-throated Robin

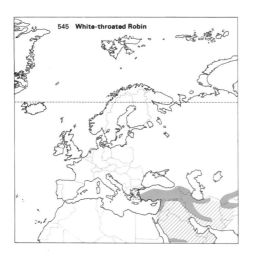

545   White-throated Robin

be spreading westwards, but keeps its south-eastern wintering area, and seems to have spread from about the Urals to northern Scandinavia in the present century.

White-throated Robin   *Irania gutturalis*
(Map 545)
Migrant; breeding in the dry Warm Temperate zone, wintering in the Subtropical zone. It occurs in broken stony terrain with scattered shrubs in open country, scrub with sparse trees on mountain slopes, and in forest edge, from lowland up to *c.* 2,000 m, rarely up to *c.* 2,350 m. It winters in north-east Africa and Arabia in dense scrub, and undergrowth along ravines and rivers.

TYPICAL THRUSHES *Turdus* and *Zoothera* species

Moderate-sized songbirds, arboreal, but mainly terrestrial in feeding. The nest is a cup in a tree or shrub, or rock crevice. There are eight species in western Eurasia and several more occur as strays. There are four species with broad distributions across most of Eurasia, a number with limited distributions in the east and south-east (maps 549, 551, 553) and several with central to eastern distributions, and with two distinct forms within the population (maps 548, 550, 551). The Blackbird has a more southerly distribution, from Europe and the Atlantic islands across to southern China, while a group of forms in India are sometimes grouped as *Turdus simillimus* but are representatives of the Blackbird and possibly conspecific with it. The Blackbird is replaced at high altitudes in Europe by the Ring Ouzel but may occur in Ring Ouzel type habitats in the Himalayas, where two other related species occur (map 551). The American Robin *T. migratorius* appears to be a member of the Blackbird subgroup. Another probably related species is the centrally distributed Red-throated Thrush, of which the north-western black-throated form reaches to the Urals. The small Eye-browed Thrush *T. obscurus*, which may occur as a stray, is part of an eastern complex (map 551) involving the Pale Thrush *T. pallidus* and Red-billed Thrush *T. chrysolaus*, the three sometimes regarded as forms of one species. The last appears to replace the Blackbird in Japan. They may, however, be closer to the redwings (map 548), the western species of which is the typical Red-

wing, overlapping widely in breeding range with the eastern Naumann's Thrush *T. naumanni*. The latter has two populations, the southern typical form and the northern Dusky Thrush *T. n. euonomus*, both of which may stray westwards. The other three spotted thrushes extend well to the east; the Fieldfare to the Lena and Aldan Rivers, the Mistle and Song Thrushes to Lake Baikal. The last has an apparent replacement species, the Eastern Song Thrush *T. mupinensis* in China; and several other thrushes have small and mainly separate distributions in the east (map 549). In addition three more *Turdus* species occur in the Himalayan region.

In the genus *Zoothera*, White's Thrush has a divided and poorly defined distribution as an eastern species extending west to the Urals and with a small Himalayan range. The Siberian Thrush *Z. siberica*, which may stray west, has a similar range in the north-east. The main stronghold of the genus is further south, with another seven species in the Himalayas and India. The north-west American Varied Thrush *Z. naevia* originates from this group.

Mistle Thrush   *Turdus viscivorus* (Map 546)
Resident and migrant; breeding in Boreal to Warm Temperate zones, wintering in Temperate to Warm Temperate zones. It occurs in all types of mature, open forest with little undergrowth, and in the south of its range is a bird of mountain forest. Where well-grown trees are present it also uses shelterbelts and rows of trees in cultivation and hedgerows; and park-

Mistle Thrush   Fieldfare   Redwing   Naumann's Thrush   Dusky Thrush

land and gardens, usually where these are associated with open grassland. It occurs more frequently in open grassland in winter.

Fieldfare *Turdus pilaris* (Map 547)

Migrant, and resident in the west; breeding in Boreal to continental Temperate zones, wintering in Warm Temperate and western warmer Boreal to Temperate zones. It is a bird of birch scrub, open conifer forest and mixed forest, forest edge, forest with grassy clearings or meadows and groups of trees in cultivated areas. In Scandinavia it occurs in parkland and gardens, occurring in urban areas. It winters in open grassland and cultivation. Its colonisation of Europe south of the Baltic has been recent, the westward spread occurring over the last century and a half, and reaching France in the 1950s. It established a colony in Greenland and nested in eastern North America in the late 1930s.

Redwing *Turdus iliacus* (Map 548)

Mainly migrant; breeding in Subarctic and Arctic/Alpine to Boreal zones, wintering in Warm Temperate and western Temperate zones. It occurs in more open habitats than the Song Thrush, being found in wooded tundra, birch scrub, mixed forest, broken forest and forest edge, riverine forest; and in the northwest in parkland and gardens. In the east it occurs more frequently in shrubby growth along watercourses and forest edge, and in thicker forest. In winter it tends to occur in open, cultivated and grassy places.

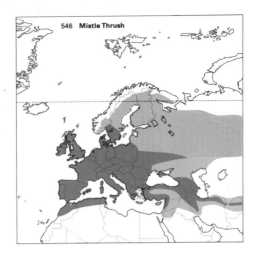

546 Mistle Thrush

547 Fieldfare

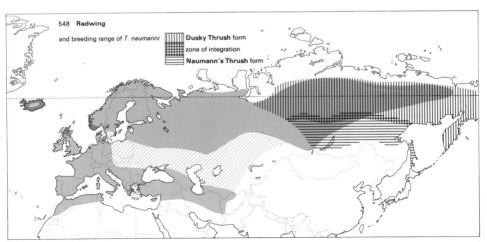

548 Redwing
and breeding range of *T. naumanni*

Dusky Thrush form
zone of integration
Naumann's Thrush form

Song Thrush

Eastern Song Thrush

Grey-backed Thrush

Kessler's Song Thrush

Japanese Grey Thrush

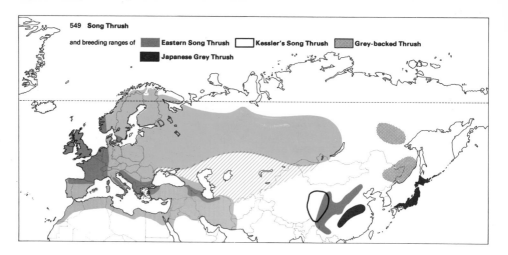

Song Thrush *Turdus philomelos* (Map 549)
Migrant and resident; breeding in Boreal to Temperate zones and wintering in the Warm Temperate, and western Temperate to cooler Boreal zones. Chiefly a bird of forest with thick, varied undergrowth and ground cover. It occurs in hill and mountain forest as well. In western Europe it has adapted to more open areas, parkland, shelterbelts, hedgerows, and gardens where some low shrubby growth is present.

Black-throated Thrush *Turdus ruficollis*
(Map 550)
Migrant; breeding from the Boreal zone to the Arctic/Alpine and Boreal altitudinal levels of the Temperate zone. The two colour forms

occur in different habitats: the Black-throated mainly in lowland open forest; the Red-throated in sparse mountain forest and on mossy scrub tundra. They winter on open cultivation, grassland, and forest edge.

Blackbird *Turdus merula* (Map 551)
Resident and migrant; breeding in warmer Boreal to Warm Temperate zones, wintering in Temperate to Warm Temperate zones. It is mainly a bird of forest edge. In the west a bird of parkland, orchards, groves and gardens, also in towns. Elsewhere in forest of all types with undergrowth, in scrub, and in hills and mountain areas up to the tree line. The Himalayan form extends into Ring Ouzel type, barer, rocky habitats.

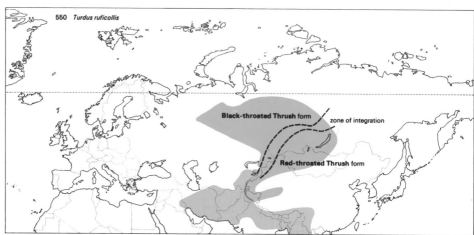

Black-throated Thrush

Red-throated Thrush

Blackbird

White-collared Blackbird

Grey-winged Blackbird

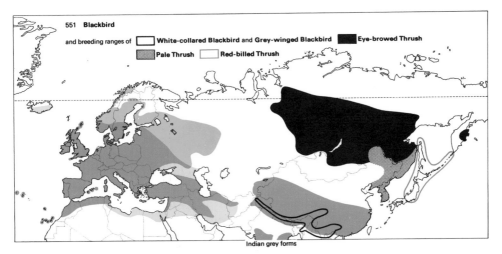

551 Blackbird

and breeding ranges of ☐ White-collared Blackbird and Grey-winged Blackbird ■ Eye-browed Thrush

▨ Pale Thrush   ☐ Red-billed Thrush

Indian grey forms

Ring Ouzel   *Turdus torquatus* (Map 552)
Mainly migrant, resident in a few places in the
south-west; breeding in Boreal and Arctic/
Alpine altitudinal zones, wintering in the Warm
Temperate zone. It breeds on alpine meadows,
grassy slopes with rocks and screes, the banks
of hill streams, heathland and moorland with
sparse shrubs, rocky slopes of coasts and islands; extending to northern birch scrub and
light and stunted tree growth around the tree
line. It replaces the Blackbird where habitat
changes. It winters in mountain areas with
patchy scrub.

White's Thrush   *Zoothera dauma* (Map 553)
Migrant; breeding in the eastern Boreal and
Boreal altitudinal zones, and wintering in the

552 Ring Ouzel

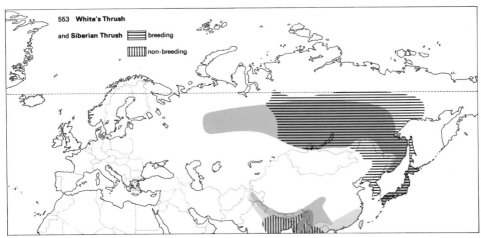

553 White's Thrush

and **Siberian Thrush** ▤ breeding

▥ non-breeding

Eye-browed Thrush   Pale Thrush   Red-billed Thrush   Ring Ouzel   Siberian Thrush

eastern Subtropical zone. In most types of forest, but usually in thick forest with shrubby undergrowth, wintering in thick cover on for-

est edge and cultivation, and along streams and in bamboo brakes.

BABBLERS   *Timaliidae*

A large and varied family, numerous in most of the Old World other than the Palaearctic. A large number of species occur in South-east Asia and from the complex of species in India and the Himalayan region a number extend into southern and western China, but only a few occur well into the Palaearctic and only five in the western part. The only species present through Europe is the Bearded Reedling, a reedbed-haunting species with a cup nest set low in reeds, extending across most of Eurasia as well where suitable habitat is present. It is an offshoot of a specialised group of eastern and south-eastern species, the Parrotbills (Paradoxornithinae), sometimes regarded as a separate family. They inhabit reedbeds and bamboo thickets, and have produced a large number of species, some with tiny ranges (map 554). Six of those shown – the Three-toed Parrotbill *Paradoxornis paradoxus*, Spectacled Parrotbill *P. conspicillatus*, Przewalski's Parrotbill *P. przewalski*, Dusky Parrotbill *P. zappeyi*, David's Parrotbill *P. davidianus* and the Chinese Parrotbill *P. hendei* – are explicable only in terms of restricted habitat, although the more southerly congeners have wider ranges. Only the Bearded Reedling extends outside the south-eastern Asian area, and within much of the latter area

Webb's Parrotbill *Paradoxornis webbianus* appears to be the main replacement species. Of the more typical babblers the genus *Turdoides* consists of a group of moderate-sized, highly sociable birds, living in small groups and mainly in low cover. The nest is a cup in a shrub or tree. They are resident, moving little, and possibly because of this have produced a large number of species. There are fourteen in Africa south of the Sahara and nine in India, and linking these is a series of four species replacing each other from North Africa to Pakistan (maps 555–558). The two western species, the Fulvous and Arabian Babblers, occur in arid country. The Iraq Babbler is found in reedbeds and moister areas. The Common Babbler, which is another species of drier areas, is present through India except the north-east and extends westwards to overlap the range of the Iraq Babbler, the two species differing a little in bill-size and to some extent in habitat preference.

Bearded Reedling   *Panurus biarmicus*
(Map 554)
Resident; in Temperate to Warm Temperate zones, but with some local and longer hard weather movements. It occurs only in large areas of reeds (*Phragmites*). This limits and localises its distribution, which is more spor-

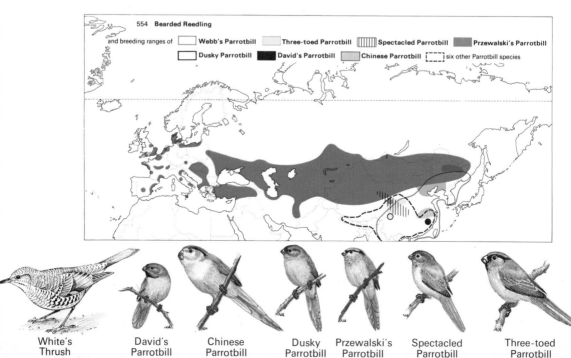

554   Bearded Reedling

and breeding ranges of ☐ Webb's Parrotbill   ▨ Three-toed Parrotbill   ▥ Spectacled Parrotbill   ▨ Przewalski's Parrotbill
☐ Dusky Parrotbill   ▣ David's Parrotbill   ▨ Chinese Parrotbill   ⌐ six other Parrotbill species

| White's Thrush | David's Parrotbill | Chinese Parrotbill | Dusky Parrotbill | Przewalski's Parrotbill | Spectacled Parrotbill | Three-toed Parrotbill |

555 Fulvous Babbler

556 Arabian Babbler

557 Iraq Babbler

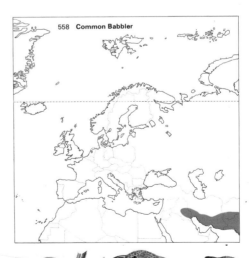
558 Common Babbler

adic than the map suggests. In hard winters it may move out of more northerly areas, and after a successful breeding season it may explore new reedbed localities.

Fulvous Babbler *Turdoides fulvus* (Map 555)
Resident; in dry Subtropical to Tropical zones. It occurs in arid, desert and semi-desert areas where scattered shrubs and thorn scrub occur, and in and around oases.

Arabian Babbler *Turdoides squamiceps* (Map 556)
Resident; in the dry Subtropical zone. It occurs in similar habitats to the previous species.

Iraq Babbler *Turdoides altirostris* (Map 557)
Resident; in the Subtropical zone. It occurs frequently in reedbeds, but also in moist cultivated areas with shrub or tree cover, such as groves, poplar thickets, orchards and market gardens. It may be found where the Common Babbler would also be expected to occur in these areas.

Common Babbler *Turdoides caudatus* (Map 558)
Resident; in Subtropical to Tropical zones. It occurs in arid and semi-desert areas and stony lower hill slopes, at times up to *c*. 2,100 m. It is found in dry thorn scrub, rocky areas with sparse shrubs, sandy regions with scattered trees, shrubs and sparse herbage, but also occurs in groves, and thick hedgerows, shrubby and tree cover in cultivation, and in orchards and gardens.

Webb's
Parrotbill

Bearded
Reedling

Common Babbler

Iraq Babbler

Arabian Babbler

Fulvous Babbler

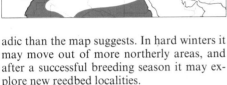

LONG-TAILED TITS   *Aegithalidae*

The family consists of tiny, insect-eating birds of only seven species. The domed nest is in a bush or tree. The Long-tailed Tit is the most widespread, occurring right across Eurasia and down through China almost to the eastern end of the Himalayas. In China its range overlaps that of the Sooty Long-tailed Tit *Aegithalos fuliginosus*, and where it is absent, in the Himalayas and west to Afghanistan, three other species are present. In western North America the family is represented by the Bushtit *Psaltriparus minimus*. The Long-tailed Tit has several colour phases in apparently latitudinal sequence at either end of the range. The white-headed form (*A. c. caudatus*)

extends right across the northern range; the striped-headed dark-breasted form (*A. c. europaeus*) in most of Europe south of the Baltic and in Britain, and at the other extreme in Korea and Japan; and the striped-headed grey-backed form (*A. c. alpinus*) in parts of southern Europe, the Middle East and Caucasus, and in China.

Long-tailed Tit   *Aegithalos caudatus*
(Map 559)
Resident, with some local and cold weather movements; in Boreal to Warm Temperate zones. It occurs mainly in mixed or broadleaf forest where some thick shrubby growth is present. It is also found in conifer forest where some broadleaf trees occur, in riverine and mountain forest where it may ascend to the limit of the broadleaf tree zone, in tree and shrub growth bordering water or along roads, in well-planted parkland and gardens, and in cultivated areas with groups or shelterbelts of trees with shrubs.

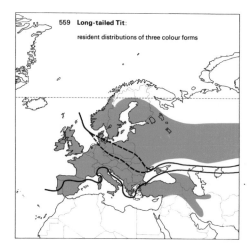

559   **Long-tailed Tit:**

resident distributions of three colour forms

PENDULINE TITS   *Remizidae*

A small family of very small insect-eaters, with a domed nest in tree or reeds. There are only nine species, mainly African with five species south of the Sahara and one in the south Sahara, the typical Penduline Tit across Eurasia, the Fire-capped Tit *Cephalopyrus flammiceps* in the Himalayas, and the Verdin *Auriparus flaviceps* in North America. The Penduline Tit shows considerable variation in head colour within its range, and in areas around the Caspian and Aral Seas is confined to reedbeds where it breeds. As a result a number of distinct forms, overlapping in range, have been recognised, and it has been suggested that more than one species is involved, but the overall picture is not clear.

Penduline Tit   *Remiz pendulinus* (Map 560)
Mainly resident, but with some dispersive, irruptive and cold weather movements; in Temperate to Warm Temperate zones. It occurs in thickets of broadleaf shrubs and small trees, or scattered larger trees, bordering freshwater and brackish lakes and rivers; in large reedbeds with or without scattered shrubs and trees; in forested flood levels, and more rarely in forest steppes and groves of taller broadleaf

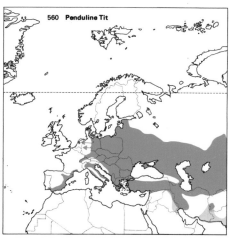

560   **Penduline Tit**

Long-tailed Tit

Penduline Tit

trees away from water. At the edge of its range occurrence may be erratic but there has been a gradual westward spread in Europe and breeding has been recorded in recent years in the Netherlands.

TITS   *Paridae*

A large family of small insect- and seed-eating birds of trees and scrub, occurring in both the Old and New Worlds. The nest is a cavity, usually in a tree, in some species excavated by the bird, and the need for this may limit distribution. Nine species occur in the area, with broad ranges that often overlap, the birds being separated by differences in preference for vegetation types and different feeding zones in them. Different species occupying the equivalent ecological niches occur in North America. In Eurasia several distinct pairs occur. The Crested Tit has a European distribution in pine forest, but the Brown Crested Tit *Parus dichrous* occurs in mountain conifer forest of the Himalayas and western China.

The Blue and Azure Tits are a west and east pair, the latter extending west of the Urals into the range of the former. This appears to have occurred in the recent past, with some hybridisation, and later evidence of a gradual retreat. The distinct form of the Azure Tit (*flavipectus*) occurring in Russian Turkestan and a small area of northern China (map 562) might, however, be a relic of a third form with a more central range. In the black-capped tits, the Marsh Tit has a split distribution, part in Europe, part in China and Japan. The very similar Willow Tit extends right across Eurasia; both this and the larger, conifer-forest haunting Siberian Tit probably originating in the east. The last has a counterpart in the Sombre Tit of the Balkans and Middle East. In addition the black-capped group have two species, the Red-bellied Tit *P. davidi* and the White-browed Tit *P. superciliosus*, confined to limited ranges in China.

The Great Tit has three distinct forms, in Europe, in India and in China; but in contrast to the Willow and Siberian Tits it appears to be the European form that has spread eastwards. The three forms now meet (map 571) and zones of interbreeding occur. In addition, along the western edge of the middle mountain zone the very closely related Turkestan Tit *P. bokharensis* occurs, and from the eastern Himalayas to Indochina the Great Tit's distribution overlaps that of the similar Greenbacked Tit *P. monticolus*, the latter preferring thicker forest habitats. The Coal Tit has a broad distribution through Eurasia, fragmented in mountain regions in the south. It is present in the eastern Himalayas but in the western Himalayas is replaced by Vigors's Black Crested Tit *P. melanocephalus* (map 565) which is similar to the eastern form of Coal Tit. A second species very similar to the western Himalayan bird but larger, the Black Crested Tit *P. rubidiventris* (map 565), also occurs in that area and extends west to the Altai and east into China, overlapping in range with the Coal Tit as well. The Japanese Tit *P. varius* has a plumage pattern reminiscent of that of the Coal Tit but differs in the large bill.

Crested Tit   *Parus cristatus* (Map 561)
Resident; in western Boreal to Warm Temperate zones. It occurs in mature and often open conifer forest, mostly in pine; and is found in both lowland and mountains, occasionally extending into marginal broadleaf forest. It occurs in drier habitats than the Coal Tit.

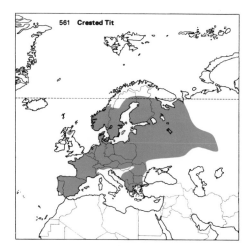

561   Crested Tit

Crested Tit

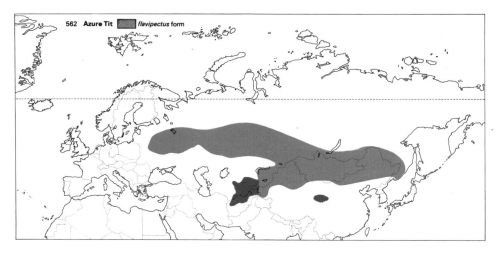

562 **Azure Tit** ☒ *flavipectus* form

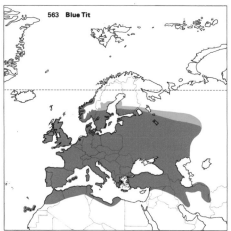

563 **Blue Tit**

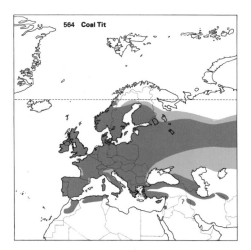

564 **Coal Tit**

Azure Tit *Parus cyaneus* (Map 562)

Resident; in the Temperate zone. It occurs in the east in similar habitats to the Blue Tit, but more frequently in broadleaf shrubs and trees bordering freshwater rivers and lakes, extending in such habitat into conifer forest and open steppes; and in broadleaf shrubby growth bordering mountain conifer forest.

Blue Tit *Parus caeruleus* (Map 563)

Mainly resident, migrating in the extreme north-east; in western warmer Boreal to Warm Temperate zones. It occurs in open broadleaf forest of all types, at low and high altitudes, and less frequently in conifers. It can utilise very open habitats with few and small trees, to a greater extent than the Great Tit. It is found frequently in small areas of trees, shelterbelts, parkland, orchards and gardens, scattered trees and hedgerows in cultivated areas, and in the south in olive groves and oases. In winter it may occur in low scrub and reedbeds.

Coal Tit *Parus ater* (Maps 564, 565)

Resident and migrant; in Boreal to Warm Temperate zones. It is mainly a bird of conifer forest, but in the extreme west and south-west of its range it occurs in mixed and broadleaf forest. It prefers moister and more mature forest with tall trees, particularly spruce in the north, and in mixed forest where it may be associated with conifers. In the south of its range it occurs at high altitudes, up to the limit of the conifer forest.

Azure Tit

Blue Tit

Coal Tit

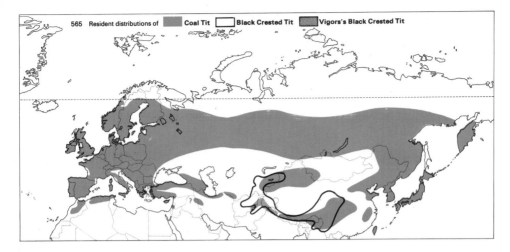

565 Resident distributions of   **Coal Tit**   **Black Crested Tit**   **Vigors's Black Crested Tit**

Sombre Tit *Parus lugubris* (Map 566)
Resident; in the Warm Temperate zone. It occurs mainly in fairly open broadleaf forest, to a lesser extent in pine forest, on hillsides and mountains, and along rivers and streams; it is also found in thickets, groves, orchards, parkland and gardens.

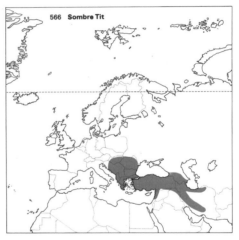

566   Sombre Tit

Siberian Tit *Parus cinctus* (Map 567)
Mainly resident, with some winter movements; in the cooler Boreal zone. It occurs in moist lowland conifer forest; being found in mature forest, and in broadleaf thickets and trees bordering fresh waters in conifer forest; and also in flooded thickets.

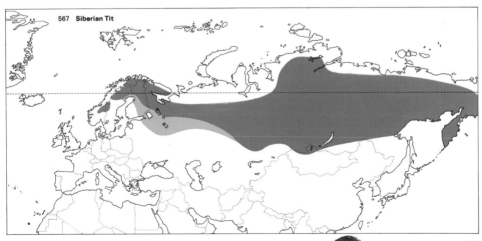

567   Siberian Tit

Black Crested Tit

Vigors's Black Crested Tit

Sombre Tit

Siberian Tit

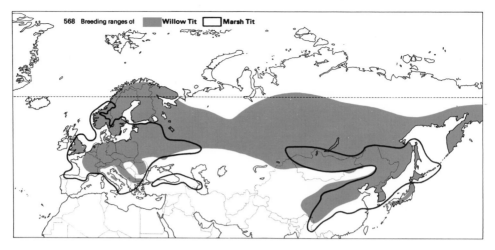

568   Breeding ranges of   Willow Tit   Marsh Tit

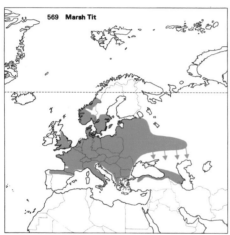

569   Marsh Tit

Marsh Tit   *Parus palustris* (Maps 568, 569)
Resident, with some local wandering; in warmer Boreal to Temperate zones. It occurs in broadleaf forest, more rarely in mixed forest, and usually in areas with thick shrubby undergrowth. It is also found in riverine forest, and elsewhere usually in more moist areas. It is mainly a lowland species, but in southern mountains may occur in broadleaf forest at up to *c*. 1,400 m. It is absent from pure conifer and dry broadleaf forest.

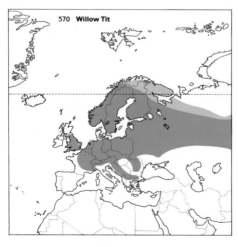

570   Willow Tit

Willow Tit   *Parus montanus* (Maps 568, 570)
Mainly resident, with some northern migration; in Subarctic to cooler Temperate zones. It occurs mainly in lowland and mountain conifer forest, and in Europe to some extent in broadleaf forest and scrub of wet areas. It is found in thick damp conifer forest, more open mountain and subalpine conifer forest; mountain scrub; subarctic birch forest; and in birch, willow and alder forest and thickets in lowland swampy areas. In mountains it may occur at up to *c*. 2,450 m.

Marsh Tit   LB

Willow Tit

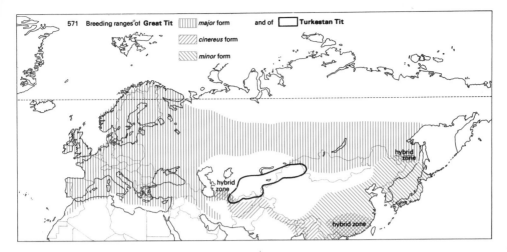

571 Breeding ranges of **Great Tit** major form   and of ☐ **Turkestan Tit**
cinereus form
minor form

Great Tit *Parus major* (Maps 571, 572)
Resident and partly migrant; in Subarctic to
Warm Temperate zones. It is a bird of open
and often mature forest, but also extends into
more scattered and shrubby growth, although
to a lesser extent than the Blue Tit. It prefers
broadleaf forest, but also occurs in conifer and
mixed forest of all kinds, and in plantations,
shelterbelts, riverine forest, groves, orchards,
thickets and hedgerows, and gardens. It occurs up to the tree line in mountains, and in
scattered trees and thickets in steppes, semi-
desert and desert areas.

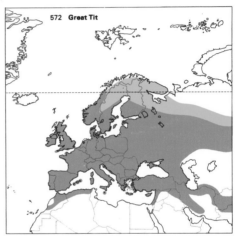

572 **Great Tit**

NUTHATCHES AND
WALLCREEPERS *Sittidae*

A group of small birds moving and feeding on
the trunks and branches of trees, and rocks.
They have woodpecker-like bills designed for
hacking open large seeds, and also probe
crevices. The nest is a cavity in a tree or rocks,
and in some species is modified by plastering
with mud. There are six species in the region,
and four subgroups can be recognised – the
small thin-billed species that do not plaster
the nesthole, the nest-plastering Common
Nuthatch complex, the two rock nuthatches
that virtually build a mud nest, and the treecreeper-like Wallcreeper. In the forests of the
Himalayas, Burma and southern China there

are another six *Sitta* species. North America
has four tree nuthatches, and one of these, the
Red-breasted Nuthatch *S. canadensis*, is sufficiently similar to some species of the first
Eurasian subgroup for them to have been con-
sidered conspecific in the past.

THIN-BILLED NUTHATCHES some
Sitta species (Map 573)
This is a group of six species with small to tiny
ranges scattered across the southern part of
Eurasia. They usually occur in isolated areas
of conifer forest high in mountains, and tend
to feed high in the trees. They are possibly
relics of a more widely distributed early form
but it has been suggested that they are not
closely related. The Chinese Nuthatch *Sitta*

Great Tit

Turkestan Tit

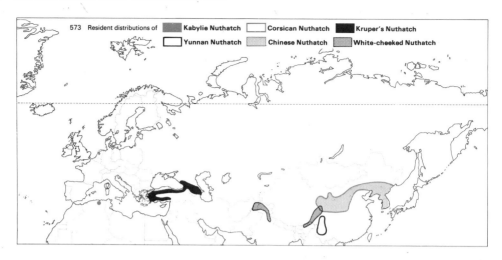

573   Resident distributions of ▨ Kabylie Nuthatch   ☐ Corsican Nuthatch   ■ Kruper's Nuthatch
☐ Yunnan Nuthatch   ▨ Chinese Nuthatch   ■ White-cheeked Nuthatch

villosus has the widest range, in conifer forest and probably mainly in pines, while the Yunnan Nuthatch *S. yunnanensis* occurs in a small range at 3,000–5,000 m in pine forest but not in thick conifers. The White-cheeked Nuthatch *S. leucopsis*, which has two separate populations at the ends of the Himalayas and occurs in alpine spruce and cedar forest, probably belongs to this group. Further west Krüper's Nuthatch occurs in the mountains of Turkey and the Caucasus, the Corsican Nuthatch in similar pine forest habitats on a single island, and the Kabylie Nuthatch in high mixed forest on a single mountain ridge.

Kabylie Nuthatch   *Sitta ledanti* (Map 573)
Resident; in cool Temperate altitudinal zone of Warm Temperate region. It occurs in a single, very limited area of mountain forest, only a few kilometres in extent, at *c.* 1,200–1,800 m. The climate is cool and wet and the vegetation is open, climax spruce, oak and cedar forest with little undergrowth.

Corsican Nuthatch   *Sitta whiteheadi*
(Map 573)
Resident; in the Boreal altitudinal zones of the Warm Temperate zone. It occurs in more mature and open conifer forest in mountain areas, and is recorded breeding at *c.* 1,000 m.

Krüper's Nuthatch   *Sitta kruperi* (Map 573)
Resident; in the Boreal altitudinal zone of the Warm Temperate zone. It occurs in mountain forest, mainly in spruce, and in the Caucasus occurs at altitudes of *c.* 1,000–2,000 m.

COMMON NUTHATCH COMPLEX
some *Sitta* species
The typical nuthatch complex has a wider tolerance of forest habitats and covers much of Eurasia. It appears to have produced three distinct forms of a species, and two more which may be separate species. In Europe (see map 574) there is a buff-breasted white-cheeked form, *S. europaea caesia*. The white-breasted form *S. e. europaea* probably originated in the east and spread to the west, into southern Scandinavia and into western Europe where it overlaps and interbreeds with the first form. In south-eastern China the buff- or grey-breasted and buff-cheeked *S. e. sinensis* form occurs, interbreeding with *S. e. europaea* where they meet. In Kashmir and northern Afghanistan is the isolate form *S. e. cashmirensis*, like *S. e. europaea* but sexually dimorphic and possibly a separate species. From India to Indochina the dark Chestnut-breasted Nuthatch *S. castanea* replaces the others.

Common Nuthatch   *Sitta europaea*
(Map 574)
Resident; in warmer Boreal to Warm Temperate zones. It occurs in broadleaf, mixed and conifer forest, usually in well-grown, more open forest with tall trees, and is present in mountains up to the limit of this vegetation. It also occurs in open hillside forest of warm regions, in plantations, parkland, orchards and groups and lines of trees in cultivated areas, and in groves and gardens; being more frequent in open and lower growth in winter. The Scandinavian population shows a ten-

Kabylie Nuthatch

Corsican Nuthatch

Krüper's Nuthatch

Yunnan Nuthatch

Chinese Nuthatch

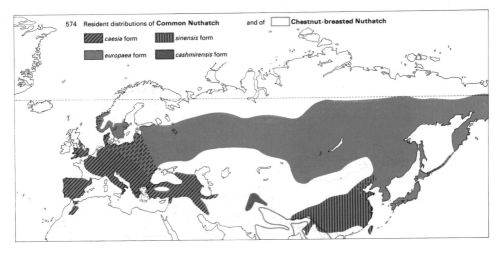

574 Resident distributions of **Common Nuthatch** and of ☐ **Chestnut-breasted Nuthatch**

caesia form *sinensis* form
europaea form *cashmirensis* form

dency to southerly irruptive and hard weather movements.

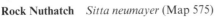

ROCK NUTHATCHES some *Sitta*
species

The two were originally regarded as a single species, and have evolved away from the tree habitat to feed in a very similar manner on irregular steep rocky surfaces. The nest, built into a crevice, may be almost entirely of mud. The typical Rock Nuthatch has a population of larger individuals in the Balkans, but a smaller form in Iran where it overlaps the very similar range of the larger Eastern Rock Nuthatch, thus reducing competition, the two presumably exploiting slightly differing food supplies.

Rock Nuthatch *Sitta neumayer* (Map 575)
Resident; in the Warm Temperate zone. It occurs in warm, arid areas, which may be sparsely forested or with scattered trees, on rock outcrops and crags, cliffs, precipices, steep sides of ravines and valleys, outcrops with basal screes of large boulders, and similar rugged places. It occurs at altitudes of 0–2,000 m. It tends to winter at lower altitudes where it may occur in more forested areas, occasionally feeding in trees.

Eastern Rock Nuthatch *Sitta tephronota*
(Map 576)
Resident; in the Warm Temperate zone. It occurs in the same habitats as the previous species, at altitudes of up to 2,600 m.

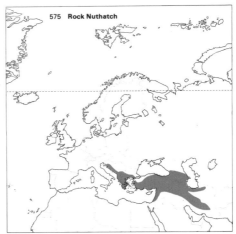

575 Rock Nuthatch

576 Eastern Rock Nuthatch

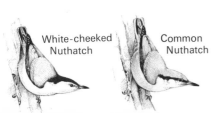

White-cheeked Nuthatch

Common Nuthatch

Chestnut-breasted Nuthatch

Rock Nuthatch

Eastern Rock Nuthatch

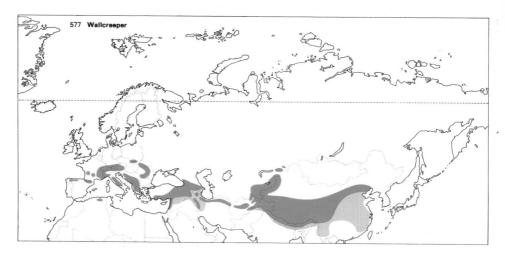

577 Wallcreeper

WALLCREEPER *Tichodroma* species

A single species, closely related to nuthatches but with a slender, curved bill and treecreeper-like habits. Like the rock nuthatches it exploits sheer rocky surfaces but usually occurs at higher altitudes than the former. The nest is a cup in a crevice.

Wallcreeper *Tichodroma muraria* (Map 577)
Mainly resident, partly migratory or vagrant; in the Alpine to Temperate altitudinal zones of the Temperate to Warm Temperate zones. It occurs in steep, precipitous rock outcrops, deep ravines, cliffs and rock walls, often in the vicinity of water, and sometimes at the snow-line. It breeds in Europe at up to c. 2,500 m and feeds at up to c. 4,800 m, in the Caucasus it occurs at up to 3,100 m, and in the Himalayas and Tibet summers at c. 3,300–5,350 m. It winters at lower altitudes and may also occur on earth cliffs, old buildings and ruins, and rocky riverbeds.

TREECREEPERS *Certhiidae*

Very small, slender-billed birds, moving up tree-trunks and branches like woodpeckers, taking insects from crevices. The nest is in a tree cavity or behind loose bark. Several tropical genera of uncertain relationship are sometimes put in this family. The genus *Certhia* appears to be Eurasian in origin, and there is a single form in North and Central America which is usually regarded as conspecific with the Eurasian Treecreeper. The latter extends across Eurasia to western Europe but appears to be eastern in origin; the Short-toed Treecreeper of the European mainland and North Africa being the western species. The Himalayan Treecreeper *Certhia himalayana* is a third, southern, species with a central range, divided (map 578) between southern Turkestan, western Himalayas and China. It overlaps that of the Eurasian Treecreeper in similar habitats, but with a tendency to higher altitudes and more conifer forest, the opposite situation to that of the European birds. In the gap in the eastern Himalayas, still within the range of the Eurasian Treecreeper, it is replaced by the Brown-throated Treecreeper *C. discolor* which mainly inhabits broad-leaf forest, and by Stoliczka's Treecreeper *C. nipalensis* in mixed and conifer forest.

Wallcreeper

Eurasian Treecreeper

Short-toed Treecreeper

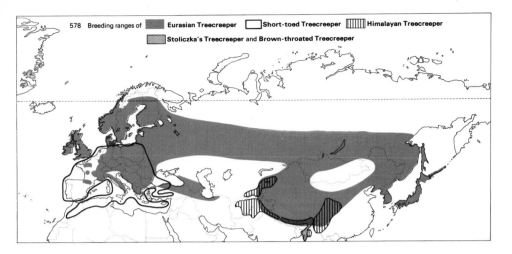

578 Breeding ranges of ▓ Eurasian Treecreeper ☐ Short-toed Treecreeper ▥ Himalayan Treecreeper
▨ Stoliczka's Treecreeper and Brown-throated Treecreeper

Eurasian Treecreeper   *Certhia familiaris*
(Maps 578, 579)
Mainly resident, with some local and limited migration; in Boreal to Temperate zones. In Europe, where it occurs with the next species, it is mainly in conifer forest and montane areas, but in places where the other species does not occur; both species may use all types of forest and occur at most altitudes. It occurs in conifer, mixed and broadleaf forest, in Europe from northern lowlands to *c.* 1,500 m in the south, in the Caucasus to 3,000 m, and in the Himalayas at 1,000–4,250 m. It prefers larger trees but will occur in tall damp scrub, and in shelterbelts, woods, parklands and well-grown gardens, occurring in more open sites most frequently in winter.

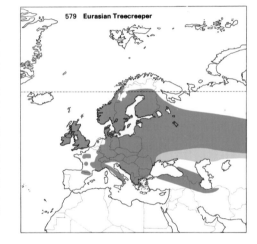

579 Eurasian Treecreeper

Short-toed Treecreeper   *Certhia brachydactyla* (Maps 578, 580)
Resident; in western Temperate to Warm Temperate zones. See the note under the previous species concerning habitat preferences in the areas of range overlap. It occurs in similar regions to the previous species, but more often in broadleaf and mixed forest, and in the south-west in the drier, open pine forest. It is found in lowland, montane and riverine forest, parkland, rows and groups of trees in cultivated areas, and groves, orchards, oases and gardens.

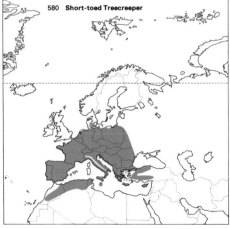

580 Short-toed Treecreeper

Himalayan Treecreeper

Stoliczka's Treecreeper

Brown-throated Treecreeper

DIPPERS *Cinclidae*

A small family of heavily built birds of flowing streams, diving and walking underwater to feed on small creatures. The domed nest is built in a crevice overlooking water. The five species mainly replace each other, with one in the mountains of western North America, two more in the Andes, and two in Eurasia. In the last region the Common Dipper occupies the western region as far as China; while the Brown Dipper *Cinclus pallasii* occurs through China to Amurland and Japan (map 581). There is an overlap of ranges in the Himalayas, western China and southern Turkestan where the latter species tends to occur at lower altitudes, and on the larger rivers, but there is

some evidence of competition. Both species show some altitudinal movements and slight migration in winter.

Common Dipper *Cinclus cinclus* (Map 581) Mainly resident, with some altitudinal and hard weather movements; in Arctic/Alpine to Temperate altitudinal zones of Subarctic to Warm Temperate zones. It occurs on clear running water, mainly with a stony or gravelly bed, and usually on rocky mountain streams and small rivers in open country or forest. It occurs in the Alps to *c.* 2,250 m, and in the Himalayas and Tibet to *c.* 5,600 m. It will winter in such areas where water is moving, even with ice on the surface, but at such times also occurs on slower lowland streams.

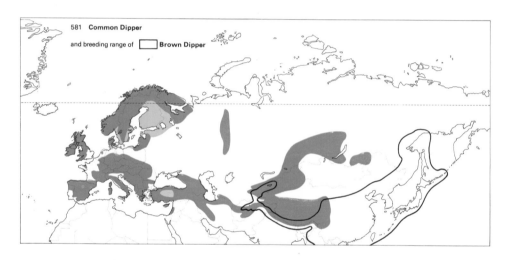

581 **Common Dipper**
and breeding range of ☐ **Brown Dipper**

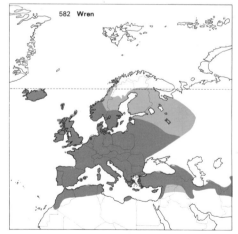

582 **Wren**

WRENS *Troglodytidae*

A family of insect-eating birds, mainly skulking in low vegetation, and building domed nests in bushes, herbage or crevices. The family is mainly in America where it appears to originate. The single, tiny Old World species, the Common or Winter Wren, may have evolved in Eurasia as the counterpart of the North American House Wren *Troglodytes aedon*, and have invaded North America later to occupy the wetter overgrown habitats not used by the House Wren.

Wren *Troglodytes troglodytes* (Map 582) Resident and migrant; in warmer Boreal to Warm Temperate zones. It occurs in low thick

Common Dipper

Brown Dipper

Wren

vegetation in moist places, ranging from thick undergrowth in all types of forest, to scrub and hillside bracken, moorland, heathland, tangled vegetation in rocks and cliff faces of mountains, shores and islands, and in broken rocks, boulder beds, moraines and screes. It extends up to the low scrub line in mountain areas, and in Europe utilises man-modified cover in parkland, hedgerows, cultivation and gardens. In the drier parts of its range it usually occurs by water.

SUNBIRDS *Nectariniidae*

A tropical Old World family of tiny, brightly-coloured nectar-feeding birds, building bag-like pendent nests in trees, shrubs or tall herbage. Numerous species occur in Africa and the Oriental region, and are connected by three African species (maps 583, 584) which extend to Egypt and Israel, while the Purple Sunbird extends westwards from India to around the Persian Gulf. The Pygmy Sunbird extends up the Nile valley and borders of the Red Sea, the Shining Sunbird occurring for only a part of the way. The apparently isolated Orange-tufted Sunbird has another population in south-western Arabia and extends across Africa south of the Sahara. The Purple Sunbird also has a more extensive range, eastwards through India and Burma to Indochina.

Orange-tufted Sunbird *Nectarinia osea*
(Map 583)
Resident; in the Subtropical zone. It occurs in dry, open grassy areas, with scattered shrubs and trees, or in rocky savannah.

Shining Sunbird *Nectarinia habessinica*
(Map 583)
Resident; in the Subtropical zone. It occurs in hot, arid areas with thin scrub and grasses, at altitudes of up to *c.* 2,000 m.

Pygmy Sunbird *Anthreptes platura*
(Map 584)
Resident; in Subtropical zone. It occurs in open, grassy areas with shrubs, or in tall open scrub, at altitudes of 0–2,000 m. It also occurs in low shrubby growth on desert edges, but will use gardens in irrigated areas.

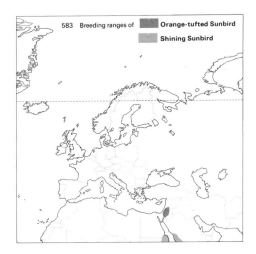

583 Breeding ranges of ▉ Orange-tufted Sunbird
 ▨ Shining Sunbird

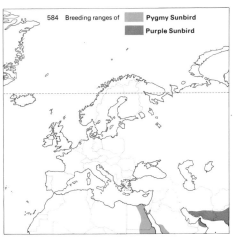

584 Breeding ranges of ▨ Pygmy Sunbird
 ▉ Purple Sunbird

Purple Sunbird *Nectarinia asiatica*
(Map 584)
Resident, with some local and altitudinal movements; in Subtropical to Tropical zones. It occurs in taller shrubs and in trees in cultivated areas, groves, oases and gardens, and extends at times into open broadleaf forest and thick scrub at altitudes of up to 1,980 m.

Orange-tufted Sunbird

Shining Sunbird

Pygmy Sunbird

Purple Sunbird

BUNTINGS   *Emberizidae*

A large group of seed- and insect-eating birds. The nest is a cup low in a bush, herbage or crevice. The large genus *Emberiza* is an Old World group, and only the northern Snow and Lapland Buntings are shared with North America which has its own large complex of buntings. Within Eurasia speciation has been more complex in the south-east where there are, in addition to those referred to here, eight more *Emberiza* species and the Crested Bunting *Melophus lathami*. Within the European buntings we can recognise a number of sub-groups roughly in succession from north to south. The Snow and Lapland Buntings are Arctic species. Then several species spread

westwards in the northern forest zone, apparently without western counterparts – the Yellow-breasted, Rustic and Little Buntings. The widespread reed bunting complex (map 591) appears closest to the last. The Temperate zone Yellow, Cirl and Pine Buntings occur across the middle region (map 592), and the Corn Bunting stands alone in the west. Next is the Ortolan Bunting group (map 597) of more open and drier country; and the Black-headed and Red-headed Buntings (map 603) in similar southern areas. Finally the Rock Bunting group (map 604) spreads across from the Mediterranean to Japan.

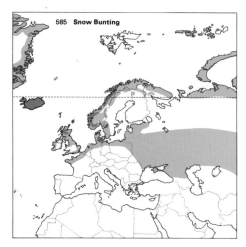

585 Snow Bunting

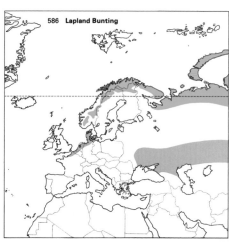

586 Lapland Bunting

SNOW AND LAPLAND BUNTINGS
Plectrophenax and *Calcarius* species
These are terrestrial Arctic species, both circumpolar in distribution. The Snow Bunting occurs on rocky areas of tundra coasts and northern mountains. The Lapland Bunting prefers shrub tundra and broken moss tundra. There are three more "longspur" species in North America, occurring on prairies as well as tundra, and the genus may have originated there.

Snow Bunting   *Plectrophenax nivalis*
(Map 585)
Mainly migrant, resident with altitudinal movements in Scotland and Iceland; breeding in the Arctic/Alpine zone, wintering in cool Temperate to coastal Boreal zones. It breeds on bare, rocky lichen tundra, rocky coasts, rock outcrops in glaciers and snowfields, and on high tundra-type northern mountain tops. It winters on the stony or sandy shores and dunes of low-lying coastal areas, on grass moorland, and open cultivated areas and grass steppe.

Lapland Bunting   *Calcarius lapponicus*
(Map 586)
Migrant; breeding in the Arctic/Alpine zone, wintering in the Temperate zone. It breeds on wetter areas than the previous species, in shrub tundra, or on moss tundra in areas of dwarf willow, tussock grass or irregular terrain. It winters on flat and open grassy areas bordering coasts and estuaries, grass moorland, grass steppes and bare, open cultivated areas.

Snow Bunting

Lapland Bunting

NORTHERN ZONE BUNTINGS
Emberiza species

Several species spread through the northern part of Eurasia from the east. The Yellow-breasted Bunting is a bird of sparse low scrub, probably closely related to the Yellowhammer-type of bunting. The Rustic Bunting occurs in swampy areas around conifer forest. The Elegant Bunting *Emberiza elegans* of eastern China and Manchuria has similarities of pattern if one discounts the yellow colour and may be related to the last species. The Little Bunting, a small species having similarities to the females of both Rustic and Reed Bunting, occurs a little further north than the other two in the shrubby growth of shrub tundra and river edge.

Yellow-breasted Bunting   *Emberiza aureola* (Map 587)

Migrant; breeding in the Boreal to cool Temperate zones, wintering in eastern Subtropical to Tropical zones. It prefers open, moist areas with shrubs and small trees. It occurs in low-lying wet or dry meadows with tall herbage and scattered shrubs, riverside thickets and shrubby willows in river flood-zones, fields and boggy areas with secondary scrub, open burnt forest with scattered trees, mountain meadows with scrub and scattered trees, birch forest edge and sparse growth of young forest. In winter it occurs in India and South-east Asia in lowland cultivated areas, hedgerows and gardens.

Rustic Bunting   *Emberiza rustica* (Map 588)

Migrant; breeding in the Boreal zone, wintering in eastern warmer Boreal to Temperate zones. It prefers marshy areas in and around conifer forest; occurring in peat bogs, broadleaf trees fringing conifer forest swamps, shrubby growth along rivers in conifer forest and birch forest, and swampy places within forest. In winter it occurs from Manchuria to eastern China and in Turkestan.

Little Bunting   *Emberiza pusilla* (Map 589)

Migrant; breeding in the Subarctic to cooler Boreal zones, wintering in eastern Subtropical to Tropical zones. It prefers damp thickets in forest tundra, shrub tundra and scattered shrubs in open tundra, usually in birch, willow or alder; and in similar growth bordering

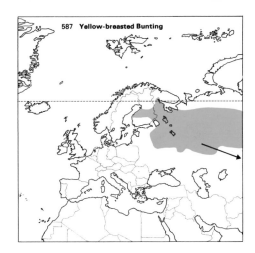

587 Yellow-breasted Bunting

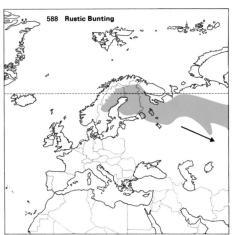

588 Rustic Bunting

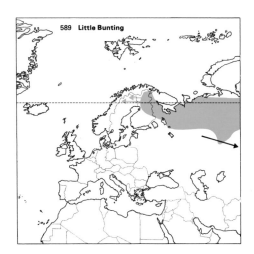

589 Little Bunting

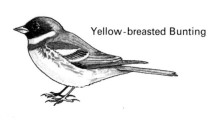

Yellow-breasted Bunting

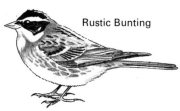

Rustic Bunting

Little Bunting

forest rivers or tundra river mouths. It winters in China, South-east Asia and Turkestan; in open cultivation, stubble and arable fields, and reedbeds.

REED BUNTING COMPLEX, some *Emberiza* species (Map 591)

A complex of three species covers most of the area. The Japanese Reed Bunting *E. yessoensis* occurs in wet meadows with tall herbage and shrubs, in Japan and nearby China, Korea and Manchuria. To the north of this over much of eastern Siberia is the eastern species Pallas's Reed Bunting *E. pallasii*, and in the west the typical Reed Bunting which extensively overlaps with the western range of Pallas's Reed Bunting. The last appears to be a bird of drier and cooler habitats, in tundra with tall herbage and shrubs, and shrubs and grass areas of steppes and semi-desert, occurring up to *c.* 2,400 m in southern mountains. The typical Reed Bunting is a bird of lowland wet areas, with altitudes of only *c.* 0–400 m. Within its range more than one bill-size occurs. The northern part of the range is occupied by a thin-billed form, and from the Caspian through the montane steppe areas to Lake Baikal a thick-billed or "parrot-billed" form occurs. In Europe around the Mediterranean a form with an intermediate bill-size is found. It is suggested that these larger bills are correlated with habitats mainly of the thicker-stemmed reeds (*Phragmites*) and reed-mace (*Typhia*).

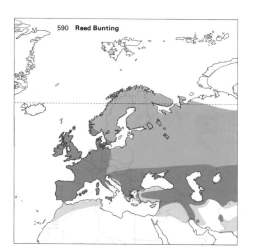

Reed Bunting   *Emberiza schoeniclus* (Maps 590, 591)

Resident and migrant; breeding in Subarctic to Temperate zones, wintering in Warm Temperate to Subtropical and western Temperate zones. It occurs in marshy areas with tall herbage and sometimes small shrubs; being found in marshland, and in tall herbage and swampy areas bordering fresh or brackish waters of all kinds, peat bogs, wet meadows with tall herbage, reedbeds, shrub tundra, swampy areas in grass steppes and wet grassy clearings in forests. It winters into the Middle East and across to northern China and Japan, in reeds, tall grass, crops and scrub along watercourses.

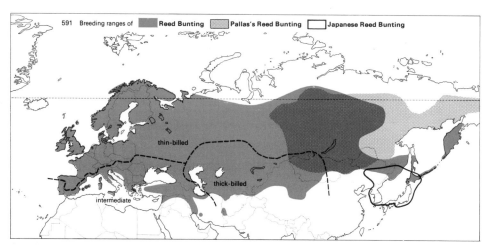

591   Breeding ranges of   Reed Bunting   Pallas's Reed Bunting   Japanese Reed Bunting

Reed Bunting   Pallas's Reed Bunting   Japanese Reed Bunting

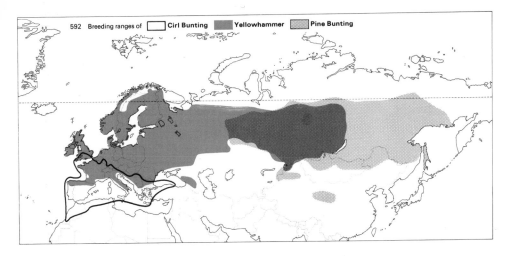

592   Breeding ranges of [ ] Cirl Bunting ▨ Yellowhammer ▨ Pine Bunting

YELLOWHAMMER GROUP AND CORN BUNTING some *Emberiza* species

These are species of open forest and partly wooded to cultivated areas. The Yellowhammer occupies the Boreal to Temperate western region of forest and cultivation. Its eastern counterpart is the Pine Bunting and the two overlap extensively between the Urals and Lake Baikal, with some evidence of hybridisation. In the drier south-western area of Europe the Yellowhammer is replaced to some extent by the Cirl Bunting. The Corn Bunting stands alone as a heavy-billed, dull-coloured species in open areas with low herbage and scrub in the European region, apparently lacking obvious counterparts elsewhere.

Corn Bunting   *Emberiza calandra* (Map 593)
Mainly resident, migrant along the south-east border; in western Temperate to Warm Temperate zones. It occurs in open grassy or cultivated areas with some tall herbage or low shrubs, and song posts; being found in the vegetation of dry, warm and semi-arid regions, grass steppes with sparse shrubs, stony steppe with sparse herbage, low maquis and grassy areas of sandy desert. It also occurs on the edges of forest, in orchards, and hilly steppe areas up to 2,600 m.

Cirl Bunting   *Emberiza cirlus*
(Maps 592, 594)
Resident; in the Warm Temperate and western Temperate zones. It occurs mainly in open areas with scattered trees and shrubs, on warm

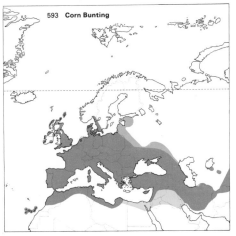

593   Corn Bunting

594   Cirl Bunting

Corn Bunting

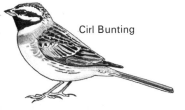

Cirl Bunting

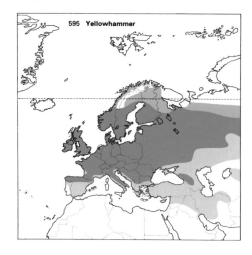

slopes in the north, sheltered and often mountain areas in the south. It is found on grassy
hillsides with scattered trees, in open broadleaf
forest and margins, cultivated areas with
groups or rows of trees or hedgerows, orchards,
groves, and vineyards. In the south it occurs at
altitudes of up to *c*. 1,000 m.

Yellowhammer   *Emberiza citrinella*
(Maps 592, 595)

Mainly resident, partly migrant; breeding in
Subarctic to Temperate zones, wintering in
warmer Boreal to Warm Temperate zones. It
is typically a bird of forest edge and clearings
in open forest with sparse herbage, usually in
drier areas. Mainly in open broadleaf or pine
forest, it also occurs in other conifers and birch
scrub. It is found from tundra forest and
shrub tundra to subalpine zones with scattered trees. It has colonised all types of cultivated land with hedgerows, groups and rows
of trees or shrubs, and shelterbelts; and occurs
on scrubby moorland and heaths. In winter it
occurs more frequently on open arable land.

Pine Bunting   *Emberiza leucocephala*
(Maps 592, 596)

Mainly migrant, except along the southern
edge of the breeding range; breeding in Boreal
to cooler Temperate zones, wintering in Temperate to Warm Temperate zones. It occurs in
similar habitats to the Yellowhammer, but
more frequently in sparse conifer forest and
scattered steppe forest; and in areas of overlapping range the Yellowhammer is more
typically a bird of forest with the Pine Bunting
in more open sites. It is found in mountain
areas at up to *c*. 2,000 m. It winters in northern
China and Pakistan and north-west India, in
open cultivation and grassland with shrubby
growth, at altitudes of up to *c*. 1,500 m.

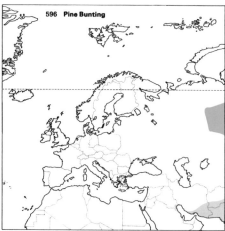

ORTOLAN BUNTING GROUP some *Emberiza* species

These are birds of mainly dry, open habitats
(map 597). The Ortolan Bunting occurs widely
in Temperate to Warm Temperate regions of
western Eurasia, and around the Baltic. It
is a species of open places with herbage and
a few shrubs or trees, and has spread north
in areas of cultivation. It may have had a
western European origin since in the Aegean
and eastern Mediterranean the closely related
Cretzschmar's Bunting occurs, usually occupying the lower and more open areas. The
Grey-necked Bunting is a bird of higher and
dry, rocky regions from Iran to the Altai,
overlapping in general range with the Ortolan
Bunting in the former area. The Cinereous
Bunting, with a discontinuous distribution in
the eastern Mediterranean and Middle East in
scrub on arid, rocky slopes, appears to be
another of this group. There do not appear to
be any obvious eastern Eurasian counterparts.

Yellowhammer

Pine Bunting

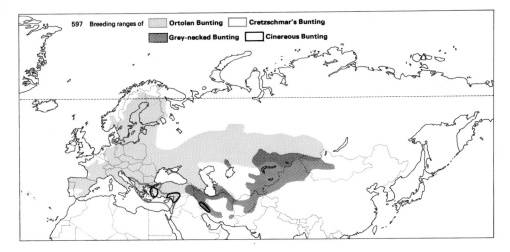

597 Breeding ranges of   Ortolan Bunting   Cretzschmar's Bunting
                          Grey-necked Bunting   Cinereous Bunting

Ortolan Bunting   *Emberiza hortulana*
(Maps 597, 598)

Migrant; breeding in Boreal to Warm Temperate zones, wintering in the Subtropical zone. It occurs in open country, with sparse or continuous herbage, or bare cultivation and some scattered trees or shrubs, on rough hillsides, level steppes, open forest edge and shelterbelts, sparse or scattered trees in grassland, orchards and gardens. It occurs in dry and semi-desert areas, but also extends into moister areas opened up by cultivation, although absent from areas of high rainfall. In the southern part of its range it is mainly a bird of hills and mountains at altitudes of up to *c.* 2,300 m. It winters in Africa on the southern side of the Sahara, and in southern Arabia, in savannah and steppe areas and cultivated regions.

Cretzschmar's Bunting   *Emberiza caesia*
(Maps 597, 599)

Migrant; breeding in the eastern Mediterranean Warm Temperate zone, wintering in the Subtropical zone. It has a limited distribution and may occur in habitats similar to those used by the previous species in dry regions, but tends to use even drier, rocky and more barren slopes; more closely resembling in this respect the Grey-necked Bunting. It occurs on hillsides and rocky islands in areas with sparser herbage and some shrub or tree growth, usually below *c.* 1,300 m. It winters in north-east Africa and southern Arabia in dry savannah, steppes, and cultivated areas and gardens of dry regions.

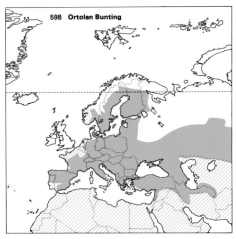

598 Ortolan Bunting

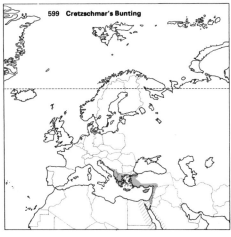

599 Cretzschmar's Bunting

Ortolan Bunting

Cretzschmar's Bunting

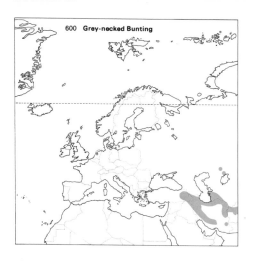

Grey-necked Bunting *Emberiza buchanani*
(Maps 597, 600)
Migrant; breeding in montane Temperate to
Warm Temperate zones, wintering in Subtropical to Tropical zones. It occurs on dry
rocky slopes of foothills and mountains up
to altitudes of *c.* 2,500 m, in areas of sparse
herbage and scattered shrubs, and on screes,
rocky outcrops and ravines. It is typical of
more barren and arid areas than the Ortolan
Bunting. It winters in Pakistan and western
India, in similar rocky and sparsely vegetated
country, and sometimes on stubbles.

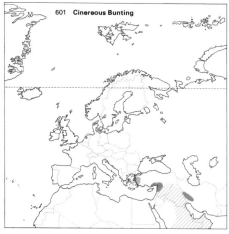

Cinereous Bunting *Emberiza cineracea*
(Maps 597, 601)
Resident and migrant; in the Warm Temperate zone, extending into the Subtropical zone
in winter. It occurs on high slopes, dry and
rocky with sparse shrubby vegetation. It
winters in north-east Africa and south-west
Arabia, often in dry coastal areas.

**BLACK-HEADED/RED-HEADED
BUNTINGS** some *Emberiza* species
These are birds of warm and dry but more
overgrown habitats (map 603). The Black-
headed Bunting occurs in lowland and hill
scrub and partly wooded areas east to the
Caspian, and between the Caspian and the
Altai is replaced by the Red-headed Bunting.
There is evidence of hybridisation at the
southern end of the Caspian. The Red-headed
Bunting is more typical of open habitats with
thickets or tall herbage. The Chestnut Bunting
Emberiza rutila is rather similar in appearance
to the last species but in habitat preference is a
bird of larch or birch forest with undergrowth
in damp areas. The first two species occur at
times as strays in western Europe.

Black-headed Bunting *Emberiza
melanocephala* (Maps 602, 603)
Migrant; breeding in the Warm Temperate
zone, wintering in Subtropical to Tropical
zones. It occurs in open lowland grassland or
scrub, and on mountain slopes, in thorn scrub
and maquis, in open forest with undergrowth,
shrub steppes, orchards, groves and vineyards, and cultivated areas with groups or
rows of trees or tall shrubs. It winters in western India, in cultivated areas with some scrub,
particularly among cereal crops.

Red-headed Bunting *Emberiza bruniceps*
(Map 603)
Migrant; breeding in the Warm Temperate
zone, wintering in the Subtropical zone. It oc-

Grey-necked Bunting   Cinereous Bunting   Black-headed Bunting

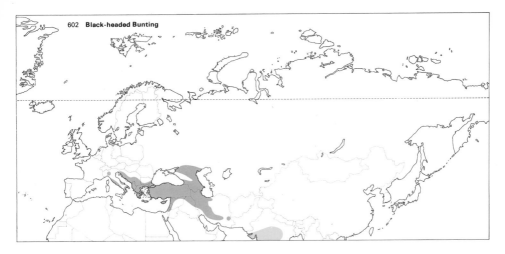

602 Black-headed Bunting

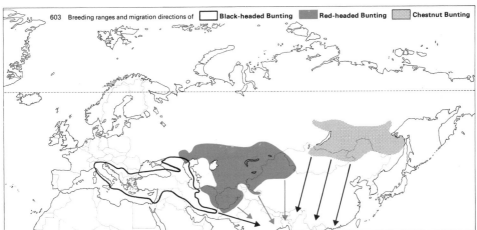

603 Breeding ranges and migration directions of ☐ Black-headed Bunting ▨ Red-headed Bunting ▨ Chestnut Bunting

curs in drier country than the previous species, with less vigorous vegetation; being found in shrubs and thickets of more open country, and in tall herbaceous growth; in steppes, semi-desert and shrubs and oases of true desert. It also occurs in similar habitats in mountains up to *c.* 3,000 m. It winters in Pakistan and northern India, in similar habitats to the previous species.

ROCK BUNTING GROUP some
Emberiza species

These are mainly birds of dry, open and rocky places in the south (map 604). The Rock Bunting occurs on rocky hillsides and has two forms, a western form with black-streaked head occurring east to the Altai and Him-

alayas, and an eastern (*godlewski*) form with more chestnut-streaked head replacing it through much of western China and Mongolia. Eastern China and Japan are occupied by the Meadow Bunting *Emberiza cioides* which occurs in similar habitats of dry hillsides but also extends into thickets and shrubs of grassland and fields, and open sapling growth. This species overlaps extensively in range with the eastern form of Rock Bunting. Within the range of the former the closely related Jankowski's Bunting *E. jankowski* occupies a very limited range of open hill habitat. Further west the White-capped Bunting *E. stewarti* occurs in mountains of Afghanistan and Turkestan, on dry rocky and sparsely vegetated hillsides in areas where the Rock Bunting is

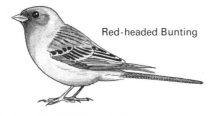

Red-headed Bunting

Chestnut Bunting

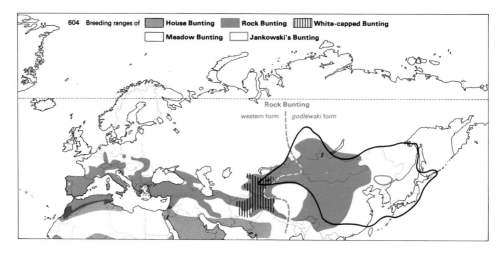

604 Breeding ranges of ▨ House Bunting ▨ Rock Bunting ▥ White-capped Bunting / Meadow Bunting ☐ Jankowski's Bunting

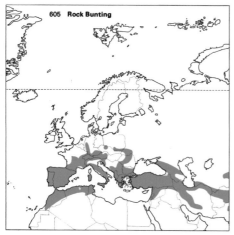

605 Rock Bunting

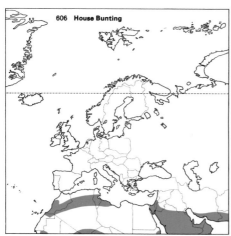

606 House Bunting

found at higher altitudes. The House Bunting appears to be close to these species and is a more southerly bird, replacing the others in arid semi-desert and desert.

Rock Bunting *Emberiza cia* (Maps 604, 605) Resident; in Warm Temperate to southern Temperate zones. It occurs on dry rocky slopes, often at high altitudes, with sparse herbage and some shrubs or trees. It is found on rocky hill slopes with scattered shrubs in arid areas, open areas at the upper forest limits, juniper scrub, subalpine meadows with shrubs and screes, stone-walled cultivated areas and vineyards on hillsides. It occurs from low altitudes in the north to higher southern ones where it is found on mountains at *c.* 2,000–4,000 m, wintering at lower altitudes.

House Bunting *Emberiza striolata* (Maps 604, 606) Resident; in Subtropical to Tropical zones. It occurs in arid areas, on rocky slopes with sparse vegetation, ravines, and ruins and buildings. It is found in desert and semi-desert but usually within reach of a source of water. It may occur in lower and more open areas in winter.

House Bunting   Rock Bunting   White-capped Bunting   Siberian Meadow Bunting

FINCHES   *Fringillidae*

A large group of small, seed-eating birds, the bills showing variation in structure and sharpness for seed manipulation and crushing. The cup nest is in a tree, shrub or on the ground. Habitats range from bare and rocky desert to forest. There are a number of subgroups – the chaffinches, Bullfinch, serins, typical cardueline finches, crossbills, desert finches, rosefinches and grosbeaks.

CHAFFINCHES   *Fringilla* species
These are more slender-billed species of forest and forest edge, more terrestrial in feeding than most other finches with the possible exception of the desert finches. The Brambling and Chaffinch appear to form an east and west pair (map 608), the former now being a boreal forest bird, spreading across into northern Europe and to some extent overlapping in range with the Chaffinch. Where one spreads the other retreats, but it is not certain if this is due to direct competition or to other factors such as climatic change. The Chaffinch shows variation within its range, and the North African and Atlantic Island form is distinct. The Atlantic Islands have been colonised twice, the earlier event having produced a distinct species, the Blue Chaffinch.

Brambling   *Fringilla montifringilla*
(Maps 607, 608)
Migrant; breeding in Subarctic to Boreal zones, wintering in the Warm Temperate to western Temperate zones. It occurs in more open conifer forest, birch forest and riverine birch and willow zones; and into shrub tundra. Like the Chaffinch it winters in flocks on more open cultivated areas and forest edge.

Blue Chaffinch   *Fringilla teydea* (Map 608)
Resident; in the Canary Islands on Tenerife and Gran Canaria. It usually occurs in mountain pine forest with undergrowth, at *c.* 1,100–2,200 m; more exceptionally in forest without undergrowth, and in dense, high-altitude scrub. In these regions the common Chaffinch occurs at lower altitudes in broadleaf forest and tree heath scrub.

607 Brambling

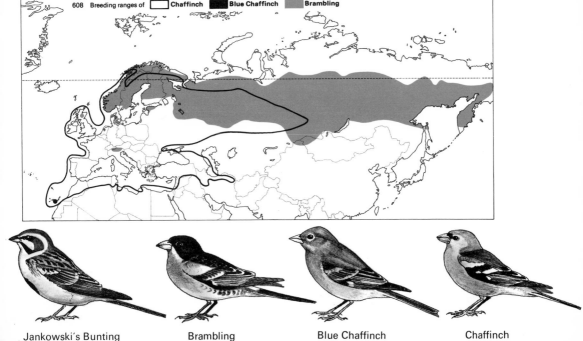

608 Breeding ranges of ☐ Chaffinch ■ Blue Chaffinch ▨ Brambling

Jankowski's Bunting   Brambling   Blue Chaffinch   Chaffinch

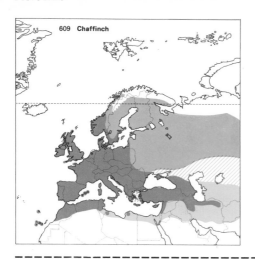

609 Chaffinch

Chaffinch *Fringilla coelebs* (Maps 608, 609)
Resident and migrant; breeding in Boreal to Warm Temperate zones, wintering in Warm Temperate and the western Temperate zones. It occurs in all types of forest, usually in more open or marginal areas, on forest edge, in small woodlands and groves and rows of trees in cultivated areas, in parkland, gardens and orchards. It is found in lowland and mountain forests, up to *c.* 2,500 m in the south-east of its range. It winters at lower altitudes, usually in flocks in more open and cultivated areas and along forest edge.

BULLFINCHES *Pyrrhula* species
These are bud-eating specialists with short, stout bills. They are mainly centred on the Himalayas where four species are present, the common Bullfinch occurring right across Eurasia to the north of these (map 610). The Brown Bullfinch *Pyrrhula nipalensis*, which occurs through southern China and the Himalayas, is brown with no black on the head. The other three Himalayan species have black only around the eyes and bill, and grey, red and orange plumages. The Orange Bullfinch *P. aurantiaca* occurs only in the eastern Himalayas, the Red-headed Bullfinch *P. erythrocephala* throughout the Himalayas, and Beavan's Bullfinch *P. erythaca* from the eastern end of the Himalayas through western China. The typical species occurs across the whole of Eurasia. The male shows variation in breast colour indicating some separation and isolation of populations at earlier periods. The main population has a pale pink breast in the male. The western European population is deep red on the breast, while an isolate in the Azores lacks the red, and at the other extreme of range, in Amurland, Manchuria and Japan, a form has a grey breast and red face.

Bullfinch *Pyrrhula pyrrhula* (Map 610)
Resident and migrant; breeding in Boreal to Temperate zones, wintering in warmer Boreal to Warm Temperate zones. It occurs in conifer and mixed forest, and in Europe in broadleaf forest, usually in thick growth with under-

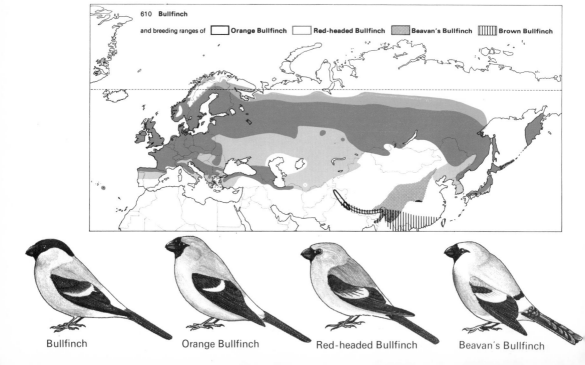

610 **Bullfinch**
and breeding ranges of ☐ Orange Bullfinch ☐ Red-headed Bullfinch ▨ Beavan's Bullfinch ▥ Brown Bullfinch

Bullfinch   Orange Bullfinch   Red-headed Bullfinch   Beavan's Bullfinch

growth. It has also adapted in the west to cultivated areas with thick hedgerows, gardens, orchards and parkland where suitable shrubs and thick foliage are present. It is found in mountain forest at altitudes of up to c. 2,900 m.

SERINS *Serinus* species

Very small birds, with short, blunt bills, usually occurring in fairly open, dry places. There are a series of six species around the Warm Temperate region, several of them being mountain forms (map 611). The main stronghold of the genus is in Africa where a further twenty-eight species occur. Of the northern birds, the Canary occurs on the Atlantic Islands. The typical Serin is found around the western and northern Mediterranean and has spread north into temperate Europe. A mountain species, the Citril Finch, occurs in the Alps and Pyrenees within the Serin's range, and has a highly discontinuous relict distribution. The Syrian Serin occurs in the eastern Mediterranean; and the Red-fronted Serin in eastern mountain regions from Turkey to the Altai, overlapping the range of the Serin in western Turkey. The Tibetan Serin *Serinus tibetanus* (previously the Tibetan Siskin *Carduelis tibetanus*) is a high-mountain species of southern Tibet, now thought to be part of this species group. In the cooler northern forest areas the group appear to be replaced by the Siskin and Redpoll.

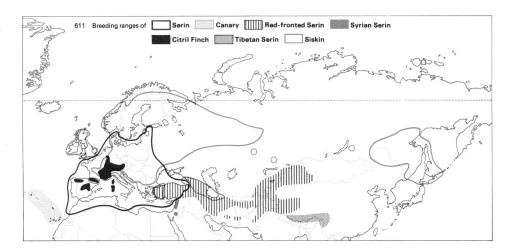

611 Breeding ranges of Serin · Canary · Red-fronted Serin · Syrian Serin · Citril Finch · Tibetan Serin · Siskin

Serin *Serinus serinus* (Maps 611, 612)
Resident and migrant; breeding in Temperate to Warm Temperate zones, wintering in the Warm Temperate zone. It occurs in warmer places on forest edge, in broken forest and scattered clumps and rows of trees on hill and mountain sides and in cultivated areas. In the southern part of its range it occurs from sea level up to the subalpine mountain zone. It has adapted well to parkland, orchards, groves, vineyards and gardens. Its northerly spread may be associated with this for it spread to central Europe in the nineteenth century and in the last fifty years has extended to its present range in northern Europe; but it is vulnerable to cold wet weather and is migratory in these regions.

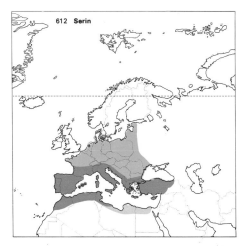

612 Serin

Brown Bullfinch

Serin　　　　　Tibetan Serin

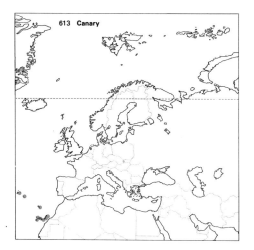

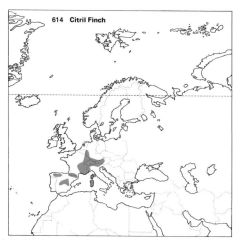

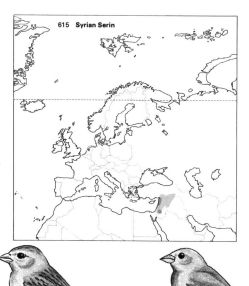

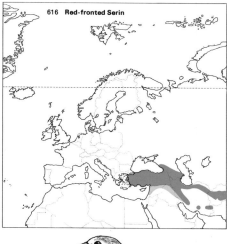

Canary   *Serinus canaria* (Maps 611, 613)
Resident in the Warm Temperate zone. It occurs in scrub and sparse forest on mountain slopes, and in trees and shrubs in and around cultivated areas.

Citril Finch   *Serinus cintrinella*
(Maps 611, 614)
Resident, with some altitudinal seasonal movements; in the Boreal altitudinal zone in the western Temperate zone. It occurs in mountain conifer forest, open subalpine forest and forest edge. In Corsica and Sardinia it also occurs in dry mountain scrub. In winter it occurs at lower altitudes in sheltered valleys.

Syrian Serin   *Serinus syriacus*
(Maps 611, 615)
Resident; in the Warm Temperate zone. It breeds in mixed and conifer forests in mountains, wintering in more open areas.

Red-fronted Serin   *Serinus pusillus*
(Maps 611, 616)
Resident; in the eastern Warm Temperate zone where it breeds in Boreal to Subalpine altitude zones and winters at lower levels. It usually breeds in rugged, rocky areas. It is found in scrub at the tree line, on screes and rocky slopes, in open birch and pine with rhododendrons, and into spruce and broadleaf forest. It breeds at *c.* 600–3,000 m in the Caucasus and *c.* 2,400–4,000 m in the Himalayas. In winter it occurs at lower altitudes in foothills and valleys, on open or rocky areas with sparse herbage and shrubs.

Canary   Citril Finch   Syrian Serin

TYPICAL CARDUELINE FINCHES
Carduelis and *Acanthis* species

These species show a greater variety in bill shape; short in *Acanthis* species, longer and sharper in Siskin and Goldfinch, and largest in the Greenfinch. The Siskin has a discontinuous distribution (map 611) with large western and eastern populations without obvious differences, suggesting that the break in continuity is recent. In North America it is replaced by the similar Pine Siskin *Carduelis pinus*, and three other species of this type occur in open habitats of the type used by the Goldfinch in Eurasia. The Goldfinch has a broad distribution east to the Altai, but within its range has ·two distinct forms apparently evolved during a period of separation. A European black-crowned form occurs east to the Caspian and northern Altai, and a Turkestan grey-headed form from north-eastern Iran through to western Mongolia, the two interbreeding where they meet. The Greenfinch shows a complex of three species. The typical Greenfinch occurs through Europe with an outlying population in Turkestan. The smaller Chinese Greenfinch *C. sinica* occurs in similar habitats in China and Japan. In similar temperate altitudes in the Himalayas and northern Indochina there are several dark brown and yellow forms, variously regarded as from one to three species, and here (map 618) treated as *C. spinoides*. In captivity all the greenfinches produce freely-breeding hybrids; with some evidence of interbreeding in the montane *C. spinoides* birds in the wild. The North American Evening Grosbeak *Hesperi-phona vespertina* looks as though it might be a giant greenfinch.

The Linnet and Twite are a species pair, with the mainly lowland European Linnet east to the Altai. The Twite is a mountain species now mainly centred on Central Asia with a north-western European population that is probably a relic of a more continuous glacial period distribution in steppe tundra. The Redpoll also has two forms, sometimes regarded as one species. Both occur across Eurasia and North America. The Arctic Redpoll is found through the tundra. The common Redpoll is mainly a bird of birch forest further south; and its forms in central and western Europe and Britain are smaller and darker than the main Eurasian form, and those of Greenland and Iceland are larger and darker.

Goldfinch *Carduelis carduelis* (Map 617)
Resident and migrant; breeding in Boreal to Warm Temperate zones, wintering in Warm Temperate and warmer western Temperate zones. It occurs where open-foliaged, mainly broadleafed trees occur by open, weed-grown ground or mixed herbage. It is found on the edges and in clearings of forests; in open forest, mainly broadleaf or mixed; and in scattered groups and rows of trees in cultivated areas and on steppes; in riverine forest, parkland and cultivated areas with trees and shrubs, orchards, vineyards, groves and gardens. In suitable habitats it occurs in mountains almost to the tree line. In winter it may occur in more open areas.

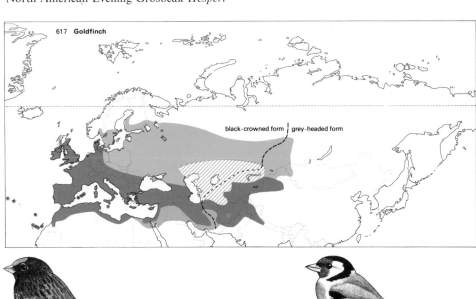

617 Goldfinch

black-crowned form | grey-headed form

Red-fronted Serin

Goldfinch

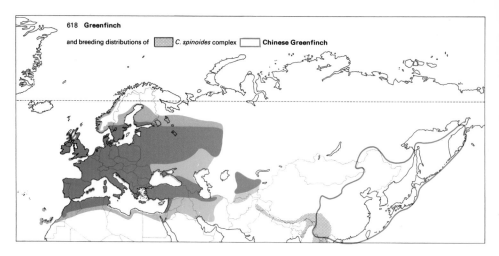

618 **Greenfinch**

and breeding distributions of [ ] *C. spinoides* complex [ ] Chinese Greenfinch

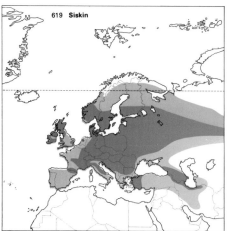

619 **Siskin**

Greenfinch   *Carduelis chloris* (Map 618)
Mainly resident, partly migrant in the north;
occurring in warmer Boreal to Warm Temperate zones. It occurs in similar habitats
to the Goldfinch, but prefers taller trees, and
during the breeding season is likely to occur in
any area with a few or scattered trees, preferably well grown. In winter it is found in more
open areas, often on cultivated land or coastal
marshland.

Siskin   *Carduelis spinus* (Maps 611, 619)
Resident and migrant or vagrant; breeding
in Boreal to Temperate zones, wintering in
warmer Boreal to Warm Temperate zones. It
occurs mainly in spruce forest, preferring open
forest with well-grown trees, but also occur-

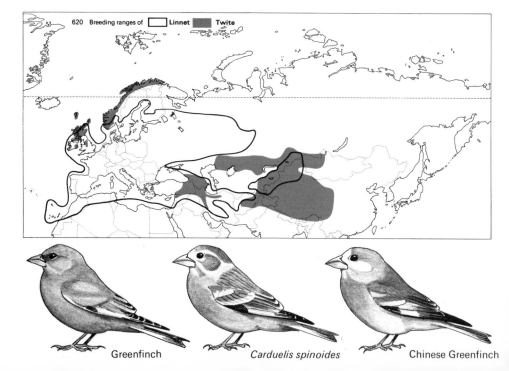

620 Breeding ranges of [ ] **Linnet** [ ] **Twite**

Greenfinch   *Carduelis spinoides*   Chinese Greenfinch

ring in other conifer and mixed forest, and broadleaf forest with some spruce, and parkland. It is found in both lowland and mountain forest. In winter it is vagrant in response to hard weather rather than migrant, and occurs in more open areas, usually in birch and alder trees bordering watercourses.

Linnet *Acanthis cannabina* (Maps 620, 621)
Resident and migrant; breeding in warmer Boreal to Warm Temperate zones, wintering in Warm Temperate and western Temperate zones. It occurs usually in open areas with low and sometimes sparse shrubby growth; being found on moorland, heathland, coastal marshes, edges and clearings of forest, dry hillsides with sparse trees or shrubs, maquis, cultivated and grassland areas with shrubs or small trees, hedgerows, orchards, vineyards and gardens. In southern mountain areas it occurs at altitudes of up to *c.* 2,400 m.

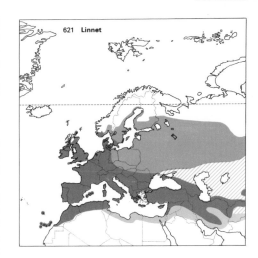

Twite *Acanthis flavirostris* (Maps 620, 622)
Resident and migrant; breeding in the Boreal altitude zones of the extreme north-western Boreal to Temperate zones, and eastern Temperate zone. It occurs on dry, open upland grasslands with very sparse shrubs. In north-western Europe it is found on moorland, rocky grassland with short herbage and few shrubs, and in dwarf birch; elsewhere in subalpine to alpine rocky meadows, mountain steppes and mountain tundra and scrub. In the south of its range it is found breeding at altitudes of 2,500–3,500 m and in Tibet up to *c.* 4,800 m. It winters at lower levels and in western Europe usually on low coastal areas.

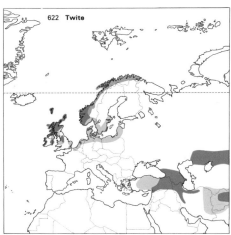

Redpoll *Acanthis flammea* (Map 623)
Resident and migrant; breeding in the Sub-arctic to Boreal zones, and parts of the western Temperate zone, wintering in the warmer Boreal to Temperate zones. It occurs in birch forest, shrub tundra, open conifer forest with some broadleaf trees; in birch, willow and alder along northern rivers, mountain conifer forest, pine plantations, and woods and gardens with some conifer or birch trees. In winter it is often nomadic in more open places, but particularly in waterside birches and alders.

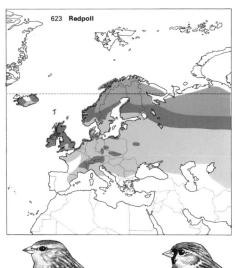

Siskin Linnet

Twite Redpoll

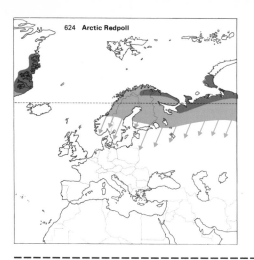

624   Arctic Redpoll

Arctic Redpoll   *Acanthis hornemanni*
(Map 624)
Resident and partial migrant; breeding in the
Arctic zone and wintering in Arctic to Boreal
zones. It occurs mainly in shrub tundra, or
where some dwarf willow or birch is present.
In winter it may occur in warmer regions with
the previous species.

CROSSBILLS *Loxia* species
This is a small genus of forest finches with
bill tips crossed to aid the extraction of seeds
from the cones of conifers. The development
of the bill, and to some extent speciation, appears to depend on the size of cones used
for food. Reliance on this food source causes
the irruptive dispersals at irregular intervals
which are characteristic of these species. It has
been suggested that the Common Crossbill,
with spruce as its typical food tree, left relict
populations in the north-west during the later
glaciations and these became adapted to exploit pine cones and gave rise to the Scottish
Crossbill of northern Scotland and the Parrot
Crossbill of Scandinavia, the Common Crossbill spreading west again in the post-glacial

period with the spread of spruce again in
Europe. The Common Crossbill (map 625)
has also differentiated to produce a large-
billed population specialising on pine cones in
the Mediterranean islands and North Africa,
which might have equivalent status to the
Scottish birds. The populations in Turkestan
and the Altai region are thinner-billed, resembling to some extent in this respect the
White-winged Crossbill, with which they do
not overlap in distribution. The White-winged
Crossbill is a slender-billed species feeding
mainly on larch and cedar cones and occurring in a narrow zone across Eurasia (map
625). Both the Common and White-winged
Crossbills also occur across North America.
In spite of the bill specialisations the species

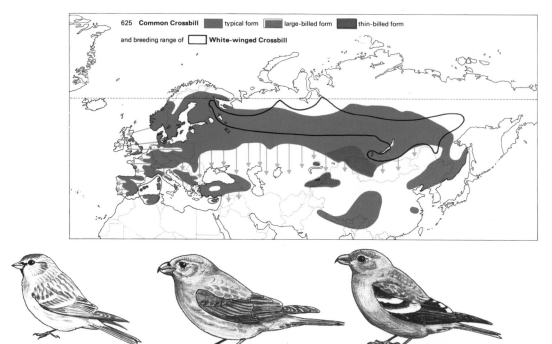

625   **Common Crossbill**   typical form   large-billed form   thin-billed form
and breeding range of   **White-winged Crossbill**

Arctic Redpoll   Common Crossbill   White-winged Crossbill

are not wholly confined to one type of conifer seed for food and may also at times utilise those eaten by the other species.

Common Crossbill   *Loxia curvirostra*
(Map 625)
Resident, nomadic and irruptive in many years; in Boreal to Warm Temperate zones. It occurs in conifer forest, usually in spruce or mixed forest; in open or broken forest, in more mature conifer plantations and shelter-belts. In the south of its range it occurs in mountain forest up to *c*. 4,500 m. The northern population is irruptive and may extend west or south in periods of fluctuating food supply, breeding at times during these movements. The large-billed form in Cyprus, Corsica, the Balearic Islands and North Africa occurs in pine forest and is sedentary.

Scottish Crossbill   *Loxia scotica* (Map 626)
Resident; in the western Boreal zone. It occurs in a limited area of Scotland in mature conifer forest and mixed forest, or in conifer plantations, mainly of Scots Pine.

Parrot Crossbill   *Loxia pytyopsittacus*
(Map 627)
Resident, nomadic and irruptive; in the Boreal zone. It occurs in mature open pine forest, and mixed conifer forest with pines, mostly on drier or mountain areas, but at times in open pine forest on marshland.

White-winged Crossbill   *Loxia leucoptera*
(Maps 625, 628)
Resident, nomadic and occasionally irruptive. It occurs through the Boreal conifer zone across Eurasia where larch, cedar or fir are present. Larch is the principal food tree, and it may occur in mature larch plantations.

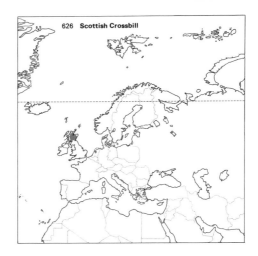

626 Scottish Crossbill

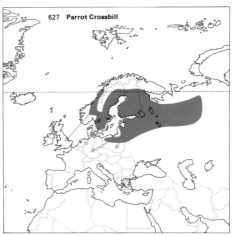

627 Parrot Crossbill

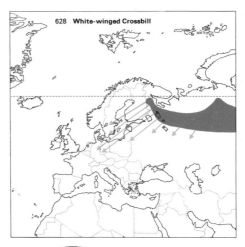

628 White-winged Crossbill

Scottish Crossbill

Parrot Crossbill

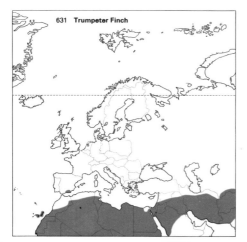

DESERT FINCHES *Rhodopechys* species
These are birds of hot, arid open spaces, and
have short stout bills. There are four species
in the genus. The Trumpeter Finch is a lowland species of the Afro-Arabian deserts and
through Iran and Afghanistan. It is replaced
on higher rocky ground by the Mongolian
Trumpeter Finch, which is sometimes regarded as a subspecies of the former, and
has a range extending from eastern Iran across
to eastern China through the upland desert
regions. The Crimson-winged Finch is a dry
mountain species with a discontinuous distribution from North Africa to the Altai,
while the Desert Finch is another lowland
species extending from the eastern Mediterranean through the Altai to western China.

Desert Finch   *Rhodopechys obsoleta*
(Map 629)
Resident; in the Warm Temperate zone. It
occurs in arid and semi-arid areas in lowland,
and to a lesser extent in foothills and mountain valleys, up to *c.* 2,000 m in the east of
its range. It is found where some open tree
or shrub growth is present, in plantations,
orchards and rows of trees in oases or areas
of irrigation, and in arid places with sparse
herbage and scattered trees or shrub thickets.
It may feed in weedy or fallow cultivated
areas. It usually occurs within reach of some
source of water.

Crimson-winged Finch   *Rhodopechys*
sanguinea (Map 630)
Resident, with some altitudinal movements; in
the Warm Temperate zone. It occurs at high
altitudes on mountains, being recorded at altitudes of 1,700–3,200 m. It is found in sparse
arid scrub on stony slopes and ridges, in the
scrub and juniper zone above the trees, on
bare stony slopes with sparse herbage, and on
almost bare, dry, eroded clay hills. It winters
at lower altitudes on bare areas and arable
cultivation.

Trumpeter Finch   *Rhodopechys githaginea*
(Map 631)
Resident and nomadic; in Subtropical desert
zones. It is a terrestrial species, occurring in
bare rocky desert areas with very sparse vegetation, stony mountain slopes with sparse
herbage, and dry steppes. It is usually within
reach of a source of water.

Desert Finch   Crimson-winged Finch   Trumpeter Finch

Mongolian Trumpeter Finch *Rhodopechys mongolica* (Map 632)

Resident, with some altitudinal migration in hard weather; in the Warm Temperate mountain zone. It occurs in arid semi-desert or desert areas of mountainous or rugged country. It is found on steep and broken mountain slopes with very sparse vegetation, or in steep-sided ravines, occurring at altitudes of *c.* 1,000–4,000 m.

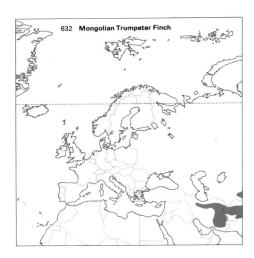

ROSEFINCHES *Carpodacus* and *Pinicola* species

These are stout-billed birds, usually occurring in shrubby mountain forest. Two species extend through the northern Eurasia region, and three more occur in southern mountain areas; but in addition there are a further thirteen species in a complex mass of overlapping ranges crowded into the Himalayan, southern Chinese and northern Indonesian region. Three other species are found in North America. The Common Rosefinch occurs through most of northern Eurasia from the Baltic eastwards (map 633). Pallas's Rosefinch *Carpodacus roseus*, which occasionally strays to Europe, is found in more forested habitats within the eastern part of the previous species' range. In the southern mountains the Sinai and Great Rosefinches have discontinuous distributions mainly centred on the Altai and Tibetan regions but with outlying populations in the eastern Mediterranean and Caucasus. In the central Asian region the Red-mantled Rosefinch *C. rhodochlamys* is found in the upper forest and scrub zones of mountain ranges (map 633). The Pine Grosbeak might be a large, blunt-billed species of this group. It occurs through the Boreal forest regions, covering a similar area to the Common Rosefinch in the east, but in a narrow northern zone west of the River Ob. It also occurs across North America. Both Common Rosefinch and Pine Grosbeak have a distribution suggesting an easterly origin, and the former may have moved westwards more recently than the other. The Common Rosefinch shows a steady tendency to westward extension of range, but performed a similar and temporary range extension early in this

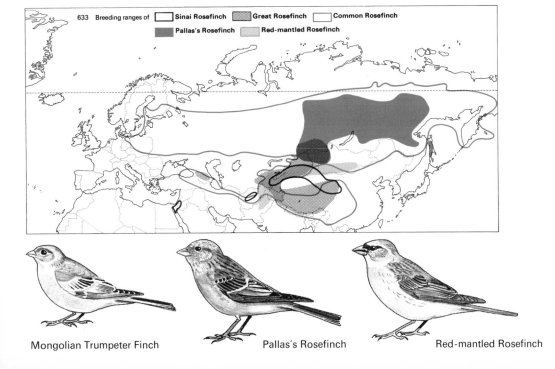

Mongolian Trumpeter Finch   Pallas's Rosefinch   Red-mantled Rosefinch

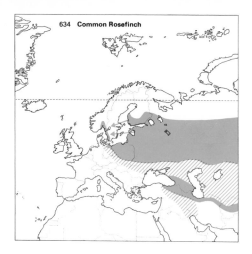

century. The Red-headed Rosefinch *Propyrrhula subhimachala* of the eastern Himalayas is at times put into the genus *Pinicola* with the Pine Grosbeak.

Common Rosefinch   *Carpodacus erythrinus*
(Maps 633, 634)
Migrant; breeding in the eastern warmer Boreal to Temperate zones, wintering in Subtropical to Tropical zones. It is a species of low scrub and shrubby growth, occurring in lowlands in the north, but in the south of its breeding range in mountains from *c.* 2,500–3,900 m. It is found on forest edge, clearings and burnt areas, swampy forest areas with low shrubby growth, broadleaf thickets and low trees bordering northern rivers, and on the edge of marshy or grassy areas, shrubs and thickets in broad grassland valleys, hedgerows, orchards, low woodland, and gardens, scrub in cultivated areas, broken forest on rugged mountain slopes, and shrubs and small trees in alpine and subalpine meadows. It winters in India, South-east Asia, and southern China, in open forest, hillside scrub and cultivated areas with shrubs and trees.

Sinai Rosefinch   *Carpodacus synoicus*
(Maps 633, 635)
Resident; in the Warm Temperate zone. It is a species of barren rocky areas, in gorges, ravines and narrow dry valleys. Near the Mediterranean it occurs at altitudes of up to *c.* 2,000 m but in Afghanistan occurs at *c.* 2,600–3,050 m.

Great Rosefinch   *Carpodacus rubicilla*
(Maps 633, 636)
Resident, with some seasonal altitudinal movements; in the Boreal or Temperate altitudinal zones. It occurs on open rocky ground on high mountain slopes, alpine meadows and partly overgrown screes of large rocks and boulders, rocky outcrops with low shrubby growth, steep rock surfaces, and boulder-strewn areas at the foot of mountain slopes. It breeds at from *c.* 2,000–3,500 m and in the Himalayas at *c.* 3,300–5,000 m. In winter it descends to *c.* 1,000–1,500 m and occurs in valley thickets and the lower ends of ravines.

Common Rosefinch   Sinai Rosefinch   Great Rosefinch   Pine Grosbeak

Pine Grosbeak *Pinicola enucleator*
(Map 637)
Resident and partial migrant, or irruptive; in
the Boreal zone. It occurs in conifer forest,
including more open subalpine forest, mixed
forest with birch and alder, and into arctic
birch scrub. Like the crossbills it shows irregular dispersal, and sometimes, but less frequently than the crossbills, irrupts over some
distance through much of western Europe,
when food supplies are poor.

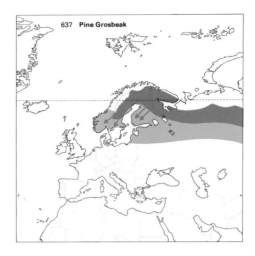

637 Pine Grosbeak

GROSBEAKS *Coccothraustes, Mycerobas*
and *Euphona* species
These are a group of large finches with very
stout bills; to some extent replacing each other
distributionally, but not necessarily related.
The Hawfinch occurs right across temperate
Eurasia. In the Himalayas and into South-east
Asia there are four species of the genus
Mycerobas (map 638). The Allied Grosbeak
M. affinis and Spotted-winged Grosbeak
M. melanozanthos occur through most of this
area with the Black-and-Yellow Grosbeak
M. icterioides confined to the western Him-
alayas. The White-winged Grosbeak *M. car-
nipes* extends from this area into most of
Tibet and through Turkestan and northern
Iran. Further east the Yellow-billed Grosbeak
Euphonia migratoria is present in China and
the Masked Grosbeak *E. personata* in north-
ern China, Amurland and Japan. The Evening

Grosbeak *Hesperiphona vespertina* of North
America is sometimes linked with this group
but might be closer to the typical cardueline
finches.

White-winged Grosbeak *Mycerobas
carnipes* (Map 638)
Resident, with some seasonal altitudinal
movements; in the Temperate to Boreal altitudinal zones of the Warm Temperate zone. It
occurs in mountain forest and scrub; being
found in juniper scrub on which it mainly
feeds, and mixed juniper and pine forest near
the tree line, and in mixed forest at lower
altitudes. It breeds at altitudes of *c.* 2,400–
3,600 m; usually, but not always, occurring at
lower altitudes in winter.

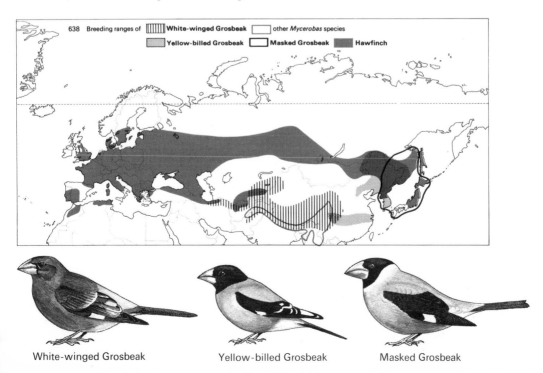

638 Breeding ranges of ▥ White-winged Grosbeak ☐ other *Mycerobas* species
▨ Yellow-billed Grosbeak ☐ Masked Grosbeak ■ Hawfinch

White-winged Grosbeak   Yellow-billed Grosbeak   Masked Grosbeak

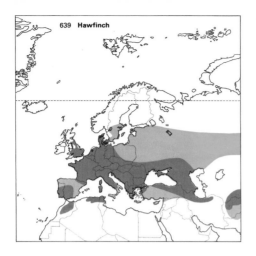
639 Hawfinch

640 African Silverbill

641 Indian Silverbill

Hawfinch   *Coccothraustes coccothraustes*
(Maps 638, 639)
Resident and migrant; breeding in Temperate to Warm Temperate zones, wintering in the Warm Temperate and western Temperate zones. It is a bird of broadleaf and mixed forest, exceptionally in some types of conifer forest, in broadleaf forest zones bordering Boreal rivers and lakes, river flood-zone thickets, riverine forest, well-grown shelterbelts, forest steppes, and parkland, groves and orchards with tall mature trees. It also occurs in scattered tall trees and thickets of open and cultivated areas. It occurs in suitable habitats in lowland and mountain areas. Migration is erratic and apparently linked to some extent with availability of food.

WAXBILLS AND MANNIKINS
Estrildidae

This is a family of mostly very small, seed-eating birds of the Afrotropical, Oriental and Australasian regions. Only the two silverbills breed in the area, and only at the edge of it (maps 640, 641). They have evolved from a common ancestor on either side of the desert zone, the Indian Silverbill in the Indian region, now extending west to the Persian Gulf, while the African Silverbill occurs in the southern parts of the Sahara and southern Red Sea coasts. The Common Waxbill is a member of the large African genus *Estrilda* and is widespread in Africa south of the Sahara. It has been introduced into Portugal where it appears to have established itself.

African Silverbill   *Lonchura cantans*
(Map 640)
Resident; in the Subtropical to Tropical zones. It occurs in dry semi-desert to desert areas where sparse herbage and some bushes and trees are present, and in areas of thornbush and *Acacia* scrub.

Indian Silverbill   *Lonchura malabarica*
(Map 641)
Resident; in the Subtropical zone. It occurs in dry areas, but usually less arid than in the previous species; in sparse scrub, grassland, open secondary forest growth, and areas of cultivation with hedgerows or shrubs. It is

Hawfinch

African Silverbill

Indian Silverbill

usually found in lowland, but has occurred up to *c*. 1,200 m in places.

Common Waxbill   *Estrilda astrild* (Map 642)
Introduced resident; in the Warm Temperate zone. This is a widespread species in open areas with grasses; being found in grassland and the edges of cultivation and into forest clearings. It roosts in large numbers in reedbeds. In Portugal it inhabits reedbeds and their overgrown edges among cultivated land where it feeds.

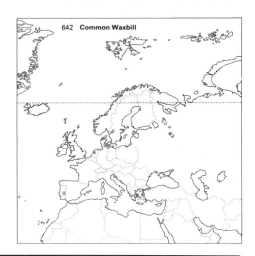

642   Common Waxbill

SPARROWS AND SNOWFINCHES   *Ploceidae*

Although the weaverbirds of the Afrotropical and Oriental regions form the major part of this family, only the three groups of typical sparrows, rock sparrows and snowfinches have successfully colonised parts of the Eurasian region. In general they nest in holes and cavities, or build domed nests in trees or shrubs. They feed mainly on seeds, and to a lesser extent on insects.

SPARROWS *Passer* species
Some of the typical sparrows are so widespread that it is difficult to detect the probable areas of origin. The Tree Sparrow occurs right across most of Eurasia, and may have spread from the east where it is the typical species around human habitations and where the House Sparrow is absent. The latter has two poorly differentiated forms, the typical one probably originating in the west and spreading from the Middle East to Europe. It has only extended across eastern Eurasia from Russia, and extended a little further northwest in Europe, since the beginning of the nineteenth century. Its southern form *indicus* probably originated in the Indian region and has spread across to Arabia, and up into Turkestan where it is a migrant. Where the House Sparrow overlaps the range of the Tree Sparrow as a resident it supplants the latter as an exploiter of human habitation. The Spanish Sparrow occurs around the Mediterranean and may have spread east from there. It is seemingly absent from part of the northern Mediterranean where the Italian Sparrow occurs. The latter appears as distinctive as some other species, but is usually regarded as a form of the House Sparrow with which it hybridises. However, the House Sparrow also hybridises with the Spanish Sparrow in parts of North Africa where they appear to have recently come together in some habitats. Where two species now occur together around the Mediterranean, the Spanish Sparrow is usually in the country habitat, in trees or scrub, and the House or Italian Sparrows in towns and villages.

There is a series of other *Passer* species (map 647) across the warmer regions. The Desert Sparrow occurs in the western Sahara with a small population in Turkestan. The Saxaul Sparrow *P. ammodendri* is the desert species replacing it in Central Asia. The Scrub Sparrow (Dead Sea Sparrow) and the Sind Jungle Sparrow occur away from human settlement in arid areas by water, the former from the eastern Mediterranean to Afghanistan, the latter in riverine growth in the Indus valley. The Cinnamon Sparrow *P. rutilans* is a species of eastern mountain villages and forest habitats, also occurring in Africa where a further six *Passer* species are found, mostly in hot, dry areas. Another species, the Plain-backed Sparrow *P. flaveolus*, occurs in Malaysia. The House Sparrow has been introduced to most parts of the world and is present as an introduced species right across North America.

Common Waxbill

Cinnamon Sparrow

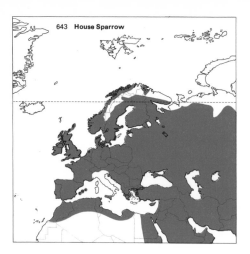

House Sparrow *Passer domesticus*
(Map 643)
Resident in Boreal to Subtropical zones, migrant in Turkestan. Throughout its range it is very closely linked with human habitation, and it appears able to survive in any urban or marginal environment where man lives. It is typically a bird of cultivated areas, grassland, orchards, parkland, gardens and similar areas, usually within reach of buildings. Its range is still spreading with cultivation. The spread right across Siberia to the eastern end of Eurasia, and into northern Scandinavia and the north-western offshore islands, has taken place since the beginning of the nineteenth century.

Italian Sparrow *Passer domesticus italiae*
(Map 644)
Resident; in the Warm Temperate zone. It occurs in niches normally occupied by the House Sparrow in Italy, Corsica, Sicily and Crete. It interbreeds with the House Sparrow in northern Italy and the Spanish Sparrow in Sicily. Populations regarded as hybrid occur on Sardinia, Malta, Pantelleria, Rhodes and Scarpanto.

Spanish Sparrow *Passer hispaniolensis*
(Map 645)
Resident and partial migrant; in the Warm Temperate zone, wintering into the Subtropical zone. It occurs in riverine scrub and thickets, shrubs and open woodland, and in date palm and olive groves in more cultivated areas. It is often in habitats bordering cultivation or grassland. In the absence of House Sparrows it may utilise habitats usually occupied by that species.

Tree Sparrow *Passer montanus* (Map 646)
Mainly resident except on the Arctic edge of the range; in Boreal to Warm Temperate zones. In the west it is a bird of cultivated areas with trees, arable land with trees and

House Sparrow   Italian Sparrow   Spanish Sparrow   Tree Sparrow

hedgerows, cultivated parkland, open and broken forest and woodland, orchards, gardens and farmyards. In more open eastern areas it occurs on rocky outcrops in the absence of trees. It is mainly a lowland species but in the Caucasus occurs at altitudes of up to *c.* 2,000 m and in Central Asia up to *c.* 3,500 m.

Sind Jungle Sparrow *Passer pyrrhonotus* (Map 647)

Resident; in the Subtropical zone. It occurs in dry riverine thickets and tall growth bordering the drier areas of the Indus plain, in scrubby thickets, tamarisk and *Acacia* scrub with tall grasses bordering rivers and swamps; and in semi-desert thickets and shrubs near water. It nests in such habitats and may co-exist with the House Sparrow where settlement occurs in such areas.

Scrub Sparrow or Dead Sea Sparrow *Passer moabiticus* (Map 647)

Resident; in the Subtropical zone. It occurs in arid areas, in trees, thick scrub and shrubs where these grow along watercourses or near a source of water.

Desert Sparrow *Passer simplex* (Map 647)

Resident; in the dry Subtropical zone. It occurs in pure desert areas, normally in sandy regions, in dunes where sparse vegetation occurs in hollows, or in shrubby growth in wadis; while in Asia it is found in more rugged and hilly desert areas with sparse shrubs and trees.

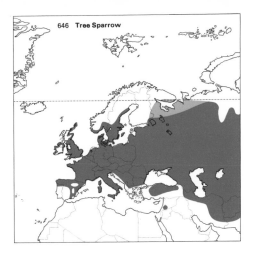

646 Tree Sparrow

Saxaul Sparrow *Passer ammodendri* (Map 647)

Resident; in the dry eastern Temperate zone. It occurs in arid and semi-desert or desert areas in the vicinity of a source of water; being found usually in river valleys where thickets of shrubs or trees such as saxaul, tamarisk and poplar occur along watercourses, and in areas of cultivation in such regions, in oases, and mountain foothills with shrubby vegetation.

ROCK SPARROWS *Petronia* species

There are three rock sparrows in the area, and a further two species occur in Africa south of the Sahara. The typical Rock Sparrow is found in drier rocky habitats from the western

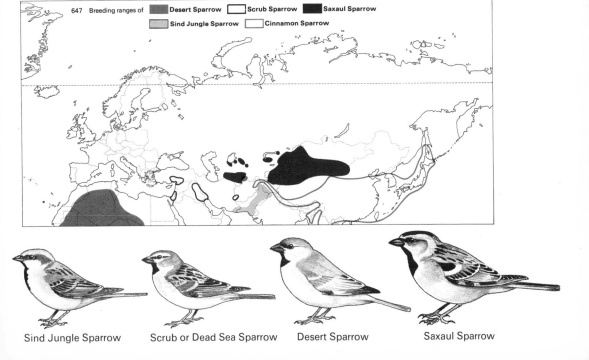

647 Breeding ranges of ▨ Desert Sparrow ☐ Scrub Sparrow ■ Saxaul Sparrow
▨ Sind Jungle Sparrow ☐ Cinnamon Sparrow

Sind Jungle Sparrow   Scrub or Dead Sea Sparrow   Desert Sparrow   Saxaul Sparrow

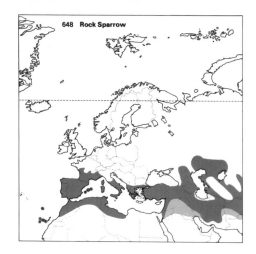

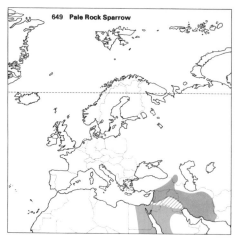

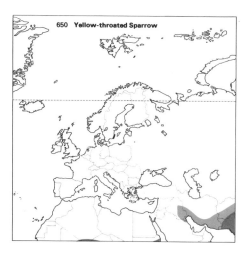

Mediterranean across to western China and Mongolia. In the warm area from the eastern Mediterranean to eastern Iran the Pale Rock Sparrow occurs, while the Yellow-throated Sparrow is in arid, more desert, areas across the Sahara and from the Persian Gulf to India. The three replace each other to some degree, but there is a considerable overlap in range.

Rock Sparrow *Petronia petronia* (Map 648)
Resident and partial migrant; in the Warm Temperate zone. It occurs on open or scrub-covered stony areas and rocky slopes and hillsides, in both well-watered and semi-desert regions, on stony or earth cliffs in grassy or shrubby areas, old buildings and ruins, ravines, screes, cliffs, crags and barren mountain areas, rocky outcrops in arid steppes, and open places with large hollow trees. It is also found in cultivated areas, vineyards and olive groves, often where these occur at higher altitudes, but also at lower levels, more especially in winter. It may occur at up to *c*. 2,600 m, and in the Himalayas has been recorded at up to *c*. 4,800 m.

Pale Rock Sparrow *Petronia brachydactyla* (Map 649)
Migrant; breeding in Warm Temperate to Subtropical zones, wintering in the Subtropical zone. It occurs in rocky, arid and very sparsely vegetated areas with widely scattered shrubs or trees or thickets; and on sparsely grassed hillsides. In some areas it occurs on mountains at altitudes of up to *c*. 2,300 m. It winters in Arabia and north-east Africa, occurring in more open and cultivated areas, particularly in cereal crops.

Yellow-throated Sparrow *Petronia xanthocollis* (Map 650)
Migrant and resident with local movements; in Subtropical to Tropical zones. It occurs in open dry forest, forest scrub, cultivated areas with scattered trees, shrubs or hedgerows, and in oases, groves and gardens. It is a mainly lowland species occurring in foothills up to *c*. 1,200 m when breeding.

SNOWFINCHES *Montifringilla* species
These are high-altitude sparrows, with superficial resemblances both to the Snow Bunting and the *Leucosticte* mountain finches. The general distribution of the genus shows some

Rock Sparrow   Pale Rock Sparrow   Yellow-throated Sparrow   Snowfinch

resemblance to that of dunnocks, with a single mountain form through southern Eurasia and a complex speciation in the Central Asian region, where six other species occur in fairly limited high-mountain habitats.

Snowfinch   *Montifringilla nivalis* (Map 651)
Resident; in the Alpine and Subalpine altitudinal zones of Temperate to Warm Temperate zones. It occurs on barren and rocky areas, on boulder-strewn slopes, level tundra-type rocky mountain tops, high screes and glacier edges, stony areas of mountain steppes, alpine and subalpine meadows with cliffs or rock outcrops, and around buildings and human settlement at high altitudes. It may occur at altitudes of 1,400–3,700 m, and up to 5,300 m in Tibet.

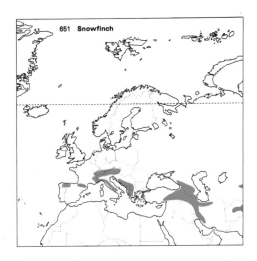

ORIOLES   *Oriolidae*

Arboreal, fruit- and insect-eating birds, mostly occurring in tropical open forest areas. The Golden Oriole occurs in western Eurasia as far east as the Altai (map 652) and has an eastern counterpart in the Black-naped Oriole *Oriolus chinensis* of China and Indochina. The Golden Oriole also extends into the Indian region where it overlaps in range with a southern species, the similar Black-headed Oriole *O. xanthornis*, which occurs through that region and Indochina. The smaller Maroon Oriole *O. traillii* occurs discontinuously in hill forest in southern China and South-east Asia. This family does not occur in North America where it is replaced by some species of the Troupial family, the Icteridae.

Golden Oriole   *Oriolus oriolus* (Map 652)
Migrant; breeding in Temperate to Warm Temperate zones; wintering in Subtropical to Tropical zones. It is typically a bird of open broadleaf forest and parkland with tall leafy trees and little undergrowth, occurring also in mixed forest, riverine forest and rows and groups of leafy trees in cultivated areas and grassland, forest steppes, plantations, orchards and gardens with fruit trees. It is not in conifer forest but may occur at altitudes of up to *c.* 1,450 m, and in the Himalayas up to *c.* 2,700 m. It winters in Africa south of the Sahara and in the Indian region.

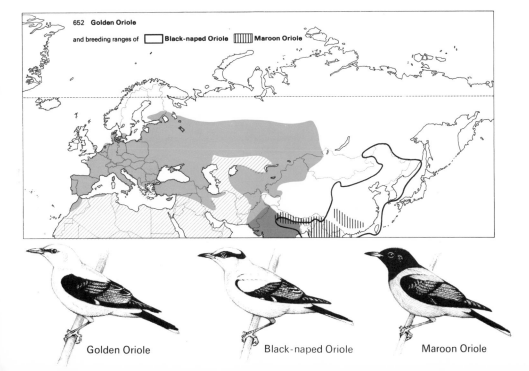

Golden Oriole   Black-naped Oriole   Maroon Oriole

STARLINGS *Sturnidae*

These are Old World small to medium-sized insect- and fruit-eating birds, usually highly sociable. The Eurasian species feed mostly on the ground and nest in cavities. The genus *Sturnus* occurs in Eurasia and the Oriental region. Only a few species have colonised the former region (map 654). The Common Starling occurs across western Eurasia as far as the Altai. In north-west Africa and the Iberian Peninsula it is replaced by the very similar Spotless Starling. In part of northern Spain the two now overlap in range without interbreeding, but may possibly compete. The Common Starling is absent from drier areas between the Caspian and Aral Seas, and in this area and over most of the steppes of this area and the drier regions immediately to the south the Rosy Starling occurs. Like other Asiatic steppe species it tends to irrupt westwards at times. The Ashy Starling *Sturnus cineraceus* appears to be an eastern equivalent of the Common Starling in northern China and Japan, and the Silky Starling *S. sericeus* occupies much of southern China. The Pied Starling *S. contra* occupies the South-east Asian region to the south of these other species. Within the range of the Ashy Starling two smaller and short-billed species occur, the Daurian Starling *S. sturnina* in northern China and Manchuria and the Red-cheeked Starling *S. philippensis* in Japan. Tristram's Starling is an outlying representative of a genus mainly occurring in Africa where a further nine species occur. The Mynahs of the genus *Acridotheres* are centred on the Oriental region with five species in the Indian region, where the Common Mynah appears to take the place occupied by the Common Starling in Europe. The Common Mynah has spread to the Persian Gulf, and has been introduced by man in various parts of the world, including California. The Common Starling has also been widely introduced, with greater success, and occurs across the whole of North America.

Common Starling   *Sturnus vulgaris*
(Maps 653, 654)
Resident and migrant; breeding in Subarctic to Temperate zones, wintering in Warm Temperate and western Temperate zones. It is

653   Common Starling

654   Breeding ranges of   Common Starling   Spotless Starling   Ashy Starling
Silky Starling   Pied Starling   Tristram's Starling

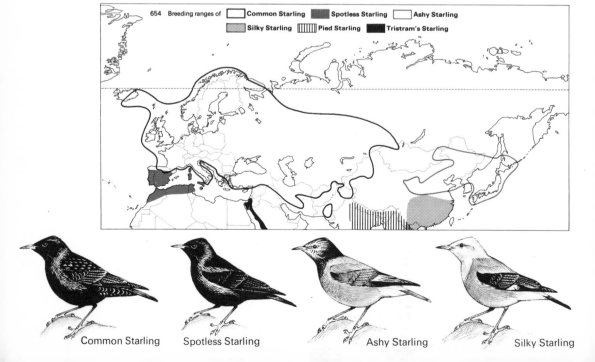

Common Starling   Spotless Starling   Ashy Starling   Silky Starling

basically a bird of open, mainly grassy areas with cavities nearby for nesting; finding this from very open forest, and forest edge, to urban areas. It occurs in open montane forest with grassy clearings, riverine forest in meadows, cultivated areas with woods, shelterbelts or scattered trees, orchards and groves, parkland, gardens, farms and towns. It extends into arctic birch scrub, usually where man is present, and into steppes. It did not spread to Iceland until 1935, and has recently spread in Spain.

Spotless Starling   *Sturnus unicolor*
(Maps 654, 655)
Resident; in western Temperate zone. Its habitat preferences are those of the previous species, which it replaces in its distribution, although the two are now coming into contact with each other in northern Spain.

Rosy Starling   *Sturnus roseus* (Map 656)
Migrant, and irruptive; breeding in Temperate steppe to Warm Temperate zones, wintering in the Subtropical zone. It usually occurs on open, grassy or sparsely vegetated steppes, semi-desert, desert, bare foothills or mountains, within reach of water and where crevices or cavities in rocky ground or outcrops allow nesting. At other times it may occur in vineyards and other fruit-growing areas. It has been found at altitudes of up to 2,835 m. It winters in the Indian region, in open areas of grassland, cultivation or low thorn scrub. It moves in large flocks and has periodically irrupted westwards into various parts of Europe, where in some areas such as Hungary and northern Italy it may nest colonially with a rapid, synchronised breeding cycle before withdrawing; while further west it occurs as a stray at such times.

Common Mynah   *Acridotheres tristis*
(Map 657)
Resident; in eastern Subtropical to Tropical zones. It usually occurs around cultivation and human habitation, in all kinds of places from forest to desert, where open ground for feeding and buildings and trees for nesting are present. In the Himalayas it occurs at altitudes of up to *c.* 3,000 m.

655   Spotless Starling

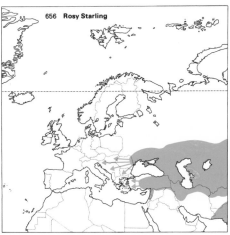

656   Rosy Starling

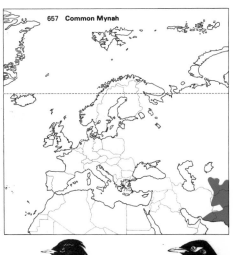

657   Common Mynah

Pied Starling   Tristram's Starling   Rosy Starling   Common Mynah

JAYS, MAGPIES AND CROWS   *Corvidae*

This is a cosmopolitan family of small to large birds, occurring in a variety of habitats. They mostly nest in bushes, trees or on rock ledges, but the Jackdaw uses cavities. Within the family there are a number of subgroups including nutcrackers, jays, magpies, ground choughs and typical crows.

NUTCRACKERS *Nucifraga* species
These are medium-sized birds feeding mainly on conifer seeds or hazelnuts. The typical Nutcracker occurs discontinuously in mountain areas in Europe, and continuously from the eastern Baltic across Eurasia, and in China and the Himalayas. In North America it is replaced by Clark's Nutcracker *Nucifraga columbiana* and possibly to some extent by the Pinyon Jay *Gymnorhinus cyanocephalus*, one of a group of American jays which has diverged to specialise on conifer seed as a food. The typical species has three forms recognisable on plumage (map 658), the main *caryocatactes* group of Eurasia, the less boldly-marked *hemispilus* group of China and the eastern Himalayas, and the distinctively spotted *multipunctata* which appears to have developed during some isolation in the western Himalayas. In addition the *caryocatactes* group appears to have had separate western and eastern forms. The western form has a heavy bill possibly correlated with using hazelnuts as a major food. It occurs in southern Scandinavia and mountain areas of Europe. The eastern form consists mainly of a slender-billed type but with thicker-billed birds toward the south-eastern limits in Tien Shan and Japan. The slender-billed type appears to have extended westwards through the forest zone as far as the Baltic, and periodically irrupts westwards over Europe, invading the range of the thick-billed birds.

Nutcracker   *Nucifraga caryocatactes*
(Map 658)
Resident, and irruptive; in the Boreal zone, and Boreal altitudinal zone of the Temperate zone. It occurs when breeding in conifer forest dominated by Arolla Pine in the south, Spruce in the west and Siberian Cedar in the east; and in mixed but mainly conifer forest; at altitudes of 800–2,150 m in the Alps and up to 3,000 or 4,000 m in the Himalayas, depending on the altitudes of conifer forest. When not breeding western birds may descend into broadleaf forest. Young birds tend to disperse more than older pairs. The slender-billed form is frequently irruptive, and occurs to a variable extent over much of eastern Europe in winter, and at times as far west as Britain. The movements depend on the crop of conifer seeds:

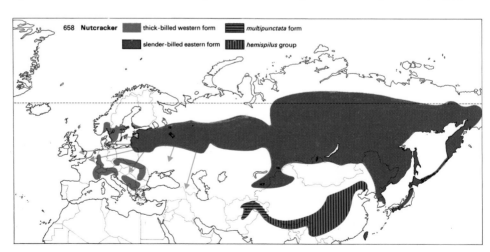

658   **Nutcracker** ▢ thick-billed western form   *multipunctata* form
slender-billed eastern form   *hemispilus* group

Nutcracker   Eurasian Jay

JAYS *Perisoreus* and *Garrulus* species

The Siberian Jay is a bird of northern forest adapted to the cold, and occurring right across Eurasia in this zone. The Szechwan Grey Jay *Perisoreus internigrans* is a relict isolate in a small region of mountain conifer forest in Szechwan and Tibet. In North America the Canada Jay *P. canadensis* occurs through the northern forest zone. The Eurasian Jay is a more southerly species occurring across Eurasia mainly in broadleaf forest. It has two related eastern species with limited ranges (map 659), the Lanceolated Jay *G. lanceolatus* in the western Himalayas where it partly overlaps in range with the pink-headed form of the Eurasian Jay, and Lidth's Jay *G. lidthi* in the northern Ryukyu Islands south of Japan. The Eurasian Jay has produced a number of local forms, which in general have striped or plain crowns in the temperate regions, and black crowns further south (map 659). Listing these from east to west: there is a striped-crowned greyish form in Japan (1. *japonicus* group), and a striped-crowned reddish-headed form (2. *brandtii* group) in Sakhalin, Amurland and northern China, which has extended from the east westwards across the forest zone of Eurasia to meet and interbreed with the greyish, striped-crowned European birds in Russia and Finland, and in the east interbreeds with the plain-crowned Chinese birds in northern China. Through most of China extending westwards through the Himalayas is a pink, plain-headed form (3. *specularis* group) which in Burma interbreeds with the black-headed South-east Asian form (4. *leucotis* group).

The birds of northern Iran appear to be a small, dark, striped-headed group (5. *hyrcanus* group), and a black-crowned, white-foreheaded form occurs from here through Turkey and into the Middle East (6. *atricapillus* group). The greyish, striped-headed form occurs through Europe (7. *glandarius* group) and a black-crowned form in North Africa (8. *cervicalis* group). In North America it is replaced by the Blue Jay *Cyanocitta cristata* in the east and Steller's Jay *C. stelleri* in the west, and possibly to some extent by the scrub jays of the genus *Aphelocoma*.

Eurasian Jay   *Garrulus glandarius* (Map 659)
Resident, and irruptive in the north; in Boreal to Warm Temperate zones. It occurs in forest, particularly in broadleaf forest with oak which is a principal food tree, but also in mixed and conifer forest, in both lowland and mountains up to the tree line. It also occurs in riverine forest, shelterbelts and plantations, parklands, orchards and secluded gardens. Northern forest birds irrupt southwards in seasons when food is scarce.

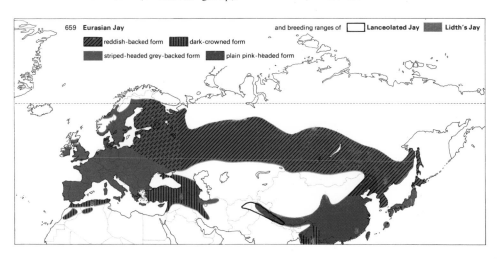

659   Eurasian Jay   and breeding ranges of [ ] Lanceolated Jay [■] Lidth's Jay

reddish-backed form   dark-crowned form
striped-headed grey-backed form   plain pink-headed form

Lidth's Jay   Lanceolated Jay

660 Siberian Jay

Siberian Jay *Perisoreus infaustus* (Map 660)
Resident and nomadic; in Subarctic to Boreal zones. It occurs in conifer forest, particularly in spruce forest in the west; and also extends into more open conifer and birch scrub.

MAGPIES *Pica* and *Cyanopica* species
Long-tailed medium to small corvids, feeding mainly on the ground in more open areas with trees and shrubs. The typical Magpie occurs right across Eurasia and through western North America, with a second species, the Yellow-billed Magpie *Pica nuttalli*, similar except for bill colour, found in California. The Azure-winged Magpie shows a widely discontinuous distribution with one form in the Iberian Peninsula, and the other in China and Japan. Many species show this east–west division but the degree of separation is unusual, and the western form appears to have a more limited habitat through either specialisation or competition with some other species. These magpies do not occur in the Indian region where they may be replaced by magpies or treepies of the genera *Cissa, Urocissa* and *Dendrocitta*, some species of which have ranges extending into southern China where they overlap the south-eastern extreme of the common Magpie's range.

Magpie *Pica pica* (Map 661)
Resident, with some local seasonal movements; in Arctic to Warm Temperate zones. It occurs in open areas and scrub where taller, dense trees or shrubs are present; being found in open forest, clearings, and forest edge, heathland, scrub on hills and mountains and into semi-desert, parkland, plantations, shelterbelts, orchards, gardens, and cultivation or grassland with scattered patches of trees, or tall shrubs, forest tundra, forest steppes, and patches of taller shrubby cover or trees in any open country.

Azure-winged Magpie *Cyanopica cyanus* (Map 662)
Resident; in the Warm Temperate zone. It occurs, in small colonies, in open broadleaf and conifer forest, hilly country with riverine trees and scrub; and open cultivated or grassy country with groups of trees, scrub or hedgerows; or in cork oak or olive groves and orchards.

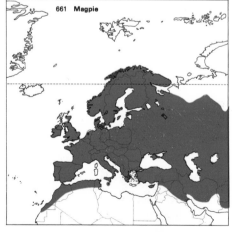

661 Magpie

Siberian Jay   Magpie   Azure-winged Magpie

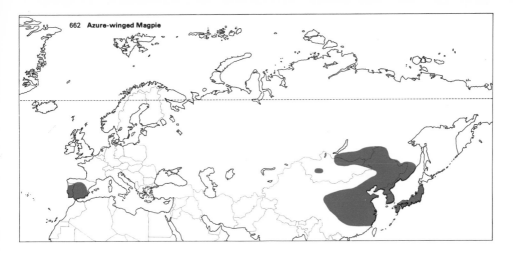

662 Azure-winged Magpie

GROUND CHOUGHS OR GROUND JAYS *Podoces* and *Pseudopodoces* species

These are a small group of aberrant corvids of central Eurasia (map 663). They are small terrestial species of open desert areas, mostly nesting in bushes. The smallest species, Hume's Ground Chough *Pseudopodoces humilis*, which nests in cavities, is now thought to be more closely related to the starlings. The other genus has four species, mainly replacing each other but with two of them – Henderson's Ground Chough *Podoces hendersoni* and Biddulph's Ground Chough *P. biddulphi* – overlapping in distribution, with the former having a preference for more stony areas that helps to separate them.

Pleske's Ground Chough   *Podoces pleskei*
(Map 663)
Resident; in dry Warm Temperate zone. It occurs in open desert areas with very sparse clumps of herbage and shrubby vegetation.

Pander's Ground Chough   *Podoces panderi*
(Map 663)
Resident, with some local seasonal movement; in dry Warm Temperate zone. It occurs in areas of shrub desert, usually in places where high dune ridges alternate with shrubby growth in the depressions between. It is found in mixed shrubs but not usually in pure saxaul growth.

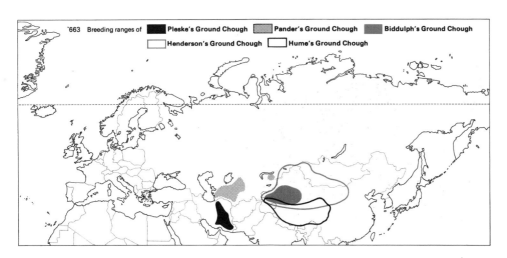

663 Breeding ranges of ■ Pleske's Ground Chough ▦ Pander's Ground Chough ■ Biddulph's Ground Chough
□ Henderson's Ground Chough □ Hume's Ground Chough

Pleske's Ground Chough

Pander's Ground Chough

Biddulph's Ground Chough

Hume's Ground Chough

Henderson's Ground Chough

TYPICAL CROWS AND CHOUGHS
Corvus and *Pyrrhocorax* species

These are the well-known medium to large black birds, widespread scavengers and eaters of small creatures. Within Eurasia the Raven and Carrion Crow are very widespread species, one large and one smaller. The crow-sized Rook is more limited in distribution by its need for open grassland and cultivation with groups of trees. The last two species have distinct eastern and western forms, and the smaller and more insectivorous jackdaws have an eastern and western species. The choughs are slender-billed ground-probers of rocky regions, having a lower altitude species with longer bill, and an alpine species with shorter bill, both with highly discontinuous distributions in mountain areas.

In more detail, the Raven is widely distributed with only slight local variations, but has disappeared through persecution in highly populated areas. It is replaced in desert areas of North Africa and the Middle East by the smaller and more crow-like Brown-necked Raven, while the Fan-tailed Raven occurs within the latter's range but appears linked to steep cliff sites. The Carrion Crow has a wide distribution but evidence of earlier discontinuity is apparent in the plumage colour (map 668). The western European black Carrion Crow extends to central Europe north of the Alps, southern Denmark and Scotland, where it is replaced by the grey-bodied form, the Hooded Crow. There is a narrow zone of interbreeding which appears stable, but has shifted a little westwards. In central Siberia, west of the Aral Sea and in Afghanistan the Hooded Crow is in turn replaced by another black form which occurs throughout eastern Eurasia except for southern China, where the species is replaced by the black and white Collared Crow *Corvus torquatus*. The Rook occurs across Eurasia but with two forms, the western bare-faced form extending east to the Altai region and an eastern form *C. f. pastinator*, with fully feathered head, replacing it in the remaining range east to Japan. The jackdaws show a similar division (map 671) involving two species. The western Jackdaw extends east to the Altai region and east of this the Daurian Jackdaw *C. dauricus* occurs. The latter resembles the Hooded Crow in having a pale body with black head, wings and tail. None of these species occurs in the Indian lowland region, where the large-billed Jungle Crow *C. macrorhynchus* is intermediate in size between Raven and Carrion Crow and occurs from Afghanistan into the area of southern China, where the other two are absent but the Collared Crow occurs. The smaller and more slender House Crow *C. splendens*, which is intermediate in size between Carrion Crow and Jackdaw, occurs from Pakistan to Indochina. In North America the Raven is present across the northern parts, and four other crow species occur, but both Jackdaw and choughs lack obvious counterparts.

664 Raven

Raven   *Corvus corax* (Map 664)

Mainly resident, with some northern winter nomadism; in Arctic to Warm Temperate zones. It is a highly adaptable species, occurring from sea coast to subalpine mountain zones, from the Arctic to semi-arid areas, and from forest to open country. Almost the only limiting factor appears to be that it normally needs a rock ledge, bush or tree for its nest, but it also usually avoids dense forest, and has been exterminated in areas of intensive human settlement.

Raven

Brown-necked Raven

Brown-necked Raven   *Corvus ruficollis*
(Map 665)
Resident, with some seasonal movements; in
the dry Subtropical zone. It is widespread
through most semi-desert and desert areas
within its range. In North Africa it is more
particularly a bird of *Artemesia* steppes with
trees, and date palm groves, but elsewhere
occurs widely in barren hilly areas, desert and
semi-desert with scrub or trees, and on arid sea
coasts, using isolated trees, rock ledges and
man-made structures for nesting.

Fan-tailed Raven   *Corvus rhipidurus*
(Map 666)
Resident; in the dry Subtropical zone. It is
limited in distribution to desert hill and mountain areas with steep cliffs, crags, escarpments
and ravines.

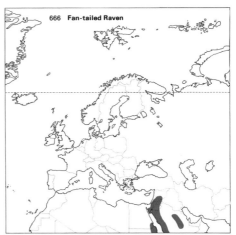

Rook   *Corvus frugilegus* (Map 667)
Resident and migrant; breeding in Boreal to
Temperate zones, wintering in Warm Temperate and western Temperate zones. It is sociable and occurs in areas of moister grassland
and cultivation where there are trees for colonial nesting. It is found in grassland and
agricultural areas, river valleys, forest edge
and broken forest with grassy clearings or
grassy marshes, forest steppes and parkland.
It is usually in lowland but in the mountain
areas of central Eurasia has been recorded at
up to *c*. 2,000 m. In winter it occurs in more
open areas in large flocks.

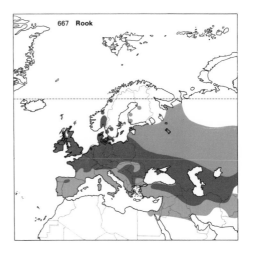

Fan-Tailed Raven

Rook

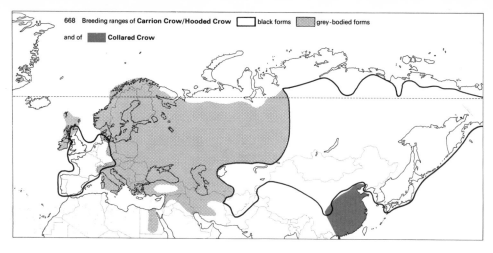

668   Breeding ranges of **Carrion Crow/Hooded Crow**   black forms   grey-bodied forms
and of   **Collared Crow**

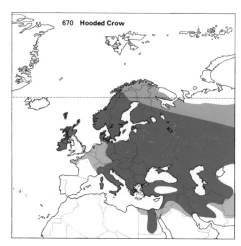

669   Carrion Crow

670   Hooded Crow

Carrion/Hooded Crow   *Corvus corone*
(Maps 668, 669, 670)
Carrion Crow *C. c. corone* resident; in Warm
Temperate zones in winter. Like the Raven it
Hooded Crow *C. c. cornix* resident and migrant; breeding in Subarctic to Warm Temperate zones, with shift from Arctic and eastern
Boreal zones to Warm Temperate and western
Temperate zones in winter. Like the Raven it
is of very widespread occurrence in a great
variety of habitats other than dense forest, but
is more limited to areas where some trees are
present. Unlike the Raven it has survived in
areas of high human population, and where
tolerated will use urban environments.

Jackdaw   *Corvus monedula* (Map 671)
Resident and migrant; breeding in warmer
western Boreal to Warm Temperate zones,
wintering in Warm Temperate to western
Temperate zones. It is a bird that mostly feeds
on the ground in open areas but requires well-
grown trees or rock outcrops for roosting and
nesting. It occurs on coasts with cliffs, rugged
hills with rocky outcrops or quarries, open
forest by grassland or areas of cultivation,
riverine forest and parkland. In open habitats
in lowland it is found near river cliffs, rock
outcrops and various types of buildings or
ruins. It occurs in farmland and urban areas.
On mountains it may be found up to the tree
line but at higher altitudes may be replaced
by the choughs. It appears to have spread in
Europe with the increase in cultivation.

Carrion Crow   Hooded Crow   Collared Crow

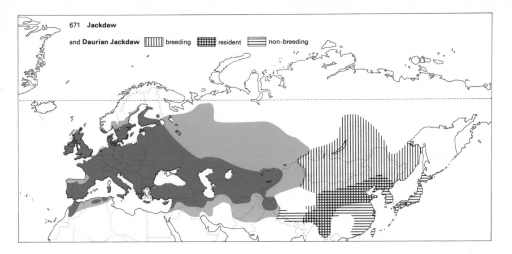

671 Jackdaw
and **Daurian Jackdaw** |||||| breeding ▦ resident ☰ non-breeding

Red-billed Chough *Pyrrhocorax pyrrhocorax*
(Map 672)

Resident, with some seasonal altitudinal movements; in the Temperate to Subalpine altitudinal zones of the Warm Temperate and western Temperate zones. It occurs where steep cliffs and crags occur close to open grassy areas, and it may utilise large man-made quarries. It is found on sea cliffs, hill crags, rocky valleys with rock outcrops, and the upper parts of mountains above the tree line. In winter it usually occurs at lower altitudes in open areas. In some areas it is at lower altitudes than the Alpine Chough, but their ranges overlap extensively. It has decreased in recent times in central and western Europe without obvious reason.

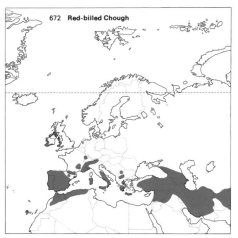

672 Red-billed Chough

Alpine Chough *Pyrrhocorax graculus*
(Map 673)

Resident, with some seasonal altitudinal movements; in Subalpine to Alpine zones of the Warm Temperate zone. Like the previous species it occurs where steep rocky slopes adjoin open grassy areas, but it may also scavenge to some extent and it is more often found around high-altitude human habitation. In high mountain areas it occurs right up to the snow line. In winter it usually occurs at lower altitudes in mountains.

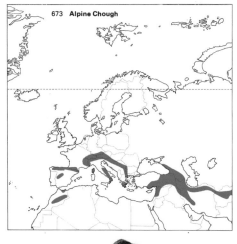

673 Alpine Chough

Jackdaw   Daurian Jackdaw   Red-billed Chough   Alpine Chough

A Selective Bibliography

In the present work reference has been made to distributions outside Eurasia. The following books contain distribution maps for some of the world's other major regions.

There are a number of books which contain distribution maps of birds and cover a part of the region dealt with in this book; and others which map a larger range but only cover a particular group of species. The list below covers most of these.

Brichetti, P. 1978. *Guida degli Uccelli Nidificanti in Italia*. F. ll. Scalvi: Italy.

Cheng Tso-Hsin, 1976. *Distributional List of Chinese Birds*. Peking Institute of Zoology: Peking. (In Chinese, with Latin and English names of species; 828 species mapped.)

Cramp, S. Ed. *Handbook of the Birds of Europe, the Middle East and North Africa. Birds of the Western Palaearctic*. 1977. Oxford University Press. (To be completed in seven volumes. Gives Europe and world distribution of species.)

Dermentiev, G. P. and others. *Birds of the Soviet Union*. Six vols. Russian edn. 1951–4, Moscow: U.S.S.R. Translated 1966–8. Israel Program for Scientific Translations: Jerusalem: Israel.

Dybbro, T. 1976. *De Danske Ynglefugles Udbredelse*. Dansk Ornitologisk Forening: Copenhagen.

Etchécopar, R. D. and Huë, F. 1964. *Les Oiseaux du Nord de l'Afrique*. N. Boubée: Paris. Translated Hollom, P. A. D. 1967. *Birds of North Africa*. Oliver & Boyd: Edinburgh.

Haftorn, S. 1971. *Norges Fugler*. Universitetsforlaget: Oslo.

Huë, F. and Etchécopar, R. D. 1970. *Les Oiseaux du Proche et du Moyen Orient*. N. Boubée: Paris.

Jennings, M. C. 1981. *The Birds of Saudi Arabia: a Checklist*. From author: 10 Mill Lane, Wittlesford, Cambridge.

Lippens, L. and Wille, H. 1972. *Atlas des Oiseaux de Belgique et d'Europe Occidentale*. Lannoo: Tielt, Belgium.

Meinertzhagen, R. 1954. *Birds of Arabia*. Oliver & Boyd: Edinburgh.

Salim Ali and Ripley, D. 1968–74. *Handbook of the Birds of India and Pakistan*. Ten vols. Oxford University Press: Bombay, London, New York.

Scott, D. A., Hamadani, H. M. and Mirhosseyni, A. A. 1975. *Birds of Iran*. Department of the Environment: Teheran, Iran.

Sharrock, J. T. R. Ed. 1976. *Atlas of Breeding Birds in Britain and Ireland*. British Trust for Ornithology: Tring, Herts.

Tuck, G. and Heinzel, H. 1978. *A Field Guide to the Seabirds of Britain and the World*. Collins: London. (Contains world maps of species.)

Voous, K. H. 1960. *Atlas of European Birds*. Nelson: London. (Contains world maps of breeding range only of strictly European birds.)

Yeatman, L. 1976. *Atlas des Oiseaux Nicheurs de France*. Ministry of the Environment: Paris.

Blake, E. R. 1977. *Manual of Neotropical Birds. Vol. 1: Penguins to Gulls*. University of Chicago Press: Chicago. (To be completed in four volumes.)

Hall, B. P. and Moreau, R. E. 1970. *An Atlas of Speciation in African Passerine Birds*. And **Snow, D. W.** Ed. *An Atlas of Speciation in African Non-passerine Birds*. British Museum: London.

Robbins, C. S., Bruun, B. and Zim, H. S. 1966. *A Guide to Field Identification: Birds of North America*. Golden Press: New York.

Slater, P. 1970–74. *A Field Guide to Australian Birds. Vol. 1: Non-passerines. Vol. 2: Passerines*. Rigby: Adelaide.

Watson, G. E. 1975. *Birds of the Antarctic and Subantarctic*. A.G.U.: Washington.

In addition to mapping birds I have also tried to provide a brief introduction to the comparative study of distribution. This aspect of wildlife study, which is known as zoogeography, is not confined to birds but includes all animals and plants, and a knowledge of what happens in one group can help us to interpret the distribution patterns in another. The following are a selective sample of the books that have helped to form the thinking behind the present work.

Bochenski, Z. 1974. *Ptaki Młodszego Czwartorzedu Polski (Birds of the late Quarternary of Poland)*. Polska Akademia Nauk: Warsaw.

Darlington, P. J. 1957. *Zoogeography*. J. Wiley: New York.

Frenzel, B. 1968. *Grundzüge der Pleistozänen Vegetationsgeschichte Nord-Eurasiens*. Erdwissenscaftliche Forschung Bd. 1. Franz Steiner Verlag: Wiesbaden.

Haffer, J. 1974. *Avian Speciation in Tropical South America*. Nuttall Ornithological Club Publications no. 14. Cambridge: Massachusetts.

Keast, A. 1961. *Bird Speciation on the Australian Continent*. Bulletin, Museum of Comparative Zoology, Harvard. Vol. 123, no. 8. Cambridge: Massachusetts.

Lack, D. 1971. *Ecological Isolation in Birds*. Blackwell Scientific Publications: Oxford.

Mengel, R. M. 1964. *The Probable History of Species Formation in Some Northern Wood Warblers (Parulidae)*. Living Bird vol. 3: pp. 9–43.

Ploeger, P. L. 1968. *Geographical Differentiation in Arctic Anatidae as a Result of Isolation During the Last Glaciation*. Ardea vol. 56.

Udvardy, M. 1969. *Dynamic Zoogeography*. Van Nostrand: New York.

Voous, K. H. 1947. *On the History of the Distribution of the Genus Dendrocopos*. Ponsen & Looijen: Wageningen.

Wattel, J. 1973. *Geographical Differentiation in the Genus Accipiter*. Nuttall Ornithological Club Publication, no. 13. Cambridge: Massachusetts.

Index of English names

Numbers in **bold** type refer to main entries. Map numbers, Maps A–T, and figure numbers are given in *italic* type.

Index of Scientific names

Numbers in **bold** type refer to main entries. Map numbers, Maps A–T, and figure numbers are given in *italic* type.